Claudio Rozzoni
The Phenomenological Image

Claudio Rozzoni

The Phenomenological Image

A Husserlian Inquiry into Reality, Phantasy, and Aesthetic Experience

DE GRUYTER

ISBN 978-3-11-221377-3
e-ISBN (PDF) 978-3-11-072576-6
e-ISBN (EPUB) 978-3-11-072588-9

Library of Congress Control Number: 2023942858

Bibliographic information published by the Deutsche Nationalbibliothek
The Deutsche Nationalbibliothek lists this publication in the Deutsche Nationalbibliografie; detailed bibliographic data are available on the Internet at http://dnb.dnb.de.

© 2025 Walter de Gruyter GmbH, Berlin/Boston
This volume is text- and page-identical with the hardback published in 2024.
Printing and binding: CPI books GmbH, Leck

www.degruyter.com

Acknowledgments

First of all, my sincerest thanks go to my publisher De Gruyter and especially Philosophy Department editors Christoph Schirmer and Mara Weber for all their support during the editorial process.

I am grateful to the Portuguese Fundação para a Ciência e a Tecnologia (FCT), which supported my work at the Nova Institute of Philosophy (IFILNOVA). This book would not have been possible without the research I developed during my time with IFILNOVA, which offered me an exceptional environment in which to exchange and test ideas, particularly in the CulturLab and the "Aesthetics and Philosophy of Art" Research Group. I am truly grateful to Maria Filomena Molder and IFILNOVA director Professor João Constâncio for their constant and inspiring support. I would like to thank several other IFILNOVA colleagues and friends for all of our stimulating philosophical discussions over the past several years: Nélio Conceição, Giovanni Damele, Marta Faustino, Nuno Fonseca, Pietro Gori, Bartholomew Ryan, Paolo Stellino, and Susana Viegas.

While developing this volume and directly related works, opportunities to present and discuss aspects of my ongoing work proved indispensable. I would like to thank the University of Bucharest, the University of Calabria, the University of Copenhagen, the University of Florence, the University of Jena, ZKM – Centre for Art and Media (Karlsruhe), the Husserl Archives (Köln), the University of Köln, the University of Lausanne, the New University of Lisbon, the Husserl Archives (Leuven), the Catholic University of Louvain, UCLA (Los Angeles), the University of Milan, the University of Murcia, Sorbonne University (Paris), the University of Parma, and Charles University (Prague) for providing these opportunities.

Thanks as well to the many insightful scholars I engaged with at these institutions, including Emmanuel Alloa, John Brough, Mauro Carbone, Marco Cavallaro, Robert Clewis, Fabrizio Desideri, Carmine Di Martino, Roberto Diodato, Serena Feloj, Christian Ferencz-Flatz, Julian Hanich, Joseph G. Kickasola, Dieter Lohmar, Stéphane Lojkine, Danielle Lories, Giovanni Matteucci, William McDonald, Andrea Mecacci, Regina-Nino Mion, Robert Pippin, Martin Puchner, Salvador Rubio Marco, Anne Elisabeth Sejten, Hans Rainer Sepp, Carlo Serra, Richard Shusterman, Paolo Spinicci, Andrea Staiti, Michela Summa, Carole Talon-Hugon, Elena Tavani, Salvatore Tedesco, Alberto Voltolini, Thomas Vongehr, Lambert Wiesing, and Dan Zahavi.

I am also grateful to the phenomenologists Elio Franzini, Vincenzo Costa, and Eduard Marbach for taking time over the past several years to discuss so many crucial issues related to the phenomenology of image and phantasy. Thank you so much for generously sharing your insights and offering constant encouragement and inspiration.

Special thanks to the Department of Cultural and Environmental Heritage at the University of Milan, where I currently teach aesthetics, for providing such a fruitful academic environment in which to think about phenomenology "outside the box," especially in relation to culture and the arts. In particular, I wish to thank the Department Director, Alberto Bentoglio, and my aesthetics colleagues Maddalena Mazzocut-Mis, Alice Barale, and Andrea Scanziani.

Last but not least, I am truly grateful to Jaime McGill for her remarkable work in revising my English and for supporting me in finding my own style in a language which I cherish but which is nevertheless not my native tongue.

An early version of this work was originally published in Italian under the title *Nell'immagine. Realtà, fantasia, esperienza estetica* (Firenze, 2017), a volume that I penned in direct correlation with my work as editor of the first Italian edition of Husserl's manuscripts on image and phantasy (*Fantasia e immagine*, Soveria Mannelli, 2017). While continuing to revise it over the last several years, I also expanded upon its ideas in the process of writing other articles, some of which I have incorporated into these pages. Even so, this work is neither to be considered a mere translation of the Italian version nor an amalgam of those subsequent elaborations. Everything in this book has been thoroughly revised and rewritten, and the final result is a work unto itself.

The research for and writing of this book was made possible by the support of the FCT – Fundação para a Ciência e a Tecnologia, as part of IFILNOVA project UID/FIL/00183/2019, Norma Transitória – DL 57/2016/CP1453/CT0065.

Contents

Preface — 1

Bibliographical Note and Abbreviations — 7

1 Phenomenology of Image and Phantasy — 10
1.1 "Again and Again" — 10
1.2 Intentionality *Inferior* — 12
1.3 Phantasy Intentionality *qua* Intuitive Presentification — 15
1.4 The Point of View of *Imaginatio:* The Triadic Structure — 18
1.5 The Ineffable Essence of Image Object — 21
1.6 Image and Sign — 25
1.7 A Potential Misunderstanding: The "Image-Theory" — 28
1.8 Does Phantasy Experience Necessarily Imply Mental Images? — 30
1.9 From Delegation to Reproduction — 35
1.10 The Phantasy Ego — 38
1.11 Universalizing Phantasy — 42
1.12 *Ficta* Complying with *Perceptio* — 44
1.13 Positional and *Quasi*-Positional Rays — 47
1.14 Images and Belief — 49
1.15 Depiction and Aesthetic Consideration — 55
1.16 The Photographic *Sujet* — 58
1.17 Photography and Reality — 61
1.18 Moving Images and Belief — 69
1.19 Iconic Belief in the Present — 71
1.20 Which Window? — 73
1.21 Seeing the Character — 79
1.22 Difference Iterability — 86

2 The Aesthetic Consciousness — 91
2.1 The Letter to Hugo von Hofmannsthal and Manuscript A VI 1 — 91
2.2 Valueception — 98
2.3 Dark Valuing Ideas — 101
2.4 The Unitary Interweaving of Acts — 103
2.5 Aesthetic Experience, Image, and Modalizations — 105
2.6 Constituting the "How": Stylistic Manifestations — 110
2.7 The Aesthetic Fold — 112
2.8 Pleasurable "How," Painful "What" — 115

- 2.9 A True Story —— **118**
- 2.10 Living in the Aesthetic Feeling —— **123**
- 2.11 The Portrait and Its *Sujet* —— **126**
- 2.12 Failed Recognitions —— **130**
- 2.13 Rise of the Mannequins? Illusion and Art —— **137**
- 2.14 Expressive Elements —— **141**

3 Toward Perspectival Images —— 147
- 3.1 What Kind of Sameness? —— **147**
- 3.2 Opening Perspectives —— **150**
- 3.3 Expressive Coherent Deformations —— **152**
- 3.4 The Silent Axiological Appeal —— **153**
- 3.5 Cinematic *Quasi*-worlds —— **155**
- 3.6 Between "Real" and "Ideal" —— **158**
- 3.7 *Quasi*-emotions as Modified Emotions —— **162**
- 3.8 Are Emotions in Fiction "Paradoxical"? —— **165**
- 3.9 *Quasi*-values and Axiological Effects —— **168**
- 3.10 Same Body, Different Persons —— **171**
- 3.11 Fragmented Reality —— **173**
- 3.12 Perspectival Truths —— **179**
- 3.13 Perspectivism, Not Relativism —— **182**
- 3.14 Shipwrecks at a Distance —— **186**
- 3.15 Actuality at an Iconic Distance —— **189**
- 3.16 A Twenty-First-Century Portrait —— **191**
- 3.17 A Temporal Portrait: Singular Expressive Qualities —— **194**
- 3.18 Images without Belief: A Double Distance? —— **197**
- 3.19 *Quasi*-Guilty: Haneke and the "Reality of Fiction" —— **199**
- 3.20 Phantasy as a Protected Field of Experimentation —— **204**
- 3.21 Dramaturgically Manipulative Presentifications —— **206**
- 3.22 *Sub Specie Sensus* —— **208**
- 3.23 By Chance, Balthazar —— **212**
- 3.24 The Polyvalence of Truth —— **216**
- 3.25 Beyond Documentary and Fiction —— **219**

References —— 232
- Husserl's Writings —— **232**
- Husserl's Writings Not Included in the Husserliana Series —— **232**
- Manuscripts —— **232**
- Secondary Literature —— **232**

Thematic Index —— 246

Preface

This volume aims to propose a phenomenology of the image, that is, to promote a return to a description of the image that starts from its fundamental characteristics, its essential features. The task I endeavor to pursue here draws inspiration from the work that the father of phenomenology, Edmund Husserl, began developing in the early twentieth century, particularly in a seminal course he taught in 1905 in Göttingen. As Husserliana Volume XXIII—which contains the bulk of Husserl's unpublished work on phantasy and image consciousness—testifies, these lectures opened up a whole series of reflections that continued for many years, yielding results that fed into his most celebrated works.

In the first chapter of this book, I have attempted to reconstruct the context of those endeavors, focusing in particular on identifying and defining those essential elements of image consciousness potentially constituting the living legacy of the phenomenology of the image. Elaborating on this legacy in order to develop a renewed understanding of our contemporary encounters with images could also prove beneficial at an interdisciplinary level. Moreover, clarifying the essential structures at work when we experience images may help unravel some of the confusion that often affects myriad disciplines when it comes to a concept that is extremely familiar yet remains nebulous in many ways. Defining imagery's essential traits can potentially reveal new avenues not only for comprehending contemporary and future image types, but also for illuminating our ongoing research into past ones.

The fundamental question that such lines of inquiry soon raise concerns whether there are structural differences between our image experiences and phantasy experiences—or, in phenomenological terms, between image consciousness and phantasy consciousness. In his 1905 course, Husserl approached defining the nature of the image as a corollary inquiry to his investigations into the nature of phantasy. At a more general level, the first two parts of the 1905 course were devoted to the phenomenology of perception and attention. In the third part, Husserl felt the need to develop a phenomenological description of phantasy as he considered it a *necessary and complementary step* to its account of perception. He set out to uncover the essential differences between perception and phantasy, eventually finding them to be two originary modes of manifestation marked by an irreducible temporal difference (hence his devotion of the fourth and final part of the course to seminal investigations of time consciousness).

Perception and phantasy are two different modes through which something can manifest itself to us. In the mode of perception, something is given to us "in the flesh," and we take it as actually present; in the mode of phantasy, something is given to us, yet we know it is not present in front of us the way it would be if we were perceiving it. Though I might phantasize a lush, green tree or a pleasant melody, that tree and that melody are not part of our shared perceptual reality. This distinction does not *eo ipso* imply a primacy of perception over phantasy (or vice versa, for that matter)—it merely serves to clarify essential differences between these two qualitatively distinct forms of experience.

As mentioned, Husserl inaugurates his research into the essence of images by investigating the nature of phantasy specifically to gain phenomenological insights into what are commonly called "phantasy images," i.e., "mental images" through which we putatively represent things "in our minds." The key question in this regard is whether phantasy consciousness is ultimately founded upon image consciousness. This is the critical issue at the heart of such a phenomenological task: are there "mental images" at all? Are there images "in our minds"—analogous to the "physical" images we continually encounter in everyday life but minus the sensible support? In other words, does phantasy *need* images in order to represent absent objects, or is our ability to produce and see images instead grounded in phantasy consciousness?

As we shall see, Husserl's response to this question reverses the terms of the first hypothesis (phantasy needs images): his phenomenological inquiries yielded the result that phantasy need not necessarily be founded on the capacity to produce mental images. In Husserl's view, the capacity for phantasy (as an originary modality of consciousness) need not be grounded in images proper; rather, phantasy consciousness is what underlies the capacity to recognize and produce physical images. He determines that phantasizing is not projection of an image medium acting as a representative for an absent object but rather is perception in the as-if, *quasi*-perception carried out by a *quasi*-subject—hence the possibility of distinguishing between real and phantasy egos from a phenomenological standpoint. In this sense, phantasy is the originary mode of consciousness that, in more strict phenomenological terms, can be called *presentification*. We can then further distinguish between "private *presentifications*" (*quasi*-perceptions without images) and presentifications in image.

Analyses in this direction have also led me to question a distinction perhaps often taken for granted, namely that images pertain exclusively to phantasy and perception exclusively to reality—in other words, that proper images (presentifications in image) are *eo ipso* considered nonreal, whereas perception involves things "in the flesh" and thus taken as real. As we shall see, elaborations upon the Husserlian manuscripts in Chapter 1 lead me to stress that perception *per se* is no guarantee of reality, nor does the image *per se* guarantee unreality: it is possible for perceptual experiences (or, more precisely, experiences complying with *percep-

tio[1]) to pertain to phantasy and for image experiences to force associations with reality. Though the image in itself is "unreal" in the sense of its presentifying nature (it shows something not present in the flesh), this is not to say that the *sujet*—the thing or person we see by "looking into the image"—cannot or should not be considered real. In short, we can have phantasies in the flesh and images imbued with belief.

Accordingly, we can experience the *sujet* of an image in either a documentary or a fictional consciousness—that is, with or without a "ray of belief" crossing the image as regards the existence of what it presentifies. The image in itself makes no absolute guarantees concerning belief or lack thereof: context is what motivates the emergence of a documentary or fictional consciousness in relation to any given image. The same can apply to perceptual, noniconic experiences: we can experience them either in a consciousness of reality (as occurs constantly in context of going about our everyday lives) or a consciousness of fiction (as is the case, to mention one paradigmatic example, when we watch events upon a theatrical stage, which represents one possible context in which fictional worlds can comply with *perceptio*).

The second chapter deepens the originary phenomenological distinctions elucidated in the first but with a specific focus on the nature of aesthetic experience. Too often, the type of consciousness associated with aesthetic experience is confused with other modalities of consciousness which, despite possibly overlapping with aesthetic experience in some ways, must nonetheless be kept distinct as regards their originary sense. Specifically, the term "aesthetic" is often used interchangeably with terms like "fictional," "artistic," or "iconic," thereby creating confusion that can fundamentally undermine research outcomes. Through the Husserlian manuscripts, I attempt to trace the roots of the "aesthetic" back to a consciousness which, though it may indeed have seminal connections to the associated terms listed above, ultimately possesses its own qualitative originality that cannot be reduced to any of those terms.

Taking Husserl's famous 1907 letter to Hugo von Hofmannsthal as a starting point as well as drawing upon subsequent Husserlian writings that develop the premises outlined in that letter (including the Husserliana XXIII manuscripts as well as, for example, *Ideas 2* and the seminal *First Philosophy*), I trace the nature of the "aesthetic" back to its crucial connection to a felt value regarding the manner of manifestation—the *how* of its *what*, in a manner of speaking. For Husserl, aesthetic experience arises from the foundational moment at which a value is felt

---

1 We shall see the sense in which Husserl draws a distinction between *perceptio* (*Perzeption*) and perception (*Wahrnehmung*).

regarding the way something appears, whether that "something" is perceived in the flesh or presentified in an image. Husserl was well aware that emphasizing the moment of the "how" rather than the "what" of a manifestation aligned with Kant's well-known characterization of "aesthetic disinterest," though he was not aiming to follow in the footsteps of the Kantian approach so much as to conduct an independent inquiry at the phenomenological level into the nature of this disinterest.

Despite entailing disinterest in something's existence in the general sense (in other words, disinterest in whether something actually exists or not), aesthetic experience does involve another form of interest: though "existentially disinterested," it is "axiologically interested." In aesthetic experience, axiological interest manifests itself through the sphere of feeling—we experience a particular value, an appreciation for the manner in which something is given, and it is necessarily given in a feeling interrelated with this value.

Clearly, talking about the "how" of manifestation, the manner of appearing, might carry the risk of reintroducing the dichotomy between content (what) and form (how) into the discussion of aesthetic experience. I propose that Husserlian analysis allows us to understand the aesthetic attitude directed toward the "how" as involving an interest that is affected by the specificity of the perspective in which the "what" is given—a portion of the world that emerges in its specific, emotionally felt value. Such an axiological encounter can then find multiple developments, and it affords the possibility to embrace belief in existence in a way that a strictly Kantian approach would not tolerate. In aesthetic experience, even the most ordinary object can emerge in the value of its manifestation—and strictly speaking, all manifestations can be aesthetically "expressive" in principle: a "zero degree" of aestheticity is only a limit point. In Chapter 2, I point out that every presentificational artistic choice posits an authorial responsibility for decisions on "*how*" the "*what*" is presented, and I examine the question of how to deal with the impossibility of remaining neutral or impartial even when confronting *sujets* that seem refractory to aestheticization.

Throughout the book, but particularly in Chapter 3, I investigate some of the ways that art can become a domain for broadening the notion of aesthetic experience to encompass the possibility of producing a perspective aesthetically (in a contemporary development of the Kantian notion of "aesthetic idea"). *Lato sensu*, I characterize this perspective as an intimate and indissociable relationship among narrative (cognitive, perspective *stricto sensu*), emotional, and axiological dimensions. In this sense, a work of art can prompt recipients to experience values exhibited aesthetically (*aisthesis*), triggering an evaluation process that is both emotional and cognitive though neither conceptually mediated nor circumscribable. Artistic experience can thus transform our conception of the world in its totality, altering the perspectives in which we *always* live. These transformations can be connoted either positively (by enlightening us to previously unknown facets of the world) or negatively (by concealing, anesthetizing, or speciously "spectacularizing" reality).

More fundamentally, I seek to demonstrate how, by acting upon sense as the foundational element of a (real or fictitious) world, art can operate in a dimension "refractory" to the distinction between documentary and fiction—*sub specie sensus*—and can even explore the thresholds between these two polarities in multiple directions; here, as in other contexts throughout the book, Marcel Proust's work provides seminal insights. Art recipients thus become participants in perspectives that force them to think at a cognitive-emotional-axiological level, whether or not they believe in the factuality of what they are seeing.

To elaborate on this point, I strive to bring the Husserlian manuscripts into dialogue with pivotal insights by French phenomenologists like Sartre and Merleau-Ponty (neither of whom have had access to the then-unpublished material in Husserliana XXIII) as well as by philosophers like Deleuze. The latter's work, despite its explicit dissociation from Husserlian thought (even if this dissociation is largely based on positions borrowed from other authors rather than direct engagement with Husserl's original texts), offers a fruitful point of comparison to phenomenology that may suggest new directions for research.

Here, such comparisons give rise to a number of observations. One is that artistic processes can delve into the possibility of *producing sujets* through images (a point I also examine in reference to painting, drawing upon Denis Diderot's refusal to recognize his portrait at the *Salons*). Another is that they can express neutral qualities impervious to questions concerning belief in existence but open to the emotional "perception" of values (*valueception*). The expressive power pertaining to artistic practices can give rise to perspectives that do not merely copy a static, self-contained world and show it to the recipient but rather open up new dimensions of sense in a constant state of interaction with, and with mutual influence upon, what we call "the world." Artistic images can vary and deform reality—not so much to offer a diversion from it as to allow new essences to emerge and thereby create possibilities for expressing new perspectives.

The third chapter examines this concept in detail, specifically in relation to *cinematographic* images. I touch upon the ideas of Robert Bresson and consider their contemporary development in the works of Austrian director Michael Haneke and Canadian photographer Jeff Wall. My aim in doing so is to highlight how these artistic practices can engage in a dialogue with the phenomenological themes elaborated here—that is, not only how phenomenology can shed light on artistic practices but vice versa as well.

These three authors all offer paradigmatic examples of what I describe as perspectives (*lato sensu*) that move beyond naïve dichotomies between reality and fiction. Their work is no mere projection of narratives, emotions, and values, nor are their perspectives relative stances, private interpretations of a self-contained and autonomous world. Indeed, perspectives are nexuses of axiologically and emotionally perceived senses that individuate their subjects rather than being subjective interpretations of the world projected onto it by allegedly autonomous individuals. If, as I propose, the condition of a world's possibility for manifestation is the essential connection among narrative (perspective *stricto sensu*), values, and emotions, these authors think of *cinematography* as a privileged field that, though purely presentificational in nature, can create new perspectives directly affecting our perpetually perspectival comprehension of what we call "the world."

More specifically, I delve into aspects of Michael Haneke's work to explore a practice of cinema that undermines the notion of cinematic fiction as an ontologically safe harbor from which the viewer can be an unaffected "spectator of shipwrecks," to borrow the famous Lucretian *topos*. Rather, Haneke suggests, the cinematographic experience "sucks spectators into" the *quasi*-actions of the world of sense. Even when they presume themselves "safe," distanced both iconically and fictionally from what they are watching, their participation in a world of interrelated meanings leads them to *quasi*-carry out some of the on-screen action, whether they realize it or not. This becomes an issue when artists take responsibility for how some *sujets* are presented (violence and death, for example). This is obviously not to say that directors are obliged to follow a normative stance or restrict themselves in what they presentify in images, however. In fact, cinematography can also provide an avenue through which to experiment with experiences we typically cannot or would not seek out in real life.

The book ends with a passage on Jeff Wall's cinematographic photography, which focuses on the threshold between documentary and fiction and re-frames aesthetic experience as an experience of value with both cognitive and emotional dimensions. Aesthetic-artistic experience is construed as both a creation of value and an agent for processes of valorization. Like Haneke, Wall expressly avoids construing artistic-aesthetic perspectives as predetermined positions through which to "feed" the passive viewer objective meanings or products. Rather, his work obliges viewers to assume the role of storyteller, to develop for themselves the fecundity of the instant expressed within his photographs. By giving life to one of the multiple perspectival narratives opened through Wall's artistic gestures, the viewer thus becomes a creator in turn.

Milan, May 9, 2023

Bibliographical Note and Abbreviations

In general, references to the works of Edmund Husserl are taken from the Husserlian critical edition *Edmund Husserl: Gesammelte Werke* as stated below (except in specific cases, all referenced in the Bibliography). The abbreviated title Hua and the corresponding Roman numeral indicating the volume are followed by the page number of the corresponding English translation. When the latter is not available, the translation is to be considered mine.

With regard to English translations of Husserlian texts, I have often introduced slight modifications aimed primarily at bringing them in line with my translation choices and rendering my text as homogeneous as possible; for readability purposes, I have dispensed with labeling each such instance as "transl. slightly modified." References to the English edition used are always provided so that readers can make their own comparisons.

Unpublished manuscripts are cited in accordance with the system used in the Husserl Archives in Leuven, including the original page number; in such cases, I have also provided the original text. As far as critical literature is concerned, page numbers refer to the English edition listed in the Bibliography. For works not translated into English, the page numbers refer to the original editions, and any translations are to be considered mine.

Husserliana: Edmund Husserl, *Gesammelte Werke*

Hua I	Husserl, Edmund (1991): *Cartesianische Meditationen und Pariser Vorträge*. Ed. Strasser, Stephan. Dordrecht/Boston/London: Kluwer Academic; – *Cartesian Meditations. An Introduction to Phenomenology*. Eng. transl. ed. by Cairns, D., The Hague: Springer, 1960.
Hua II	Husserl, Edmund (1973): *Die Idee der Phänomenologie. Fünf Vorlesungen*. Ed. Biemel, Walter. Den Haag: Martinus Nijhoff; – *The Idea of Phenomenology*. Eng. transl. Alston, W.P., Nakhnikian, G., Dordrecht/Boston/London: Kluwer Academic, 1990.
Hua III/1	Husserl, Edmund (1976): *Ideen zu einer reinen Phänomenologie und phänomenologischen Philosophie. Erstes Buch: Allgemeine Einführung in die reine Phänomenologie*. Ed. Schuhmann, Karl. Den Haag: Martinus Nijhoff; – *Ideas Pertaining to a Pure Phenomenology and to a Phenomenological Philosophy. First Book. General Introduction to a Pure Phenomenology*. Eng. transl. Kersten, F., The Hague: Martinus Nijhoff, 1983.
Hua IV	Husserl, Edmund (1952): *Ideen zu einer reinen Phänomenologie und phänomenologischen Philosophie. Zweites Buch: Phänomenologische Untersuchungen zur Konstitution*. Ed. Biemel, Marly. Den Haag: Martinus Nijhoff; – *Ideas Pertaining to a Pure Phenomenology and to a Phenomenological Philosophy. Second Book. Studies in the

	Philosophy of Constitution. Eng. transl. Rojcewicz, R., Schuwer, A., Dordrecht/Boston/London: Kluwer Academic, 1989.
Hua VI	Husserl, Edmund (1976): *Die Krisis der europäischen Wissenschaften und die transzendentale Phänomenologie. Eine Einleitung in die phänomenologische Philosophie.* Ed. Biemel, Walter. Den Haag: Martinus Nijhoff; – *The Crisis of European Sciences and Transcendental Phenomenology. An Introduction to Phenomenology.* Eng. Transl. Carr, D., Evanston: Northwestern University Press, 1970.
Hua VIII	Husserl, Edmund (1959): *Erste Philosophie (1923/24). Zweiter Teil: Theorie der phänomenologischen Reduktion.* Ed. Boehm, Rudolf. Den Haag: Martinus Nijhoff; – *First Philosophy. Lectures 1923/24 and Related Texts from the Manuscripts (1920–1925).* Eng. transl. Luft, S., Naberhaus, T.M., Dordrecht: Springer, 2019.
Hua X	Husserl, Edmund (1966): *Zur Phänomenologie des inneren Zeitbewusstseins (1893–1917).* Ed. Boehm, Rudolf. Den Haag: Martinus Nijhoff; – *On the Phenomenology of the Consciousness of Internal Time (1893–1917).* Eng. transl. ed. by Brough, J.B., Dordrecht: Kluwer Academic, 1991.
Hua XVI	Husserl, Edmund (1973): *Ding und Raum. Vorlesungen 1907.* Ed. Claesges, Ulrich. Den Haag: Martinus Nijhoff; – *Thing and Space. Lectures of 1907.* Eng. transl. Rojcewicz, R., Dorderctht: Springer, 1997.
Hua XIX/1	Husserl, Edmund (1984): *Logische Untersuchungen. Zweiter Band: Untersuchungen zur Phänomenologie und Theorie der Erkenntnis, Erster Teil.* Ed. Panzer, Ursula. Den Haag: Martinus Nijhoff; – *Logical Investigations.* Vol. 1 and 2. Eng. transl. ed. by Moran, D., London/New York: Routledge, 2001.
Hua XXIII	Husserl, Edmund (1980): *Phantasie, Bildbewusstsein, Erinnerung. Zur Phänomenologie der anschaulichen Vergegenwärtigungen. Texte aus dem Nachlass (1898–1925).* Ed. Marbach, Eduard. Den Haag: Martinus Nijhoff; – *Phantasy, Image Consciousness, and Memory (1898–1925).* Eng. transl. ed. by Brough, J., Dordrecht: Springer, 2005.
Hua XXIV	Husserl, Edmund (1984): *Einleitung in die Logik und Erkenntnistheorie. Vorlesungen 1906/07.* Ed. Melle, Ullrich. Dordrecht: Martinus Nijhoff; – *Introduction to Logic and Theory of Knowledge. Lectures 1906/07.* Eng. transl. Ortiz Hill, C., Dordrecht: Springer, 2008. The "Personal Notes" from 1906 and 1907 (appeared as *Beilage IX* in Hua XXIV, German edition, pp. 442–452) have been translated in Husserl, Edmund (1994): *Early Writings in the Philosophy of Logic and Mathematics.* Eng. transl. Willard, D., Dordrecht: Springer, 490–500.
Hua XXV	Husserl, Edmund (1987): *Aufsätze und Vorträge (1911–1921).* Eds. Nenon, Thomas; Sepp, Hans Rainer. Dordrecht: Martinus Nijhoff.
Hua XXXVIII	Husserl, Edmund (2004): *Wahrnehmung und Aufmerksamkeit. Texte aus dem Nachlass (1893–1912).* Eds. Vongehr, Thomas; Giuliani, Regula. Dordrecht: Springer.

Other Abbreviations

AI	Artificial Intelligence
HBO	Home Box Office
IKB	International Klein Blue

MoMA   Museum of Modern Art, New York
VR   Virtual Reality

1 Phenomenology of Image and Phantasy

1.1 "Again and Again"

The present study is philosophically rooted in the manuscripts on *Phantasy, Image Consciousness, and Memory* that Edmund Husserl (1859–1938) elaborated over a period of more than 20 years. These texts were published in 1980 in Husserliana XXIII, which was edited by Eduard Marbach and is, indeed, entitled *Phantasie, Bildbewusstsein, Erinnerung*. These writings serve as testimony to the father of Phenomenology's style of work—evidence that is all the more significant because it concerns themes Husserl considered crucial to the destiny of the entire phenomenological project, despite having devoted comparatively little space to them in works published during his lifetime. In fact, though Husserl never published these manuscripts, that does not mean that they are not of great importance: they offer valuable insights into published passages devoted to phantasy and image consciousness, offering beneficial context through which we can appreciate their relevance more fully.

More generally, as we shall see, the *Nachlass* writings shed light on the specific (and difficult) genesis of some of the most significant results Husserl published within his lifetime, and even directly explore the complex (and problematic) nature of these processes of perpetual development. Another seminal aspect immediately relevant to our work is that these manuscripts on image and phantasy (and, more generally, on reality and unreality) invite others to embark upon their own explorations of these topics.

Such paths are never easy, of course—and worse yet, they are perennially menaced by aporetical results. Despite treading arduous ground, however, the material in these manuscripts offers us a unique opportunity to describe the iconic and imaginative dimension of our time in the spirit of phenomenology. Echoing a well-known Merleau-Ponty essay, this would mean striving to develop the "shadow" (Merleau-Ponty 1959) of Husserl's legacy—a shadow that still looms large today, inviting us to take up the challenge and shed new light on these elusive domains (while simultaneously generating new and productive obscurities, as an essential counterpart of every process of clarification (Franzini 2009, pp. 37–47)).

Of course, referring to such analyses in context of "modernity" is not meant to suggest simply checking whether they "literally" apply to the new and radically different forms of images populating our *Umwelt*, our modern environment. Indeed, were we to insist on subjecting any phenomena that Husserl did not *specifically* describe (for example, image material found on the various electronic devices that have now become part of our everyday lives) to static limits defined before such phenomena existed, it would betray the very spirit of phenomenology.

By the same token, however, there is no reason to insist that conducting a Husserlian inquiry into the *essence* of images implies an obligation to limit the scope of our work to aspects explicitly thematized by Husserl himself. Rather, we ought to be asking which *new horizons and descriptions* such an approach could potentially reveal today, and how we might use Husserl's legacy—which he encouraged others to test "again and again [*immer wieder*]," especially through variations—as a starting point for new inquiries.

As has been rightly noted, the phenomenology of image has been "an underappreciated theme in" Husserl's "vast corpus of writings" (de Warren 2010, p. 305). Whereas Husserl's phenomenological analyses concerning theory of judgment, logic, perception, and time are well-known, his contributions toward a phenomenology of phantasy and image might be described as relatively unknown, or at least lesser known until recently. One reason for this is the aforementioned lack of space devoted to the topic in Husserl's published works (see, for instance, Hua I; Husserl 1939, especially §§ 39–42), even though Husserl famously declared that "*feigning [Fiktion]*," exercised by our "free phantasy," "*makes up the vital element of phenomenology as of every other eidetic science*" (Hua III/1, p. 160). Moreover, Husserliana XXIII, which collects the bulk of Husserl's unpublished work on *Phantasy and Image Consciousness* (Hua XXIII), was only published in 1980, and John B. Brough's English translation was not released until 2005. Now, however, several aspects previously overlooked or misunderstood by many contemporary theories of image can be addressed more thoroughly with the help of these richly complex writings, and these implicit potentialities are on the verge of finally taking their rightful place within philosophical debate on the subject (Brough 2012; Ferencz-Flatz/Hanich 2016; Wiesing 2005).

Though the *Nachlass* represents a corpus of posthumous manuscripts, it would be a mistake to discount the enormous potential within these pages for that reason alone. Rather than construing this as some insurmountable obstacle to the contemporary revival of such research, let us think of it as a precious—albeit complicated—opportunity to develop a *new field of study* concerning *new types of descriptions* for *new phenomena*. The due caution readers must obviously exercise when examining this Husserlian legacy is counterbalanced by the strong, even urgent invitation it extends to readers to embark upon investigative processes of their own. Research concerning the value of unpublished philosophical manuscripts is receiving more and more attention, both revealing these manuscripts potentially seminal role in shedding light on the genesis of an author's published *corpus* and providing a treasure trove of new avenues through which to explore and develop the author's thoughts.²

The present study does not pretend to be all-encompassing regarding the different ways in which such a task might be undertaken; presenting a few concrete possibilities in this direction would already constitute a major achievement. Moreover, as mentioned, the fact that these manuscripts were published only in 1980 clearly means they remained equally unknown to great thinkers of the twentieth century who drew heavily upon Husserl's published works and those manuscripts available to them at the time when developing their own concepts of images. (Such thinkers include phenomenologists and nonphenomenologists alike, of course: in France, for example, we might point out Sartre and Merleau-Ponty—as well as Deleuze, in a contrast that may offer fruitful angles for further analysis.) As such, renewed awareness and examination of these ideas could yield retrospective potential for new dialogues between Husserl and these philosophers, thereby opening up novel possibilities for interpretation, development, and critique that can and must serve as an avenue toward productive perspectives on our contemporary understanding of images.

1.2 Intentionality *Inferior*

Among the texts collected in Husserliana XXIII, the first (*Phantasy and Image Consciousness*) is probably both the best known and the most systematic. This text was a lecture manuscript of the third part of *Principal Parts of the Phenomenology and Theory of Knowledge* (*Hauptstücke aus der Phänomenologie und Theorie der Erkenntnis*), a course Husserl taught in the winter semester 1904/05 in Göttingen. The first two parts of the course were devoted to the phenomenology of perception and attention;³ the fourth famously introduced Husserl's phenomenology of time and was later significantly elaborated and published as the well-known "lectures

---

2 Regarding the increasing recognition afforded the philosophical relevance of manuscript study, see the issue of *Aisthesis* (13/2, 2020) devoted to "Reading Philosophy Through Archives and Manuscripts," particularly the contribution by Caminada (2020), which provides an introduction to the recent Husserl archive digitization project in Leuven and its potential for generating new awareness of the Husserlian way of thinking.
3 See Hua XXXVIII, "Erstes Hauptstück: Über Wahrnehmung," pp. 8–67; "Zweites Hauptstück: Über Aufmerksamkeit, spezielle Meinung," pp. 68–123.

on time consciousness" in 1928 in Volume 9 of the *Jahrbuch für Philosophie und phänomenologische Forschung* (edited by Martin Heidegger).[4]

Notably, the general title of these *Vorlesungen* echoes the one Husserl used for the second part of his 1900–01 *Logical Investigations*. As Husserl explains at the beginning of this seminal course, he initially intended to devote the lectures exclusively to "the superior intellectual acts, [...] the sphere of the so-called 'theory of judgment.'" Later, however, he felt compelled to instead conduct an analysis at a "lower level," i.e., of "those phenomena that, under the somewhat vague titles of *perception, sensation, phantasy representation, representational image, memory*, are well known to everyone, yet have still undergone far too little scientific investigation" (Hua XXXVIII, p. 3). This testifies to Husserl's belief that a "science of knowledge" would inherently entail analyzing the "aesthetic ways in which this knowledge is articulated" (Franzini 2002, p. XIV); in this sense, this third *Hauptstück* may provide a capital contribution to the study of aesthetics as *gnoseologia inferior*.[5]

It is in this context of inquiry into the lower experiential strata that Husserl confronts the challenging task of providing an account of the concept of *phantasy*, which he considered a necessary counterpoint to the account of perception he gave in the first two parts of the course (see Hua XXIII, p. 1).[6] This would ultimately

---

[4] "The manuscript of the 'Lectures on time' was not preserved"—unlike those relating to the first three parts of the course—"in its original form. Husserl not only subsequently added appendices and additions, but also cut and threw away parts insufficient as regards content or even form, partially replacing them with more precise and organic descriptions" (Boehm 1966, p. xviii). It is also worth remembering that the text published in the 1928 *Jahrbuch* (pp. 367–498) is the result of a subsequent elaboration by Edith Stein, one Husserl made directly available to Heidegger in 1926 after Heidegger offered to edit the research. For a detailed account of the genesis of the 1928 text and a discussion of its relationship with the original exposition of the 1905 lectures, see also Boehm (1966, pp. xxiv–xxxvi).

[5] In an important diary note dated September 25, 1906, Husserl states that the overarching task of phenomenology is a "critique of reason" (Husserl 1956, p. 297), saying that it requires not only analysis of superior acts, but also analysis of the underlying "problems of a phenomenology of perception, phantasy, time and the thing" (Husserl 1956, p. 298). The entry also refers to the analyses carried out in his 1904–05 Göttingen course, in the context of a systematic discussion aiming to resolve the analyses' many imperfections (cf. Hua XXIV, p. 445, Eng. transl. in Husserl 1994, pp. 494–495).

[6] "We have been occupying ourselves up to this point with the phenomenology of perception. We cannot attempt to carry out a phenomenology of perception in a fully adequate way and complete it on its own account without taking into consideration the phenomena closely related to perception. By taking these phenomena into consideration in the analyses to which we now turn, what we have learned thus far will be freshly illuminated, supplemented, and enriched. Our immediate aim is the phenomenology of *phantasy*" (Hua XXIII, p. 1).

prove crucial to defining the particular form of intentionality pertaining to phantasy and image consciousness under scrutiny in this book.

Some clarification is in order regarding this particular form of intentionality. On the one hand, we must bear in mind that when, in this third section of the 1904/05 course, Husserl begins delving into the specific type of intentionality involved in our phantasy experiences, he explicitly indicates that the work of Franz Brentano serves as the general background to his analysis; this is undoubtedly part of the reason why Aristotelian motives play such a prominent role throughout the investigation.[7] Specifically, Husserl draws upon Brentano's lectures on "selected questions from psychology and aesthetics" (Hua XXXVIII, p. 4), which Brentano held in Vienna in the mid-1880s (see Brentano 1959, pp. 3–87). Phenomenology's father-to-be numbered among the course's auditors, and Husserl refers to Brentano as his "brilliant teacher" (Hua XXXVIII, p. 4; see also Hua XXV, p. 304 ff.). On the other hand, however, this process of philosophical realignment is far from linear and proves decidedly problematic: revisiting these topics also provides Husserl with an opportunity to distance himself from Brentanian views (see, for instance, Hua XXIII, §§ 4, 45). Husserl's attempt to break every prejudicial link with previous notions of phantasy and image consciousness in order to pursue a strictly phenomenological account thereof also leads to a harsh confrontation with some of his mentor's theses. Indeed, Husserl's declaration of gratitude toward Brentano comes across as a prelude to a great reckoning, through which Husserl seeks to move beyond those Brentanian positions he considers unsatisfactory.[8]

Husserl's extensive ties to Brentano are widely known. In fact, he was led into philosophy by Brentano, who famously reintroduced the medieval notion of "intentionality" into his contemporary philosophical reflections. Husserl later developed this concept autonomously in his *Logical Investigations*, the work that marks the inception of phenomenology. Intentionality, the essential law of consciousness, represents the core of the phenomenological enterprise (Husserl 1910, pp. 90–91). Our experience of the world cannot be merely subjective or objective; rather, it essentially involves subjective and objective sides whose intimate relation precedes abstract consideration of either. As Brentano puts it, "in presentation something is presented, in judgement something is affirmed or denied, in love loved, in hate hated, in desire desired and so on" (Brentano 1874,

---

[7] Regarding the Aristotelian heritage of Brentano's ideas, see, for example, Besoli (2007) and Taieb (2018). Regarding the Aristotelian roots of Husserl's terminology, see, for example, Tinaburri (2011) and Breuer (2017). See Ferrarin (2015) for an analysis drawing attention to critical points of difference between the two philosophers.

[8] For a comparison between Brentano and Husserl on the theme of imagination, see Rollinger (1993).

pp. 92–93). Phenomenological description must be capable of rendering a satisfactory account of the different modes in which our acts (and, correlatively, their objects) and our objects (and, correlatively, their acts) are given to consciousness. When we say our acts are intentional, it implies the necessary corollary that there can be no "consciousness" that is not a "consciousness of." The relationship between consciousness and object manifests itself in different ways depending on the particular act involved—for example, perception of a tree, phantasy of a tree, etc.—and such relationships are "expressed by the little word 'of'" (Hua XVI, p. 12; Hua I, p. 33).

1.3 Phantasy Intentionality *qua* Intuitive Presentification

For Husserl, analyses concerning phantasy and image consciousness are *fully* within the sphere of a phenomenology of "intuitive presentifications [*anschauliche Vergegenwärtigungen*]" (Hua XXIII, p. 6). In perception, we see things and people "in flesh and bone" and posit them as existent; in phantasy, on the other hand, we do not posit that the people or things in question are *actually* standing before us. Rather, Husserl writes that they "hover before [*vorschweben*]" us (see Hua XXIII, *passim*). They are given to us intuitively, i.e., through a peculiar form of intentionality in which an object "appears [*erscheint*]" to us yet is not "present [*gegenwärtig*]" but merely "presentified [*vergegenwärtigt*]" (Hua XXIII, p. 18).

These are *objectivating* experiences in which, according to the eidetic laws of phantasy, I can see a friend, a tree, a table, etc. without them being actually there —or even fictitious creatures (such as Husserl's oft-mentioned water nymphs and centaurs) that I have never seen "in the flesh" and presumably never will.

It must be emphasized that this first characterization of phantasy presentification as an objectivating experience, in which something "hovers before us," prompts us to recognize an essential affinity with presentifications of memory (one of several Aristotelian insights echoed in Brentano's work).[9] These, too, are

---

9 "There are good reasons to associate memory and imagination. Both these faculties present things that are not given to perception 'here and now'; they make them the object of attention even in their absence. As an initial approximation, one can say that the Aristotelian formula applies in both cases: we have the form without the matter in front of us, like an inner eye. We do not surrender and subjugate ourselves wholly to the datum of perception; we maintain a certain freedom to disregard its physical presence, to distance ourselves from it, and we can approach it in that vicarious way that we call image, which places aspects and contents of the thing before our eyes" (Ferrarin 2007, p. 160). Our analyses in this work will examine whether and how one can properly speak of phantasy or memory image.

intuitive, objectivating representations of something that is not "there" but merely "hovers before us." In Husserl, however, this "*Vorschweben*," or "hovering," refers to the "phantasy's lack of roots in objective space and objective time"(Dufourcq 2011, p. 84).[10] For example, the tree, the friend, and the table hovering before me in a memory might be "the friend I met up with *last night*," "the tree I saw outside my house *this morning*," and "the table where I ate dinner *three hours ago*." Broadly speaking, the objectivities we see in memories are objectivities we recall having experienced in a temporally distinct situation, at a specific *moment* that can be pinpointed within the temporal course of my experiences. Were I to phantasize about the same friend, tree, or table, however, I might well choose to see them on some distant planet, outside of time. We will analyze this distinction in greater detail later on.

These initial considerations are enough to suggest that Husserl's primary interest lies in discerning *qualitative* differences between our experiences, a question that drives him to seek out an essential distinction between what he calls "modes of consciousness." Perception is only one such mode; objects are given to us in several other modes as well—such as when we see objects either through images or, as they say, "in our minds." As indicated, phenomenology must be able to provide an account of the essential differences among these *modes of consciousness* as well as of the particular nature of each mode's inherent intentionality—the essential correlation between its subjective and objective poles. After dedicating his efforts to the perceptual dimension in the first two parts of the course, Husserl uses the third part to attempt to define the eidetic differences that distinguish phantasy consciousness from perceptual consciousness.

In perception, objects are given to us in a dimension of presence (*Gegenwärtigung*). The intentional act pertaining to perception gives the object not only as "there in the flesh" but, as Husserl more precisely explains in his 1907 *Dingvorlesung*, "as actually present, as self-given there in the current now" (Hua XVI, p. 12). Husserl explicitly construes the dimension of perception as implying a "character of belief," that is, perception (*Wahr-nehmung*) as "taking-for-true [*Für-wahr-Nehmen*]" (Hua XVI, p. 13). He thus draws a distinction between perception and *perceptio* [*Perzeption*], which we will examine in detail later. For now, suffice it to say that *perceptio* can be roughly described as perception not implying a moment of belief.

---

10 On the "temporal indeterminacy" of the "products" of phantasy, see also Piana (1979, pp. 162–165).

Accordingly, *nota bene*, expressions like "in the flesh" or "in person [*leibhaft*]" do not *eo ipso* mean "perceptual" (in the sense of *Wahrnehmung*).[11]

When analyzing phantasy through a phenomenological lens, we are soon confronted with a phenomenon that will prove challenging: it seems that any description of the ways in which phantasy manifests itself must necessarily *involve the notion of image*. Indeed, it is in this context that Husserl comes to examine the issue of defining the particular type of manifestation pertaining to image and the related form of intentionality called "image consciousness." In the third part of the Göttingen course, when seeking to define the nature of intentionality pertaining to phantasy acts, Husserl begins by describing this intentionality in terms of "pictorialization [*Verbildlichung*]" (see, for example, Hua XXIII, § 8). Let us remark that he had already adopted this approach in an 1898 text devoted to "phantasy and representation in image" (see Appendix 1 to Hua XXIII, pp. 117–152)—a text that did, indeed, serve as a starting point for his later Göttingen analysis.[12]

---

[11] For this reason, I prefer to translate the word "*Perzeption*" using the Latin word "*perceptio*"—and the corresponding adjective "*perzeptiv*" as "complying with *perceptio*"—in order to keep it separate from the term "perception," the usual translation for the German word *Wahrnehmung*. Even though Husserl sometimes uses these terms interchangeably, in Hua XXIII we can find more than one reason to maintain Husserl's actual distinction between *Wahrnehmung* and *Perzeption* in the English translation. *Perzeption* is *Wahrnehmung* without belief, and, as Husserl says, any *Wahrnehmung* that does not take (*nimmt*) something as true (*wahr*) is no longer *Wahrnehmung* in the proper sense of the word. It is legitimate to say that an object given perceptually (*wahrnehmungsmäßig*) is also given as complying with *perceptio* (*perzeptiv*), but the converse is not true: we cannot state that what is given when complying with *perceptio* (*perzeptiv*) is automatically given perceptually (*wahrnehmungsmäßig*). Though these terms may overlap in some cases, this does not change the fact that such a distinction can be rightfully (and not pleonastically) introduced in the English translation, thus allowing the reader to feel the distinction between *Wahrnehmung* and *Perzeption* that plays a seminal role in these analyses. This is why Husserl's references to illusion claiming the status of reality are not, in principle, cases of phantasy complying with *perceptio* (*perzeptiv*), but rather of perceptual (*wahrnehmungsmäßig*) illusions that, once discovered, become canceled perceptions (*Wahrnehmungen*)—canceled realities only apprehended *après coup* as perzeptive *Phantasien*. Accordingly, we can also think of *perceptio* as a *genus* encompassing the species of positional *perceptio* (or *Wahrnehmung*) and positionless *perceptio* (or *perceptio* in the strict sense).

[12] He also integrates a segment dating back to that period (cf. Hua XXIII, p. 60, note 1): the phenomenological characterization of the child's photograph (which we shall discuss soon) also appears in the 1898 elaboration. In that instance, however, Husserl is expressly talking about the photograph of his son (cf. Hua XXIII, p. 118).

1.4 The Point of View of *Imaginatio:* The Triadic Structure

To understand phantasy consciousness as a pictorializing consciousness means construing the form of intentionality pertaining to phantasy consciousness as essentially analogous to the form of intentionality pertaining to the experience of what Husserl calls "physical images" (Hua XXIII, *passim*), such as the ones commonly involved when we view paintings, photographs, cinematic images, sculptures, etc. (These are all Husserl's examples, but it is important that we extend our exploration of these differentiations to include other types of images that either did not exist in Husserl's day or were not discussed at length in his work). Under this perspective, the phantasy object—which, as we have seen, does not actually manifest itself "in the flesh" but is merely presentified—also "appears to us in *image*. The Latins say *imaginatio*" (Hua XXIII, p. 18).

Husserl picks up his subsequent analyses from this point not so much as a linear progression of philosophical thought but rather as a way of reckoning with his early approach. In fact, his aim is "to try to pursue as far as possible the point of view of *imaginatio*" (Hua XXIII, p. 18). By clarifying its essence, Husserl hopes to determine whether the concept holds up in the face of several "objections" of which he is already aware.[13]

This soon leads Husserl to aim his scrutinizing phenomenological lens at the idea of a commonality of essence (*Wesensgemeinsamkeit*; see Hua XXIII, § 10) between *physical images* (i.e., images whose manifestations have a supporting material dimension) and *phantasy images* (those that are often known as "mental images," though that term could prove uncomfortable or prejudicial for reasons we shall soon explore). Under this approach, a photograph of the palace in Berlin would be structurally analogous to a phantasy image of it; the sole difference between the two would be the physical structure supporting the former. In fact, the photograph and the phantasy image would both be instances of the image consciousness *genus*, and both would be construed as results of a process of pictorialization (Hua XXIII, pp. 18–20).

According to "the point of view of *imaginatio*," our experiences of objects given in both phantasy and physical images are rooted within the intentional struc-

---

[13] See Hua XXIII, p. 18, note 2: "We intend to try to pursue as far as possible the point of view of *imaginatio* and the notion that *phantasy representation* can be interpreted as *image representation* —although there is no dearth of objections to this attempt, objections that subsequently turn out to be justified." Significantly, the clause "objections that subsequently turn out to be justified" was only added later, probably around 1917 (see the "Textkritische Anmerkungen" of the Hua XXIII German edition, p. 617), by which point Husserl had long abandoned his concept of *imaginatio* construed as *Verbildlichung.*

1.4 The Point of View of *Imaginatio*: The Triadic Structure — 19

ture of "image consciousness" (construed as pictorialization, that is, as "conversion into image"). Neither phantasy nor physical images offer us the actual thing in the flesh (the actual palace, in this case); rather, both are *intuitive presentifications in image* of the thing.

Thus, unlike in perception, objects and events are not given directly—*without iconic mediation*—in image consciousness. In this kind of intentionality, we can distinguish between the "thing" and the "image." This intentionality involves *a mediating iconic moment:* what is intended is not the image manifesting itself *before* a subject's eyes, but rather the absent thing for which the image functions as a "representant [*Repräsentant*]" (Hua XXIII, p. 20). Against *this* background, the same would hold true for phantasy acts as well: "if the palace in Berlin hovers before us in the phantasy image, then the palace in Berlin is precisely the thing meant, the thing presented. From the palace in Berlin, however, we distinguish the image hovering before us, which naturally is not a real thing and is not in Berlin" (Hua XXIII, p. 20). From *this* viewpoint, phantasy representation implies "*a certain mediacy*" (Hua XXIII, p. 25).

If image consciousness intentionality involves two objectivities (i.e., "image" and "thing"), then phenomenological description must account for two different objectifying "apprehensions, one built on the other." Husserl specifies that apprehension constituting the image is insufficient for image consciousness to arise: it requires a second apprehension through which alone the relationship to the pictorially presentified image *sujet* can be established. Our act is directed not at "the image hover[ing] before [us]" but rather at the represented *sujet*, thanks to a "second apprehension [...] founded in the image apprehension" (see Hua XXIII, p. 25).

The schema emerging from this description can also be defined as a *delegation model* in the specific (legal) sense of "standing in place of" or "acting in another's name." The image acts as a *representant* (*Repräsentant*) for the absent original, which is not present but merely *presentified* (*vergegenwärtigt*) through a third party. The image serves as its deputy, as its *Stellvertreter*.[14]

Early on in the Göttingen course, as we have seen, Husserl tends to ascribe this structure of *imaginatio* to both mental images and physical ones. Both, he says, involve an image consciousness conceived on the model of delegation, and in both cases the thing does not give itself directly, as in perception. Rather, one can "distinguish image and thing" (Hua XXIII, p. 19). The "delegative" approach initially seems to affect Husserl's understanding of the phantasy experience, whose *prima facie* description indicates a structure analogous to the one characterizing physical images. However, as mentioned, deeper analysis of this form of intention-

---

[14] See, for instance, Hua XXIII, p. 26.

ality will uncover additional differences between these two types of images—differences that will ultimately call their alleged structural commonalities into question.

In fact, Husserl remarks that describing physical images phenomenologically seems "more complicated" than the "parallel case" (Hua XXIII, p. 20) of phantasy images. For one, he notes that the meaning of the word "image" is twofold with physical images (Hua XXIII, p. 20): it can refer to both (i) "the image as physical thing, as this painted and framed canvas, as this imprinted paper, and so on" and (ii) "the image as the *image object* [*Bildobjekt*] appearing in such and such a way through its determinate coloration and form." Within the point of view of *imaginatio*, Husserl construes the image object as the *"precise analogue of the phantasy image"* (Hua XXIII, p. 20, my italics).

For simplicity's sake, let us consider an ordinary photograph depicting a friend of ours—a paradigmatic example we shall be using throughout the book. When looking at this photograph, we can easily repeat the experience Husserl describes in his Göttingen analysis, in which he wonders *how* a photograph is capable of presenting an absent child:

> For example, there lies before us a photograph representing a child. How does it do this? Well, primarily by sketching an image that on the whole does indeed resemble the child but deviates from it markedly in appearing size, coloring, and so on. Of course, this miniature child appearing here in disagreeably grayish-violet coloring is not the child that is meant, not the represented child. It is not the child itself but its photographic *image*. If we speak of the image in this way, and if we say in criticism that the image fails, that it resembles the original only in this or that respect, or if we say that it resembles it perfectly, then naturally we do not mean the physical image, the thing that lies there on the table or hangs on the wall. The photograph as physical thing is a real object and is taken as such in perception [*Wahrnehmung*]. (Hua XXIII, pp. 20–21)

Husserl's description of this photograph brings to light the well-known phenomenological tripartition among
a) the "physical image," i.e., a "real object" that "is taken as such in *perception*"—in our example, the photograph as a thing made of paper that we can store in an album;
b) the "image object," or "representing image," i.e., "something appearing that has never existed and never will exist and, of course, is not taken by us for even a moment as something real," which holds a "depictive function"—in our example, the "miniature" friend, which "is not the [friend] itself but [her] photographic *image*"; and
c) the "image *sujet*," i.e., the "represented or depicted object"—in our example, the friend herself (Hua XXIII, p. 21).

1.5 The Ineffable Essence of Image Object

What turns out to be particularly difficult to grasp is the nature of the image object: it is not the perceivable (as *wahrnehmbar*) image thing, nor is it the absent image *sujet*. Although image objects might seem to involve a material dimension, they are not perceptual objects in the proper sense. Images as things *can* be considered perceptual in that we say an image is hanging on the wall, that it is lightweight, that it has been damaged, etc. The absent *sujet might* also have been perceived in the past or be perceived in the future (or, for that matter, in the present, if the friend is standing beside her photograph).

Conversely, the image object can never be perceived. It is a veritable "medial-threshold" that simultaneously differentiates itself from the other two "objects" on account of what Husserl calls the phenomenon of "conflict [*Widerstreit*]." As he puts it,

> The image object as image object must be the bearer of conflict in a double sense. In one sense (a), it is in conflict with the actual perceptual present. This is the conflict between the image as image object appearance and the image as physical image thing; (b) in the other sense, there is the conflict between the image-object appearance and the presentation of the *sujet* entwined with it or, rather, partially coinciding with it. (Hua XXIII, p. 55)

Let us explore each of these in greater detail.

(a) Physical image consciousness requires a *consciousness of conflict* between the image object properly manifesting itself and the perceived material substratum found in the physical image (mere physical colors, for example). In the same sense, the image object also conflicts with its surrounding perceptual reality; with a painting, for example, the boundary between the two *might* be delimited by the frame, which thus ideally marks the point of discontinuity between the synthesis of the perceptual dimension and that pertaining to the space of the image (cf. Hua XXIII, p. 50). *Nota bene:* I emphasize "might" because the presence of a frame is not a necessary prerequisite to the image object's appearance—I could simply draw a face on the wall without having to frame it (Figure 1). Parietal art offers a similar example.

In any case, there is a *disjunctive conflict* between the apprehension of the image object and the apprehension of the physical colors: the "spatialit[ies]" of the image object and the physical image are "incompatible" (see Hua XXIII, p. 153). Apprehension of the image object is only made possible by "us[ing] up" (Hua XXIII, p. 28, note 4) all sensible content that would otherwise be employed in apprehending the image thing. *These two apprehensions cannot be simultaneous.* Husserl rightly points out (see Hua XXIII, p. 49) that, although it is possible in principle for us to turn our focus away from the picture and think of the lines and col-

Figure 1: "Simple drawing" of a face without a frame

ors comprising it as mere lines and colors, it is usually difficult for us to do so. Conversely, the contrast between material substrate and image object is evident in (for example) paintings done using what Diderot, in keeping with art vocabulary, called the "contrasted manner" (*manière heurtée*), in which the image object becomes visible to the viewer only at a certain distance. Up close, we see only a confusion of matter on canvas, but when we take a few steps back, the image suddenly appears.[15]

As Husserl points out, the initial apprehension that consumes the sensible content and produces the image object does not yet constitute "the relation to the image *sujet*" (for which the image object inherently acts as a representative) necessary for manifestation of the image "in the proper sense" (Hua XXIII, pp. 23, 24). Therefore, such moments of apprehension do not pertain exclusively to the manifestation of the image object, i.e., to that first apprehension that "steals" or subtracts the content available for perceptual apprehension. For an image to manifest itself, there needs to be a second apprehension capable of bringing a second object to light: the image *sujet*, the object properly meant in image consciousness.

(b) Physical image consciousness requires a *consciousness of conflict* between the image object properly manifesting itself and the represented image *sujet*: the former must present not only "moments of resemblance" (Hua XXIII, p. 33) to the latter (thereby enabling the relationship between the two) but also "moments of difference" (Hua XXIII, p. 44). These divergent moments must allow the image object to manifest itself as an image object—that is, to prevent its illusory perception as the thing itself (see Hua XXIII, p. 22). As such, the difference between image object and image *sujet* should not be conceived as a deficit, a lacuna that a "perfect image" should be able to bridge. Rather (based on Husserl's initial framing of the

---

[15] "Chardin's technique [*le faire*] is particular. It has in common with the contrasted manner [*manière heurtée*] that from near one does not know what it [*scil.* the object represented] is, and that as one moves away the object is created and ends up being that of nature" (Diderot 2009 [1765], p. 59).

issue, at least), these moments of difference are a necessary condition for the two apprehensions (image object and image *sujet*) to build upon one another. The conflict here is not disjunctive but *conjunctive:* these two apprehensions *are simultaneous.* The object meant is the image *sujet*, but only *qua* presentified by the image object.

Nevertheless, caution is warranted here as Husserl has forced us onto a slippery slope. Although phenomenological description allows us to distinguish between these different moments, Husserl emphasizes that, in image consciousness, the object properly meant is, from the very beginning, the *depicted* object (the *sujet*) and not its representative (the image object, such as the image on the surface of a painting or photograph, or those "superhuman"-sized figures we see on the movie screen).

Even after clarifying this point, however, we are still far from determining the precise nature of the intentional relation between image object and image *sujet*. In keeping with the delegation model, one can reasonably say that, for image consciousness to subsist, some form of disparity or distinction must arise, thereby allowing one to establish what the image is and what, for example, the object meant or the *sujet* is. Without this distinction, our image consciousness might shift into a consciousness of reality, which we might subsequently recognize as an illusion. We will return to this point several times later on; for now, let us merely note that this theme dates back at least as far as Plato, whose paradox of the two Cratyluses touched upon the need for such a distinction.

In *Cratylus* (432b), Plato pointed out that differences between a thing and its image were necessary in order for the latter to exist as such. If the image of Cratylus imitated Cratylus in *every* respect, Plato said, we would no longer have Cratylus and his image but rather two Cratyluses:

> SOCRATES: [...] I should say rather that the image, if expressing in every point the entire reality, would no longer be an image. Let us suppose the existence of two objects: one of them shall be Cratylus, and the other the image of Cratylus; and we will suppose, further, that some God makes not only a representation such as a painter would make of your outward form and color, but also creates an inward organization like yours, having the same warmth and softness; and into this infuses motion, and soul, and mind, such as you have, and in a word copies all your qualities, and places them by you in another form; would you say that this was Cratylus and the image of Cratylus, or that there were two Cratyluses? CRATYLUS: I should say that there were two Cratyluses. (Plato 1980, 432b, p. 466)

As has been noted, this *topos* also recurs in Descartes' *Dioptrics*,[16] and it has found a considerable echo in both analytical and continental fields in the debate regard-

---

[16] "In no case does an image have to resemble the object it represents in all respects, for other-

ing the role resemblance plays in depiction.[17] While this approach rejects the notion of an image resembling the object it is purported to depict in *every* respect, instead postulating the necessity of a *moment of difference*, it must still account for the nature of that resemblance, the supposed basis for the possibility of depiction.

In many ways, this debate has already shown how difficult resemblance is to define, despite its seemingly immediate comprehensibility. We all think we know what it means to say that A resembles B, but trouble arises when we try to specify what exactly that resemblance entails or how it makes depiction possible.

As Husserl points out in *Logical Investigations*, resemblance—unlike depiction—is a reciprocal relationship (see Sokolowski 1992, p. 5; Zahavi 2003, p. 18). For instance, two trees might closely resemble one another, but this does not *eo ipso* make one a representation of the other. Even being identical cannot change things in this respect (Hua XIX/1, Vol. 2, p. 124): identical twins do not represent each other. In other words, the capacity to represent something is not a quality that can be exhaustively grounded in an object; we can only fully account for this capacity by turning to consciousness—namely, to the particular *act* of *presentifying* one object through another.

Although similarity alone is not a sufficient condition of representation, it remains one necessary condition under this "delegation model." Besides mentioning the moment of difference, Husserl also discusses "moments of resemblance" (Hua XXIII, p. 33), referencing the latter when characterizing the intentionality of image consciousness as an *intuitive* form of presentification in which the image object acts as a visual representant of the image *sujet*: "we see the *sujet* in the image itself; we see the former in the latter" (Hua XXIII, p. 54). This, he says, is why the intentionality of image consciousness can be characterized as a "seeing-in" (*hinein-*

---

wise there would be no distinction between the object and its image. It is enough that the image resembles its object in a few respects. Indeed, the perfection of an image often depends on its not resembling its object as much as it might" (Descartes 1637, p. 165). In this regard, see also Scholz (2004, pp. 26–27), who rightly notes that "Descartes goes further than Plato" since he "disputes the idea that the greatest possible similarity should be pursued in images." Later in the quoted passage, Descartes notes that "it often happens that in order to be more perfect as an image and to represent an object better, an engraving ought not to resemble it." For a comparison of Plato and Descartes on this point, see also Voltolini (2013, pp. 26–29). For a more detailed contextualization and discussion of Descartes' positions within a theory of depiction, see Hyman (2006, p. 114 ff.).

[17] See, for example, Scholz (2004, pp. 17–81); Spinicci (2008, pp. 23–31).

schauen) (Hua XXIII, p. 57)[18] which is supported by "these moments of resemblance" insofar as "the *sujet* presents itself to us *in them:* through them we look into the *sujet*" (Hua XXIII, p. 33).

The image *sujet*, the represented object, is to be seen *in* the image itself. Crucially, however, this specific intentionality need not necessarily be a one-way street: the *sujet* we intend when viewing the image may simultaneously "look (back at) us" (Hua XXIII, p. 31), starting from an orientation arising *in the* image—as often is the case with portraits.

1.6 Image and Sign

The fact that image consciousness allows us to see the *sujet* through a seeing-in that *interprets* some specific characteristics as *resemblant* allows Husserl to distinguish it from symbolic or "signitive consciousness" (Hua XXIII, p. 56). Image consciousness, he remarks, is not a signitive relationship: the object represented, the image *sujet*, must be intuited in the image itself. Husserl makes this point very early on in the Göttingen analyses: the image object, he says, does not function as a *symbol* for, or a *signifier* of, the image *sujet*. Qualities of symbolism or signification do not pertain to the essence of image consciousness (see Hua XXIII, pp. 56, 185, 361, 518; see also Marbach 2000, p. 295).

Admittedly, image consciousness and symbolic/signitive consciousness do indeed share one property: neither involves a "simple" form of intentionality (like the one involved in perception) since they "*both* point beyond themselves" (Hua XXIII, p. 37). However, whereas "symbolic apprehension and […] signitive apprehension point beyond to an object *foreign* to what appears" (Hua XXIII, p. 37), image consciousness requires us to *see in* the image object in order to see the image *sujet*.[19] Accordingly, Husserl draws a sharp distinction between intrinsic (immanent) *imaginatio*—i.e., the "genuine" ("seeing-in")—and extrinsic, "external

---

18 Only "who looks purely into the image lives in the character of the image and has, in the image, the presentification of the object" (Hua XXIII, p. 38). See also Hua XXIII, pp. 33, 37, 57. On the characterization of Husserl's image consciousness as *seeing-in*, see also Brough (2012, § 4).

19 See, in particular, Marbach (2000), where the editor of Hua XXIII "stress[es]" how "this inner iconicity is by no means restricted, as one might perhaps think at first, to so-called realistic or naturalistic pictorial representations. Instead, […] inner iconicity is a matter of attitudinal stance, set, or turn of mind, which can be alive in the presence of representations that are even relatively 'impoverished' as regards their iconifying moments. […] Outer iconicity, too, is a matter of attitudinal stance, set, or turn of mind. The outward-turn may be triggered more readily by certain types of pictures, but according to Husserl it is in principle always possible to adopt this stance on the presence of pictorial representation" (Marbach 2000, pp. 294–295).

(transeunt)" *imaginatio*, which he construes as symbolic/signitive consciousness founded on image consciousness (see Hua XXIII, p. 56). To draw upon an earlier example, seeing the palace of Berlin *in* a photograph (genuine) is not the same as seeing a small palace-shaped icon on a street sign indicating that it is nearby (external).[20]

Though image *can* function as a sign, it does not necessarily have to do so. Even when they do function as signs, images must be constituted as such before they can be assigned a signitive function. In this sense, image consciousness precedes signitive consciousness (cf. Hua XXIII, p. 56). Once we have identified this primary intrinsic character, we can then, "in the second place, distinguish this internal imaging from external, transeunt imaging—a different mode of representation by means of resemblance, which belongs in a series with representation by means of signs, or at least mediates *imaginatio* consciousness with signitive consciousness" (Hua XXIII, p. 56). In this latter case, images "divert interest from themselves and seek to turn it away, as it were" (Hua XXIII, p. 56).

Husserl gives several examples to help clarify this point. He starts by pointing out that an image primarily constituted as an intrinsic image—say, a photograph—can serve as an "engine [...] of memory" (see Hua XXIII, p. 56):

> A photograph [...] can also *bring to mind* a person in a manner similar to that in which a *sign* brings to mind something signified. If it does that, the image is characterized, phenomenologically, as that which brings something to mind. The person himself, however, who exists for us intentionally in a second and separate, though related, representation—for example, in a phantasy representation (but perhaps also in a merely empty intention)—the person, I say, then appears as what the image brings to mind. (Hua XXIII, p. 56)

To return to another previous example, we can see our friend by looking at a photograph of her, but the photograph can also serve as the "engine" for a different, intuitive representation of her—for example by prompting me to recall the first

---

20 Sartre's *The Imaginary* draws this essential distinction between image and sign as well. He mentions "a placard nailed above a door of the station" referring to the "Assistant Manager's Office" as an example of sign consciousness: "I *read* the words on the placard and I now know that I must go in here to make my claim." In this case, we "take [...] a certain attitude of consciousness": when *reading* what is manifested on the placard surface, we are prompted to "aim" our gaze at another object that *need not resemble* that manifestation (in other words, the office need not resemble the word "office"). In keeping with Husserl's remarks, Sartre clarifies that "in the case of the sign, as in that of the image, we have an intention that aims at an object, [...], an object aimed at that is not present. At first glance it might seem that we are dealing with the same function. It is to be noticed, moreover, that classical psychology often confuses sign and image. When Hume tells us that the relation between the image and its object is extrinsic, he makes the image a sign" (Sartre 1940, p. 21).

time we met, thus causing me to intuitively presentify her in a "memorial representation [*Erinnerungsvorstellung*]": "Whoever makes use of the image as an aid to memory seeks and perhaps finds another presentification of the object, which may offer him a richer presentification of it" (Hua XXIII, p. 38).

Husserl also brings up the case of "pictorial indices," referring to "volumes containing complete series of works by Dürer, Raphael, and so on, in the most minute reproductions" whose "chief object [...] is not to awaken internal imaging and the aesthetic pleasure" (Hua XXIII, p. 38). Those tiny images, he says, are not aimed at an "intrinsic" look purported to receive them aesthetically; "their point, instead, is to supply pictorial indices of the works of those great artists. The reproductions are repertories of memory. They are *illustrative captions*, aids to memory, so to speak" (Hua XXIII, p. 38). Similarly, a museum website might refer to the physical works on display using small thumbnail images (which, of course, might also serve as links to larger and more detailed digital reproductions on the site).

There are any number of possible examples in this vein; the important point here is that, in such cases, an image serves as the trigger for *another* presentification or presentation. Just as "a wood engraving of a Raphael Madonna, for example, can remind us of the original that we have seen in the Dresden gallery," (Hua XXIII, p. 38) the tiny image of the *Madonna Sistina* on our computer screen when we load the *Gemäldegalerie Alte Meister* homepage might prompt us to think about the actual work.[21]

Conversely, genuine image consciousness does not push us to aim our gaze elsewhere; it draws our gaze in rather than driving it away. It can also strike the subject in many ways, but always with itself as the visual source of the experience. With representational images, we see the represented object in the image itself: "in order to represent the object, we are supposed to see *in* the image" (Hua XXIII, p. 37).

---

21 Husserl also elaborates on this idea in Appendix IX (probably 1905) to *Phantasy and Image Consciousness*: "I look at this small advertising reproduction of the *Pietà* of Fra Bartolomeo. I grasp the image at one glance. The consciousness of agreement does not fill me. I do not live in the image; on the contrary, I feel pulled outward. I experience the image as a *sign* for the original, which I have seen at an earlier time. The meaning is not inherent in the image; rather, it is inherent in a second meaning-consciousness grounded on the image consciousness and connected with the image consciousness in the way in which a symbol and an intention that points beyond it are connected" (Hua XXIII, p. 185).

1.7 A Potential Misunderstanding: The "Image-Theory"

At this point, it should be clear that the function Husserl assigns to the image object (namely, deputing it to a representative role within the "delegation model") can give rise to a dangerous misconception. As stressed, the potential difficulty appears to lie in grasping the *nature* of the image object, the "interceding" element in this form of intentionality. The image object is not the image thing that can be *perceived*, nor is it the image *sujet*, which is absent despite being the ultimate and proper object of the intentional process. Husserl qualifies the image object as "*a nothing [ein Nichts]*" (Hua XXIII, p. 50), but it is an odd "nothing" insofar as it is a visible one, a "figment [*Fiktum*]" (Hua XXIII, p. 59). This unreal *yet visible* mediality functions as a representative; by looking *into* it, we are given to see the presentified *sujet*. Properly speaking, then, when we experience a physical image, it is not the image as a "thing" that fills that role but rather the image object, i.e., a "semblance thing" (Hua XXIII, p. 21) that "truly does not exist" (Hua XXIII, p. 23) but "makes its appearance to us on the basis of color sensations, form sensations, and so forth" (Hua XXIII, p. 21).

Let us dispel a potential misunderstanding here. From the outset, Husserl rejects the possibility of construing the image object—whether in physical or phantasy image consciousness—as a "mental image" hidden *in* our head. Years later, in *Eye and Mind*, Maurice Merleau-Ponty references the image's "bad repute," saying that images are all too often construed as "a tracing, a copy, a second thing," a mere intermediary between a self-contained "I" and the world, located somewhere in our mind—as if "the *mental image was such a drawing*, belonging among our private bric-a-brac" (Merleau-Ponty 1960–1961, p. 126, my italics).

Even as early as his *Logical Investigations* (1900–01), Husserl warns us against falling prey to a naïve and "erroneous *image-theory* [*Bildertheorie*], which thinks it has sufficiently explained the fact of representation [*des Vorstellens*]—fully present in each act—by saying that: 'Outside the thing itself is there (or is at times there); in consciousness there is an image which does duty for it [*Im Bewuȷ̈stsein ist als sein Stellvertreter ein Bild*]'" (Hua XIX/1, Vol. 2, p. 125).[22] This assertion upends the notion of needing iconic mediation at the core of our perception—Husserl categorically rejects any model of perception that requires an intervening deputy-image (a deputy for the object "in" the subject's head—or the subject's "private bric-a-brac," as Merleau-Ponty puts it) to explain the subject-object relationship.

---

[22] On the critique of *Bildertheorie* in the *Logical Investigations* see Saraiva (1970, pp. 45–46) and Alloa (2011, pp. 244–249). See Jansen (2005, pp. 222–226) for a discussion specifically related to Hua XXIII.

1.7 A Potential Misunderstanding: The "Image-Theory" — 29

This criticism of the "images theory" clearly echoes the criticism of consciousness as a representational device as construed under the "'theater of the mind' approach in early modern philosophy, wherein," as Pippin rightly notes,

> what we were conscious of in ordinary consciousness could not be said to be spatio-temporal external objects in any immediate sense but sensory effects, "ideas," "impressions," "representations," and so forth, such that the work of the understanding left us either, for the empiricists, "fainter" and, because more generalized, vaguer "ideas" or, for the rationalists, "clearer and distincter" versions of what was only imperfectly and deceptively apprehended immediately. But for both camps, *consciousness itself was reflective*. (Pippin 2005, p. 87)

This approach is already at work in Humean empiricism, as if perception were given through the "theater of the mind,"[23] or as if consciousness were a screen upon which a cinematic parade of things unfolded.[24]

Yet although the *Logical Investigations* reject all forms of naïve iconic hypostatization and mediation as regards the phenomenological account of perception, they still construe phantasy through a pictorializing model; an exhaustive elaboration of phantasy intentionality remains a *desideratum* at this stage. Despite having already ruled out the notion that explaining intentional acts might require iconic internal mental mediation, Husserl does not elaborate this point extensively in relation to a "phenomenology of phantasy." Several key related questions still warrant further development: what about the nature of what we might call, at least at an early stage, phantasy images? How do we experience them? And how do they relate to those "other" images we all see, use, and share in everyday life?

At the time of the *Logical Investigations*, Husserl seems to foresee the complexity and acknowledge the provisional nature of such an approach, though he postpones any decisive examination of this slippery issue to future analyses. In a certain sense, the "seeds" for Husserl's future developments (which we shall now examine in detail) are evident in his criticism of "image-theory". The third part of his Göttingen lectures represents a critical threshold: it can be considered the paramount moment of confrontation with unresolved issues that threatened to undermine proper elaboration of the phantasy experience.

---

23 For another sense of the expression "theater of the mind" in relation to imagination, see Ferrarin (2018), who elaborates on Wollheim (1984, p. 63 ff.) rather than Hume (as such an expression might initially suggest). In this other usage, the expression "theater of the mind" can stand for the plurality of perspectives and voices we can put into motion to form a sort of theater. This other direction points to phantasy's ability to create its own dramas (*quasi*-worlds).

24 Cf. Saraiva (1970, p. 47), who explicitly revisits the critical analyses conducted in Gurwitsch (2009 [1940]; as specifically regards the idea of "consciousness" as a "cinematic screen," see p. 145).

1.8 Does Phantasy Experience Necessarily Imply Mental Images?

Thus, when Husserl sets out in 1905 to inquire into the essence of phantasy experience, he is already well aware of the pitfalls of any naïve "theory of phantasy" purporting to explain phantasy representation using a mediating image hovering in mental space like a "thing in a box" (which is in keeping with his previous warning against "image theory"). Moreover, he rightly specifies that even accepting any such theory purely for the sake of argument would not exempt that theory from providing a plausible account of *how* this mental image *were capable of depicting* something absent: "If I put a picture in a drawer," he sarcastically asks, "does *the drawer* represent something?" (Hua XXIII, p. 23). Let us remark that this holds true with regard to physical images as well. Though Husserl stresses that the image object is actually a "nothing" and remarks on multiple occasions that it "truly does not exist" (Hua XXIII, p. 23), this in no way implies that the image object is instead existent in the perceiver's mind: "not only [...] it has no existence outside my consciousness, but also [...] it has no existence inside my consciousness; it has no existence at all" (Hua XXIII, p. 23). What properly exists, as mentioned, is the image as a physical thing.

Even so, Husserl still needs a satisfactory account of what a "phantasy image" *is*, a description of its essential structure. In particular, difficulties arise when it comes to determining whether or not the triadic structure identified through analysis of the physical image can be truly recognized in phantasy as well—and, accordingly, whether the image/phantasy consciousness parallel drawn in the name of *imaginatio* (in the sense of "conversion into an *imago*") holds.

Under Husserl's early account of *imaginatio*, we might claim that, just as we can see a friend presentified in an image object by pulling a photograph out of a drawer and looking *into* it, we see a friend presentified in an image by forging in phantasy its mental (*geistige*)[25] image object, a sort of mental proxy grounding the intentionality directed to the absent *sujet*. This approach can be found in his 1898 dissertation, making it nearly coeval to *Logical Investigations*.

As an example, Husserl offers a phantasy of the palace in Berlin (*das Berliner Schloss*). Under this delegation structure, the presence of an image object—a phan-

---

[25] "Now the situation is certainly more complicated in the case of physical *imaginatio* than it is in the case of ordinary phantasy representation, but we do find that both have something essential in common: In the case of physical *imaginatio*, a physical object that exercises the function of awakening a 'mental image [*geistiges Bild*]' is presupposed; in phantasy representation in the ordinary sense, a mental image is there without being tied to such a physical excitant. In both cases, however, the mental image is precisely an image; it represents a *sujet*" (Hua XXIII, p. 22).

tasy image (*Phantasiebild*) that "hovers before us"—serves as the basis for the intuitive presentification directed at the absent object, i. e., to the actual palace that is not *hic et nunc* before us but rather is in Berlin (Hua XXIII, p. 20). Above, we mentioned the first difference that seems to jump out at us when we seek to distinguish between the structures of phantasy and physical representations: the former lacks the moment of the image thing and thus lacks the conflict between image thing and image object.

However, his efforts to give a phenomenological account of this alleged greater simplicity eventually lead Husserl to radically rethink his initial perspective on *imaginatio*. As noted earlier, raising these crucial doubts is one of the most relevant results of the third part of his course. Ultimately, the pictorializing structure does not appear to be involved in the phantasy experience. Considering phantasy using the delegative paradigm, as elaborated through the phenomenological description of physical image, leads to a veritable cul-de-sac. In his Göttingen lectures, Husserl maintains his distinction between image object and image *sujet* regarding physical images, saying that the former acts as an iconic device allowing presentification of the latter. As far as phantasy images are concerned, however, he challenges and ultimately rejects this distinction. "Could it not be the case," Husserl asks, "that phantasy apprehensions might function without any character of image [*Bildlichkeit*]?" (Hua XXIII, p. 53). He calls into question the *necessity* of assigning any role whatsoever to a mediating image object, an iconic deputy, in the essential characterization of phantasy experience: "Does an image object through which an image *sujet* is intuited actually become constituted in phantasy? I must confess that again and again I was seized by serious doubts here" (Hua XXIII, p. 60).

In fact, the difficulties he encountered while working toward a phenomenological description of the "phantasy image" structure soon revealed several key factors distinguishing phantasy images from physical. Husserl comes to suggest that phantasy consciousness can arise without needing a *fictum* that manifests itself on sensuous content and "bears on itself the brand of nullity" (Hua XXIII, p. 61) —in other words, a *fictum* representing the image *sujet*, that is, a *fictum* of the type we find in physical images.

Accordingly, Husserl proposes that phantasy presentification *does not involve the constitution of an image object at all*. This is tantamount to affirming that we do not need mediating image objects when considering a phantasy-*sujet*; rather, we experience the *sujet* in an *immediate consciousness of presentification*.

Yet even as he highlights the differences characterizing phantasy experience, Husserl seems to imply that a seeing-in consciousness is still at work. A *"modified"* consciousness allowing us to "see [...] what is meant *in* what is experienced" is still necessary for the phantasy object to appear. Unlike under the previous delegative account, however, in this case this happens "without [...] first taking what is sensuously experienced as something existing independently" (Hua XXIII, p. 85, my italics).²⁶

Difficulties also arise when it comes to defining phantasy's sensory content: what specifically can we say *is there* in phantasy to serve as the basis for the image object's emergence? This "nothing" does seem to be made of *something*, after all. In physical images, the image object arises on a perceptual ground (despite conflicting with it); as such, under this paradigm, a phantasized image object ought to be based on corresponding sensuous content, that is, on the "phantasms" (Hua XXIII, p. 11). Under the specific variant of the "content-apprehension schema" informing Husserl's work at this stage of his phenomenological journey (see Jansen 2005, which also points out the "empiricist vestiges" of this "early" account of phantasy), these phantasms should form the basis for the constitution of image objects in an analogous role to their perceptual equivalents. As such, it stands to reason that they should somehow be "present" in the first place.

When it comes to phantasy, however, Husserl questions the double objectivity allegedly required to see the image *sujet* in the image object and ultimately abandons the hypothesis. For one, this would amount to viewing the phantasm as disposable, something "present" in the service of an "unrealizing" apprehension. Husserl, however, ultimately concludes that construing the phantasm as present, sensuous content underlying the image object's emergence in phantasy is highly problematic and gives rise to unresolvable contradictions (see Husserl XXIII, § 37). Rather, Husserl suggests, it is only *après coup* through a process of abstraction that we are able to conceive this specific sensory content as equivalent to present content,²⁷—for example, "by grasping it as simultaneous with a datum of perception." In such cases, however, the referenced "present" is only "a present objectified by means of mediations, not a present that is immediately sensed" (Hua XXIII, p. 85).

Therefore—and this is a fundamental point—the phantasy image's lack of a physical dimension equates to no element of presence *at all*.²⁸ Unlike in apprehen-

---

26 Husserl's considerations do not seem sufficiently precise in this instance. In fact, following on from his earlier descriptions, we can say that even with physical images, there is not something that is first taken as existing and then perceived as an image. Rather, in the case of "physical images," the sensible material is used from the beginning by the unrealizing phantasy consciousness, which sees it as something not present (not present at the point where it manifests itself).
27 See also the analyses in Richir (2000, pp. 80–84). The Belgian phenomenologist's reflections are also examined and developed further in Schnell (2007, pp. 148–153).
28 "In phantasy, we do not have anything 'present,' and in this sense we do not have an image object" (Hua XXIII, p. 86).

sion of the physical image (at least as Husserl understood it up to this point),²⁹ phantasy apprehension does not entail consciousness of something present being deputed to convey image consciousness: "the *phantasm*, the sensuous content of phantasy, gives itself as not present. It defends itself against the demand that it be taken as present; from the beginning it carries with it the characteristic of unreality. Primarily it has the function of being taken as something else. Only indirect reflection bestows on it an acquired present" (Hua XXIII, p. 87). In other words, no conflict emerges between a present physical dimension and an image object. Constitution of the phantasy object does not require the consciousness to steal sensible content from a "phantasmically" present "thing." Phantasms are given as "not there" from the very beginning, without a mediating representative.

Thus, Husserl eventually rejects the notion that the intentionality of phantasy consciousness implies the manifestation of an image object, i.e., a depictive "figment" (constituting itself on "phantasms") representing the *sujet* (see Hua XXIII, pp. 59–60). In light of this, he abandons the hypothesis of parallelism between phantasy and physical images. Crucially, Husserl comes to recognize that what "hovers" before us in phantasy is *"immediately [unmittelbar]"* (Hua XXIII, p. 85) given as *nonpresent*, without requiring a conflict between an allegedly present phantasm and an image object obtained on its basis. The "point of view of imaginatio," in the sense of conversion into *imago*, does not fit phantasy intentionality. Husserl clearly refuses to ground phantasy experience in the *imaginatio* as a pictorializing model. As shown in the following quotation, the same holds for memory presentifications: "If our phantasy playfully occupies itself with angels and devils, dwarves and water nymphs, or if our memory displaces us into a past that passes before our mind in intuitive formations, then the appearing objectivities are not taken as image objects, as mere representatives, analogues, images of other objectivities" (Hua XXIII, p. 92).³⁰

---

29 "When an imagining consciousness is brought about on the basis of sensations of whatever sort, this happens under the mediation of perceptual apprehensions that constitute a present, an image object standing before me as present. If we were to ask on what this depends, the answer would be: The sensation defends itself, so to speak, against the demand that it be taken as the mere image of something. It is itself the mark of reality; all reality is measured against it; it is a primary, actual present. But while it makes a present appear, it can at the same time direct consciousness to something analogous, and simultaneously permit us to see in what is present something else, something not present" (Hua XXIII, p. 87). Still, some Husserlian passages seem to imply lingering uncertainty regarding whether and to what extent this present element comes to the fore with so-called physical images.
30 This point is reiterated in Appendix IX (probably 1905) to Text no. 1, again in reference to memory: "if, living in phantasy, I go back in memory, if, for example, I think back on the Wolfgangsee, on a watering place, on the trip in the boat, on the Gellow, on the blacksmith and his hammers, and

If an objectifying apprehension constituting the image object is no longer required in phantasy consciousness, then phantasy intentionality is no longer to be understood as involving a double objectivity. Like perception, phantasy acts involve a direct form of intentionality, not one mediated through an image object that serves to ground a second layer of objectivation (namely, the image *sujet*). Husserl eventually comes to describe the intentionality characterizing the phantasy experience as an immediate, unmediated consciousness of presentification, "a modified consciousness of seeing what is meant in what is experienced" (Hua XXIII, p. 85).

These distinctions constitute a substantial realignment of the whole approach Husserl had developed up to that point. His rejection of the structural parallel between image consciousness and phantasy consciousness conceived in terms of *imaginatio* proper—of "conversion into an image" (*Verbildlichung*)—leaves room for a *new parallel* between *phantasy* and *perception*. Following up on his above-mentioned criticism of the image-theory in *Logical Investigations*, Husserl affirms that "the word '*imaginatio* [*Imagination*],' the talk of phantasy images, and so forth, ought not mislead us here any more than talk of 'perceptual images' does in the case of perception. [...] The phantasy appearance, the simple phantasy appearance unencumbered by any imaging built on it, relates to its object just as *straightforwardly* [*einfältig*]"—in "one fold"—"as perception does" (Hua XXIII, p. 92). Thus, phantasy consciousness does not experience its own object through a mediating image, it "does not contain a manifold [*mehrfältige*] intention." Accordingly, "*presentification* [*Vergegenwärtigung*]" reveals itself to be "*an ultimate mode of intuitive representation* [*Vorstellung*], just like perceptual representation [*Wahrnehmungsvorstellung*], just like presentation [*Gegenwärtigung*]" (Hua XXIII, p. 93).

We can take these ideas a step further and suggest that Husserl considers *phantasy* inherently *aniconic* in a sense that overturns his initial Göttingen approach.[31] Phantasy is a mode of consciousness involving a specific temporality rather than something we experience through images. In other words, *the fact that we can see images is not what allows us to have phantasies; rather, the fact that we can trigger a phantasy consciousness is what allows us to recognize and create images.*

---

so forth—if, I say, I *live in phantasy*, then I do not notice anything at all in the way of a representative [*repräsentativen*] consciousness; I do not see an appearance before me and take it as a representant of something else. On the contrary, I see the thing itself, the event, and so on" (Hua XXIII, p. 178).

31 Husserl definitely clarifies this point as early as 1905. I would therefore disagree with Aldea (2013) by maintaining that, *properly speaking*, Husserl no longer "struggles" with the concept of "mental images" from that point onward.

Just as we do not perceive objects through image copies of them, we do not intuit objects through representative images in phantasy. As Husserl notes in *Ideas I* (see Hua III/1, pp. 218–219), a tree I perceive is not given to consciousness through any form of mental representation that would mediate my encounter with it. Analogously—and in keeping with the new perception/phantasy parallel that we have just raised—when I phantasize a tree, that tree is not the *sujet* of a mental image hovering within my consciousness.

In this third part of the Göttingen lecture course, Husserl comes to realize that, in order to make any further progress in this direction, he will need to delve deeper into the phenomenology of time—a subject that, as he recalled at the beginning of the first part of the lecture series, he skipped in *Logical Investigations* because he did not yet feel ready to confront it (see Hua XXXVIII, p. 4). Incorporating time analysis into his investigations will lend Husserl new insights into his previous work, creating new possibilities for development.

1.9 From Delegation to Reproduction

Faced with these perplexing questions, Husserl ultimately refuses to ground phantasy experience in the *imaginatio* as a pictorializing model; rather, his phenomenological analysis quickly reveals "[a]n essential distinction […] between […] *imaginatio* [*Imagination*] in the proper sense, representation by means of an *image*," wherein "an appearing object is taken to be a depictive image for another object perfectly like it or resembling it," and "*imaginatio* [*Imagination*] in the sense of simple phantasy [*schlichte Phantasie*]," which is "sharply set apart from the genuine image function" insofar as it "lacks an *image* object that becomes constituted in its own right" (Hua XXIII, pp. 89–90).[32] Husserl thus goes as far as to question whether this latter case can even be described in terms of phantasy image at all.

This "breaking point" Husserl reaches in the seminal Göttingen course serves as an impetus for new elaborations. His work in this direction ultimately undermines the delegation or *Repräsentation* model, which he had previously considered a key element of the structure of image consciousness and had initially assumed to be integral to phantasy as well.

---

32 In keeping with the second (loose) meaning of the term *imaginatio*, Husserl uses the terms *imaginatio* (*Imagination*), imagination (*Einbildung*), and phantasy (*Phantasie*) interchangeably in the Hua XXIII manuscripts subsequent to those on the Göttingen course (Text no. 2, for example), while also referring to *imaginatio* in the more general sense of phantasy as in Appendix L to Text no. 16 (likely dating to around Spring 1912) entitled "On Imaginatio [*Zu Imagination*]" (Hua XXIII, pp. 569–573). We will return to this text later.

After Husserl rules out the possibility of interpreting *phantasy representation* (*Phantasievorstellung*) as *imaging representation* (*Bildlichkeitsvorstellung*) (see Hua XXIII, p. 79), his research manuscripts over the next several years make it clear that his revised concept of phantasy consciousness will shift from the double objectivity implied under the delegation (*Repräsentation*) model to the "immediate" paradigm of reproduction (*Reproduktion*).[33] This is evidenced, for instance, in Text no. 2 (1904–1909) and Text no. 8 (1909) of Hua XXIII, as well as in the intense analyses carried out in Texts nos. 15, 16, and 17 of the same volume—all dating from 1912, one year before the publication of *Ideas I*, which would benefit significantly from the results of these investigations as well.

Despite being marked by "editorial silence," the period between 1905 and 1913 represents a crucial phase of Husserl's endeavors, one in which he not only develops the notion of phenomenological reduction (see Hua II) but also significantly revises the content-apprehension schema that still informed his 1905 analyses. In this context, it is worth considering another Hua XXIII manuscript, probably penned sometime in the summer or early autumn of 1909, in which Husserl explicitly blames the content-apprehension scheme as the main reason for his repeated failures to account for the difference between perception and phantasy (see Hua XXIII, p. 323).[34] Accordingly, Husserl dramatically revises his content-apprehension scheme during this period, which in turn leads him to re-examine[35] his previous approach to sensory content *in both perception and phantasy.*

On the one hand, Husserl claims, perception does not involve *first* having neutral content and *then* an apprehension constituting the perceptual manifestations; for instance, "we do not first of all have a color as content of apprehension and then the characteristic of apprehension that produces the appearance" (Hua XXIII, p. 323). Analogously, when it comes to phantasy, "we do not again have a color as content of apprehension," i.e., a pure phantasm, "and then a changed apprehension, the apprehension that produces the phantasy appearance" (Hua XXIII,

---

[33] "The word 'imaging' [*Bildlichkeit*], however, is itself only a figurative term, and here etymology supplies us with an image that is quite dangerous. At present, therefore, I prefer 'reproductive,' which, of course, must also be merely a word and not a concept derived from its ordinary and etymological sense" (Hua XXIII, p. 394).
[34] Regarding Husserlian self-criticism concerning the scheme and the corrections he makes to his previous positions, see also Hua X, "For the Dissolution of the Apprehension-Content Scheme" (p. 279 ff.).
[35] Concerning the actual scope of this revision, see also Lohmar (2006, pp. 404–407), and Lohmar (2010, p. 118), which seek to mitigate positions that construe Husserl's rejection of this model as absolute. In this respect, see also Mensch (2010, p. 154), where we read, "one has to agree with Lohmar that Husserl's criticism of the model [*scil.* the schema "content-there-to-be-interpreted – interpretation"] is not general, but directed to specific points and ends with a positive result."

p. 323). Earlier, we mentioned that Husserl had already raised the thorny question of the nature of the phantasy's sensory content at the end of the third *Hauptstück* of the Göttingen course, noting that the phantasm could not be understood as something present and merely waiting to be interpreted by consciousness. What emerges here is that there is no neutral sensual content *at all*, and this applies to perceptual content as well. In other words, all content is already consciousness: "'Consciousness' consists of consciousness through and through, and the sensation as well as the phantasm is already 'consciousness'" (Hua XXIII, p. 323), and both give themselves in a specific temporal mode. Against this background, the notion of "pure content" would only be the result of a gesture of abstraction, of an abstraction process.

Under these modified terms (and following on from his fundamental analyses concerning consciousness of time, which he inaugurated in the fourth part of the 1905 Göttingen course), Husserl comes to conceive "perception as *impressional* (originary) consciousness of the present, consciousness of what is there itself, and the like" and phantasy as its "reproductively modified" pendant, as a *quasi*-experience (*quasi* in the sense of the Latin *quam si*, "as if"), "as the *reproductively modified consciousness of the present*, consciousness of what is there itself as it were, of what is present as it were, of the phantasy present [*des gleichsam Gegenwärtig, der Gegenwartsphantasie*]." From this perspective, phantasy can benefit from a specific form of presence, a *Gegenwartsphantasie*, but not the one pertaining to a "concrete individual [...], which now exists and endures for its time, and so on" (Hua XXIII, p. 323). Thus, we have perceptual acts—positionally characterized as real, stamped by "the moment of *belief*" (Hua XXIII, p. 106)—on the one hand, and phantasy acts—not positional but *quasi*-acts as modified reproductions of perceptual acts—on the other.

Described in these terms, phantasy is no longer construed as a specific mode of apprehension applicable to enigmatic sensory contents (i.e., phantasms), but rather as a reproductive modification of a corresponding act of perception; this can be viewed as an answer to the aforementioned questions raised at the end of the third *Hauptstück* in 1905. It is now presentification itself that Husserl characterizes as a reproductive act rather than a representative one. A phantasy act, we might suggest, does not merely imply the intuitive presentification of an object. There is no qualitatively unique consciousness capable of grasping either a perceptual object (perceptual act) or a phantasy object (phantasy act).

Indeed, as Husserl's critique of Brentano in the third *Hauptstück* makes clear (see Hua XXIII, § 46), determining the quality of the object is not sufficient for determining the quality of the act; a shift of consciousness is required as its essential correlate. As we shall see in subsequent chapters, the subjective and objective sides are not to be construed as abstracted and separate but rather as facets of a more originary experience. What is reproduced in phantasy (and memory)[36] is not the object or the occurrence, but rather the act of consciousness presentifying the object or the occurrence in the mode of "as it were."

As we have seen above (see note 33), Husserl is well aware that the term "reproduction" might give rise to misunderstandings, and so he specifies that it is not to be understood in "its ordinary and etymological sense." Similarly, he remarks that the reproduction itself should not be thought of as a copy, a repetition, or "an echo, reflection, afterimage" of an "originary experience," but rather as a "new kind of *act*" with its own structure and its own "as it were" temporality (Hua XXIII, p. 372).[37]

1.10 The Phantasy Ego

Nonetheless, this is not Husserl's final word on phantasy intentionality. As early as 1911–12 (see Marbach 2006, p. LXVI), through additional inquiries into this perception/phantasy parallel (and, most importantly, his well-known analyses of time), his phenomenological lens uncovers another "fold" of phantasy intentionality construed as reproductive presentification. (Lest there be any misunderstanding, he does not reinstate iconic mediation into the essential structure of phantasy intentionality, which he still views as the reproductive parallel to perceptual intentionality.)

One of the manuscripts grouped under Text no. 15 takes us directly to the heart of a theme that will play a seminal role in this book: the phenomenon of *Ichspaltung*, or the division of the ego into the real ego and the phantasy ego.[38] We have already touched upon one directly related aspect of the structure of phantasy experience, namely that rather than solely entailing the intuitive presentification of the phantasized object, phantasy acts imply the reproduction of a subjective act *quasi*-perceiving that object—a process qualitatively different from the one involved with reality.

---

[36] As specifically regards the structure of recollection, see Text no. 14 in Hua XXIII (pp. 363 ff. and 368). See also Bernet (2006, p. 420) for a discussion of the differences between phantasy and memory reproduction.

[37] See also Bernet (2004, p. 94; pp. 111–112). For more on phantasy reproduction and its synthetic, productive character, compare Casey (1971, pp. 479–480).

[38] The phenomenon of ego-splitting (*Ichspaltung*) does not concern the relationship between real and phantasy experiences exclusively. It goes to the very heart of the possibility of the phenomenological *epoché*. Cf. for example Luft (2004, p. 212); Cavallaro (2017, p. 168).

Even as early as the 1905 Göttingen lectures, Husserl referred to the kind of experience in which "we give ourselves up to the attractions of phantasy to such an extent that we begin to react to the phantasy appearances in actions *just as if* perceptions were at stake: our fist clenches, we hold audible dialogues with the imagined persons, and so on" (Hua XXIII, p. 45). We now know that such cases do not involve perception in the proper sense—it is not by chance that, even in that early text, Husserl stresses the "as-if" quality of those particular perceptions. In the manuscript now under consideration, he characterizes this type of phantasy absorption in terms of "self-forgetfulness": "When I phantasy in a living way, when I am completely absorbed in phantasy, I am 'self-forgetful'" (Hua XXIII, p. 412). Indeed, these manifestations of *quasi*-acts seem to reinforce the hypothesis of the split-self phenomenon, i.e., that a different self (not the real one) seems to be at work in phantasy. The person who performs these actions is a "phantasy ego [*Phantasie-Ich*] [...] perform[ing] [...] phantasy reproductions" (Hua XXIII, p. 412).

Uncovering this phenomenon raises two linked issues of paramount importance: i) the nature and degree of distinction between these two egos and ii) whether and to what extent there is any relationship between them. Assuming a clear separation between real and phantasy egos would lead us to question whether the subject perceiving their actual surroundings and the one phantasizing alternative worlds are in fact *not* the same subject.

Several important authors have pointed out the importance of this splitting (*Spaltung*) or doubling (*Verdoppelung*). Properly speaking, the existence of two terms would seem to suggest two different concepts. For our purposes here, deeming one term more accurate than the other is less important than exploring the phenomenon both are variously used to describe. For now, let us mention one seminal facet to this *possibility* of scission, namely that it seemingly allows us to live different lives, experience possible worlds. In a genuine and originary way, our ability to imagine otherwise enables us as human beings to vary or transform or "fold" what we experience; without this ability, we would lack even the capacity to desire. The possibilities phantasy opens up can also be construed as the transcendental phenomenon, as the "structure [...] that many art forms are grafted onto. To read a book, to watch a film or a play is to take part in this life, to enter into this fear before the dragon, to feel the pain in your leg: all in the way of the as-if" (Costa 2010, p. 138). Of course, not every phantasy experience or narrative is *ipso facto* an art form.

Husserl's 1912 manuscript examines the essential structure of the ego-split phenomenon by highlighting the different temporalities it implies. In order to provide a phenomenological account of the aforementioned common experience in which we are *absorbed* in the performance of *quasi*-actions taking place in phantasy, Husserl establishes a distinction between impressions (perception) and reproductions (phantasy or memory). From an "internal consciousness" perspective, the same self "impressionally" experiences all types of acts, i.e., the "self" writing now is the same "self" that, say, stopped writing a moment ago and imagined being elsewhere. Similarly, I could reconstruct an experience of mine not long ago, saying that *I* went for a walk, that *I* got on the train, that *I* sat down; that *I*, almost involuntarily, began phantasizing about playing in a Champions League game; that *I* got off the train, where *I* saw a "person" smiling at *me* from a billboard, looking *me* in the eyes and encouraging *me* to buy a new model of smartphone.

On the one hand, all these acts, including phantasies, have an "impressional" quality with respect to internal consciousness of time (hence "I, I, I..."), as Husserl restates in his later *Experience and Judgment*: "as lived experiences, phantasies [*Phantasien*] are ordered in the unity of the ego, just as all acts are—which means that internal consciousness constitutes intentional connection" (Husserl 1939, p. 168). On the other hand, in keeping with what we have said so far, we can say that a splitting or doubling took place when it came to experiencing the phantasy acts: the production of a "phantasy ego" that lived its *quasi*-acts in a reproductive way, not an "impressional" way.[39] This is, in effect, a *double* experience in a specific sense: it is impressional in that I remember having phantasized about something at a certain moment while on the train, but I also remember being absent from myself at that moment. To a certain extent, I forgot myself while carrying out phantasy actions that cannot be viewed as equivalent to the first series of experiences I described (the actions I actually carried out—getting on the train, etc.). I actually carried out a phantasy in which I was playing in a Champions League game, but I did not actually play the game. Significantly, as suggested above, this point is confirmed later in *Experience and Judgment*, where Husserl reaffirms the idea of a qualitative splitting between actual acts and *quasi*-actual acts, stressing that the latter occurs in *quasi*-time, i.e., "*a time without actual, strict localization of position*" (Husserl 1939, p. 169).

The emergence of this implicit fold in phantasy consciousness finds an important reformulation in *First Philosophy*, the seminal lecture course Husserl taught in the winter semester of 1923/24 at the University of Freiburg. This is a text of great significance: Husserl "composed" it "to serve as the basis for his repeatedly planned but never completed 'Systematic Work' that would introduce and summarize his mature thought" (Luft 2019, p. xiii), and even though it did not see the light of day within Husserl's lifetime, he repeatedly expressed intentions to publish it (see Luft 2019, pp. xiii–xiv).

---

[39] See also Bernet (2006, pp. 419–420).

On the *noematic* (objective) side, as we have come to assert, both perception and phantasy give their object in unmediated ways. By shifting his phenomenological analysis to the *noetic* (egological) side of the act, however, Husserl reveals a "peculiar mediacy" (Hua VIII, p. 319) implicitly at work within phantasy intentionality. Unlike perception intentionality, in which acts pertain to a unique egological flow, phantasy intentionality essentially entails a subjective divide, a *doubling of consciousness* between "actual" and "phantasy-I" (see Hua VIII, pp. 320–321; see also Bernet 2004, pp. 93–117; de Warren 2009, p. 149, pp. 156–157). In other words, phantasy acts are carried out by a phantasy-I distinct from the real one (although a consciousness of reality, albeit minimal, always marks these *quasi*-experiences, thereby distinguishing them from hallucinations).

In fact, though Husserl continues to characterize perception in terms of a "simple intentionality" (Hua VIII, p. 333), he also remarks that the structural components of phantasy experience include not only the phantasy object but also a "peculiar mediacy" (Hua VIII, p. 319) that usually goes unnoticed. In other words, the manifestation of a phantasy object *necessarily* implies that the "consciousness reproduces, or replicates, its own perceptual activity in a modified form," (de Warren 2009, p. 151) thus giving rise to a veritable "doubling of consciousness" (de Warren 2009, p. 149). This modified form of perception is not a copy of perception but rather the original form of a modified experience in the sense that it is temporally different and proteiform.

This particular mediacy does not undermine what we have said thus far, nor (as mentioned above) does it imply the reinstatement of any iconic mediation whatsoever. Rather, as Husserl puts it, it means that "the *actus* 'I phantasize a scene of centaurs' is only possible in the form that I enact, in the mode of the 'as if,' the *actus* 'I perceive the scene of centaurs'" (Hua VIII, p. 320). This, of course, highlights the need to clarify the nature of this "as if," of the "quasi (*quam si*)" eidetically implied in phantasy acts under this perspective.

Thus, in *First Philosophy*, Husserl remarks that phantasy is not simply one act among others; rather, it is given through a folding that opens onto peculiar worlds. Phantasy intentionality, he says, "is not such a simple matter, as if I had nothing but the act of phantasizing and in it the scene with centaurs as its simple intentional object in the mode of the 'as if'" (Hua VIII, p. 319). Having a real subject who simply happens to perform a phantasy act is not sufficient for a phantasy experience to arise. Rather, the act of phantasy itself also presupposes a phantasy subject performing it, and the rise and resurgence of such a subject presents itself as a break within the real self's progression of experiences.

1.11 Universalizing Phantasy

In the spirit of phenomenological inquiry—in which every "step forward" offers new perspectives through which concepts "originally" construed as "simple and undivided" may well prove "complex and full of distinctions"[40] (or vice versa)—Husserl's results regarding phantasy presentifications *qua* reproduction seem to prompt him to reconsider his phenomenological account of presentification in physical image, which had previously reached a sufficiently stable form in his Göttingen analyses.

Similarly, some of research he conducted on phantasy during this period (and his corresponding emancipation from the *imaginatio stricto sensu* point of view) inspired him to "change direction" from his initial approach of 1904–1905 and re-examine image consciousness. Husserl already hints at this shift, albeit *in nuce*, at the conclusion of the third *Hauptstück* of the 1904–1905 course, where he notes that "phantasy makes up the most essential moment even in common imaging" (Hua XXIII, pp. 93–94).

My thesis is that the research outcomes on phantasy consciousness that led Husserl to characterize it as a reproductive presentification—an "as-if" counterpart of perception, a *quasi*-perception—eventually do impact his understanding of image consciousness. Significantly, a manuscript from 1912 questions image consciousness "once again," asking "what that can mean" (Hua XXIII, p. 560). In another manuscript dated that same year, Husserl comes to *"universalize the concept of phantasy"* as *presentification* and to distinguish between *"two fundamental forms"*: 1) *"reproductive"* phantasy and 2) phantasy "complying with *perceptio* [*perzeptive*], that is, presentification in image [*im Bild*], in pictorial [*bildlich*] exhibiting" (Hua XXIII, p. 565), which then includes *image consciousness itself* (see also Hua XXIII, p. 605).

This appears to diverge from his previous approach to the relationship between image and phantasy consciousness. To put it bluntly, his early account (*imaginatio* as "conversion into image") might lead us to describe image consciousness (then known as picture consciousness) as a genus containing two species, i.e., physical and phantasy image consciousness. Under his subsequent *universalization* of the concept of phantasy, on the other hand, phantasy consciousness would be the genus, with its two species being phantasy *with* and *without* the involvement

---

[40] "Indeed, this is universally the peculiarity of phenomenological analysis. Every step forward yields new points of view from which what we have already discovered appears in a new light, so that often enough what we were originally able to take as simple and undivided presents itself as complex and full of distinctions" (Hua XXIII, p. 19).

of physical/iconic dimensions (phantasy involving *perceptio* and reproductive phantasy, respectively).

When characterizing image consciousness as a case of phantasy consciousness ("presentification in image"), Husserl introduces the notion of *perzeptive Phantasie*. In keeping with what we noted above (see note 11), it is not by chance that Husserl avoids referencing "perceptual phantasy" (*wahrnehmungsmäßige Phantasie*), which would constitute an oxymoron. In fact, the consciousness of unreality is already at work in pictorial exhibiting *qua* phantasy (consciousness of presentification), preventing its object from being taken-as-true (perception as *Wahrnehmung*), i.e., perceived as existent. Just as in reproductive phantasy, pictures exhibit their objects as appearance without consciousness of presence—consciousness of perception proper—ever arising.[41] As I proposed, it is not our capacity to create images that founds our capacity to phantasize but the other way around.

Accordingly, such appearances are not "perceptual illusion[s]" (Hua XXIII, p. 563) either. Husserl is categorical on this point: *"the image is not an illusion"* (Hua XXIII, p. 581). *An image is not* "a perceptual appearance [*Wahrnehmungserscheinung*]" (Hua XXIII, p. 584). Although the image object can be characterized as a figment, it is not "an *illusory* figment" (Hua XXIII, p. 585) since illusions proper "posit" their objects as existent. An image, meanwhile, shows itself as an image (conflicting with perception) and does not, in principle, claim to be actually there in the way a deceptive semblance might. As Merleau-Ponty will later remark, "it is of the nature of illusion not to present itself as such" (Merleau-Ponty 1945, p. 344).

This seems to suggest the possibility of experiencing image consciousness as a "one-fold" intentionality as well (on the noematic, objective side) insofar as what is experienced on a physical basis is directly apprehended in the phantasy modification (see, for instance, Hua XXIII, p. 562). In this vein, Husserl ultimately comes to recognize that his early understanding of image consciousness (*Bildlichkeitsbewusstsein*) was still too caught up in the depictive model, whereas he now understands image consciousness intentionality to have a more originary structure than depiction (*Abbildung*) intentionality, i.e., "representation by means of more or less imperfect copies [*Abbilder*]" (Hua XXIII, p. 183). Rather than being the final word on image consciousness, depiction is thus merely *one* of its possible articulations. These aspects are particularly evident in Husserl's explorations of aesthetic and artistic considerations in images. (Note: though Husserl occasionally uses the

---

[41] That is why, properly speaking, I would not categorize Husserl's approach under "perception theory," as proposed in Wiesing (2005, p. 19).

terms "aesthetic" and "artistic" interchangeably, it is important to avoid presuming the two concepts to be identical).[42]

As we shall see in greater detail in the next chapter, aesthetic consciousness is a form of intentionality that focuses on *how* something appears (see Hua XXIII, p. 461). In one sense, it does not even seem fundamentally related to image consciousness given that iconic status does not pertain exclusively to it. In principle, we can experience anything aesthetically—not just images but also, for example, a "landscape" or even an "ashtray [...] in the drawing-room" (Hua XXIII, p. 168). In another sense, however, aesthetic consciousness does seem to imply an essential relationship with image consciousness in that Husserl suggests that parts of the actual world (say, a landscape) can "act as an 'image'" when considered aesthetically. In such cases, we can take them "not as present: but precisely as images" (Hua XXIII, p. 167, note 4), thus operating in a phantasy consciousness that, as with *perzeptive Phantasie* (see Hua XXIII, p. 616), does not entail the "position taking" regarding existence that occurs in perception.

1.12 *Ficta* Complying with *Perceptio*

Two Husserlian texts on theater (dated 1912 and 1918, respectively) may prove useful to our examination of the adjective *perzeptiv*. Having updated his characterization of phantasy, Husserl assigns it a new role in aesthetic experience in these texts. Specifically, he elaborates upon his previous characterizations of works of art.

In his 1912 text, Husserl asserts that, when watching "performances in a stage play," we have a particular *attitude* toward the on-stage action from the very beginning: we do not perceive "bodies" in the proper sense but rather "*fict[a]* complying with *perceptio* [*perzeptiv[e] Fikt[a]*]" (Hua XXIII, p. 456). From the outset, we experience a type of consciousness that does not imply either the existence or the nonexistence of what we are watching. As Husserl puts it, we are "living in the iconic consciousness" (Hua XXIII, p. 457), here to be understood as "iconic phantasy [*eikonische Phantasie*]" (Hua XXIII, p. 456). Husserl refers to instances of "imagery complying with *perceptio*, specifically, iconic imagery" to describe the experiences of watching "the performances in a stage play" or "contemplating a painting." (Note that, in this artistic context and in keeping with the generalized concept of phantasy, Husserl refers to "a painting" *qua* artistic image not in terms of a del-

---

[42] See also Rozzoni and Conceição (2021), especially as regards the distinctions between aesthetic and artistic value.

egative representant, but rather as one possible form of phantasy complying with *perceptio*.)

Husserl's 1912 analyses do not seem to call the representational function of theatrical images into serious question. Here, he seems to say that these particular *ficta* serve to presentify something that is nonpresent on a sensible basis. In such instances, the actual things—the physical bodies or images—work in service of a phantasy process employing sensible material for its own purposes. As we have seen, referencing the dimension of *perceptio* (instead of that of *perception*) is Husserl's way of indicating that something not present is made *sensible* without requiring belief in its actual existence, i.e., that these experiences are *neutral* (at least at the level of their manifestation) in that the marker of belief (in reality) is not our primary concern. It is important to note that this suspension of interest in existence or nonexistence can apply to sounds: the voice we hear *is* the voice of King Lear, or of Hamm and Clov.

The key point here concerns the spatial and temporal nature of the on-stage action. We are called to experience these occurrences in the mode of as-if, in a temporality different from what we ordinarily experience outside the theater: we enter into and participate in a "suspended world."[43] We can allow ourselves to participate in the various *quasi*-worlds offered to us, and we can leave them whenever we like. We can let ourselves be involved with the entities on stage (or, more generally, within the space of the play). In principle, of course, this space need not be delimited by a stage or a frame—phantasy space is *proteiform*, just as children can continually change the spatial boundaries of their make-believe. When we enter a consciousness of play (not to be uncritically equated to phantasy as presentification), we are always aware, for example, that the two actors fist-fighting onstage are not actually hurting each other. It seems legitimate to draw similar conclusions regarding a fistfight presentified in a fictional film.

In a documentary film, of course, the situation would certainly be different. As we will attempt to show, the cinematic experience in such cases implies a certain dimension of belief. Documentaries are a form of cinema seeking to present an object that has been captured, recorded, taken-for-real by the camera—all expressions that we shall have to characterize from a phenomenological standpoint.

Like fictional films, however, documentaries involve a form of *perzeptive Phantasie* (albeit one without a consciousness of play), since objects we see within documentaries are given in image consciousness, not as perceptual objects we au-

---

[43] "In the fictionalizing experience, or in the attitude in which we live in the 'image' world, we have not carried out anything belonging to the real world of actual experience, and specifically of the experience of the realities serving for presentation; this world, for us, is not a posited but a suspended world" (Hua XXIII, p. 619).

tomatically take as part of our surrounding perceptual context. ("*Phantasie*" refers to the unreality of the sensible manifestation itself, not to whether I believe in the existence of the *sujet* I am observing, as is generally the case in a documentary attitude.) Here again, our goal is to identify subtle differences between phenomena often presumed similar or even interchangeable. Though we can also describe documentary cinema in terms of belief (in the *sujet*'s existence), the experience is not identical to the one characterizing the position of existence in the perceptual dimension. When I watch a documentary, I can believe that what is happening on the screen is real without being lured into thinking that it is actually happening *on* the physical screen itself.

As we shall see, in the aesthetic attitude, the issue of belief in a *sujet*'s actual existence is removed from the equation (at least in principle). We view film images without primarily considering them a proxy for the things being depicted. We are "interested" in their particular manner of manifestation without needing to question their relationship to any external *sujets* they may be presumed to represent. To put it roughly, the "unusual" skin color of a face in a black-and-white portrait might be considered a "conflicting" moment (compared to real skin color) under a purely depictive consciousness, whereas an aesthetic attitude might instead experience the black and white nuances as essential expressive elements of *that* photograph and *that* face. Analogously, when viewing a close-up of a face in a movie, we do not perceive it as conflicting with a life-size head; rather, we experience the expressive power of *that* iconic manifestation (we shall address the notion of "expression" in more depth in the second chapter).

All of these aspects become evident in the 1918 manuscript referenced above (see Hua XXIII, Text no. 18b, p. 616) in which Husserl defines art as "the realm of phantasy that has been given form" and feels the need to revisit his previous characterization of artistic images, which he now recognizes as overly reliant on the dimension of depiction. Here again, Husserl turns to theater as a paradigmatic case: when we watch a stage performance, he writes, we live in a "world" of *perzeptive Phantasie* within which "depictiveness is not the *primary* concern." The images actors "produce," the images their bodies become—for instance the "image of a character in the play"—are not "image[s] of [*Bild(er) von*]" in the sense of "depiction[s] of [*Abbild(er) von*]." Husserl references the notion of "immediate imagination," which we might think of as a "one-fold" *perzeptive Phantasie* (without iconic mediation) whose noetic correlate is the phantasy-I living in the "as-if" world (Hua XXIII, pp. 616–617).

In order to see such characters in a nonmediated way, we as spectators experience an I-doubling. From the beginning, we live in a phantasy consciousness, in the world of "play [*Spiel*]." Above, we noted the need to distinguish between phantasy and play consciousness, though there are certainly points of overlap between the two and Husserl sometimes uses the term "phantasy" in reference to the dimension of play. In theater, the consciousness of play elicits the setting of an immediate phantasy. It is true that actors are there "in person," but we do not carry out the perception of them, we do not take them as real. Rather, we experience them as a form of *phantasy in the flesh*—we see characters directly. Reality "changes into reality as-if" (Hua XXIII, p. 615), not posited but *quasi*-posited. At this juncture, let us note that this process is triggered through the institution of a narrative, however simple: an elementary action, a *drama*.

As spectators to a performance, we do not produce the phantasies this "play" offers. Rather, we are invited to participate in them as phantasy egos. Narrative and actions "are [...] forced upon us," analogously to what occurs in reality, "only" here it occurs in the realm of as-if. In this sense, the "image worlds" shaped by phantasy can obtain "intersubjective 'existence,'" offering us the possibility of a shared *quasi*-experience. Our discussions of this experience, our opinions on it and so forth, then have a "kind of objective truth" (Hua XXIII, p. 621).

1.13 Positional and *Quasi*-Positional Rays

The aforementioned Texts nos. 15, 16, and 17 in Hua XXIII, all dated 1912 (one year before the first book of *Ideas* was published), are fundamental to understanding how Husserl's reflections on *reproductive* experiences developed. In this first chapter, we have limited ourselves to the ideas in these manuscripts that are instrumental to the points discussed thus far; Chapter 2 will elaborate on other key concepts, especially when we begin considering the aesthetic experience in greater detail.

Let us consider a passage in Text no. 15 passage that draws a distinction between impressional experiences (which fall under the domain of perception) and reproductive ones (which include phantasy and memory). Husserl distinguishes between phantasy and memory on several occasions by describing the latter as a form of reproduction with a "ray positing factual existence" running through it (see, for example, Hua XXIII, pp. 407, 502, 503). Husserl reiterates this distinction in the first volume of *Ideas*, once again explicitly differentiating memory from phantasy by mentioning the positional ray running through the former but not the latter.[44] In this view, phantasy would be a modified memory—that is, a memory deprived of the ray of existence. At a very general level, therefore, this

---

[44] There, phantasy is defined as "neutrality modification of 'positing' presentification, therefore of memory in the widest conceivable sense" (Hua III/1, p. 260).

suggests a qualitative similarity between the reproductive experiences involved in recollection and phantasy, with the characteristic of belief acting as a discriminator between the two.

Without this discriminating element, it might be difficult to tell the difference between phantasy and memory. Indeed, there are borderline experiences in which we are unable, or at least initially unable, to determine whether a reproduction offers a past actual experience or something merely phantasized. In such cases, we may call upon other memories to help us reconstruct a chain of events we believe true and see whether that reproduction fits into it. If we are successful in establishing such a plausible—*qua* "taken-as-true"—narrative, we may decide that it was indeed a memory, a reproduction of an actual experience; if not, we might conclude that it was all "just" a phantasy.

Husserl's 1912 manuscripts also testify to his efforts to identify phenomena often overlooked or misidentified. One such example would be differentiating phantasizing from merely "thinking-of [*Sich-denken*]," which designates a specific type of modification in which the character of belief is subtracted from "position-taking [*Stellungnahme*]" (Hua XXIII, p. 450). "For every position taking," he says (Hua XXIII, p. 451), there can be a corresponding apositional modification aimed at suspending the positional ray (*belief*) running through that experience, thereby yielding a "'corresponding' modification" (Hua XXIII, p. 451). Note, however, that suspending belief in something's existence (i.e., neutralizing something) is not tantamount to phantasizing in the sense of a *quasi*-position—these are two distinct phenomena.

The reason I am highlighting this distinction is because it allows us, for instance, to separate instances where we merely think of something (present or reproduced) while experiencing it as neutral from experiences not only neutralized but also dramatized, in the Greek sense of the term δρᾶμα, or "action." Dramatized experiences involve *quasi*-narratives eliciting the phantasy-I to take a "*quasi*-position," making them phantasy experiences in the sense of playful experiences—not only in the "once upon a time" sense, but also in the sense of "there is now" (or as Husserl later puts it in *Experience and Judgment*, "there *quasi*-is now"[45]), in a presence that is not actual, i.e., a presentification.

This "*quasi*" is not to imply that these experiences are somehow deficient or diluted "slightly less than real" acts or "almost-acts." Rather, as we have seen, they are experiences in the etymological sense of "*quam si*," of "as if" (a sense

---

[45] "The object of imagination is present to consciousness as temporal and temporally determined, enduring in time; but its time is a *quasi-time*. [...] It is a temporal object, it has its time. And yet it is not in time" (Husserl 1939, p. 168).

that still predominantly informs the use of the Latin loaner word *quasi* in both English and German). Accordingly, we can now call the prefix *quasi* a qualitative "sign" denoting phantasy experiences in which we "carry out this or that *quasi*-perceiving, *quasi*-judging, *quasi*-distinguishing and comparing, *quasi*-wishing, willing, etc." (Hua XXIII, p. 413), i.e., in which we carry out *quasi*-acts developing in the realm of possibility rather than that of actuality.[46]

Along these lines, it seems legitimate to say that we are not mere inactive spectators in phantasy; rather, we perform *quasi*-acts. These can either be reproductive acts or, when they find a sensible manifestation of sorts (in theater and cinema, for example), phantasy acts complying with *perceptio*. It is important not to let the notion of "reproduction" lead us to view reproductive acts as copy-acts, mere reflections of other previous acts (of perception, for example). Instead, we should view reproductive acts in the sense of *re + production*, where the prefix "re" refers not to a servile "again" so much as to creative repetition in a new temporal horizon. As we have observed, these repetitions may (as in memory) or may not (as in phantasy *stricto sensu*) bear the mark of something that "has been." Reproductive acts can maintain a relationship not only with past reality but also with present and even future reality; the latter occurs, for example, in memorative anticipation (*Vorerinnerung*), in which we produce an intuitive presentification of something we expect to actually happen in the future—a possibility we take as bound to become real.

1.14 Images and Belief

Our analyses thus far were intended to give us the tools necessary for a phenomenologically grounded characterization of images; having defined such a horizon through these investigations, we can now develop these ideas further. More precisely, it will be important for us to examine how these phenomenological descriptions of image and phantasy consciousness can assist us in shaping a philosophical account of the relation between images and reality—a line of research essential to contemporary debates. The notion of belief is of paramount importance in this context. We have seen that the notion of belief plays a primary role in the consti-

---

[46] One small but important caveat is that we cannot simply take phantasies as possibilities—although, as we shall see, there is an essential connection between the "phantasized" and the "possible." See Brough (2005, p. xliii), which underscores how Husserl ultimately "came to view the consciousness of possibility as a higher-order act distinct from phantasy itself." Properly speaking, "in the fictionalizing experience, or in the attitude in which we live in the 'image' world, we have not carried out anything belonging to the real world of actual experience" (Hua XXIII, p. 619).

tution of "flesh and blood" perception, in which the concrete object is perceived in the sense of *"wahr-genommen,"* or "taken-as-true, as real" (cf., for instance, Hua XVI, § 5). Properly speaking, on the other hand, an image is never "perceived [*wahr-genommen*]" in itself: it is merely a *"figment"* (Hua XXIII, p. 52). Even so, it would be incorrect to conclude that the dimension of belief does not pertain to images; on the contrary, belief plays a pivotal role (for instance) in our experience of *film images* claiming to represent reality.

As previously remarked with respect to the tripartite structure of image consciousness, describing the ontological status of images becomes a particularly thorny question when we turn to the *image object*. As noted, the "image thing" made of paper and ink (or canvas and paint, etc.) is a "physical thing" that can be perceived and said to *exist* as an object within the perceptual flow of recognitions constituting our real environment[47] with its own "normativity."[48] The *image sujet* (the "depicted" object) *can* be said to exist in some cases and not in others; either way, however, it cannot be said to be actually present in front of us. Conversely, as we have seen, the *image object* "has never existed and never will exist and, of course, is not taken by us for even a moment as something real" (Hua XXIII, p. 21)—it is neither *existent* nor *nonexistent*.

From this point of view, one might say that the depictive image inevitably puts the *sujet* at a certain ontological *distance* (even in the case of close-up images), in the specific sense that the *sujet* is never actually *in* the location of its manifestation —it manifests itself *in absentia*. Physical images are not purported to show the actual perceptual objects; they show images, not "flesh and blood" things "in themselves," which is how we experience people and things perceptively.

Along these lines, filmic images, *qua* physical images, do not show perceptual objects: what we see on the screen are images in themselves, not things "in the flesh." We could not touch the objects on the screen even if we wanted to—they are intangible, exclusively visual (and auditory) in nature. Turning to theater, one might object that we could, technically, touch theater actors' bodies. However, this still would not constitute touching the characters proper; only by stepping into the play, entering the *quasi*-world in which the characters exist, could we *quasi*-touch them. (For more on the constitution of "*quasi*-worlds," see also Husserl 1939, §§ 39–40). Images are not inserted into the material flux of actuality surrounding us (images *qua* things are not the image objects manifested on their sur-

---

[47] "The consciousness that 'it agrees,' the consciousness of reality, is living and is genuinely explicated in the harmonious transition of concordant perceptions and not in the latent background of conflicting perceptions" (Hua XXIII, pp. 439–440).
[48] On the Husserlian account of the "kind of normativity […] inform[ing] perceptual intentionality" cf. Crowell (2013, pp. 124–146).

faces). There is a conflict (*Widerstreit*) between the iconic objects emerging in the peculiar space manifesting itself on-screen and the real objects surrounding the screen (which would include the screen itself as a "thing"). In other words, if someone spills milk on-screen, no one worries about stains on the movie-theater floor. We cannot grab the objects we see on the screen and perceptively share them with the people around us because image objects within the screen space do not pertain to the domain of perception.

This also bears upon the nature of the *act* of viewing, which raises the question: what type of act pertains to viewing these images? When we look at an actual thing, is it a different act of seeing from when we view an image of the "same" thing? On the one hand, we can affirm that, say, we *see* a knife (image *sujet*) *in* a "cinematographic depictive image."[49] On the other hand, this *seeing is not the same seeing* we experience in perception when we see a knife "in the flesh" in a kitchen. We know that the latter must be handled with care, while the former cannot physically hurt us—it is merely an image object showing a knife. What

---

[49] In a Hua XXIII text likely dating back to 1917, Husserl explicitly recognizes that the constitution of an image object also concerns moving images: "It pertains to an image that the depictive image, understood as image object, has a 'being' that persists and abides. This persisting, this remaining unchanged, does not mean that the image object is unchanging; indeed, it can be a cinematographic depictive image" (Hua XXIII, p. 645). Accordingly, it can legitimately be stated that "the changing image object is synthetically identified and intended as 'the same' throughout all of its changes, and thus allows an identical pictorialization [*Verbildlichung*] of the same image subject [read: *sujet*]" (Ferencz-Flatz 2008–2009, pp. 95–96). Defining the "image thing" can become more complicated with cinematic projection than it is with paintings or photographs, and doing so pushes us onto slippery ground. For instance, does the division between film strip/projector and screen/projection complicate the idea of the "image thing"? On the one hand, one could say that the latter does not exist without the former, but at the same time, we do not see the film strip and the projector as physical parts of the image. In John Brough (2011)'s insightful article "Showing and Seeing. Film as Phenomenology," we read that "Husserl finds three moments in image consciousness: the image itself, the characters I see on the screen, for example; the image's physical support, such as the projector and film stock; and the subject [read: *sujet*] of the image, what it is about. Image consciousness is unique in that it has a foot in both the perceptual and imaginative worlds" (Brough 2011, p. 198). But are we sure we can truly say that "projector and film stock" (Brough 2011, p. 198) are part of the image thing from a phenomenological point of view? Although I do think this question requires further, specifically phenomenological, development (especially as regards the new kinds of cinematic experiences made possible by new media), I would be inclined to say that the projector and film are not part of the image thing in Husserlian terms simply because they are not part of our movie theater experience, nor are they intended to be. For the moment, I would restrict my definition of the "image thing" to the illuminated screen itself. (Of course, the projectionist might look at the film strip and discern the threefold structure of image we have been discussing, but this is a different experience from the one the director intended for me as a viewer.)

we experience on-screen is not a presentation (*Gegenwärtigung*) of a knife, but rather a *presentification* (*Vergegenwärtigung*) of it: the knife is *presentified* in the movie, not actually *present* in (for example) the movie theater.

Still, even though it seems that the question of existence is *always* neutralized at the image-object level (the image object is a *"nothing"* (Hua XXIII, p. 50), a *"nullity"* (Hua XXIII, p. 51), neither existent nor nonexistent), we must ask what our attitude toward the image *sujet* is. As noted earlier, image consciousness does not *eo ipso* imply a consciousness of unreality regarding the image *sujet*, which, though not present, can be intentioned as existent or nonexistent.

Examining our belief in photography phenomenologically recalls some of the key issues explored by Roland Barthes in *Camera Lucida*, his famous final essay from 1980 (which is, incidentally, the same year the Husserlian manuscripts on image were published in Hua XXIII). Barthes explicitly states that the work draws inspiration from phenomenology (and, specifically, from Sartre: *Camera Lucida* is dedicated to his *The Imaginary*[50]).

Say, for example, that we know we are about to watch a documentary film, one in which the photographic nature of the image could serve to testify that—as Barthes puts it—the person or thing manifesting itself on the iconic surface *"has been there"* (Barthes 1980, p. 76). In what we might call a documentary attitude, even though what we see before us are only images and not things "in person," we believe in the existence of what we see *in* them (seeing-in). "Show your photographs to someone," Barthes writes, and "he will immediately show you his: 'Look, this is my brother; this is me as a child,' etc.; the Photograph is never anything but an antiphon of 'Look,' 'See,' 'Here it is;' it points a finger at certain vis-à-vis." He goes on to say that a "photograph always carries its referent with itself" (Barthes 1980, p. 5).

We can now characterize Barthes' references to "'Look,' 'See,' 'Here it is'" in terms of "looking in," and we accordingly surmise that it is only through this "looking-into" the photograph that we can see the "referent" "carried" by the image (the presentified image *sujet*, to use Husserl's language). Properly speaking, the image *sujet* is not located outside the photograph; rather, we see it in the photograph itself. The previously mentioned distinction between internal (immanent) and external symbolic (transeunt) imaging can lead us to the same conclusion.

Along these lines, we might now reformulate the issue of our belief in what we see in photographs as follows. We know that what we see in the image is not present but presentified. Yet, for example, when we look at a photograph of a friend,

---

[50] See Lotz (2010a) for a discussion concerning the peculiar phenomenological approach adopted by Barthes' text.

even though the image is not reality (reality being the domain of perception), we believe in the real existence of the friend we see in it. In such cases, even though we are operating within a regime of image consciousness rather than perceptual consciousness (i.e., we know that the friend in the image is not physically in front of us), there is a form of belief affecting what we see in the image: we believe that the friend was there "in the flesh" at the moment the photo was taken. To put it in Barthes' terms, we could say that we typically look at photographs with a certainty that the person or thing shown therein "has been there," even if we might not be able to encounter it again in reality. In view of Husserl's remarks that the image *sujet* presentified in a physical image can be either real or fictive, we can now propose a distinction between *images characterized by belief* and *images free of belief.* Photographs in the Barthesian sense seem to be of the first kind: they are always accompanied by certainty that what we are seeing in the image "has been there."

When referencing photographs in a manuscript published as Appendix XLII to Husserliana XXIII (probably around 1911–12), Husserl offers an important insight into the possibility of experiencing an image with a "positional"[51] connotation—not toward the image object, which is a *"figment,"* "a nullity of a unique type" (Hua XXIII, p. 586), but rather toward the *sujet* presentified in the image:

> Let us consider judgments that are made on the basis of *impressional images* [*von impressionalen Bildern*]. I contemplate the photograph of a zeppelin and confirm on its basis certain of the zeppelin's striking features. Here we again have pictorial exhibiting and, indeed, *positing.* My description moves in the image space, in this image world. It possesses the character of judgment with respect to the depicted *sujet.* But it expresses above all the image *sujet* (only with respect to the exhibiting moments, of course; the color is not included, and so on). (Hua XXIII, p. 533, my italics)

This undeniably opens up the possibility for phenomenological distinctions between *positional* and *apositional* images—and thus between the positional and apositional attitudes in which we can experience image consciousnesses. On initial consideration, these terms might seem to contradict that neutrality regarding existence or nonexistence that we have seen to be consubstantial to image consciousness. Caution is clearly warranted here.

It is crucial to specify that this distinction between positional and apositional images primarily concerns what we have called the image *sujet*—not the ungraspable "nothing" of the image object. In fact, regardless of whether we view images

---

51 "Positional experiences are experiences of consciousness in which the Ego accepts something, in which a belief is involved" (Hua XXIII, p. 696). Husserl himself seems to allude to this possibility of discussing image in terms of positionality: "We must note that image consciousness can be either positing or nonpositing. The *sujet* is posited" (Hua XXIII, p. 564).

in a positional or an apositional consciousness, the image object is still considered a nothing. Nevertheless, I propose the notion that image consciousness can involve interaction between *presentification* and *belief*,[52] as is the case with those images Husserl described as "impressional." Experiencing impressional images means potentially confronting the issue of the *sujet*'s existence, a question that can then develop in several directions.

In *Camera Lucida*, when discussing an André Kertész photograph entitled "Ernest, Paris 1931," Barthes writes: "it is possible that Ernest [...] is still alive today (but where? How? What a novel!)" (Barthes 1980, p. 84). The fact that he can ask this points to the particular nature of his experience when viewing this photograph due to the belief characterizing that experience. We might well experience similar surprise and ask ourselves similar questions when seeing someone depicted in an old movie—provided that we believe in the existence of the actor we see in the on-screen image object.

For purposes of our initial analysis, we can say that, when viewing film footage or looking at a photograph, our experiences are marked by a belief in the existence of what we see in the image. Despite operating in image consciousness rather than perceptual consciousness in such cases, we nonetheless believe in the real existence of what is presentified. It is interesting to note that *presentification* and *belief* are two of the elements this form of iconic consciousness has in common with memory consciousness: if we recall our friend having bought us coffee the previous afternoon, we are experiencing presentification as well as belief about what we are presentifying (we believe that our friend did, indeed, buy us coffee the day before).

We will have to return to this subject later to conduct a more in-depth investigation of the genesis and foundation of this belief: for example, under what conditions are we prone to say that we believe in the existence of what an image presents? And what are the implications of this particular form of belief? Before that, let us return our attention to the concept of the aesthetic attitude, another fundamental attitude through which we can experience images—albeit one that does not pertain to images exclusively.

---

[52] "There are, however, mixed experiences, and they are very common. Such mixed experiences can be positional, and, particularly as acts, actually bring about a position, and yet include phantasies in themselves. And they can be phantasies and yet include positions in themselves" (Hua XXIII, p. 696).

1.15 Depiction and Aesthetic Consideration

Up to this point, we have mostly discussed phantasy and image nature in a general sense. We must now begin to ask ourselves how these notions of phantasy and image can help us i) reflect upon the nature of aesthetic experience and ii) characterize some of the essential aspects of works of art. Due caution must be exercised here, of course, especially in attempting to apply Husserl's original analyses (many of which were dedicated to forms of artistic expression specific to his time) when examining media forms largely or entirely unknown in Husserl's day. As stated before, however, this work also aims to bring some of Husserl's (often fragmentary) insights to light to critically measure their scope and thereby unearth potential areas of development in our contemporary reflections.

Aesthetic considerations of phenomena feature intermittently in Husserl's analyses of phantasy and image consciousness. Significant examples of his interest in this theme can be found in Husserliana XXIII; specifically, Husserl touches upon the topic in the third part of his 1905 Göttingen lectures, albeit while prioritizing other issues, primarily that of defining the essential structures of *phantasy* and *image consciousness*. Appendix IX to Text no. 1 (probably 1905) addresses aesthetic issues in a more specific way. When discussing the nature of a photographic reproduction of Titian's *Sacred and Profane Love* (Figure 2), Husserl inquires into whether *depiction* plays a role in the artistic field. This also allows him to introduce, albeit *in nuce*, the question of the different attitudes an observer can take—whether actively or passively, with varying degrees of awareness—when responding to different types of images.

Clearly, looking at Titian's original painting is not the same as looking at a black-and-white photograph of the painting in a book or a digital color image of it on a screen. However, Husserl observes that even when encountering a representation of this work of art, one can look *into the image* and "immerse [one]self visually in" it as though viewing the Titian itself, thereby seeing the *Sacred Love*, the "glorious, superterrestrial female figure, and so on" (Hua XXIII, p. 183). Thus, it seems that the *sujet* of a painting can also be seen in depictions of the original painting. As we shall see, this is possible through an *aesthetic consciousness*, "an entirely different consciousness than" (Hua XXIII, p. 183) the one involved if that same depiction were to function as a representative for the painting, "point[ing] to the painting in which the same objects appear 'in different dimensions' and, above all, as colored" (Hua XXIII, p. 178)—in which case the proper *sujet* might be considered the original painting.

His efforts to define the specific qualities of aesthetic attitude prompted Husserl to introduce a distinction between an "*inauthentic* [*uneigentlich*] *representation*" (Hua XXIII, p. 183) and a representation wherein the "feeling of inauthenticity with respect to what is presented does not come up at all" (Hua XXIII, p. 184). The former Husserl subsumes under the category of depiction proper[53]—the same category applicable to photographs purported to depict people, such as the photograph of a child we mentioned earlier (see Hua XXIII, p. 183). The latter he associates with the moment of aesthetic consideration.

At the time of his 1904–05 lectures on *Phantasy and Image Consciousness*, Husserl holds that experiencing a consciousness of image requires a *conflict* between *image sujet* (the object depicted) and *image object* ("the appearing object that is the representant for the image *sujet*" (Hua XXIII, p. 20)). At this stage of his explorations, Husserl still defines *image consciousness* (*Bildbewusstsein*) almost exclusively in terms of *depiction consciousness* (*Abbildbewusstsein*). In the *Ab-bildung* construed this way, the particle *ab-* seems to stand for an essential gap, for the indispensable distance between image and thing that allows the former to act as a "representant" for the latter. We might therefore suggest that the depictive image proper is always lacking by definition. Here, the *ab-* of *Ab-bildung* can also be understood to have a *temporal* connotation, in the sense that the copy *imitating* the original is that which has to come *after*. In a manner of speaking, the former chases the latter without ever truly catching it—nor is it ever supposed to, as we illustrated using the example of Plato's *Cratylus*.

Figure 2: Titian, *Sacred and Profane Love* (ca. 1515)

Aesthetic consideration, on the other hand, does not emphasize the moment of lacking, of inauthenticity. In all likelihood, no one has seen every single original work depicted in every image they have ever viewed in catalogs or art history books. However, even if we only ever encounter depictions (without seeing the

---

[53] *"These are inauthentic representations, though on the basis of images.* The imaging consciousness is connected with intentions that refer to an object that is different from the object appearing in the image object and stands to it in certain characteristic relations, which, in addition, can serve to establish another representation, more direct and more authentic. We do best to say *depictions*, representation by means of more or less imperfect copies or depictions. (Hence copies of pictures belong here as well)" (Hua XXIII, p. 183).

works themselves), this does not necessarily prevent us from growing familiar with the style expressed through those representations, and even being profoundly influenced by them. This alone may be enough to suggest that, when viewing pictures in a museum catalog, we do not necessarily experience them as mere depictions of original works, as inherently deficient "images of" pieces in the museum's collection. What we experience in such cases is thus not necessarily a consciousness of depiction, of an *"inauthentic"* representation (Hua XXIII, p. 183).

On the contrary, as we have seen, it is possible for the viewer to "see the *sujet in* the image" (see Hua XXIII, p. 184, my italics). A viewer may find the style expressed through these "depictive" pictures attractive and admirable; they might absorb that style, so to speak, and learn to recognize it. In this case, the mode of consciousness is essentially akin to what we would experience when viewing the original. This obviously is not tantamount to calling the two experiences identical, but in principle they may involve the same basic attitude.

Against this background, Husserl asks rhetorically whether the original Titian itself is "a *depictive* being [*ein* Abbild-*sein*]" (Hua XXIII, p. 183), whether its "*sujet* is an object whose representant is the image understood as a *depictive image*, which is supposed to serve as the foundation for an inauthentic representation relating to it" (Hua XXIII, pp. 183–184). When it comes to images understood as depiction, we can always look for a "more authentic representation" that would be a worthier "representative" of the thing, but the Titian painting is a different matter. When it comes to "what is meant in aesthetic image consciousness," Husserl poses a question as simple as it is decisive: can there be "another intuition" that might offer us "a more authentic representation of" it? (Hua XXIII, p. 184). This question, too, is evidently rhetorical: in the aesthetic attitude, having a representation of the object "from all sides" (for example) would not provide us a "more authentic representation" as our "interest" is not "directed toward the object as such, […] but toward the *object's exhibiting of itself in the image object*" (Hua XXIII, p. 184).

In aesthetic consideration, we are focused not on what the image is lacking *qua* depiction, but rather on the specific manner of its manifestation. While in the aesthetic attitude, we are *"interested"* in the way the object is presented to us, in the way it "appears," in the specificity of its "how" (*wie*) rather than the generality of its "what" (*was*): "Titian's picture represents to me sacred and profane love. From a definite standpoint. For this standpoint there is a representation such that *a feeling of inauthenticity with respect to what is presented does not come up at all.* What *interests* me in this case is there; it is not indirectly represented" (hua XXIII, p. 184, my italics).

Keeping in mind our earlier remarks on the *ab-* in *Abbildung*, we might say that the aesthetic regime nullifies the need for contrast in order for a depiction to be recognized—the distance essential to depiction consciousness is put out of play. We shall discuss this point in greater detail in the second chapter, which will investigate the essence of aesthetic experience.

1.16 The Photographic *Sujet*

Having expounded upon our initial introduction to aesthetic consciousness, let us now rewind and take a closer look at two elements: *belief* and *presentification*. Though we have already touched upon these to some extent, there is a great deal more ground to cover in the general sense (i.e., how these discriminating elements enable us to identify different types of images) as well as specifically regarding the role these elements play in the aesthetic and artistic dimensions. We have mentioned how the general concept of phantasy allows us to think of physical image consciousness as a case of phantasy complying with *perceptio* (which should allow us to establish a more specific understanding of the senses in which we can refer to image objects, image *sujets*, and image things). In fact, at the time of his Göttingen courses (in 1904–05), Husserl had not yet fully defined and consolidated his triadic description of image consciousness; he would return to the topic several times over the coming years, re-examining and re-defining his three "moments of image." Dissecting these three instances further and further, down to their most subtle implications, reveals the incredible complexity of what originally seemed a relatively straightforward task.

Our inquiry, for its part, seeks to measure the extent to which these distinctions can be applied to various forms of images, such as paintings (including the considerations raised in connection with Titian's *Amor Sacro*), theater (which, as we have seen, seems to serve as a new paradigm for rethinking the artistic image[54]), and cinematography (which Husserl rarely explored, and even those few instances referred to a simpler form of moving image than what we know today as "movies").[55] Cinematographic images, in particular, can potentially become emblematic with regard to the aims we have set ourselves.

---

54 In this regard, see, for example, Rodrigo (2006, pp. 97–98). Pierre Rodrigo, too, pays particular attention to Text no. 18b. He sees it as the point at which Husserl's interpretation of works of art begins to undergo a paradigm shift from the model of the marble bust in *Logical Investigations* (Hua XIX/1, Vol. 2, "sixth research," § 14) to the painting and engraving in *Ideas I* and then, in 1918, to the paradigm of the theater, which proves instrumental to his development of the notion of phantasy complying with *perceptio*.

55 This investigation might also be extended to virtual images, which we will occasionally mention here, though our primary focus will remain on pictorial, photographic and filmic images. I am currently working on a separate inquiry dedicated specifically to virtual imagery. Restricting our en-

1.16 The Photographic *Sujet* — 59

In its classical form (without wanting to relativize or deny specific exceptions), cinematographic imagery shares several essential traits with photography, theater, and painting, the image forms Husserl examined more thoroughly through his phenomenological lens. Before we untangle some of these essential features with regard to the filmic image, it may be useful for us to continue exploring examples drawn from photography first so that we can later draw parallels and contrasts to their moving-image equivalents. Let us go back to what we—with a certain conscious naïvete—have called a "common" or "ordinary" photo of our friend. As mentioned, when we look at this photograph, we can say that we see our friend in it (as the image *sujet*), but this is not the same type of "seeing" that we exercise in perception when our friend is beside us "in the flesh."

We have seen above how Husserl describes the act of viewing images in terms of "seeing-in": in genuine physical image depiction, the referent (the image *sujet* depicted) is seen *in* the photograph. However, although this initial level of analysis may seem to define the notion of *sujet* with sufficient clarity, it in fact entails several pitfalls that cast doubt upon its very nature. The question of *what exactly* the *sujet* of the photograph *is* might not be as simple as we might expect. Properly speaking, for example, the image *sujet* of the aforementioned photograph of a friend is not necessarily the actual friend in the actual world. What we have called the "image object" need not necessarily resemble an "original" external to it, which is why characterizing a *sujet* as real or fictitious is not tantamount to assigning a defined ontological status to something external to the image, i.e., to a *sujet* that we might have good reason to experience as *factually* existent or nonexistent.

Though "Husserl insists on resemblance as the irreducible core of visual representation: an image depicts (*abbilden*) its object through resemblance (*Ähnlichkeit*)," it must be emphasized that "resemblance" in this case "is not taken to be a type of natural faithfulness, a causal interaction between copy and original." Rather, "Husserl examines image-consciousness as a specific form of intentionality." Although he "retains the idea of resemblance as central to depiction, image-consciousness is not construed narrowly as the consciousness of imitation—as a relation between two separate appearances, a copy and its original" (de Warren 2010, p. 306). More specifically, as we have shown when referring to the universal-

---

deavors in this work to the apparently more "conventional"—though still contemporary—varieties of images is not an effort to avoid this issue, however. Rather, we do it with the awareness that this analysis represents a seminal step that can provide important phenomenological tools for use in further inquiries into virtual environments or other emerging forms of images.

ized concept of phantasy, it is the possibility of image consciousness itself that seems to be rooted in phantasy consciousness, rather than vice versa.[56]

Brough echoes de Warren's sentiments, saying that "the kind of resemblance at work in image consciousness [in Husserl] differs from resemblance as it is commonly understood, which involves an external relation. The resemblance in imagining is instead an internal matter bound to 'seeing-in'" (Brough 2012, p. 555).[57] In other words, the depiction similarity that Husserl considers necessary for a depictional image consciousness to arise does not seem to be construed purely in terms of similarity between the image object of the friend appearing on the surface of a photograph and the real friend in the real world. Similarly, Eduard Marbach notes that even though "the pictorial relation must be anchored in or based on the physically present picture" in Husserlian image consciousness, this same "pictorial relation must not be established between the physically present picture as a thing and its depictum" (Marbach 2000, p. 304).

What, then, is the status of the *sujet*? Let us try to obtain some clarity by framing the question of belief vis-à-vis photography as follows: when looking at a photograph, we know that *that* image is not reality, that what we *actually* have *in our hands* is photographic paper or an illuminated screen. Yet even though the image object (the image of our friend) does not constitute anything genuinely present, we can say we *believe* in the existence of what we see in it. We have a specific attitude toward reality in this situation, usually one implying belief by default: we believe in our friend's actual existence even though they are not in the room with us. We may even find ourselves *existentially* absorbed in the image, gazing at it as though gazing into the eyes of the person herself, and it may even seem as though the person in the photograph were looking back at us.

---

[56] In similar fashion, de Warren asserts that "the constitution of resemblance, on this phenomenological picture, calls upon the work of the imagination within image-consciousness" (de Warren 2010, p. 307) and that "the constitution of depiction is based on what Husserl identifies as the 'perceptual imagination'"—i. e., what we have called phantasy complying with *perceptio* (given that no perceptual intentionality proper is carried out in this case)—"or the manifestation of the imagination *in* perceptual [read: *perzeptiv*] experience" (de Warren 2010, p. 307).

[57] The same article (p. 550) recalls that the notion of "seeing-in," conceived as an essential moment of representation, has been disseminated widely within Anglo-American aesthetics, in particular through Richard Wollheim's *Painting as an Art*. For a comparison between Husserlian and Wollheimian "seeing-in" see Brough (2012, pp. 550–553) and Voltolini (2013, pp. 83–85). On the analogies between the Wollheimian descriptive method and the phenomenological one, see Matteucci (2013, p. 6): "to speak of a [*scil.* Wollheim's] phenomenological exercise is not a stretch. It is Wollheim himself who sometimes uses the term phenomenology to account for his speculative attitude." I elaborated on this further in Rozzoni (2020), also extending the comparison to Kendall Walton's positions on depiction.

Clearly, we are operating in the regime of image consciousness rather than perceptual consciousness since we know that touching the image constitutes touching either paper or a screen, not our friend. Even so, there is certainly a form of belief at work regarding what we see in the image: despite being well aware that our friend is not in the room with us, we believe that she was in front of the lens "in the flesh" at the moment she or someone else took her picture.

Above, I have suggested the possibility of distinguishing between images affected by belief and images without belief, or positional or apositional images (in the specific sense outlined). Photographs in the Barthesian sense seem to fall under the former category as they are always essentially accompanied by the *certainty* that the person or thing shown "has been there where I see it" (Barthes 1980, p. 115). Obviously, the "there" in question is not "on the surface of the photograph support," but rather the "elsewhere"—where the image was "taken"—presentified by every photograph. (As we have remarked, this certainty holds true even if we have never seen this person or thing in the flesh in our lives, and even if, for whatever reason, it would now be impossible for us to do so.) Next, let us delve more deeply into the nature of this certainty as regards *sujets* of impressional images.

1.17 Photography and Reality

We all think we know what photographs are; defining these "familiar," "common" objects and their extensive roles in our day-to-day lives seems as though it would pose no particular difficulty. Were someone to ask us how this particular type of image is different from others—paintings, for example—we might *prima facie* consider having at our disposal numerous arguments demonstrating distinctions we probably consider self-evident. Barring a few specific instances involving deliberate efforts to deceive us, none of us would have a problem separating the photographs from the paintings in a set of images.

One way we might attempt to describe what, exactly, differentiates photographs from paintings might be to point out the former's privileged position vis-à-vis reality compared to the latter. Susan Sontag famously notes, for example, that "a photograph is not only an image (as a painting is an image), an interpretation of the real; it is also a trace, something directly stenciled off the real, like a footprint or a death mask" (Sontag 1977, p. 120). Thus, a photograph seems to have the value of a document (*documentum*). This connection to reality, which to us appears perfectly natural, seems to distinguish it neatly from a painting.

Sontag's quote also suggests that photographs' favorable relationship with reality is not merely a function of resembling reality more closely, despite what we might initially expect. Indeed, if degree of similarity were the only distinction between the two, a hyperrealistic color painting might well be more accurately described as "photographic" than a blurry black-and-white photograph. Instead (for example), a photograph of a crime scene, however imperfect, would most likely carry more weight in determining the outcome of a trial than a sketch of the same scene, even one by an eyewitness with a talent for drawing. Similarly, passports use photographs as identity verification rather than painted or drawn portraits, though these might well resemble the passport holder with incredible accuracy. Besides the obvious practical considerations at work there, this is primarily due to the primacy generally afforded the photographic "spoor" (although this does not rule out the possibility of other signs or representations eventually replacing the photograph in this function). As Sontag says,

> While a painting, even one that meets photographic standards of resemblance, is never more than the stating of an interpretation, a photograph is never less than the registering of an emanation (light waves reflected by objects)—a material vestige of its subject in a way that no painting can be. Between two fantasy alternatives, that Holbein the Younger had lived long enough to have painted Shakespeare or that a prototype of the camera had been invented early enough to have photographed him, most Bardolators would choose the photograph. This is not just because it would presumably show what Shakespeare *really* looked like, for even if the hypothetical photograph were faded, barely legible, a brownish shadow, we would probably still prefer it to another glorious Holbein. Having a photograph of Shakespeare would be like having a nail from the True Cross. (Sontag 1977, p. 120, my italics)

One might certainly retort that paintings can also be construed as a "spoor" to the *act* of their own creation in a certain sense—the *hand* that applied the paint to the canvas, as it were. But this very aspect is what allows us to pinpoint the difference between pictorial (*pictorium*) and photographic trace more specifically: as Barthes suggests, the latter can be defined as "acheiropoietos," or—following the etymology of the word—"not made by the hand of man" (Barthes 1980, p. 82).[58]

All these considerations refer to a feature often presented as photography's essential element, namely the so-called "indexical" dimension to which Rosalind Krauss has famously drawn attention (see Krauss 1985). The reference to "indexicality" as a characteristic feature of the photographic image originated in the revival of the term "index" as developed by the American philosopher Charles Sanders Peirce. In context of his "classification of signs" (Peirce 1998, p. 500), which

---

[58] "Always the Photograph *astonishes* me, with an astonishment which endures and renews itself, inexhaustibly. Perhaps this astonishment, this persistence reaches down into the religious substance out of which I am molded; nothing for it: Photography has something to do with resurrection: might we not say of it what the Byzantines said of the image of Christ which impregnated St. Veronica's napkin: that it was not made by the hand of man, *acheiropoietos?*" (Barthes 1980, p. 82).

includes the basic categories of "icons," "indices," and "symbols" (Peirce 1998, p. 5), Peirce emphasizes the importance of the moment of "physical *constraint*" in characterizing the photographic sign:

> Photographs, especially instantaneous photographs, are very instructive, because we know that they are in certain respects exactly like the objects they represent. But this resemblance is due to the photographs having been produced under such circumstances that they were *physically forced to correspond* point by point to nature. In that aspect, then, they belong to the second class of signs, those by *physical connection* [*scil.* Indices]. (Peirce 1998, pp. 5–6, my italics)

This is certainly not the place to examine whether the debate over the indexicality of photography actually does justice to the complexity of Peirce's notion of "index," nor to discuss the more subtle objections that might call into question its applicability to a definition of the nature of photography.[59] What I want to focus on is rather this exclusive relationship to reality that photography seems to inhabit in a manner *qualitatively* different from any other image.

We might define an "ordinary" photo—a snapshot any of us could take with a regular camera—as the "zero degree [*degré zéro*]" of photography. This seems to represent the elementary photographic gesture: the "shot," a minimal action that sets off a process. All it requires is the will to shoot (though not necessarily even that, given that one can certainly snap a photo unintentionally) and then let reality do the rest, so to speak. Here, the "shot" seems to function as a purportedly neutral device opening to receive the real.[60] Thus, the snapshot can take on the role of an *ideal* starting point for meditating on the relationship between photography and reality—as the ideal of an image we experience reflected in a mirror or on the water, or reflecting something that "has been" in front of the camera.

We can then say that we usually experience this type of photography with a documentary attitude characterized by the dimension of certainty. The photograph seems to tell us that something has happened, to offer clear evidence of its occurrence. And yet, as has been pointed out, the photograph itself "says" nothing, nor does it "show" us anything in the strictest sense. The expressions we sometimes resort to, such as "the photograph tells us" or "the photograph shows us," can lead to inappropriate "anthropomorphi[zation]" (Wiesing 2013, pp. 86–90) of the photograph. In this vein, under the aegis of photographs' indexicality, of their

---

59 In this regard, see Gunthert (2019, pp. 20–24). The author also points out that "even in the case of an analog signal neither the optical dispositive nor the carrier of the recording are neutral mediators of a flux emanating from the object" (Gunthert 2019, p. 23).

60 Gunthert also remarks that "a photographic apparatus cannot be described as a transparent mediator of the real" (Gunthert 2019, p. 23).

physical reference to reality, it is not unusual to hear that photography *documents* that something has taken place.

However, one oft-unnoticed aspect warrants mentioning: that photographs always acquire their documentary "authority" within a certain context, a horizon of sense constituted by interrelated meanings, and only within that horizon can they be "animated," perceived, and used in a certain way. In short, the "privilege of reality" usually ascribed to photography—as Barthes puts it, the fact that a photograph always "says" that something "has been"—actually extends beyond the photograph itself, both preceding and accompanying it. Photographs are always shown within a network of practices and senses, without which we would often have trouble recognizing their *sujets* (even those that commonly seem very familiar, natural, and immediately understandable to us).[61]

This is not to say that meanings can be ascribed to photographs arbitrarily but rather that they do not possess absolute inherent meaning from the moment of their creation, irrespective of their field of application or connection with the values operating either explicitly or implicitly in that context. This is also true with respect to the *certainty* that seems to be an essential characteristic of our "photographic consciousness."

The capacity to "ratify"[62] that Barthes ascribes to photography cannot, in fact, be attributed entirely to the image in itself; rather, it pertains to a *knowledge* concerning a process that must ground it. In Barthes' view, the fact that we already *know* photography comes into being through an impressional chemical process ("the discovery that silver halogens were sensitive to light"[63]) is what fosters belief

---

[61] In the words of photographer Jeff Wall, to whom we will address our analysis in the third chapter: "People tend to relate to photographs by looking at what's in them and saying what's going on, and they might get frustrated if they immediately can't recognize what's going on like they can recognize what's going on in the news. [...] a picture [....] has [...] this character that it seems to disclose an actuality very simply, but it is not that simple. Most people think that photographs are simple because they are accompanied by a lot of description, verbal: take away the verbal description, you get into the pure picture, then you have to relate to it as a poem" (Wall 2015a).
[62] "Photograph's essence," Barthes also writes, "is to *ratify* what it represents" (Barthes 1980, p. 85, my italics).
[63] "It is often said that it was the painters who invented Photography (by bequeathing it their framing, the Albertian perspective, and the optic of the *camera obscura*). I say: no, it was the chemists. For the *noeme* 'That-has-been' was possible only on the day when a scientific circumstance (the discovery that silver halogens were sensitive to light) made it possible to recover and print directly the luminous rays emitted by a variously lighted object. The photograph is literally an emanation of the referent" (Barthes 1980, p. 80). Like Sontag, Barthes talks about the image object as an "emanation." Later in the same text, he refers to her directly: "From a real body, which was there, proceed radiations which ultimately touch me; who am here, the duration of the transmission is insignificant; the photograph of the missing being, as Sontag says, will touch me like the

in the "*Spectator.*" Still, it must be stressed that nothing in the image itself seems capable of grounding our belief on its own. "Impressional images"[64] are not *eo ipso* trustworthy. Belief in an image always seems to presuppose a certain knowledge about it.

We know that images can be manipulated or doctored, thereby eliciting our position of reality through deception. This is not to say, however, that our customary belief in photographed reality is unfounded and warrants systematic questioning; rather, the issue concerning our belief in photography is whether there are good reasons to undermine that sense of momentary calm that typically characterizes our faith in them. After all, as Peirce says, the "belief" is "the demi-cadence which closes a musical phrase in the symphony of our intellectual life," and it possesses "just three properties: First, it is something that we are aware of; second, it appeases the irritation of doubt; and, third, it involves the establishment in our nature of a rule of action, or, say for short, a *habit*" (Peirce 1992, p. 129).

How, then, do we relate to photographic images? In Husserlian terms, we might also ask: how do we relate to "impressional images?" What "habit," what "rule of action" do they awaken in us? As stressed above, we are generally prone to believing in the *sujet* we see in photographs without questioning this type of certainty. In this regard, one might raise the question of how the advent of digital photography may have affected our usual responses to images and, more importantly, changed the sense in which we characterize them as impressional images. For example, many people predicted that digital technology would make it impossible to continue trusting photographs the way we do the analog variety. Yet the effects of the digital transition have proven less predictable than expected (see Gunthert 2019, pp. 17–20), and experience has shown that we do not lend photographs less credence merely because the "silver halogens" have given way to matrices. In fact, in some cases, there may be reason to consider digital photographs more believable testimony of an occurrence than their analog counterparts.[65] Once again, the image in itself—the manner in which an image object manifests itself, we might also say—is not the sole determinant of whether we believe in the *sujet* presented through it.

---

delayed rays of a star. A sort of umbilical cord links the body of the photographed thing to my gaze: light, though impalpable, is here a carnal medium, a skin I share with anyone who has been photographed" (Barthes 1980, pp. 80–81). Note how the "umbilical cord" metaphor converges with Peirce's construal of the photograph as an image by physical connection.

[64] Peirce's characterization of photographs by physical connection converges with Husserl's denotation of impressional images introduced above.

[65] See, for example, the analysis of the Abu Ghraib images in Gunthert (2019, pp. 31–41).

To return to our "common photograph" example, when our friend sends us a selfie she took in front of a monument, we ordinarily immediately believe in what we see in the image. In other words, even if the photograph is digital and thus theoretically easy to alter, we tend to trust its authenticity: we do not hesitate to believe that our friend really was or is at the monument and that she really did take the picture of herself in front of it. We already have a belief concerning the process used to generate these types of impressional images, and this knowledge strongly informs our beliefs and habits just as it does with the analog chemical development process. This is not to discount the possibility of differences between the two processes as regards belief, nor is it to suggest that these habits might not change if new doubts were to emerge in the future—I might, for example, be more suspicious about the veracity of digital photos since I know they are typically easy for anyone to modify. In principle, however, what impacts my belief in both cases is my knowledge of the relevant processes and practices.

We have attempted to characterize photography in its most elementary form and to emphasize its "witness value" (ratification, i.e., *ratum facere*, make valuable, confirmed). At the same time, however, we have seen that the "zero degree" of photography—that of a "neutral," "indifferent" photograph that reproduces reality "as it is"—is ultimately a borderline concept since even the simplest photograph does not inherently convey absolute meaning, let alone a determinate and univocal message. Rather, a photo's sense always arises within a context, a system of cross-references that can, for example, lead us to believe or doubt the reality the photograph presentifies.

In the course of its comparatively short history, photography has risen to the rank of art form, and we now encounter many photographs within artistic practice as well. It seems clear that, in order for a photograph to be considered artistic, it must be possible to recognize a value within it that is not merely reducible to its being "a trace"—the quality which, in the Barthesian view, would be considered its essence. Indeed, Barthes would consider this a betrayal of the nature of photography, of its "indexical soul":

> Society is concerned to tame the Photograph, to temper the madness which keeps threatening to explode in the face of whoever looks at it. To do this, it possesses two means. The first consists of making Photography into an art, for no art is mad. Whence the photographer's insistence on his rivalry with the artist, on subjecting himself to the rhetoric of painting and its sublimated mode of exhibition. Photography can in fact be an art: when there is no longer any madness in it, when its *noeme* is forgotten and when consequently its essence no longer acts on me: do you suppose that looking at Commander Puyo's strollers I am disturbed and exclaim "That-has-been!"? (Barthes 1980, p. 117)

Thus, it seems that photography's process of *artification* (a term I use in the sense of an object's transition from a nonartistic to an artistic status; see Shapiro/Heinich 2012) must necessarily come to terms with that "physical constraint" connecting photography to reality. Photography has always struggled for artistic recognition in its own right. Its indexical character seems insufficient—photography refuses to settle for being merely a faithful, resemblant trace of the *sujets* posing before its lens.

On the one hand, this visceral relationship that photography maintains with reality is an aspect that gives it something more than painting: it appears to be qualitatively more faithful to reality than the latter. On the other hand, this same prerogative appears to prevent it from "rising" to a further stage and in many cases becomes a burden to its artistic ambitions: one can always reproach photography by saying that its *essential* function is to bear witness and that any other ambition for it is purely *contingent* or even against its nature.[66]

As such, we might say that photography's progressive acceptance as art seems unable to completely dampen the echo of its indexical dimension, which threatens to come back into play even when we might prefer that it fade into the background, as if the photograph were condemned to preserve the memory of its impressional nature. A "click," even one made with purely artistic intentions, can always surprise us and reveal something that the naked eye missed, something that we are then immediately ready to believe. Conversely, a painter working *en plein air* can hardly "accidentally" paint an object they have not noticed despite it being in their field of vision.

In Michelangelo Antonioni's classic *Blow-up* (1966), photographer Thomas takes snapshots of a random couple in the park but encounters unanticipated images manifested on the finished photographs. In order to understand what they are about—to clarify what kind of *sujets* they presentify—, he begins blowing up the images in an effort to determine who or what was really "in front of the lens." This leads him to construe a possible *narrative* that might *truthfully* explain those impressional images—a narrative produced by a "physical connection," to return to Peirce. Everything seems to indicate that a man has been killed, but the enlarge-

---

[66] When photography was first admitted to the Salon in 1859, it was famously the target of Baudelaire's pungent criticism. But the authoritative indictment was not enough to slow down the (laborious) process of artification now underway. Further institutional recognition was in the offing. Beaumont Newhall organized the first major historical exhibition on photography at Museum of Modern Art in 1937 (Photography: 1839–1937), and John Szarkowski, Director of the Department of Photography at MoMA from 1962 to 1991, played a role in the "final institutionalization of photographic art" (Brunet 2012, p. 33 ff.). Brunet's full contribution offers an articulate reconstruction of the artification of photography.

ments result in increasingly blurred figures, exploding their contours (in a second sense of "blowing up," of course); eventually, the blown-up images mockingly take on the appearance of an abstract painting (Figure 3).

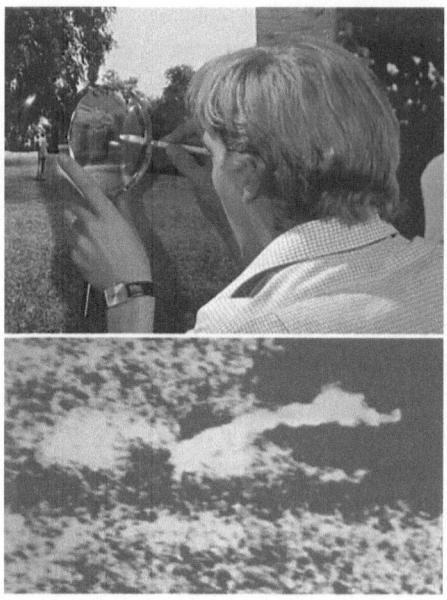

Figure 3: Stills from Michelangelo Antonioni's *Blow-up* (1966)

More specifically, what I want to highlight here is the process by which the emergence of these details provokes Thomas's sudden *change of attitude* based on what he knows about the genesis of the photographic image objects—that is, about the intrinsic connection between photography and reality. He shifts to an investigative level, devoting his attention to searching for "what really happened." Tension arises between figures imposing themselves on the strength of their "acheiropoietic" nature—not made by the hand of man, and therefore allegedly objective—and human subjectivity, which might have been distracted, might not remember or remember incorrectly, yet is always the ultimate recipient of these impressional images: a subjectivity that is prompt to believe and yet has to interpret. In recalling an experience of his own, Barthes defines this kind of tension as a "'detective' anguish [*angoisse policière*]," and relates it explicitly to *Blow-up*'s theme:

> One day I received from a photographer a picture of myself which I could not remember being taken, for all my efforts; I inspected the tie, the sweater, to discover in what circumstances I had worn them; to no avail. And yet, *because it was a photograph*, I could not deny that I

had been *there* (even if I did not know *where*). This distortion between certainty and oblivion gave me a kind of vertigo, something of a "detective" anguish (the theme of *Blow-Up* was not far off); I went to the photographer's show as to a police investigation, to learn at last what I no longer knew about myself. (Barthes 1980, p. 85)

1.18 Moving Images and Belief

We can now delve more deeply into this issue as regards moving images: how and to what extent do they demonstrate an analogous relationship with reality? We have said that Husserl's tripartition (which, as mentioned, he developed by describing a photograph) similarly applies to film images, especially as regards the possibility of construing them in terms of image objects.

To develop an analogous example to the one we used with photographic images, when I view film footage of my friend—as I look into her image object moving around on the surface the film is projected upon—I see my friend, and I believe that she actually was there when the film was shot. This attitude can characterize several disparate types of film-related experiences. For instance, when I watch footage of the Rolling Stones rehearsing "Sympathy for the Devil,"[67] I believe that Mick Jagger is playing the guitar and singing; when watching the recent footage from Peter Jackson's documentary series *The Beatles: Get Back* (2021), I believe that it constitutes presentifications of the process by which the eponymous song was created. I may not recognize everyone else who appears in the footage, but I believe in their individual existence.[68] The Lumière Brothers' first films provide another famous example of moving images in which what we see are "real person[s]." Even though the people filmed had been "prepared" to be filmed,[69] when we are looking at the image objects moving on the screen, we presume them to show "real people" who were there in front of the camera when the film was shot.

From here, it is a short step (though, as we shall see, a potentially complicated one) to so-called cinéma vérité,[70] direct cinema, or documentary films. Let us ex-

---

[67] See J.-L. Godard, *The Rolling Stones: Sympathy for the Devil* (1968).
[68] See P. Jackson, *The Beatles: Get Back* (2021).
[69] See for example Nichols (2010, p. 119).
[70] For some key insights concerning the relationship between camera and reality in *cinéma vérité*, see Mamber (1974, pp. 4–5): "Cinema verite is a practical working method based upon a faith in unmanipulated reality, a refusal to temper with life as it presents itself. [...] Still, cinema verite is more than a mutant offspring of documentary techniques. It deserves a place of its own as an alternative kind of cinema—neither documentary (as usually practiced) nor fiction (though often telling a story)."

amine this group of images now; we will turn our attention to fiction films (and their photographic pendants) later. Although these types of cinema are profoundly different from one another in certain respects, for the sake of our argument, we can say they are similar in that they are all *presentifications of* an alleged *reality*. The key here is that the audience's belief in the actual existence of what they see in these images is a major component to these forms of cinema. To the directors of such films, giving audiences a "faithful" image of reality is—at least in principle—a major consideration. In turn, we as spectators have a specific attitude toward these works: we are supposed to believe what we are being shown, to see reality through the images on screen (even though we are "merely" seeing presentifications of that reality). Here, too, Barthes's description seems to apply: "given that I am seeing it now in the image, [this] must have happened."

Even at this early juncture, it is worth noting that, with respect to the question of belief in filmic images, our phenomenological approach yields results diverging from other classical approaches. Christian Metz, for example, wrote a 1974 article counterposing cinema with photography on this very point; in it, he states that there is "a great difference between photography and the cinema, which is an art of fiction and narration and has considerable projective power. The movie spectator is absorbed, not by a 'has been there', but by a sense of 'There it is'" (Metz 1965, p. 6). In my view, however, Metz's argument confuses two different levels that phenomenological analysis keeps distinct. The dichotomy he establishes is not, in fact, his declared one between "has been there" and "there it is" so much as between "has been there" and "as if there it were." This latter dichotomy does not represent a distinction between photography and cinema; *in fact, it can apply to both*. The Barthesian "has been there," to which Metz explicitly refers as well, concerns a genuine *belief* in the reality presentified in image—a connection to a form of actuality, to use the Husserlian and Peircean terms outlined above. Were one to attempt (as Metz does) to draw a parallel between this type of belief and the "impression of belief" of the filmic modality, caution would be warranted when defining the type of belief defined in the latter. As we are seeing, the cinematic experience associated with moving images can assume different forms. For instance, this "impression of reality" might take on different connotations depending on whether one is watching a fictional movie, a documentary, or old footage of a person no longer living.

Of course, we can certainly obtain an "impression of reality" when watching a fictional movie despite not believing that the events on the screen are actually happening, have ever happened, or will ever happen. Denis Diderot offers excellent contributions in this context concerning the "effet de réel" that unreal images can (and, according to Diderot, should) effectively produce in art.[71] However, such belief should neither be equated nor confused with the belief associated with positional images (for example, the belief implied when watching a documentary claiming to presentify something that actually happened through impressional images). It is therefore no coincidence that Metz is eventually forced to acknowledge this difference by distinguishing between a "'real' reality" and a "reality of the fiction" (Metz 1974, p. 11). When he states that "cinema participates in this domestication of Photography," Barthes is thus explicitly referring to "fictional cinema, precisely the one said to be the seventh art," and only in this sense can he denote it as "illusion" (Barthes 1980, p. 117). As we shall soon see, in Husserlian terms, we might also refer to this particular case as an "artistic illusion" (Hua XXIII, p. 617).

For Barthes, however, this "domestication" of photography is not a possibility exclusively set in motion by cinematography as such. Rather, it arises from transitioning to a different *form of consciousness*. In fact, it can still occur without photography going beyond the confines of its own sphere, as Barthes makes explicit when referencing Commander Puyo's work cited above: "do you suppose that looking at Commander Puyo's strollers I am disturbed and exclaim 'That-has-been!'?" (Barthes 1980, p. 117).

1.19 Iconic Belief in the Present

The notion of belief also characterizes our experience of moving images manifesting themselves on a TV screen (or any of the other types of mobile screens now ubiquitous in our society). Against this background, one important task emerging in contemporary philosophical discussion concerns defining the status of the screen, a particular kind of "space" we encounter with ever-increasing frequency in the most disparate forms (Carbone 2016; Chateau/Moure 2016; Cometti 2010). The boundaries among cinematic screens, televisions, and computer screens are gradually breaking down (Friedberg 2006). Their related forms of spectatorship seem to have abandoned the darkness characteristic of the conventional movie theater "cave," allowing external creation of new "windows" opening onto very different experiences—thereby influencing the specific senses in which the "window" metaphor might still prove productive in the context of images.

If we take an initial phenomenological look at the elements characterizing live broadcasts, for example, we can see that they, too, can be described in terms of the

---

71 Consider, for example, the *Éloge de Richardson* (Diderot 1875 [1761]). I discuss this point in greater detail in Rozzoni (2016).

presentification/belief conceptual pair, but in the *present tense*. In this context, it is worth noting that Husserl also mentions "memory of the present [*Gegenwartserinnerung*]"[72] as a form of presentification in which what is posited is the *current existence* of something not being perceived—the Colosseum, for example, which we know (or have good reason to believe) is now in Rome.

In the same vein, when we experience live images, we are in a regime of consciousness wherein we position something as existing *now*, in the present, although in fact we are only seeing it in image, through a tele-vision (*Fern-sehen*), essentially a specific type of seeing-at-a-distance (tele/fern).[73] When we look at the television screen, we can see something presentified in it, and we also believe that what we are seeing is actually happening. The viewer can see something presentified on screen while believing that it is happening in the present. According to Lambert Wiesing, this is the defining characteristic of television. Of course, "it is possible to watch movies on TV, but that is not a specific capacity of the TV; we can do that in the movie theater as well. When we watch a movie on TV, we use the TV not as television but as home cinema, as a movie theater substitute. Only when we watch live transmissions do we use the TV as television," in which case "we let ourselves be shown something that only television can show, something that is not a film but a broadcast" (Wiesing 2005, p. 83). We might go as far as to reserve the term "television" not for the television set as a specific object, but rather for the specific act of seeing the present from an iconic distance; this would also describe, for example, watching live streams (e.g., Instagram Live) on our mobile devices.

What is phenomenologically distinctive here is that consciousness involves the possibility of seeing at a distance combined with a belief concerning the present. A similar presentifying consciousness seems to be at work in the video calls that have become increasingly common in the wake of the recent pandemic: instead of meeting up with others in the flesh, we encounter them through a presentification in the present. Here, again, when viewing image objects presentifying our work colleagues, we see *sujets* and believe in their existence.

---

72 On the "memory of the present," see, for example, Hua X, § 29 and Hua XXIII, pp. 280–281: "Well, not every memorial consciousness [*Erinnerungsbewusstsein*] (memorial consciousness in the widest sense) is consciousness of the past. I recall the Roons: the Roons that stands before me as now existing, though merely presentified [*vergegenwärtigt*]" (the Roons was a restaurant on a hillock near Göttingen, evoked several times by Husserl when formulating examples related to experiences of presentification).

73 "For the name *television* suggests that the apparatus of this name possesses the capacity to afford a view into the distance" (Wiesing 2005, p. 82).

In this last example, of course, we are not merely viewers but are also agents, in the sense that we can talk to each other. Accordingly, based on what we know about these types of connections, we would not normally question our belief in one another's existences when video chatting. Unlike television *stricto sensu*, video calls involve interaction, which, in principle, can reinforce this belief (or perhaps undermine it, should something about the interaction run counter to our expectations). These conversations take place in our reality, in the web of cross-references that constitutes our actual world. After the call, people can easily recall what really happened during the exchange (or perhaps even rewatch it), and they might well get together later on and continue their on-screen conversation while standing face-to-face and making eye contact.[74]

Wiesing chooses to characterize TV consciousness (which we considered *lato sensu*) in terms of looking through a window.[75] Interestingly, the Husserlian manuscripts under discussion here also describe image consciousness in terms of "looking through a window."[76] Some general clarification is in order regarding this important metaphor, which must be kept in mind for all the window-references we shall make in this work.

1.20 Which Window?

Clearly, using this window metaphor to characterize image consciousness could influence our approach to the inquiry. It is important that we avoid overgeneralizing it in order to prevent potential misunderstandings. Both Husserl and his pupil Eugen Fink[77] use "windowness" as an illustrative example in their writings con-

---

74 Of course, they could not have made eye contact during the video call, which (at least for now) does not allow the gazes in the image to meet: each participant can look into the other's eyes, but not simultaneously in the same manner as when they are looking at each other in the flesh.
75 "The invention of the TV is the actualization of windows that are even better than those we are familiar with from normal houses" (Wiesing 2005, p. 82).
76 "The picture on the wall gives a perceptual figment, as if I were looking through a window" (Hua XXIII, p. 612).
77 See, for instance, Fink (1930), where he speaks of the "windowness [*Fensterhaftigkeit*] of an image." However, Fink also specifies that "the speech about the window is only a metaphor. [...] What we want to emphasize when we talk about the window form of the image is this: every world of the image opens up for reasons of essence within a real world. The image is the place of this opening" (Fink 1930, p. 77). It is in this sense that "an image world without a window is in itself a nonsense" (Fink 1930, p. 77). Fink's remarks are more oriented toward the idea of an image opening onto worlds of phantasy, while here I am arguing for a double possibility of such an openness, both to a phantasy world and to an actual world taking place elsewhere.

cerning the essence of images (see, for example, Hua XXIII, pp. 50, 612), but the fact that the metaphor has been used in the past does not necessarily render it outdated, as some scholars have suggested. In particular, occasionally referencing windows in our work need not automatically constitute applying other historical uses of that metaphor, though they should of course be taken into account. At any rate, categorically reducing Husserl's intricate analyses to a single, determinate interpretation of this window paradigm would be a perilously hasty oversimplification, especially since it is entirely possible to describe his concept of image without mentioning windows at all. Instead, we should strive for a more precise definition of what the metaphor expresses to explore the role it actually plays in eidetic description of the image.

Gottfried Boehm and successors elaborating upon his work have called the window paradigm obsolete in its usefulness as a line of inquiry into the nature of images. Boehm considers Husserl to have resorted to such an "elementary model of consciousness" (Boehm 1994, p. 19), which later informed his students' reflections as well (including Fink's).[78] According to Boehm, this allegedly out-of-date paradigm finds in "Diderot's *Lettre sur les aveugles* [...] [its] most famous theoretical demonstration" and, "especially in the French debate, also the classic starting point of criticism" (Boehm 1994, p. 19).

Similarly, Boehm (1986, p. 289) asserts that "the phenomenology of Edmund Husserl [...] has remained significantly fruitless with regard to problems related to artistic seeing and its possible categories," and he claims that Husserl passed these "limits" on to his students, who were "forced" to study images starting "from the general structures of intentional consciousness" (Boehm 1986, p. 289).[79] Boehm points to Maurice Merleau-Ponty as the one to make the most progress toward overcoming this "outdated" model; unsurprisingly, Boehm claims that this required the French to "revise [...] the phenomenological foundations of his [*scil.* Merleau-Ponty's] thought, and deconstruct the perceptive axis of inten-

---

[78] "Phenomenology proved fruitful for our problem only when Merleau-Ponty began to question its theoretical foundations. Husserl himself was barely interested in the problem of the image in the sense we understand it; his students Roman Ingarden, Fritz Kaufmann and Eugen Fink took up this thread, starting, however, from the barely sufficient premise that images should be understood according to the model of a window" (Boehm 1994, pp. 17–18). Hans Rainer Sepp remembers, however, that Fink "does not limit himself to assuming the topos of the window, which has recurred in art theory since Leon Battista Alberti, but also subjects it to a radical problematization" (Sepp 2014, p. xv).

[79] Here, too, he speaks of "the attempts of Eugen Fink and Roman Ingarden, for whom the all-too-historically conditioned notion of the 'open window,' which Leon Battista Alberti in 1436 had first assumed as the model of a discursive consciousness, remained the distinctive element of the image" (Boehm 1986, p. 293).

tionality with its bipolar accentuation (of *noesis* and *noema*)," so as to "obtain an adequate understanding of eye and image" (Boehm 1994, p. 19). This position, of course, overlooks the fact that Merleau-Ponty's work does not abandon intentionality at all—though he rethinks the foundations of intentionality, his work is built upon and develops Husserl's rather than undermine it.[80]

Likewise, it seems misleading to read Husserl's use of this paradigm as derived from a specific, allegedly outdated concept of vision (in the tradition of Leon Battista Alberti, that is[81]), or to apply meanings borrowed from that tradition to terms used by Husserl as though he had merely inherited this concept without questioning it.[82] Of course, it would be equally improper to ignore the possibility of these meanings being present in or having influenced Husserlian ideas, but it is crucial to remember that, for Husserl, phenomenological analyses alone are what define the actual boundaries of the notion of the image and the specific senses in which one can refer to its windowness.

Moreover, even if there *were* a conventional, unambiguous interpretation of Alberti's window, Husserl's intermittent references to windowness ought not lead us to reduce his work to an outdated approach derived from the Albertian matrix. Rather, what seems to interest Husserl most is the problem of difference, the search for an essential distinction between what he calls modes of consciousness.

---

[80] Consider also the analyses by Zahavi (2002).
[81] Carbone (2016, p. 59) relegates Husserl's approach to this obsolete level by relying on Richir (1971), quoting the latter as follows: "To him [*scil.* Husserl], the world is a *picture* that is cut within the frame of the window." In the article Carbone references, Richir argues that Husserlian philosophers' fidelity to the "window" model makes their work still Albertian and Cartesian (Richir 1971, pp. 31–32). Against this background, Richir contends that Merleau-Ponty was the one who subverted this paradigm (a "defenestration," so to speak) by implying that "'beings' are no longer fortresses that protect their riches from the gaze of the world" (Richir 1971, p. 38). However, Richir later rediscovered the enormous potentiality of Husserlian manuscripts on the image (in 1971, as we know, they had not even been published yet); they ultimately became one of his primary sources when reflecting on images. He edited the French critical edition of Husserl's writings on *Phantasia, conscience d'image, souvenir* in 2002 and he dedicated several of his own works to them (including two seminal monographs dated 2000 and 2004).
[82] In his aforementioned drawing on the Husserlian window paradigm, Wiesing specifies that Husserl is "able to determine the limits of Alberti's metaphor of the open window. The comparison to the window does not do justice to the conflictual mode of givenness of an image object. A thing depicted in an image 'appears,' Husserl writes, 'in the way in which an actual physical thing appears, but in conflict with the actual presence (*Gegenwart*) that conflict-free perception brings about.' This means that looking at the image does not lead us to feel 'as if the person were there himself' at all. [...] The appearance of a thing in the image does not possess the unbroken character of the immediate presence of that thing, which presence is characteristic of the view through a window" (Wiesing 2005, p. 81). In this regard, see also Ferencz-Flatz (2009a, p. 239).

Let us therefore examine the degree to which the window paradigm may prove useful, at least at this initial stage. Their individual differences notwithstanding, we might describe our belief-experiences concerning moving on-screen images (documentary cinema, television broadcasts, Instagram Live, TikTok videos) as a "seeing-into" a presentifying window looking out onto (past or present) realities. Live broadcasts through such windows could constitute intersubjective experiences of real occurrences, for example when millions of people follow coverage of a major sporting event, or when the entire world sat riveted to their screens watching the events of September 11 unfold. "Viral" videos on social media are another example in which thousands or millions of people experience and share presentified occurrences.

In these and similar cases, our experiences of such images are characterized by an attitude of belief in what is presentified through them. Of course, this also opens up another topic for discussion, namely the unprecedented ways in which major world events are depicted and at times co-constructed—take, for example, the ways the Gulf War was presented and "reconstructed," "re-assembled," through the medium of television.[83] The style and mode in which these positional images are presented can dramatically impact how we experience the reality they presentify; in some cases, they can even narcotize our experience of reality and our perception of real violence, a phenomenon that can be summarized by Baudrillard's position that a proliferation of images can lead to iconoclastic outcomes.[84] (We shall discuss this in greater detail in Chapter 3, especially when addressing Michael Haneke's stylistic approach to the relationship among cinematic images, TV images and reality.)

Even so, this does not change the fact that, when confronting these kinds of images, our natural attitude is to believe in the existence of what we are seeing, though this assertion opens up opportunities for analyses investigating possible deviations, degenerations, or simulations capable of anesthetizing the claims and effects of such a belief.[85]

---

[83] See Baudrillard (1991); Sontag (2003, p. 65).

[84] "Modern iconoclasm no longer consists in destroying images, but in manufacturing a profusion of images where there is nothing to see. These are literally images that leave no trace. They have no aesthetic consequences to speak of. However, behind each of them, something has disappeared. There lies their secret, if they have one, and there lies the secret of simulation. On the horizon of simulation, not only has the real world disappeared, but the very question of its existence has no meaning" (Baudrillard 1997, pp. 118–119).

[85] In this regard, see also Sontag (2003), which contains a passage of self-criticism regarding her thesis in *On Photography* (1977) on the anesthetizing consequences of image proliferation; this passage is worth quoting extensively: "In the first of the six essays in *On Photography* (1977), I argued that while an event known through photographs certainly becomes more real than it would have

Positional images are continuously involved in shaping what we call our present, and they contribute to the constitution of our common past. Say, for example, that Robert Drew's *Primary*—a 1960 documentary following the Democratic primaries in Wisconsin between John F. Kennedy and Hubert H. Humphrey—is playing on screen, and we freeze the film on the frame shown in Figure 4. When we look at this image, we see Kennedy; we believe that it "was" him smiling faintly at Jackie's side, and we recognize this as the same man that we have all seen brutally assassinated in the tragic footage that has now become part of our collective positional phantasy, that is, our collective memory.

Like Barthes when viewing Alexander Gardner's *Portrait of Lewis Payne* (1865), we might also view images of Kennedy in *Primary* with a temporality shifted to a retrospective or "anterior future" (see Barthes 1980, pp. 96–97)—knowing that he will be shot on November 22, 1963, as testified through Abraham Zapruder's well-known film[86] of Kennedy's assassination (Figure 5).

In other words, positional images participate in the constitution of what, in a Husserlian vein, we might call the only world we agree we share: an ever-changing world that can be experienced from potentially infinite, mutually irreducible perspectives, comprised and given life also through impressional images intersubjec-

---

been had one never seen the photographs, after repeated exposure it also becomes less real. As much as they create sympathy, I wrote, photographs shrivel sympathy. Is this true? I thought it was when I wrote it. I'm not so sure now. What is the evidence that photographs have a diminishing impact, that our culture of spectatorship neutralizes the moral force of photographs of atrocities? The question turns on a view of the principal medium of the news, television. An image is drained of its force by the way it is used, where and how often it is seen. [...] The whole point of television is that one can switch channels, that it is normal to switch channels, to become restless, bored. Consumers droop. They need to be stimulated, jump-started, again and again. Content is no more than one of these stimulants. A more reflective engagement with content would require a certain intensity of awareness—just what is weakened by the expectations brought to images disseminated by the media, whose leaching out of content contributes most to the deadening of feeling" (Sontag 2003, pp. 105–106). She also offers a criticism of Baudrillard's positions, saying that he "claims to believe that images, simulated realities, are all that exist now [...]. To speak of reality becoming a spectacle is a breathtaking provincialism. It universalizes the viewing habits of a small, educated population living in the rich part of the world, where news has been converted into entertainment" (Sontag 2003, pp. 109–110).

86 Zapruder's film, of course, is but one fragment of the fact of "Kennedy's assassination," a fragment that, as we have seen, can undergo new analysis and interpretations (see, for example, Strauss 2020, p. 24, along with Vågnes 2011 for a discussion of Zapruder footage in the context of visual culture). Moreover, the question remains open regarding what it means to experience a death through such types of presentifications (see Sobchack 2004, pp. 233–235, for a discussion of this issue in relation to the discussed Zapruder film). We will return to this latter point in the third chapter.

Figure 4: Still from Robert Drew's *Primary* (1960)

Figure 5: Still from Abraham Zapruder film of John F. Kennedy's assassination (1963)

tively recognized as historical (whether analog or digital). Specific eidetic laws govern how occurrences we see in images with positional valence are inserted into what we call the "history of the world," which is in a continuous state of narrative and definitional flux. We shall revisit this fundamental point later on, when we delve into the narrative facet of how we understand both positional and apositional images.

Images can certainly also be modified or removed, not unlike what happens in perception. In principle, it is always possible for us to question our belief in the facts presentified by images: we know that images can be falsified, that we can be deceived. This is part of our current *knowledge*. Nowadays, in fact, the technology with which one can alter photographs capable of eliciting belief seems more commonplace than ever. At the same time, however, the very technical proliferation allowing unprecedented possibilities of deception has also brought us new tools with which to defend ourselves against it. The challenging task we face is to describe the unprecedented variety of phenomena with which we are confronted. In our contemporary environment (*Umwelt*) and lifeworld (*Lebenswelt*) (see Hua VI), which are increasingly taking on characteristics of an iconosphere, the scope of what we are disposed to call reality is changing radically. The dimension of perception may well come to lose its primacy over the image; in fact, our analyses of image consciousness even lead us to question the belief we assign seemingly automatically to the quality of being "in the flesh."

Against this background, a philosophical description of the new and changing relationships between image and reality becomes all the more necessary. At the same time, formulaic observations like "image is becoming more and more reality" and "reality is becoming more and more image" are insufficient. Even though we might agree with these observations for multiple reasons, they are like baggy clothes—poorly tailored (to paraphrase Bergson) to the phenomena they are intended to describe—so they end up fitting disparate points of view that ought to be kept distinct.

What we as phenomenologists should investigate instead are the *conditions under which* we can describe the differences between what we call reality and what we call image. How do we characterize the essential elements of each dimension? How might we describe the circumstances under which the relationship between them can change? When it comes to iconic presentifications, under what conditions are we willing to believe what we see in images?

1.21 Seeing the Character

We have just outlined the background for a Husserlian description of images that we believe represent something real. We have also qualified them as positing images—images that, even if not real in themselves, nonetheless posit the existence of something or someone. As we have shown, the positional is a *noetic* moment. Our analyses on the previous pages underlined how photographs in the Barthesian sense—what Husserl calls impressional images, or what Peirce describes as images produced by constraint—are tendentially qualified as positional images. Still, not all impressional images are *eo ipso* positional.[87]

What about images that, despite their photographic nature, were never intended to represent something as existent? In other words, what about "image objects" that are not held to be concerned with whether the presentified "image *sujets*" actually exist? According to my hypothesis, such images presuppose a

---

[87] Of course, as we shall see in Chapter 2, not all positional images are impressional either, as is the case with a painted portrait experienced positionally.

different kind of consciousness from the one involved with images characterized by "*sujet* position taking." With film images, for example (whether analog or digital, in keeping with our earlier remarks[88]), how does our belief approach change when, instead of watching a documentary grounded in impressional images or footage of our friend's birthday party, we watch a movie that we know to be fiction? What essentially changes in our approach when the figures we see in these images are not "real people" but characters?

Restricting our initial inquiry to "conventional" photographic (live-action) movies is not a matter of avoidance, of course; rather, this initial examination of the question can provide important phenomenological tools for use in further inquiries into animation, or into movies made using more recently developed imaging technologies (motion capture, for example,[89] or even what is now being called post-cinema; see, for instance, Denson/Leyda 2016 and Chateau/Moure 2020).

To begin our endeavors, let us remark that the Husserlian characterization of image consciousness as "triadic" becomes more problematic when applied to fictional film images. Phenomenological description can help uncover new levels of analysis in this regard; first, however, it is worth defining a few essential points to consider when approaching this complicated issue.

When we watch fictional movies, we do not take any actual position regarding the existence of what we see on the screen, even when the images that pass before our eyes are of a photographic nature. This photographic nature also seems to permit us to adopt a positional attitude toward what is presentified in those images. We might say that, when watching a fictional photographic film, it is always possible to experience an astonishment similar to what Barthes felt when viewing the photo of little Ernest—an eventuality that Barthes himself seems to point out:

> the (fictional) cinema combines two poses: the actor's "this-has-been" and the role's, so that (something I would not experience before a painting) I can never see or see again in a film certain actors whom I know to be dead without a kind of melancholy: the melancholy of Pho-

---

[88] Clearly, the advent of digital technology has also multiplied the possibilities for easily producing images of a photographic nature without a direct impression of reality: they are photographs without the "writing light" having a role in their production, without physical constraint, not "impressional" (consider, for example, photographs produced through artificial intelligence). The possibility of still considering these photographs proper is outside the scope of our analysis here. In this case, images give a sense of impressionality without being "impressional" in the proper sense. In keeping with what we argued above about belief, it is plain that, should those kinds of images become common, this might also affect our usual response towards photographic images.

[89] See, for example, Manovich (2001, p. 293): "Computer media redefine the very identity of cinema."

tography itself (I experience this same emotion listening to the recorded voices of dead singers). (Barthes 1980, p. 79)

Perhaps when watching *Citizen Kane* (1941), we might be seized with a similar "melancholy" to what Barthes described upon seeing little Ernest's photo, and find ourselves wondering about Buddy Swan (the child who played eight-year-old Charles Foster Kane; Figure 6) just as Barthes wonders about Ernest: "It is possible that Buddy is still alive today: but where? How? What a novel!" Nowadays, of course, we can unearth the "plot" of this "novel" quickly by simply googling Buddy Swan. His Wikipedia page, for example, tells us that "Paul Benjamin 'Buddy' Swann (October 24, 1929–March 21, 1993; also credited as Buddy Swann [Buddy Swan]) was an American child actor, best known for playing the title character of the 1941 film *Citizen Kane* as an eight-year-old boy" and that he died "March 21, 1993 (aged 63) in Colorado Springs, Colorado, U.S." Perhaps we might then grow interested in Buddy's own story and, for example, shoot a documentary about the man who was (and will always be) the young Kane in the world of cinematographic art.

This approach shares several points of overlap with the "documentary consciousness" discourse developed in Sobchack (1999).[90] Most relevant to our inquiry

Figure 6: Still from Orson Welles' *Citizen Kane* (1941): Buddy Swan/Charles Foster Kane

---

90 Significantly, this text dialogues explicitly with the phenomenological—notably Merleau-Pontyan and Sartrian—approach to film image proposed in Meunier (1969): an "undeservedly neglected [...] volume," as Sobchack writes, that "offers the premises and potential for an enriched understanding of how dynamic and fluid our engagement with the cinema really is" (Sobchack 1999,

is Sobchack's focus on the role of the viewer's attitude in distinguishing between documentary and fictional images. Sobchack stresses that the term "documentary" does not refer to the objects of our experience so much as to our experience of those objects ("documentary is less a thing than an experience"). Accordingly, she makes reference to a *"documentary consciousness"* (Sobchack 1999, p. 241), a consciousness that is "charge[d] with real" (Sobchack 1999, p. 242). Against this background, Sobchack takes an unequivocal stance on the subject we have just introduced regarding the shift of consciousness between actor and character (Buddy Swan/Charles Foster Kane). "In some cases," she says, the "existential echo"—that is, references to something's actual existence—"can be raised to a shout and fictional consciousness ruptured" (Sobchack 1999, p. 246). She raises the example of Renoir's *Rules of the Game*, with "the rabbit's death leap as it is shot" and "the viewer's extratextual knowledge suddenly *positing* the rabbit's existence beyond the frame of the fiction into the documentary space of an 'elsewhere' where it lived its rabbit life" (Sobchack 1999, p. 246, my italics). Likewise, "our cultural knowledge of the Burton/Taylor off-screen romance puts us in a different and less focused relation to the specific images on the screen" and "watching a fiction film such as *Cleopatra*, we cease to bracket the existence of the performers and suddenly find ourselves watching not Cleopatra but Elizabeth Taylor kiss not Antony but Richard Burton" (Sobchack 1999, p. 252).

This is not to say that the line between documentary and fictional attitudes is always perfectly clear and that the viewer is always completely free to choose one over the other: even though documentary consciousness can be "solicited," for example, it "is never determined a priori" (Sobchack 1999, p. 253). The same image might be a documentary image for one viewer and a fictional image for another.[91]

In this regard, it is worth briefly mentioning how celebrity can play such a prominent role that a theater or movie actor's "real" identity outshines the characters they play. It is clear how a director could use such hybridization as an "easy"

---

p. 242). Meunier's text has now received renewed interest in the wake of the English translation edited by Julian Hanich and Daniel Fairfax, along with several critical essays (see Meunier 1969).
91 This "switch of consciousness" is clearly possible with photographs as well. See Wiesing's remarks on a photograph of Woody Allen (2010, p. 47): "As soon as the title *Zelig* is placed underneath a photograph of Woody Allen, we will use the visible image object (which could still well be used as a pictorial sign for Woody Allen) as a sign for a different, in this case fictional, person. [...] In a biography of Woody Allen we could once more refer the image already mentioned, which was previously used as a sign for Zelig, to Woody Allen; then, perhaps, the caption would read *Woody Allen in* Zelig, *1983.*" However, note that while using a Husserlian approach to depictive photography—one also underlined by the use of the concept of image object—Wiesing maintains that the image functions as a sign in such cases. As we have previously remarked, this is not compatible with Husserl's characterization of image consciousness.

way of reaching larger audiences—"easy" in the sense that it bypasses the need for artistic considerations. Merleau-Ponty wrote in 1948 that the *"infatuation with stars, the sensationalism of the zoom, the twists and turns of plot and the intrusion of pretty pictures and witty dialogue, are all tempting pitfalls for films which chase success and, in so doing, eschew properly cinematic means of expression"* (Merleau-Ponty 1948, p. 97, my italics).

On the other hand, a director may also choose to try to avoid these forms of hybridization at all costs, for example by opting to work with nonprofessional actors—as in the case of Robert Bresson, whose work we will analyze in the third chapter. Other directors may elect to use these superimpositions between actor and character in provocative ways. For example, when Michael Haneke did a shot-for-shot remake of his already highly provocative and unsettling 1997 film *Funny Games* for American audiences (*Funny Games U.S.*, 2007), he deliberately cast two very famous actors, Naomi Watts and Tim Roth, as the victimized protagonists, thus pushing the tension between audience expectations and film developments to an even greater extreme (more on this in Chapter 3).

In keeping with this possibility of switching between documentary and fictional consciousness, when looking at a cinematographic image, we can enter into a consciousness of depiction under which we see Buddy Swan as an image *sujet* in the image object that appears on the screen (whether a giant movie-screen-sized image object or a miniature smartphone-screen-sized one). Though this consciousness can be reawakened at any moment, however, it is clear that while watching Orson Welles' masterpiece we are not encouraged to focus on the nature of the photographic relationship between the film and the *actors* "in the flesh," i.e., the real people *who were actually* in front of the lens during filming (although, as we shall see in Chapter 2, the specific *kind* of images involved, i.e., impressional, is not a complete nonfactor in our experience). Rather, we are invited to tune into the film's *quasi*-world and its characters, which in turn means tuning into its sense and its emotional openings (*Stimmungen*). We use "tune into" here in the etymological sense of being in accord with it, resonating with it; this dimension innervates much of Husserl's original terminology (derived from the German word *stimmen*) for describing modes of consciousness. We do not see little Buddy Swan (although we can do so at any moment), but rather little "eternal" Kane, who is outside our shared chronological world. We shall return later to the artistic sense of this "eternity."

Through the synthetizing sense developed by the *quasi*-world unfolding before our eyes with its own unique narrative, we can also see the same character (fictional *sujet*) depicted through multiple image objects. For obvious reasons, for example, many films use different actors to portray a single character at different ages. As observed above, we can choose to see Buddy Swan when viewing the image object of little Kane, and Orson Welles when looking "into" the image object of adult Kane.

One notable exception is Richard Linklater's *Boyhood* (2014), wherein the "passage of time" is instead made visible through the actual transformation of actors' bodies, a result achieved by stretching the filming process out over *twelve years* (which was also the provisional title). In contrast to sagas (such as François Truffaut's "Doinel cycle") or television series (in which the actors age gradually from season to season), the changes in the bodies themselves over the course of *Boyhood*'s two-hour and 46-minute runtime create a complex time-lapse phenomenon that makes the passage of time keenly visible, almost "palpable." Technologically speaking, it is also possible for the same actor to render manifestations of the same character in different life stages (as with *Boyhood*) through computer programs (nonimpressional images)–, or even by using AI to create photographic-like age-progressed images of people who never existed. Here, however, our extra-filmic knowledge would be crucial in determining the attitude we took when viewing the images: for example, it might be quite difficult to trigger a reference to the "has been," which would keep us from shifting to a documentary consciousness.

The film world is rife with examples in the opposite direction as well—that is, where a single actor plays more than one character. In Woody Allen's 1985 *The Purple Rose of Cairo*, for example, Jeff Daniels plays both Tom Baxter and Gil Shepherd; at one point, the two characters even have a conversation.[92]

To return to our question regarding the nature of *sujet* in fictional films, we can say that, in such cases, the matter of belief in the reality of what we are seeing is put out of play. Properly speaking, we do not even "suspend" it. Rather, we never allow it to emerge in the first place, instead giving precedence to a *quasi*-belief whose validity is circumscribed to the space of that particular phantasy. The positional attitude gives way to the *quasi*-positional attitude; in the "realm [...] of play," we begin by *quasi*-believing, in the attitude of phantasy (or, we might add, of free possibility; cf. Hua XXIII, p. 695).

When watching a film we know to be fiction, we instantly enter into a form of presentification free of belief: we are not concerned with whether the *sujet* we see in the image or the events unfolding on-screen really exist. Instead, these are what we might now call *quasi*-positional images. Naturally, the "faithful" recall of the photographic grain might come to elicit in us an attitude of belief as regards actual existence (shifting to the actor, for instance). However, I would suggest that when

---

[92] For a dedicated phenomenological account of Allen's *The Purple Rose of Cairo*, see Brough (2011, pp. 198–205).

we are properly living in the film's *quasi*-world, that same grain is recomposed and relived in the overall *quasi*-world of the image, "passive[ly] cancelle[d]" (see Hua XXIII, p. 612) with regard to its possible identification and its actual location in the shared actual world around us.

Against this background, what the audience is supposed to see is not the ordinary body, but the character's. As Diderot writes, actors must be "marvelous puppets" (Diderot 1951 [1830], p. 1035) who let spectators see not their everyday bodies but the powerful "phantom" arising from their performative creations (Diderot 1951 [1830], p. 1031). This *topos* is a common thread among twentieth-century reflections on the actor developed by authors of phenomenological origin, such as Ortega y Gasset, Merleau-Ponty and Eugen Fink.[93] Proust notes that the actor's body must become "transparent" (Proust 1920–21, p. 44) in order to let the character's body be seen; significantly, he describes great actors as "a *window [fenêtre]* opening upon a great work of art" (Proust 1920–1921, p. 44, my italics).

Although there are good reasons to evoke this dimension of transparency, we must remember that it has the potential to mislead us. In keeping with the notion of *sensible ideas* that Merleau-Ponty observed in Proust's work (see Merleau-Ponty 1964, p. 149), let us stress that the actor's "becoming transparent" is not a matter of somehow annulling their own (sensible, physical) body in favor of a purely ideal dimension. Rather, it implies working on and with their body in order to create new areas of sense, novel idealities that do not run counter to the sensible dimension but rather act as its expressive side (see, for example, Merleau-Ponty 1964, p. 152). It is through this *expressive* work that the actor's *body* becomes the character's *body*.

Even if we want to talk about such cases in terms of transparency, we must specify that this is a *sui generis* transparency. Actors have various processes by which they do away with their habitual mannerisms and produce their characters, a consideration Proust highlighted in his famous passage on Berma's acting. On the one hand, he notes, in order for spectators to be able to see the character Phaedra, the "ordinary Berma" (the actress's everyday attitude) must disappear on stage.[94] Poor actors, he says, are incapable of controlling their bad habits, of governing their bodies, and some rebellious mannerism can unwittingly emerge on stage, thereby impeding creation of the character (see Proust 1920–21, p. 42). On the other hand, Phaedra does not appear as a Phaedra who no longer has any relation-

---

93 I explored this important line of continuity in Rozzoni (2012).
94 Merleau-Ponty (1945, p. 212) also stresses this point: "the actress becomes invisible, and it is Phaedra who appears. The meaning swallows up the signs, and Phaedra has so completely taken possession of Berma that her passion as Phaedra appears the apotheosis of ease and naturalness."

ship with the actress Berma, as an "absolute" character completely separate from the actress giving her life. Rather, she manifests herself as a Phaedra created through Berma's peculiar *accent*. This is an important clarification.

Accordingly, as Diderot also points out (Diderot 1951 [1830], p. 1005), the character becomes a great actor's "masterpiece." "Thus," Proust writes, "into the prose sentences of the modern playwright as into the verse of Racine Berma contrived to introduce those vast images of grief, nobility, passion, which were the masterpieces of her own personal art, and in which she could be recognised as, in the portraits which he has made of different sitters, we recognise a painter" (Proust 1920–1921, p. 48). These reflections of Proust on the theatrical body are analogous to Vivian Sobchack's insights on film actors' bodies when she discusses our ability to recognize "Dustin Hoffman for his 'Hoffman-ness'" and "Meryl Streep for her 'Streep-ness'" (Sobchack 2012, p. 437). This seems to corroborate our initial hypothesis that such considerations can apply to both theatrical and film acting (possible differences notwithstanding).

In context of the *productive* fiction of theater and cinema, the actor's body need not represent or refer back to a particular pregiven *sujet*, nor pursue any previous model as its ultimate self-contained (real or imaginary) goal. Here, rather than depicting a *sujet*, the image creates it: the *Bildung* of a character *expressed* in the *how* of the image world. Later on, we will explore how the artistic-fictional screen can essentially become a productive space, one that gives life to characters and atmospheres of an order that goes beyond issues concerning the actual existence of an individual reality—or, as Aristotle might say, beyond concerns of historical order (*Poetics*, 1451b 10–33). What can arise through fiction (including artistic fiction, our particular focus) are experiences of a *quasi*-world, an "image world" (Hua XXIII, p. 619) that, as we have seen, has intersubjective value: our judgments about these worlds "*have a kind of objective truth, even though they refer to fictions*" (Hua XXIII, p. 621).

1.22 Difference Iterability

Before we continue to the next chapter, another clarification regarding the productive power of phantasy is in order. Husserl specifies that, unlike the mere modification of neutrality in the broader sense, the modification of phantasy can be reiterated at multiple levels. His student Eugen Fink elucidates this point convincingly.[95] It is phantasy's eidetic, essential structure that underlies the

---

[95] More than once, Fink uses the example of the famous "play within a play" in *Hamlet:* "the Dan-

ideal possibility of an infinite *mise en abyme*. Though the phenomenon is obviously not limited to art, numerous examples abound in the art world; Husserl describes one in § 100 of *Ideas I:*

> A name reminds us, namingly, of the Dresden Gallery and of our last visit there: we walk through the halls and stand before a picture by Teniers which represents a picture gallery. If, let us say, we allow that pictures in the latter would represent again pictures which, for their part, represent legible inscriptions, and so forth, then we can estimate which inclusion of objectivations and which mediacies are actually producible with respect to objectivities which can be seized upon. But such very complicated examples are not required for *eidetic insights*, in particular for the insights into the ideal possibility for continuing *ad libitum* the encasement of one objectivation into another. (Hua III/1, pp. 246–247)

Under this eidetic law, the *quasi*-reality of a *quasi*-world-in-image can contain, in turn, *quasi*-images distinguishable from that *quasi*-reality. The ability to iterate the differences between reality and unreality, of playing out the image-reality conflict ad infinitum like a series of nesting dolls, belongs intrinsically to phantasy (*a fortiori* for a phantasy complying with *perceptio*). Here, too, cinema can offer interesting insights, specifically as regards the relation between "fictional" and "positional" dimensions. Let us note how the initial attitude with which we approach a film's "world" influences the sense of contrast and iteration we potentially glean from it.

For example, say we watch a *documentary* in which a man (whom we believe was physically in front of the camera) shows us a photograph of his daughter (whose existence we also believe in, because we believe that this photograph was in the man's hands at the moment he was filmed, and that, in turn, the daughter was in front of the camera used to take her photograph). In the documentary, this man tells us about a fictional movie he has shot, and he shows us a scene from it. As we watch the documentary, we apprehend both the reality of the room from which the man is speaking to us and the unreality of the fictional movie playing on a screen beside the man.

The example above involved beginning in a documentary consciousness. If, on the other hand, a play-attitude (with its *quasi*-position of *quasi*-reality) is establish-

---

ish prince has the event of the king's death presented on the open stage, so that the culprits will understand that he knows of their guilt. There thus comes to be another theater played out in the theater, and a double 'nonactuality' is introduced. What kind of remarkable and strange 'appearance' is this, an appearance that belongs to the kind of play that involves playing a role, indeed in a certain way to play in general, which is, to be sure, actual but presents nothing actual? Can the 'nonactuality' of such worlds of appearance be arbitrarily repeated? How can a nonactuality be actual at all?" (Fink 1960, p. 79).

ed from the very beginning, the situation changes. Consider how this same example would unfold if we were to experience it in play consciousness—a fictional film in which a character shows us a picture of his daughter. Here, two rays of *quasi*-reality are at work (one toward the man, the other toward the presentification of the daughter) as our *quasi*-ego or phantasy ego—the subjective correlate that allows us to participate in this *quasi*-world—observes the scene. If the man then sits down to watch a fictional film on television, those images would then constitute a *quasi*-phantasy *contrasting* with the *quasi*-reality of his room.

These are only two simple examples of a process that can ideally be reiterated *ad infinitum* and in copious combinations (e.g., actuality in play contexts, as-if phantasies in actual settings). It is important to notice that, according to an eidetic law, it is always possible in this structure *en abyme* to imagine another level "behind" any alleged reality or *quasi*-reality, another layer that calls the reality or *quasi*-reality of its "predecessor" into question. Various affirmations along the lines of "life is a dream"—beyond the specific meaning that each time can assume in specific contexts—are based on this very possibility.

These inquiries give rise to the understanding that the concept of reality cannot be given without the concept of phantasy, in the specific sense that the ability to imagine something different from reality, to deform reality, is the counterpoint to every conception of reality that every age has had. The very phrase "concept of reality" necessarily implies the possibility of its variation: a reality that could not conceive of something different from what "there is" would not be a reality—it would constitute unambiguous imposition on a subjectivity incapable of even knowing itself as such.

These horizons of imagination are also what open up the possibility of skepticism—that is, of imagining a supposedly privileged position from which one can choose to deny the reality of this world. Even so, no such privileged position can posit itself as absolute, beyond the possibility of iteration (note the convergence here with the Husserlian argument against skepticism—see, for instance, Hua III/1, §20). As such, every place posited as reality can later be considered a "cave" in the Platonic sense, a fiction. Every position of place construed as real always essentially implies the possibility of imagining another, "truer," "more real" one "behind" it.

The rudimentary "experiment" depicted in the Peter Weir film *The Truman Show* (1998) offers one of the best-known mainstream cinematic examples in which the world someone considers real turns out to be an illusion. In this case, Truman's shift from real to illusory is made possible only through the emergence of a new system of meaning that includes and falsifies the first system, deeming it a fiction; in other words, his world undergoes an *après coup* phantasy modification. Of course, the relationship between true and false worlds is not as metaphysically naïve as this popular film suggests: Truman's "exit from the cave" would, in fact, merely constitute entry into another level of sense, one that could obviously give rise to further perceptions or beliefs that could in turn prove illusory as well. After all, the differences between image and perception, between real and possible, were already operative even in the *show* of which Truman was the unwitting protagonist.

Jokes, pranks, and simulations planned in the perceptual context show this well. Consider, for example, candid-camera programs in which someone is made to believe something and then shown that it was merely an illusion. Setting aside the question of such programs' "authenticity," it is clear that such experiences involve the unfortunate person perceiving—taking literally for true—a set of "facts" that have been staged by other people. A similar dynamic of belief is at work in Hitchcock's *Vertigo* (1958), in which John "Scottie" Ferguson, a retired detective, is lured by a former college friend, Gavin Elster, into *believing* that his wife Madeleine suffers from a serious condition, and thus into accepting the task of following her around to make sure nothing bad happens to her. However, the reality Scottie takes as true—and as fitting into the perceptual flux of his everyday life—is "only" a performance by Elster's mistress, Judy Barton, who impersonates Madeleine as part of a *plot* she and Elster have devised in order to murder Elster's wife. (It should be clear by now that the distinction between *perceptio* (*Perzeption*) and image does not *ipso facto* correspond to the distinction between reality and unreality. I can see Othello's "perzeptiv" body on stage as unreal (cf. Husserl 2005, 616–620) and also "take as true" a person's somatic features when viewing her/his photograph).

Theater, film, painting, novels: all of these art forms rely on the eidetic possibility of staging or playing beliefs. Fink notes that play, one of the "fundamental phenomena of human existence," has the privilege of being able to play, to stage, the other fundamental phenomena (death, work, power, love[96]) and, not least, itself (iterability of phantasy positions).[97]

---

[96] "We denote by play the fifth of the fundamental phenomena of human existence. If it is mentioned last, this does not mean that it is in an order of importance, less important and significant than death, work, power and love. Play is just as original as the other phenomena" (Fink 1955, p. 264).

[97] "The peculiar world of play not only distances itself from habitual reality, it even has the possibility of 'repeating' once again in itself, in a fictitious way, its own distance and contrast to reality. Just as there are paintings within paintings, there are plays within plays and spectacles within spectacles. Repetition can consist of several stages, yet it remains contained in all iterations in the same medium of the semblance of the world of the game. These are not pure artifices" (Fink 1971 [1968], p. 14).

Art can obviously also "play itself" by interweaving its different forms. The cinema can, for example, incorporate a theatrical representation which in turn is taken from a literary work—whether actually published, as in Roman Polanski's *Venus in Furs* (*La Vénus à la fourrure*, 2013),[98] or merely imagined, as in François Truffaut's *The Last Metro* (*Le dernier métro*, 1980). Similarly, it is not uncommon for a fictional character in a TV series to mention following a different TV series that is actually broadcast in our shared world (a fictional product of our world).

---

[98] This movie is in turn based on David Ives' *Venus in Fur*, a two-person play in which a theatrical *mise en abyme* is already at work. In this pièce, as in Polanski's film, Thomas Novachek is the writer and director of a new play based on Sacher-Masoch's *Venus in Furs*, and he is casting for the role of Vanda von Dunayev (unlike in Polanski's film, which is set in a theater, Ives' pièce takes place in an audition room).

2 The Aesthetic Consciousness

2.1 The Letter to Hugo von Hofmannsthal and Manuscript A VI 1

We touched upon the theme of considering phenomena aesthetically in the preceding analyses. As we have seen, Husserl delved into the topic as early as the Göttingen course, albeit in a context prioritizing other problems, primarily that of clarifying the structure of phantasy and image consciousness. The Appendix on the *Sacred Love*, written around the same time as he gave the course, focused more specifically on aesthetic issues. On January 12, 1907, about two years after the course in Göttingen on *Phantasy and Image Consciousness* and his related observations on *Sacred Love,* Husserl wrote a famous letter to Hugo von Hofmannsthal that would ultimately represent one of his best-known contributions on aesthetic issues. The Austrian poet had visited the philosopher in December 1906 while in Göttingen for a conference and had presented Husserl with an unspecified literary gift—presumably his *Kleine Dramen*.[99]

While formally conceived as a response to this gift, Husserl's letter affords him an opportunity[100] to draw comparisons between the attitudes of the phenomenologist and the artist—as well as the attitudes of the artist's audience, for as we shall see, Husserl opens the letter by considering the effects of Hofmannsthal's work on his readers. Within the confines of the conditions at hand (limited epistolary space, that is), Husserl attempts to pin down several essential traits that he considers common to the phenomenological and artistic dimensions.

His "phenomenological method," he explains, "demands an attitude toward all forms of objectivity [...] which is closely related to the attitude and stance in which [Hofmannsthal's] art, *as something purely aesthetic,* places us," the audience, "with respect to the presented objects and the whole of the surrounding world" (Husserl 1994, p. 2, my italics). More specifically, the "intuition of a purely aesthetic work" entails a "suspension of all existential attitudes of the intellect and of all attitudes relating to emotions and the will which presuppose such an existential attitude." Better still, Husserl continues, in the case of such an aesthetic experience, this suspension is something to which we surrender nearly passively: we are "almost

---

[99] On Hofmannsthal's journey to Göttingen and the conference he held there entitled *Der Dichter und diese Zeit*—which Husserl was apparently able to attend—see Hirsch (1968, pp. 108–111).
[100] "What a hopeless and typical professor! He cannot even open his mouth, without giving a lecture" (Husserl 1994, p. 2).

force[d] [...] into [...] a state of aesthetic intuition that excludes" any existential attitude (Husserl 1994, p. 2).

Husserl's point here seems clear enough: the relationship between existential concern and aesthetic purity is inversely proportional (see Husserl 1994, p. 2). In other words, the more concerned we are with the existence of what we are contemplating, the less open we are to purely aesthetic contemplation. In fact, according to this view, even having such existential concerns could potentially compromise the purity of aesthetic experience. The parallel Husserl draws between phenomenological and aesthetic attitudes is thus first grounded in the suspension of position-taking as regards the existence of objects that, in our natural attitude, we would normally assume to be part of our reality.

We have said that Husserl speaks of aesthetic attitude in terms of both the artist and the recipient.[101] Like phenomenologists, artists and their recipients experience the world as pure manifestation. None of the three *deny* the existence of what they experience, which would amount to taking a position *against* the world's existence; rather, they experience the world as *neutralized*. Here, too, Husserl's position clearly resonates with Kant's account of aesthetic judgment in the third *Critique*, particularly as regards the notion of *disinterest*. Husserl points out that, in both phenomenological and aesthetic attitudes, one experiences the world as a pure appearance (*Erscheinung*); questions regarding the existence or nonexistence of the world are set aside. In *this* sense, one can rightly call both phenomenological and artistic practices "disinterested." Even so, as we shall see, this is not to say that such practices imply the suspension of *all* interest; it would be more appropriate to describe them in terms of a *shift* in interest. Despite suspending interest in the existence of the "fact" world, the phenomenologist and the artist (as well as the recipient) are interested in the *sense* that makes such a "fact" possible, in its various modes of manifestation.[102]

Of course, there are significant differences between artists and phenomenologists as well. Husserl holds that the phenomenologist clearly "serves" no "purpose of aesthetic pleasure, but rather the purpose of continued investigations and cognition, and of constituting scientific insights in a new sphere (the philosophical sphere)" (Husserl 1994, p. 2); the artist, meanwhile, "does not attempt to found

---

101 As mentioned, Husserl does not always differentiate between "aesthetic" and "artistic" and sometimes uses the words interchangeably; we shall attempt to make the proper distinctions here wherever necessary.
102 "Only one thing remains: to clarify, in a pure intuiting (in a pure intuiting analysis and abstraction), the meaning which is immanent in the *pure phenomena*, without ever going beyond them, i.e. without presupposing any transcendent existences that are intended in them" (Husserl 1994, p. 2).

the 'meaning' of the world-phenomenon and grasp it in concepts, but appropriates it intuitively, in order to gather, out of its plenitude, materials for the creation of aesthetic forms" (Husserl 1994, p. 2). Unlike the philosopher, therefore, the artist works without concepts. Here, too, we might detect an implicit echo of Kant's third *Critique*, one clearly reinforced when Husserl claims that the artist must possess "genius" and "follow, purely and solely, his *daimonion*" that "drives him to an intuiting-blind production" (Husserl 1994, p. 2)—an intertwining of passivity and activity.

Significant insights for the development of this topic can also be found in an important Husserlian manuscript entitled "Aesthetics and Phenomenology [*Ästhetik und Phänomenologie*]," preserved at the Husserl Archive in Louvain under the signature A VI 1. The twenty-page manuscript was (largely) written between 1906 and 1918 and likely compiled in August 1918. Three of its pages are published in Hua XXIII: pages 4 and 5 as Appendix LIX (Hua XIII, pp. 651–654; likely written in either 1916 or 1918), and page 12 as Appendix VI (Hua XXIII, pp. 167–169; likely written in 1906). It is also worth observing that page 7 is basically a sketch of the 1907 letter to Hofmannsthal.

Pages 8 and 9, on "Aesthetic objectivity [*Ästhetische Objektivität*]," were published in Scaramuzza and Schuhmann (1990), whose own introduction to these pages notably states that "Husserl has scarcely addressed aesthetic questions" (Scaramuzza/Schuhmann 1990, p. 165). Despite its title of "Aesthetics and Phenomenology," they do not consider the collection sufficient evidence that aesthetics played a significant role in Husserl's overall phenomenological project. As regards the two pages they edited, they claim that the aesthetic considerations presented in them do not represent "original reflections" but rather "notes about a conversation that took place between [...] the two Munich phenomenologists Johannes Daubert and Aloys Fischer" and the father of phenomenology when Daubert and Fischer visited the latter on April 17, 1906 (Scaramuzza/Schuhmann 1990, p. 165). "According to Husserl," Scaramuzza and Schuhmann write, "the 'main part' of the thoughts expressed therein came 'from his two friends'," primarily Fischer (Scaramuzza/Schuhmann 1990, p. 165).[103] Despite acknowledging that "the greater part of these ideas stem from [his] two friends," however, Husserl notes near the end of his reflections that "the conversation has given rise to relevant insights and rigorous analyses" (Scaramuzza/Schuhmann 1990, p. 173).[104]

---

103 For a detailed account of the theoretical and practical context in which the meeting takes place, see Scaramuzza/Schuhmann (1990, pp. 165–167).
104 Fitzner (2014, p. 13) makes this clarification as well.

Regardless of the overall significance we assign this single encounter (and the role the two young Munichers played within it), what we will try to show in this second chapter is that Husserl's interest in aesthetics is less sporadic than scholars initially assumed and that his reflections can make significant contributions to contemporary aesthetic debate. Even these brief pages considered in Scaramuzza and Schuhmann's study clearly resonate with several points made consistently throughout the Husserlian corpus, thereby delineating an aesthetic constellation of autonomous reflections that go well beyond this auspicious encounter.

More precisely, the central question here concerns the consciousness involved when considering phenomena *aesthetically*. As mentioned, though Husserl's Göttingen lectures (i.e., his more general discourse on image consciousness) devote some attention to aesthetic consciousness and phenomena's "manner of appearing [*Erscheinungsweise*]" or manifesting themselves (see Hua XXIII, p. 40), they do not give this issue the space it deserves. In the 1905 lectures, Husserl's primary goal is to find an essential commonality among *all* physical images; he does not yet fully draw the additional distinctions necessary when investigating more specific stances (for example, the pleasure associated with *how* images look or works of art are experienced). Indeed, under Husserl's generalized approach of 1904–1905, a photograph of a child, a Dürer woodcut, a Veronese painting, and a digital image manifesting itself on a screen might all fall under the same category of "image consciousness," insofar as they share the same iconic structure. Though this approach is perfectly legitimate in that context, such an analysis clearly leaves some questions unspecified; only later will Husserl return to explore them in greater depth.

Ms. A VI 1 sheds light on the *axiological* dimension, a point that is crucial to a deeper understanding of aesthetic experience. Husserl explicitly brings up the notions of value (*Wert*) and *Wertnehmen*, a neologism he coins as a parallel to the German *Wahrnehmen*, "to perceive." As Husserl suggests in a passage from his 1907 *Dingvorlesung*, *Wahrnehmen* can be construed as a "taking as true [*Fürwahr-Nehmen*]"; *Wertnehmen* can analogously be understood to mean "taking as valuable [*Für-wert-Nehmen*]," with the corresponding substantive, *Wertnehmung*, thus implying "*value-taking*" (see, for example, Hua VIII, p. 307)—or, to coin an analogous neologism in English, *valueception*.

More specifically, this manuscript yields significant insights into a phenomenological account of aesthetic attitude in that it establishes an *essential connection* between the suspension of existence outlined above and the moment of value-taking. In the aesthetic experience, Husserl writes, we have 1) "value-taking [*Wertnehmen*]," whose correlate is an "aesthetic-axiological object" (as opposed to perceiving [*Wahrnehmen*], whose correlate would be an existent object); 2) specific *feelings* of the kind mentioned in the letter to von Hofmannsthal—that is, feelings not motivated by an existential stance: "delight in the *beautiful* [*Freude am Schönen*]" (see Ms. A VI ½a).[105]

Having identified the relevance of these moments, however, Husserl says that we now need a phenomenological account of the nature of their (complicated) relationship. For one, despite not being dependent upon the existence of the object, aesthetic values and feelings are essentially related to its "way of appearance, in and for itself [*Erscheinungsweise, an und für sich*]" (see Ms. A VI ½a, in which Husserl discusses the *appearance* of Raphael's *Madonna* using similar terms as in his earlier considerations of Titian's *Sacred and Profane Love*,[106] which we examined in the first chapter). Nevertheless, as Husserl emphasizes in the Ms. A VI 1 page on aesthetics (later published as Appendix VI of Hua XXIII), it is not that being "in the aesthetic attitude" constitutes rendering appearance itself an object of study (as might be the case "in the psychological attitude"). When aesthetically attuned, we do not "make" appearance "into a theoretical object" or a "practical" one, "tak[ing] delight [*zu freuen*] in it as something actual." Rather, aesthetic experience concerns "a pleasure [*Gefallen*]" that "leaves existence out of play and is essentially determined by the mode of appearance." Significantly, Husserl adds, "see [...] Kant's theory" (Hua XXIII, p. 168, note 6).

Nonetheless, as I suggested above, even though the phenomenological attitude we have described thus far might be justifiably filed under the heading of "aesthetic disinterest," from a phenomenological perspective (as arguably already suggested by Kant[107]), aesthetic experience cannot be defined as disinterest *tout court*. Rather, this disinterest specifically references the *actual existence* of the object under contemplation. In the section on "aesthetics" quoted above, Husserl distinguishes between "interest in the thing [*Interesse an der Sache*]" (Hua XXIII, p. 168),

---

[105] I would like to thank the Husserl Archives in Leuven for permission to reference and quote from Husserl's *Nachlass*.

[106] In this manuscript, singling out the example of Raphael's *Madonna*, Husserl recognizes that "value" can have multiple meanings in context of art, including several that might initially be construed as external to the work itself—such as its technical value or its commercial value (see Ms. A VI 1/2a. On this point see also Zecchi 1984, pp. 113–115). However, the most critical issue is the one we are discussing here concerning the relationship between the originary aesthetic pleasure we feel in enjoying the work and the intuition of values (*Werterschauen*) this experience brings about (see Ms. A VI 1/2a).

[107] We cannot linger here on the complex nature of the disinterest inherent in Kant's judgment of taste. For our purposes, suffice it to recall that Kant, too, spoke not of disinterest *lato sensu*, but rather of disinterest in the existence of the object under consideration. For a discussion of seminal issues concerning Kantian disinterest, see, for example, Guyer (1978). For a discussion of the continuities and discontinuities between Husserl's and Kant's aesthetic disinterestedness see Crowther (2022).

or more precisely interest concerning its existence, and "interest in the appearance" (Hua XXIII, p. 168). Aesthetic disinterest concerns the former, whereas the latter is the key factor in aesthetic experience.

It is also worth stressing here that "aesthetic consciousness is not restricted to works of art" (Brough 2005, p. xlix).[108] As we have remarked, "artistic" and "aesthetic" are not synonymous; we have numerous occasions throughout this work to specify areas of intersection and distinction between the two. In principle, at the most general level, *any* object or situation can be appreciated aesthetically—including nonartistic contexts such as nature or scientific practices.[109] Even in a "drawing-room," Husserl writes, "different appearances of the same object," "the disposition of vases, ashtrays, and so forth," cannot be said to be "equivalent" in aesthetic feeling (Husserl XXIII, p. 168). What is at stake in aesthetic experience proper is the possibility for phenomena to elicit *pleasure* purely through their mode of manifestation.

Another important point regarding disinterest "in the thing" is that even though the aesthetic experience is not about directing our interest toward the object in its concrete actuality, this does not necessarily require us to hide or deny the "function of the object, its purposes, and so on." Rather, Husserl argues that such functions and purposes "are co-excited, they must be there in clear fashion" in order to avoid the emergence of a "conflict between the form of the object and its function" (Hua XXIII, p. 168).[110] He subsequently develops this insight using the example of "the presentation of human beings" (Hua XXIII, p. 169), uncovering at least two aspects that I consider particularly relevant to the phenomenological analysis of aesthetic value:

> Groups. Not masses of human bodily members, in the presence of which one would not really know where or to what the members belong. To which head do these legs, these arms, and so on, belong? What is she doing, where is he standing? Characteristic position. Instant photography: Among the innumerable particular positions that actually occur, which is the one "no-

---

[108] "It can also occur in the contemplation of an object in nature, such as a mountain (648) or a landscape (615). It can even occur in the case of something I phantasy (649). The essential point about aesthetic consciousness is that the object that gives me aesthetic delight, whatever that object may be, does so because of the way in which it appears (462, 522)" (Brough 2005, p. xlix). Bracketed numbers in this quotation refer to passages found in Hua XXIII.
[109] See for example Stecker (2006, p. 1), and Matteucci (2017, p. 226).
[110] The latter is a clarification that may strike us as extremely—and anachronistically—normative for our taste more than a century later (especially after a century like the twentieth). This, I repeat, is no obstacle to the production of new descriptions, even in areas where Husserlian analysis did not go as far as it perhaps could have (for one reason or another, though more often due to historical contingencies and the defined boundaries of the artistic field in his day rather than mere impossibility "on principle").

ticed"? And among those that are noticed, which is the "best"? Every nerve, every muscle, attuned to the action. Nothing indifferent, nothing random. Etc. *As much expression as possible*, that is to say: the excitation with the greatest possible wealth of appearance, the most powerful and most intuitive excitation possible of the consciousness of the object—specifically, not of the "human being" as a physical thing but of the human being in its function, in its activity (a pugilist), in its doing and suffering, which is supposed to be precisely the object of presentation. With as much unity as possible. The pugilist can, of course, simultaneously have a stomachache, and the gripes can express themselves in his grimace. Now that would be a beautiful aesthetic object: A pugilist or discus thrower who simultaneously has a stomachache. (Hua XXIII, p. 169, my italics)

The first aspect I would like to highlight is Husserl's emphasis of the term "expression [*Ausdruck*]." In a note in the margins of this passage, he underscores the key role that "expression" plays in the emergence of aesthetic feeling, as well as its essential connection to the manner of appearance. While he insists that "the 'things,' that is, the thing appearances, *always* express something," he goes on to specify that "they do not do this in the manner of an empty sign. They always express from within" (Hua XXIII, p. 169, note 7, my italics). What Husserl outlines here is the idea of an intensive "scale of aesthetic expressivity," according to which one sees things as *more* or *less* beautiful or ugly (see Hua XXIII, p. 169, note 7). The best and most beautiful aesthetic effect corresponds to the maximum amount of expression, while "what expresses nothing is the aesthetic *adiaphoron* [ἀδιάφορον]," the "aesthetic indifferent," the limit point of a "zero degree of aestheticity."[111]

The second aspect deserving specific mention here is the expressive "characteristic position" that can be offered, for example, by instant photos—that is, through presentifications in image. Choosing just the "right" moment to show—the "pregnant instant," to recall Diderot and Lessing[112]—does not necessarily require us to look for an image resembling reality in terms of shared moments (color, shape) and depictive relationships (with a *sujet* external to the image); rather, the image needs to express something "from within," untouched by existential concern: an action, a tension, a feeling, an atmosphere, a force. In other words, the expressed moment cannot be reduced to the factual components we actually perceive,[113] and the quality of the expressed is not correlated with our belief in

---

[111] For a discussion of this important passage on "expression," see also Rodrigo (2009, pp. 103–105).
[112] Regarding this "pregnant moment" or "pregnant instant" along the Diderotian-Lessingian lines described here, see also Barthes (1973, p. 73) and Barthes (2003, p. 107).
[113] "With regard to the expressivity of a face one can say that it presents a specific quality that does not simply reside in individual features, just as the expressive qualities of a melody do not

the existence of what expresses it.[114] Even so, what is expressed cannot be construed as wholly independent of what expresses it (Cometti 2002, p. 79). This point is fundamental to our work; we shall explore it in greater detail in the third chapter.

For now, we might summarize Husserl's point as follows: aesthetic experience, which can emerge in relation to both what we call perceptive reality and the dimension of inactual (artistic or nonartistic) presentification, focuses on the mode of appearance. As Husserl explains in his letter to Hofmannsthal, this attitude suspends interest in the actual existence of the source of aesthetic pleasure. We become interested in the object because of its capacity for *expression*, and this potentiality can work independently of our belief (or nonbelief) in its existence.[115] To return to the terms introduced above, we can now say that the *ab-* of the *Abbildung* is rendered irrelevant from the perspective of expression. What counts as expressive is instead the poetic (*poiesis*), shaping power of the *Bildung*.

2.2 Valueception

In this context, then, it becomes clear why we can claim that aesthetic experiences involve not annulled interest, but a *qualitative* shift in interest. As Husserl states in another 1912 manuscript (Hua XXIII, p. 521), rather than living in the object itself and taking it as *existent*, we "live in the appearing." Our interest shifts from the existential "what" to the aesthetic "how." Text no. 15h of Hua XXIII (probably dated 1912) is expressly devoted to "aesthetic consciousness" and sheds further light on this intricate nexus. Once again, the text primarily focuses on the intimate relationship between the aesthetic and the axiological-emotional dimensions: "*the manner of appearing is the bearer of aesthetic feeling-characteristics*" (Hua XXIII, p. 462). More specifically, Husserl says that "aesthetic valuation [*ästhetische Wertung*] is essentially connected with the distinction [*Unterschied*] between the con-

---

reside in the sum of notes belonging to a given musical sequence" (Cometti 2002, p. 74). More generally, see Cometti (2002) for a productive attempt to reconcile Merleau-Ponty's and Wittgenstein's positions on expression.

114 "The expression of soul in a face. One really needs to remember that a face with a soulful expression can be *painted*, in order to believe that it is merely shapes and colours that make this impression. It isn't to be believed, that it is merely the *eyes*—eyeball, lids, eyelashes etc.—of a human being, that one can be lost in the gaze of, into which one can look with astonishment and delight. And yet human eyes just do affect one like this" (Wittgenstein 1980, p. 267).

115 See also Appendix XL of Hua XXIII (to nos. 15c and d), p. 521: "Let us consider *aesthetic contemplation* [...]. In this case, 'the taking of a position in relation to being or nonbeing is excluded. That is not what is at stake.'"

sciousness of an object as such and the object's *manner of appearing*" (Hua XXIII, p. 461).

We previously asserted that the object is not irrelevant to aesthetic experience. Accordingly, despite reaffirming that aesthetic feeling is directed at the appearance itself, rather than at the object "through the appearance," Husserl emphasizes that this does not mean that the object (and its many connections to other objects and meanings) is rendered insignificant. In fact, the aesthetic feeling is concerned with "the object" as well, albeit *"only 'for the sake of the appearance'"* (Hua XXIII, p. 464). In principle, any given manifestation of an object is equal to any other in a practical attitude. In an aesthetic attitude, on the other hand, each of an object's individual manifestations (for example, a visage viewed from a specific angle against a specific background) expresses something unique, something not expressed by its other manifestations (that same visage viewed from another angle or against a different background).

As we shall soon see more clearly, the subject experiences a sort of "turning back [*Rückwendung*]" toward the manner of appearance, a *folding* of the focus from the "what" onto the "how" and *vice versa*, creating a dynamic equilibrium between the object and its unique appearance. Husserl suggests that aesthetic feeling arises from this very oscillation back and forth. This shift of interest opens up another crucial issue: the question of whether or not such an apositional attitude (apositional, again, meaning "neutral" regarding existence) involves another sort of position-taking: namely, an axiological position-taking carried out in terms of the previously mentioned "value-taking [*Wertnehmung*]" or valueception. Husserl seems to suggest that this is the case. In Appendix XL (from 1912, quoted above), despite again asserting that we "do not [...] carry out any position taking with respect to what appears" in aesthetic experience, he also states that we have an "aesthetic position taking that belongs to feeling" (Hua XXIII, p. 521) inherent to the sphere of value—in other words, we "carry out" an "aesthetic valuing" (Hua XXIII, p. 522).

In another research manuscript from Hua XXIII (Appendix LVIII, likely dated 1917, "on the theory of depiction"), after remarking that the depiction aesthetically considered "concerns what is presented only with respect to the moments (and the How of the moments) presented," Husserl asks: "Is it the case that I am not interested in existence here? To what extent am I not interested in it? I am not interested in the existence of what is presented *per se*. But I am interested in the existence of the *ideal* presentation of what is presented, in which case the positing of the existence of what is presented, if it occurs at all, plays no role in the consciousness of its value" (Hua XXIII, p. 647, my italics).

It thus seems that, in the aesthetic experience, we grasp [*nehmen*] beauty as a value [*Wert*]. Husserl refers to "the object of the beauty-evaluation [*Schön-Wer-*

tung]" (Hua XXIII, p. 649) as an "ideal" object that, though unaffected by existential positions, is nonetheless given through a position-taking: the value is posited yet neutral as regards the different "modalizations" (see, for example, Hua XXIII, p. 544) concerning any existential claim. Indeed, "if the actual object were to turn into a semblance object and consequently the actual mode of appearance into an inactual mode of appearance (hence one not existing in its stratum of being either)," this would not change the fact that "we would then nevertheless have something beautiful that exists, a mere figment, an 'image': which is precisely an *ideal object* and not a 'real' object (in which case we comprehend the actual modes of appearance themselves under the title of what is real)" (Hua XXIII, p. 649, my italics). Again, such appreciation need not necessarily take place within the artistic sphere as recognition of beauty is not exclusively linked to art; rather, it involves feeling a value.

Proposing an intimate relation between the expressive and axiological dimensions of aesthetic experience obviously raises further questions that we shall address more thoroughly in the third chapter. For now, we might suggest that such an "ideality" in "aesthetic valuation [*ästhetische Wertung*]" is what is *expressed* through the way of appearance, in a manner that is neutral toward "attachment" of modes of appearance "to actual *sujets* (and to *sujets* projected into the world by phantasy), and mediately to natural space and natural time and the natural world itself" (Hua XXIII, p. 649). In keeping with what we said above about the irreducibility of the expressed to the actual appearances expressing it, Husserl affirms that "beauty-value" cannot be reduced to the manner of appearance in itself.[116] What is felt as a value *is an ideality that can be presented through other manifestations*, other variations of the "first" appearance (which is then first only from a chronological viewpoint, not an ideal one): "the value remains for me even if I no longer have the respective semblance; if I can reproduce the semblance through memory or fiction, then I have it again, enjoy it again, although the presentification may not produce its full givenness" (Hua XXIII, p. 649). In Chapter 3, we shall attempt to address a potential issue arising from this last point: how does an individual manifestation's uniqueness (the unique visage in a unique context, visualized from a unique standpoint) relate to the possibility of varying that unique manifestation in order to reiterate its value (which, as we have said, renders it one variation among many)?

---

[116] "It must be observed here that the beauty-value in question does not lie in the mode of appearance that I am having impressionally and that I enjoy while I am having it. Enjoyed value is not value itself, which can exist without being enjoyed" (Hua XXIII, p. 649).

2.3 Dark Valuing Ideas

The issues we have considered up to this point are all effectively reformulated in *First Philosophy*, the 1923–24 lecture course we drew upon in the first chapter. Of particular relevance in this context is "Part Two: Theory of the Phenomenological Reduction," which Husserl taught in the second half of the winter semester in Freiburg, and which was posthumously published in 1959 in Husserliana VIII. Here, many years after his letter to Hofmannsthal and Ms. A VI 1, Husserl again draws a parallel between philosophical and artistic/aesthetic attitudes. Of course, this occurred in the context of an overall broadening and maturation of Husserl's analytical efforts;[117] the lecture course draws upon some of the most substantial results obtained through the earlier manuscripts discussed thus far. Here again, Husserl characterizes the artistic/aesthetic experience in terms of an intimate connection between value and feeling.

Husserl concludes his 1907 letter with a *post scriptum* listing the "three golden rules for the artist (in the widest sense), which at the same time are the public secrets of all true greatness" (Husserl 1994, p. 2). One concerns the passage we quoted above, where we read that the artist must "follow, purely and solely, his *daimonion*," which "drives him to an intuiting-blind production" (Husserl 1994, p. 2). It is highly significant that Husserl develops this "intuiting-blind" dimension in *First Philosophy* through the notion of *value*, specifically the notion of a "*dunamis* [δύναμις]," a sort of "dark [...] purposive idea" that "must hold valid for me" (Hua VIII, pp. 303–304). Though aesthetic intuition "gropes along blindly" (no determinate concept leads it), it can still "see" in an axiological (value-oriented) way. The artist works to shape this valuable "dark idea" through "pleasure" (moment of approval) and "displeasure" (moment of rejection; Hua VIII, p. 304). Again, this validity must originally manifest itself as felt, since the aesthetic attitude is one of feeling (another echo of Kant's third *Critique*). This is why Husserl suggests that, properly speaking, art historians operate not in an aesthetic attitude, but in a theoretical one (see for example Hua VIII, pp. 304).

These pages also offer a more clearly articulated formulation of the critical relationship between interest and disinterest in the aesthetic dimension—what one might call "disinterested interest." The key here is "*emotional interest* [*Gemütsinteresse*], a valuing interest [*wertendes Interesse*] in the broadest sense of the term" (Hua VIII, p. 307), which is characterized as the theme of aesthetic intention. Significantly, the difference between existential and emotional (*Gemüt*) interests

---

[117] Such a treatment can be said to "spread over" "Section Three" of this "Part Two" on the "Theory of the Phenomenological Reduction." See Hua VIII, pp. 286–333.

correlates to the one introduced above between *Wahrnehmung* as "taking as true [*Für-wahr-Nehmen*]" and *Wertnehmung* as "value-taking," which Husserl restates here as follows: "the value itself in its value-truth [*Wertwahrheit*] is not perceived [*wahrgenommen*], but as it were taken as value; and what *perception* [*Wahrnehmung*] achieves for the mere object, is achieved for the value by *value-taking* [*Wertnehmung*]" (Hua VIII, p. 307).[118] As noted, we might also call this *valueception* to stress the parallel with perception.

This perception/valueception analogy was already highlighted in another important *topos* of the Husserlian corpus, namely the second volume of the *Ideas*.[119] In a passage dated around 1915, Husserl writes:

> each *consciousness which originally constitutes a value-Object* as such, necessarily has in itself a *component* belonging to the *sphere of feelings* [*Gemütsphäre*]. The most original constitution of value is performed in feelings [*im Gemüt*] as that pre-theoretical (in a broad sense) delighting abandon on the part of the feeling Ego-subject for which I used the term "valueception [*Wertnehmung*]" already several decades ago in my lectures. The term is meant to indicate, in the sphere of feelings, an analogon of perception [*Wahrnehmung*], one which, in the doxic sphere, signifies the Ego's original (self-grasping) being in the presence of the object itself. Thus in the sphere of feelings what is meant by this talk of delighting [*Genießen*] is precisely that feeling in which the Ego lives with the consciousness of being in the presence of the Object "itself" in the manner of feelings [*fühlend dabei zu sein*]. (Hua IV, p. 11)

As mentioned, while not entailing perception proper, artistic and aesthetic experiences can be said to imply a positional, axiological dimension. Again, this applies not only to the artist, but also to the recipient, i.e., "the aesthetic contemplator" who "lives in a valuing interest," an "*emotional interest*" (Hua VIII, p. 307). As Husserl puts it, art can cause us to experience value as a *telos* holding the productive power of an attractive *dunamis*. The aesthetic subject is driven by this *dunamis*, "wants to fulfill within itself, in the mode of the full and pure artistic pleasure [...], the aesthetic object as this concrete value in itself," and the object felt in

---

118 On this parallel between the two forms of position-taking, see also Hua IV, pp. 10–11.
119 *Ideas II* was drafted between 1912 and 1915 and published posthumously as Husserliana IV. However, as is well known, it was available in manuscript form prior to its posthumous publication, and important authors could access it (among them Heidegger and Merleau-Ponty). On Merleau-Ponty's encounter with Husserl's text and manuscripts see, for example, Van Breda (1962). As recalled by Vongehr (2007, p. 105), "the first visitor to take a philosophical interest in Husserl's *Nachlass* in Leuven was Maurice Merleau-Ponty, whose visit in April 1939 came on the suggestion of Jean Hering, one of Husserl's former students. During his stay, he read *Ideas II*, *Experience and Judgment* and sections 28 to 72 of the *Crisis*, as well as the transcription of what was shortly afterwards to be published as *Umsturz der Kopernikanischen Wende: Die Ur-Arche Erde bewegt sich nicht.*"

the "pure and sated artistic pleasure" is *"energeia* [ἐνέργεια]" of the earlier *"dunamis* [δύναμις]" (Hua VIII, p. 307). This yields a more specific explanation of the sense in which, within aesthetic experiences, we can still be said to be "interested" despite our disinterest in the existence of what we are experiencing. It also reaffirms that our ability to "take value" from an object's way of appearance is essentially unaffected by its actual existence or nonexistence: in principle, aesthetic value can be expressed equally through reality and phantasy, through objects "in the flesh" and images.

To touch briefly upon an issue that we will develop further in Chapter 3, art can *aesthetically* open up or express a *horizon* of values—*whether aesthetic or not* —in ways that can in turn expand our scope of axiological interest. This is not a matter of merely conveying existing values in an aesthetic manner. Instead, art offers original presentations of emotional *tele* as values that "attract the subject [...] insofar as the self feels [them] as something whose existence concerns our very existence" (Costa 2014, p. 140). This is clearly another way in which, even when "enjoyed" in the neutrality of an experience "from a distance," art can *interest* us directly, influencing our conceptions of what we call the "real world."

2.4 The Unitary Interweaving of Acts

As we have seen, Husserl underscores that the art historian—and, similarly, the art critic—are attuned to the artistic object from a theoretical standpoint; in principle, aesthetic attitude would not be their primary concern. Even so, he says, for this to happen, the value as *"telos* [τέλος] of the emotionality" must already be generated and available, "ready to hand, so to speak, as already valued, as self-valued through value-taking" (Hua VIII, p. 308). Once again, let us note that Husserl previously discussed this passage between one attitude and another (specifically, between the aesthetic and theoretical attitudes) in *Ideas II:*

> there is an essential phenomenological modification of the pleasure, and of the seeing and judging, according as we pass over from one attitude to another. *This characteristic change of attitude [Einstellungsänderung] belongs, as an ideal possibility, to all acts*, and accompanying it is always the corresponding phenomenological modification. That is, all acts which are not already theoretical from the outset allow of being converted into such acts by means of a change in attitude. We can look at a picture "with delight." Then we are living in the performance of aesthetic pleasure, in the pleasure attitude, which precisely is one of "delight." Then again, we can judge the picture, with eyes of the art critic or art historian, as "beautiful." Now we are living the performance of the theoretical or judgmental attitude and no longer in the appreciating or pleasure-taking. (Hua IV, p. 10)

Note the sharp divide Husserl tends to draw between these two moments in time, as if to say that, in principle, the act of value judgment follows the act of value-taking. The potential risk in distinguishing too neatly between the emotional and the cognitive is that it might suggest that the original emotional value-taking lacks a cognitive dimension. I would be inclined to say that it does indeed have such a dimension, even if only in the form of a blind judgment. We will need to return to this seminal point.

In any case, it is clear that "'value-feeling' remains the more general term for value-consciousness, and, as feeling, it lies in every mode of such consciousness, the nonoriginary included" (Hua IV, p. 12). However, emotional and cognitive experiences need not necessarily be kept separate, as this would imply that each attitude (Husserl envisages three here: "theoretical," "axiological," and "practical" attitudes; Hua IV, p. 9) were a hermetically sealed component, and that passing from one to the other amounts to flipping a switch, with no potential for overlap or interweaving.

For example, we have the *"doxic theoretic"* attitude of the *"natural scientist,"* whose intentional correlate is the *"nature"* (Hua IV, p. 4). This does not imply that no other "experiences, e.g. feeling experiences" can be "lived" within such an attitude. There can be other "intentional lived experiences […] *constituting* […] new *objective strata* for the object in question, but ones in relation to which the subject is not in the theoretical attitude, and thus they do not constitute the respective theoretically meant and judgmentally determined object as such" (Hua IV, p. 6). On the one hand, Husserl says, when we look at

> the radiant and blue sky, living in the rapture of it […], then we are not in the theoretical or cognitive attitude but in the emotional [*Gemütseinstellung*]. On the other hand, while we are in the theoretical attitude, the pleasure may very well be present still, as, for example, in the observing physicist who is directing himself to the radiant blue sky, but then we are not living in the pleasure. (Hua IV, p. 10)

Thus, living in one attitude does not preclude the involvement of any others. As might be expected, there is also potential for pendant experiences to the one just mentioned: "doxic lived experiences also occur in the valuing and practical attitude" (Hua IV, p. 5). Put another way, one can say that,

> in the sphere of *spontaneous* performances of acts […] different spontaneities, which overlap each other, can arise with different phenomenological *dignity* [*Dignität*]: on the one hand, as the so-to-say *dominating* [*herrschende*] spontaneity, the one in which we prefer to live, and, on the other hand, as the supporting or collateral spontaneity, the one which remains in the background, the one, therefore, in which we do not prefer to live. (Hua IV, p. 14)

Notably, after first outlining this concept in *Ideas II*, Husserl returns to it and develops it in *First Philosophy*, stating that "what we normally call an act becomes questionable and requires a making-comprehensible-to-oneself, which makes understandable inwardly (phenomenologically) the naive self-evidence of using this terminology" (Hua VIII, p. 303). He therefore proposes expanding the concept of "*theme*, which, while common in the theoretical sphere," (Hua VIII, p. 303) exists in other attitudes as well, including—in another echo of the *Ideas II* passages referenced above—"axiological" and "practical" attitudes (see Hua VIII, p. 303). From this, we can glean the notion of each act being the result of "interwoven acts" and that this interweaving is "held together" by a combining force, an "interest, which unifies, overarchingly, all special interests" (Hua VIII, p. 306).

The act is thus constituted around the cohesive power of a "*domineering action*" that incorporates acts having "*function[s] of service*" or "*side action[s]*" (Hua VIII, p. 304). Such possibilities of combination manifest themselves differently from case to case, and describing them can help us develop an account of the rich complexity of what we call actions. This essential point is one we should use as a general line of inquiry for our research, and the same certainly also applies when we discuss how we experience images, fiction, or art. All of these areas, in turn, imply specific acts that can be interwoven in various ways but that must not simply be treated as equivalent.

Before returning to our final, definitive exploration of aesthetic experience in this chapter, let us attempt to address a doubt that our analyses thus far may have raised.

2.5 Aesthetic Experience, Image, and Modalizations

Examining aesthetic experience's "refractoriness" to distinctions between art and nature also means investigating how it articulates the difference between reality and image. The two pairs do not coincide; our analyses here have shed light on how concepts we might inadvertently use interchangeably must be put under the phenomenological lens, to identify peculiarities distinguishing the two.

As regards the distinction between reality and image, Husserl's emphasis on the mode of manifestation's aesthetic value seems to suggest that experiencing a perceptual object (a mountain, for example) aesthetically might be characterized as experiencing an image, as if the aesthetic experience affected the perceptual nature of the object under aesthetic consideration. Indeed, how does our *perception* of things change when we experience them aesthetically? How can we characterize *wahr-nehmen*, "taking as true" (in the sense of "really existing"), when—as is the case in the aesthetic attitude—interest in existence is put out of play? In Appendix VI (probably 1906) to Text no. 1 (§ 17) of Hua XXIII, Husserl asks:

> Why does nature, a landscape, sometimes act as an *"image"*? A distant village. The houses "little houses." These little houses have a) an altered size in comparison with houses as we ordinarily see them; b) a shallower stereoscopic quality, altered coloring, and so on. Like toy houses, they are apprehended as we apprehend images. Likewise the human beings: tiny little dolls (Hua XXIII, p. 167).[120]

From a temporal view, when we allow a landscape to "act as an 'image,'" it means that we do "not" take it "as present." The presence (*Gegenwärtigung*) of perception is modified not into a "nonpresence" (which would mean taking the position of denying its existence) so much as into "the nonpresent present" (a term whose paradoxical nature Husserl was quick to note) of the landscape's "pure manifestation," which acts as an image (Hua XXIII, p. 167)[121]—what we might also call a *perzeptive Phantasie*.

To consolidate what we have discussed so far, we might say that the aesthetic experience—which may concern both what we call reality and what would properly be described as the unreal presentificative dimension—is offered in the living interest we feel toward the mode of manifestation, which specifically leaves interest in the source of enjoyment's factual existence out of the equation. What we experience is an object having a certain *value* independent of any "index of reality," neutral as regards the difference between reality and unreality. To continue with Husserl's example, when considering a landscape depicting a mountain, we would not assign less value to *that* manifestation as a result of learning that the mountain under consideration did not actually exist.

We can now return to Section H (1912) of Text no. 15 in Hua XXIII, which we mentioned earlier in the context of clarifying the "aesthetic evaluation" process, to attempt to gain insight into the issues raised thus far. This manuscript explicitly dedicated to "aesthetic consciousness" echoes many of the points we have addressed here, particularly the crucial one concerning the relationship between mode of manifestation (*Erscheinungsweise*) and feeling (*Gefühl*). Within the specific context of Hua XXIII, Section H presents itself as a deeper look into the considerations introduced at the end of Section G, in which Husserl brings up the question of how to characterize an aesthetic experience that arises on a perceptual basis: "When an aesthetic consciousness is based on an intuition that is character-

---

[120] Here, the quoted text accounts for the changes Husserl made to the transcript (see Hua XXIII, p. 167, notes 1, 2, and 3).
[121] Here, the quoted text accounts for the changes Husserl made to the transcript (see Hua XXIII, p. 167, notes 4 and 5).

ized doxically, on the perception of nature, and so on"—as in the real landscape example mentioned above—"the feeling there does not have its basis in the doxic position taking." In other words, the feeling is independent of the landscape's actual existence: "we do not live in the latter when we are comporting ourselves aesthetically. We do not *live* in the doxic but in the valuing intentions" (Hua XXIII, pp. 458–459). Such is the specific sense in which Husserl asserts that we can contemplate the landscape as an image, as a painting.

In Section H, Husserl starts by addressing this same disinterest in existence that we have shown to be characteristic of the aesthetic attitude. Several times within this short but complicated text, Husserl returns to the problem of describing aesthetic feelings, approaching his previous positions from new directions. With each new "confrontation" with himself, he attempts to find a new perspective through which to reveal an essential aspect of the phenomenon in question. As Marc Richir (1999, p. 19, note 2) has pointed out, here Husserl's "analytical acrimony" obliges him to continuous, tireless refinement, like some form of meticulous hand-to-hand combat with the *"Sache selbst* [thing itself]."

In the course of re-examining themes previously discussed, Husserl soon brings up a matter requiring delicate consideration. We previously suggested that putting existence out of play in aesthetic interest might apply to not only the perceptual dimension but to image consciousness (presentifications in image) as well since, as shown in the first chapter, image consciousness may or may not be accompanied by a position concerning the existence of the *sujet* presented: "We can live in memory, in actually experiencing presentification. The objectivities stand before us as nonpresent 'actualities,' hence are characterized doxically, in the manner peculiar to belief. [...] The situation is the same in the case of iconic acts" (Hua XXIII, p. 460). I can live positional iconic acts, i.e., I can relate to a *sujet* with an existential interest:

> If I have the picture of a person before my eyes, I can make judgments about her character, about her mind and temperament, about her way of dressing, and so on. I take the picture precisely as the presentification of the person; I posit her as someone actual and judge about the actual person. I also judge about the person by means of affective predicates; I comport myself before the person as liking her, disliking her, valuing her ethically, and so on. (Hua XXIII, p. 460)

These considerations align with what we proposed in Chapter 1, namely that the positional condition does not pertain exclusively to perceptual experience—it can also apply to how we experience images. Despite being marked by an intrinsic neutrality concerning its manifestation as image object, image consciousness can be experienced positionally (concerning *sujet* consciousness). As such, in aesthetic consideration, image consciousness can undergo a disabling of interest in existence, a neutralization of the possible ray of belief passing through it. This means firstly that looking at an image does not automatically imply being in an aesthetic consciousness—we may or may not adopt one. In the event that we do, "we ask no questions about the being and nonbeing of what [...] appears in [the] image" (Hua XXIII, p. 459).

As these pages explicitly observe, the position of belief can pass through all presentificational acts. In examining this particular Husserlian passage, we can now also note that this applies not only to perception and iconic presentification, It also concerns memory (which, in *Ideas I*, is distinguished from phantasy precisely through the positional ray passing through the former but not the latter[122]) and even what Husserl calls objects experienced "symbolically": the signifying or symbolic (as opposed to intuitive) dimension mentioned in Chapter 1. We find examples of the latter case in language when "I hear an assertion about a person: I take the assertion objectively as the truth and condemn the person's behavior expressed in it, without having had an intuition of the behavior" (Hua XXIII, p. 460).

To sum up, we can have positional experiences (e.g., experiences imbued with a belief concerning existence) toward:
1) flesh-and-blood actualities, as is the case with perceptual objects/occurrences;
2) objects/occurrences experienced through a positionally reproductive phantasy, as is the case with memory presentification;
3) objects/occurrences presentified in images; and
4) signitively/linguistically narrated objects/occurrences.

Plainly, positional experiences happen all the time in everyday life. We have them when conversing with our friend face-to-face, when remembering her, when viewing a selfie she has just texted us from somewhere else (or posted to social media, etc.)—and also, to draw upon Husserl's own example, when another friend complains that she offended him the other day. More generally, any time we hear what we believe to be a true account of another person's good (or bad) deeds, we assign a positional hallmark to what we have been told, even in the absence of an intuitive experience. In a way, all of this articulates our daily struggle to sift through innumerable experiences (of varying degrees of perceived importance or gravity) to determine what is true and what is not, what really happened and what did not.

According to eidetic laws, each of these beliefs can be disavowed:
1) On a perceptual level: I thought I saw my friend in a crowd, but it turned out to be someone who looked a lot like her.

---

[122] See above, note 44.

2.5 Aesthetic Experience, Image, and Modalizations — 109

2) On a reproductive level: I remembered telling my friend about my new camera, but when I showed it to her, she seemed surprised, which prompted me to wonder if perhaps I did not mention the camera to her after all.
3) On an iconic level: I came to suspect that the selfie my friend just texted me was in fact cleverly Photoshopped, or that it was a photo of someone who looked just like my friend. Or perhaps I found out that the selfie was taken last year and that my friend texted it to me from home, not from the distant country where she originally took it.
4) On a signitive/symbolic level: upon speaking to my friend, I concluded that she never actually offended our mutual friend, who has an unfortunate propensity for believing his own fairytales.

These would all be instances of *modalization*, specifically of the type where a belief is discovered to be unfounded and is thus supplanted by a new belief. Of course, as the reader may have already deduced from our analyses thus far, modalizations need not always automatically result in a new position of reality replacing the old one. In some cases, our position concerning reality may instead be neutralized, in the sense of "quarantined" or "taken offline." Indeed, we can experience any of these four levels from a neutral perspective, suspending our interest in whether the event or object actually exists, "*exclud[ing] the consciousness of reality*" (Hua XXIII, p. 460). These acts would then become neutralized acts of phantasy, in the sense of unreality (but not denial of reality)—in other words, neutralized presentification acts (*perzeptiv* (1), reproductive (2), iconic (3) or signitive (4), respectively).

Thus, the aforementioned shifts in consciousness lead us to different results. Starting on the perceptual level yields a *perzeptive* phantasy; on the reproductive level (positional reproduction), a simple phantasy; on the iconic level (an image presentifying a real *sujet*), a pure "iconic phantasy"; and on the symbolic level (a story deemed true), "purely symbolic presenting and thinking" (Hua XXIII, p. 460). In each of these four cases, once we have put reality out of play, we can continue developing our phantasy experience by performing new phantasy acts in context of that experience—though, as mentioned in Chapter 1, these new acts carried out on a modified basis will be modified acts: "a man stands before my eyes in phantasy; he kills another man: I react to this by taking a position of abhorrence, and the like. The act, however, is modified" (Hua XXIII, p. 460): we know that no one has *actually* killed anyone.

2.6 Constituting the "How": Stylistic Manifestations

To sum up, with belief-acts of each of these four types, we have an essential, eidetic option to transform them into (modified) phantasy acts, rendering them neutral in terms of possible reference to actual existence. Crucially, however, the resulting phantasies do not yet constitute aesthetic experiences merely by virtue of having left reality out of play; rather, the distinguishing element in aesthetic experiences is the particular mode of manifestation in which the phenomenon is given (among many possible such modes). To continue with Husserl's example, an iconic phantasy of one man killing another may take the form of a mere iconic presentification of a *quasi*-fact—with no attention to its mode of manifestation—or it may employ precise phenomenal modalities whose specific manner of appearance yields an aesthetic effect.

For example, in the duel scene near the end of *For a Few Dollars More* (*Per qualche dollaro in più*, 1965), the *specific stylistic choices* Sergio Leone makes when depicting one man killing another allow us to feel not only the *what*—the *quasi*-occurrences on-screen that could just as easily be recounted through a purely iconic sequence, advancing the plot without artistic pretensions—but also the *how*, the value of this particular scene as it unfolds. Our aesthetic experience is affected by the fact that the different phases of the duel are depicted in this particular way, with this specific "rhythm."[123] Husserl rightly takes care to emphasize what may seem like an obvious point, namely that things are always given in accordance with a mode of manifestation (in the aesthetic sense just described), a mode that may or may not elicit aesthetic pleasure or displeasure—what we might describe as "positive" or "negative" aesthetic valence.[124]

The mode of manifestation is what determines the aesthetic feeling that can arise when we experience an object or an occurrence. As Husserl explains,

---

[123] On this point cf. what Merleau-Ponty says about this relationship between the how (style, rhythm) and value in cinema: "Beauty, when it manifests itself in cinematography, lies not in the story itself, which could quite easily be recounted in prose, and still less in the ideas which this story may evoke; nor indeed does it lie in the tics, mannerisms and devices that serve to identify a director, for their influence is no more decisive than that of a writer's favourite words. What matters is the selection of episodes to be represented and, in each one, the choice of shots that will be featured in the film, the length of time allotted to these elements, the order in which they are to be presented, the sound or words with which they are or are not to be accompanied. Taken together, all these factors contribute to form a particular overall cinematographical rhythm" (Merleau-Ponty 1948, p. 98).

[124] "Every object, in being given in a consciousness, is given in a manner of appearing; and it can then be the manner of appearing that determines aesthetic comportment, one appearance inducing aesthetic pleasure, another inducing aesthetic displeasure, and so on" (Hua XXIII, p. 461).

2.6 Constituting the "How": Stylistic Manifestations — 111

when we are merely experiencing something, primarily focused on the objective what ("objective position taking"), it is less relevant "whether" something "appears in this or that orientation." We perceive (or phantasize, for that matter) the *same* object through manifold perspectives. Even so, as discussed in Chapter 1, this "is not irrelevant aesthetically" (Husserl XXIII, p. 461). In this important Text no. 15h, Husserl specifies that "aesthetic valuation is essentially connected with the distinction between the consciousness of an object as such and the object's *manner of appearing*" (Hua XXIII, p. 461).

Let us explore the potential impact this clarification may have on the development of our discourse. For one, Husserl specifies that "mode of manifestation" means more than simply the object's "mode of presentation [*Darstellung*]," i.e., the mode of its aspectual course. Focusing on the "mode of presentation" could just as easily be accomplished through a phenomenological analysis accounting for the different aspects through which a single object gives itself to consciousness. (Eidetically, we always see an aspect of an object despite intending the whole object—an object is never effectively [*reell*] given to consciousness completely). Here, however, we are concerned with "mode of manifestation" or "mode of appearing," which does not concern an "isolated object, but precisely [...] the object in the nexus of objects in which one is conscious of it, and the manners of appearing belonging to this nexus" (Hua XXIII, p. 461).

Moreover, modes of manifestation are always given according to an emotional tone, though that emotional tone may be one of indifference. Things are always given in a pathic dimension, in a context of problems, even if the mode in question is "everything's all right." Life, we might say, always unravels in a horizon of *caring*, which always has an emotional characterization.[125] Even when we are not aesthetically attuned, the objects and events we encounter continue giving themselves according to emotional nuances intimately connected to their modes of manifestation—in certain atmospheres, we might say. As we shall see, this also concerns fictional art. This is obviously not to call emotional or atmospheric perception equivalent to artistic feeling,[126] but understanding a film or a novel nonetheless implies

---

[125] A clear reference on this point remains Heidegger, who showed how it is not possible to think of a "being-in-the-world" that is not emotionally situated, seeing in that of the "emotional tonality" one of the moments characterizing the *"Da* [there]" of *Dasein*. See in particular Heidegger (1927, § 29).
[126] Griffero (2010, p. 136) points out, for example, *"a double asymmetry"* between art and atmosphere: *"art is not only atmosphere and atmosphere is not only art."*

a certain level of *emotional comprehension* as immersing ourselves in the fictional world requires us to be "transposed into emotion" (Costa 2014, p. 34).[127]

Emotional tonalities are a way of feeling the world, and this also holds true for the *quasi*-worlds created by phantasy. A world gives itself as a system of nexuses that always present themselves with emotional and axiological qualities (once again, including not only approval but also indifference or rejection). The aesthetic *how* of manifestation can open up a specific emotional tonality, cause us to feel a particular atmosphere, and put us in an axiological situation from the outset. There is an essential connection between emotion and value: *in its genuine manifestation, value must be felt*. Art can make us experience this process as something akin to a discovery or a revelation of values—or, better, a creation of values.

2.7 The Aesthetic Fold

We previously noted that, although they are justified for the sake of analysis, absolute divisions among different modes of consciousness are more regulative ideas than concrete separations between one act and another. Acts are often experienced through a dominant mode of consciousness, but with other modes interwoven. In the manuscript currently under examination, Husserl remarks that the process of describing the structure of aesthetic experiences reveals how they often manifest themselves in combination with other, not necessarily aesthetic, forms of consciousness (see Hua XXIII, p. 389). Here, the task of giving an account of such an "amalgamated" aesthetic consciousness is what prompts Husserl to refine some of the positions on aesthetic experience we outlined earlier. Though the Husserlian text currently under consideration does revisit this question, it is merely for purposes of reworking it in order to obtain new and more comprehensive results. His efforts in developing this manuscript lead him to characterize aesthetic experience in terms of a *shift* in *interest* instead of a generic *disinterest*. As mentioned, it would be unproductive to characterize aesthetic and artistic experiences in terms of disinterest in a general sense (regardless of whether one might consider such an interest essential or preposterous) as specific interests and disinterests are at play simultaneously. Earlier, for example, we discussed the possibility of an

---

[127] As far as cinema is concerned, see also the analyses developed starting from Husserl in Deodati (2010, p. 71): "when the voice-over begins to proceed slowly and solemnly, accompanied by images of a breathtaking sunrise over the Pacific Ocean, the spectator immediately finds himself inside *Big Wednesday* (J. Milius, 1978). Not simply into its story, but right into its atmosphere. He does not yet know exactly what will happen, but in a way, he feels how it will happen."

axiologically connoted aesthetic (or artistic) interest combined with an existential disinterest.

To paraphrase a question Husserl asks in these same pages, what is aesthetic consciousness directed toward (Hua XXIII, p. 462)? Though aesthetic consciousness is apositional (unconcerned with the existence or nonexistence of the object/occurrence), we can still say—in keeping with our earlier remarks on *Ideas II* and *First Philosophy*—that it takes a position in aesthetic evaluation: *valueception* (Hua XXIII, p. 462).[128] When "read[ing] a drama" (or watching a movie), our attention is certainly directed toward the "persons, actions" being "presented" to us (Hua XXIII, p. 462), but this is not *eo ipso* aesthetically relevant. We could certainly experience fictional dramas or novels (or movies) without being aesthetically postured; we can simply follow the plot as we would any other phantasy. We can take a position (albeit a modified position, a *quasi*-position) and merely observe as the story unfolds, focusing our attention entirely on the *quasi*-facts of that story (the "what" rather than the "how"). If someone asks me what *Othello* is about, I can recount the plot in any number of ways. In that context, at least in principle, the "how" I chose would not matter—I can tell the story without aesthetic interest being a major focus.

Awakening aesthetic consciousness, on the other hand, requires that one be attuned to "*the manner of appearing*" (Hua XXIII, p. 462), the mode of the manifestation. This mode is the "bearer" of "aesthetic feeling-characteristics" that we may or may not grasp depending on whether we are aesthetically attuned, whether our attention is directed to the *how* of the phenomenon (*nota bene:* in principle, aesthetic consideration can either be deliberate—when one makes a conscious effort to adopt it—or catch a subject off guard, so to speak). It is this "fold" in attention, this moment of turning back (*Rückwendung*) to consider the *how* of the manifestation, that causes the qualitative change in experience that "gives birth to the original (aesthetic) feeling" (which, as mentioned, ideally has a zero degree, namely the aesthetic *adiaphoron*). This passage is not static but dynamic; we can think of it as "a shift from the focus on the object to this *reflective* focus and *vice versa*" (Hua XXIII, p. 464, my italics). There is an enjoyable mutual tension between the "what" and the "how," resulting in a dynamic equilibrium between object and appearance: "The appearance is the appearance of the object; the object is the object in the appearance" (Hua XXIII, p. 462). It is within this very back-and-forth movement vis-à-vis the object's way of appearance that the aesthetic feeling devel-

---

[128] *"To live in it is surely to take a position, to value something aesthetically"* (Hua XXIII, p. 462).

ops.¹²⁹ I would suggest that such a "turning back" or "folding" can then be dynamically understood as a "reflective" movement that—in Kantian terms—never finds a concept capable of circumscribing it. This is a "circular" movement whereby the aesthetic object becomes both "origin" and "term" of the feeling, without the dynamism of this movement ever being locked up in the static nature of a determinate concept (lest its aesthetic power dissolve).¹³⁰ Such a "turning back," in principle, can occur for any object since "however displeasing" the object "may be in itself, however negatively I may value it," it can "receive [...] an aesthetic coloration *because of its manner of appearing*" (Hua XXIII, p. 462).

Crucially, this idea of movement and dynamism then allows us to elaborate upon the role that the manner of manifestation plays in aesthetic experience. This manuscript points out the need to provide a more precise description of the (legitimately drawn) distinction between the *wie* (how) and the *was* (what) of experience and to elucidate how each is articulated. In short, this manuscript highlights the need to account more thoroughly for their fundamental correlation because, even though the question of existence is put "out of play" in aesthetic experience, "*the content of the object itself is not aesthetically insignificant*" (Hua XXIII, p. 462).

Echoing and expanding upon the 1906 remarks we highlighted above, Husserl stresses that the fact that Hamlet is the Prince of Denmark is indeed relevant to our aesthetic reception of the figure. For example, the character may acquire a different value through his royal status, which the recipient may associate with "emotional effects" like "loyalty" or "respect" (Hua XXIII, p. 462). Though the feelings, atmospheres, emotional tones, values, etc. aroused through these *quasi*-positions are not properly aesthetic in themselves, Husserl recognizes that they can help constitute the axiological-emotional mixture that characterizes aesthetic experience and can thus be categorized, "*transfigured*" (Richir 1999, p. 19), under the heading of "manner of appearing."

---

129 Marc Richir also emphasized this aspect in his important commentary on this Text no. 15h of Hua XXIII. See Richir (1999).

130 "It is not the same to say 'there is a square table in the room' and 'in the same room there is a beautiful table.' In this last example [...] the statement assumes someone's aesthetic point of view. [...] The aesthetic object, to use the terms Kant used in his *Critique of the Power of Judgment*, is the occasion (the origin) but also the term of a feeling, of an emotional-affective timbre of perceiving, of a subjective reflection, that is, of an aesthetic reflection in perceiving itself" (Desideri 2004, p. 34). However, there is "the caveat that outside of this pleasure—of this internal reflection of perceptive life in a pure feeling (of pleasure or displeasure)—the aesthetic object is in a state of latency: of pure possibility" (Desideri 2004, p. 37).

Similarly, when we are watching a movie, the *quasi*-fact that a character in danger eventually manages to escape the clutches of a *quasi*-villain can trigger *quasi*-relief in us as viewers. As before, though this *quasi*-relief is not aesthetic in itself, it may nonetheless be linked to aesthetic appreciation for the manner of manifestation; as a result, "the whole has the character of an enhanced aesthetic delight" (Hua XXIII, p. 462). In Chapter 3, we will explore specific ways in which aesthetic and artistic consciousness can act upon such modes of manifestation to potentially open up the possibility of experiencing new processes of valorization.

2.8 Pleasurable "How," Painful "What"

The question of the "how" becomes more complicated when its corresponding "what" concerns a painful situation—even more so when we believe the pain in question positionally, i.e., believe it to be real. Cinematic history abounds with examples in which the gravity of the "what" and the virtuosity of the "how" can give rise to substantial conflicts in combination. Consider, for example, the now-emblematic tracking shot in Gillo Pontecorvo's *Kapò* (1959), which Jacques Rivette famously condemned in a June 1961 review in *Cahiers du cinéma:* "Look […], in *Kapò*, at the shot where Riva kills herself by throwing herself on an electric barbed-wire fence; the man who decides, at that moment, to have a dolly in to tilt up the body, while taking care to precisely note the hand raised in the angle of its final framing —this man deserves nothing but the most profound contempt" (Rivette 1961; see Figure 7).[131]

Beyond the specific debate concerning Pontecorvo's shot and Rivette's accusations against the Italian director (subjective conclusions regarding the merits of said accusations are left to the reader), Rivette's review raises the issue concerning

---

[131] As Laurent Jullier and Jean-Marc Leveratto (2016) point out, Rivette's harsh critique of Pontecorvo's tracking shot in *Kapò* did "not appear out of nowhere". On the occasion of a round table (July 1959) dedicated to Alain Resnais' *Hiroshima mon amour*, Godard, objecting to the distinction between ethics and aesthetics, claimed that "tracking shots are a question of morality" (Hillier 1985, p. 62). Actually, this claim was a reversal of Luc Moullet's earlier statement (March 1959), in his article for the *Cahiers* dedicated to Sam Fuller, that "morality is a question of tracking shots" (Hillier 1985, p. 148). Rivette, who explicitly mentions both formulations in his review of *Kapò*, reiterated the point made by Godard that ethics and aesthetics cannot be separated, clarifying that the relation between these two domains is not a question of mere formalism but rather of "the attitude that [the auteur] takes in relation to that which he films" (Rivette 1961). Since 1961, the year in which Rivette published his review, the paradigm of *Kapò*'s tracking shot has been subject to variations, developments, and revivals—among others, in the equally well-known essay devoted to *Kapò*'s tracking shot written by French critic Serge Daney (1992).

Figure 7: Still from Gillo Pontecorvo's *Kapò* (1959)

the possibility of representing subjects—such as death—that "should not be addressed except in the throes of fear and trembling" (Rivette 1961). In essence, the French director's review poses the question of the authorial responsibility implied in choices related to the *how* (which cannot be abstracted aproblematically from the object, from the *what*, because as we have seen there is no "what" without a "how"). Recalling the etymology of the term "responsibility," we might instead frame this as a question of responding to the impossibility of remaining neutral or impartial when confronting subjects seemingly refractory to any sort of exhibition.

According to Rivette, there is no escaping the obligation to show something *in a certain way at all times:* "to make a film is to show certain things, that is *at the same time,* and by the same mechanism, to show them with a certain bias; these two acts being thoroughly bound together" (Rivette 1961). Nonetheless, he seems to say, certain objects or events defy any sort of representation; attempting to do so would constitute a "violation." As the controversial subject par excellence, death (especially when it comes at the hands of other humans, as in murder or even genocide) continuously raises questions of whether and how it can be represented appropriately.[132] Bazin, for example, writes that representation of death constitutes an "obscenity."[133] On the other hand, the desire to represent it may also be seen

---

[132] On this, see Didi-Huberman (2004).
[133] "Like death, love must be experienced and cannot be represented [...] without violating its nature. This violation is called obscenity. The representation of a real death is also an obscenity, no longer a moral one, as in love, but metaphysical" (Bazin 1949–1951, p. 30). Thus, Bazin seems to construe the "obscene" as an "out of the scene," as what cannot and should not enter

as symptomatic of the will to save tragedy from oblivion—thus counterbalancing the "sacrilegious" character of that need.[134]

As Kundera recalls, Céline even saw an ever-present looming insinuation of a theatrical, unnecessarily aestheticizing element in the production of all human acts, even death, whether or not presentifying media are involved. Céline spoke of the world as a stage, a real stage on which people exhibit themselves even when they should not—thereby once again framing the issue as one involving both aesthetics and ethics.[135] As we have seen, these fundamental questions run through all modes of consciousness—at the perceptual, iconic, reproductive, and symbolic levels—and warrant further investigation here, specifically with regard to image and phantasy consciousness, i.e., with regard to our experiences of images and phantasy.

Céline's provocation is intended to denounce a spectacularizing tendency that he claims affects even the most ordinary deaths. It is worth citing most of the brief text Kundera devotes to Céline's *Castle to Castle* (*D'un château l'autre*), significantly entitled *Death and the Fuss* (*La mort et le tralala*):

> In Céline's Novel *From Castle to Castle*, a story of a dog; she comes from the icy north of Denmark, where she would disappear for long escapades in the forest. When she arrives in France with Céline, her roaming days are over. Then one day, cancer:
>
> "I tried to lay her down on the straw ... just after dawn ... she didn't like me putting her there ... she didn't want it ... she wanted to be in some other place ... over by the coldest part of the house on the pebbles ... She stretched out nicely there ... she began to rattle ... it was the end ... they'd told me, I didn't believe it ... but it was true, she was facing toward what she remembered, the place she'd come from, the north, Denmark, her muzzle toward the north, pointed north, ... this very faithful dog, in a way ... faithful to the forests where she used to run off, Korsør, way up there ... and faithful to her harsh life there, ... these Meudon woods here meant nothing to her ... she died with two, three small rattles ... oh, very discreet ... no

---

the scene, in keeping with a popular etymology that has not (to my knowledge) been confirmed, but one whose meaning can be functional in characterizing the terms of our discourse.

134 As Didi-Huberman puts it, "to remember, one must imagine" (Didi-Huberman 2004, p. 30), and presentifications, as we have seen, can be experienced in all their documentary power (and reasons) in order to try to intuit "how something might have been" even when we know no presentification—iconic or reproductive—might wholly suffice for this task.

135 Dostoevsky also presents an extreme example of this human drive toward *theatricalizing* death in *The Idiot*, with the failed suicide attempt of Ippolit, a seventeen-year-old dying of consumption. Ippolit reads his "explanation" (a confession whose revealing title is *Après moi le deluge!*) in front of an audience, secretly planning to commit suicide once he finishes, when "the sun will probably already be risen and 'resounding in the sky,'" as he puts it (see Dostoevsky 1869, p. 414). Ippolit clearly thinks of suicide as a *coup de théâtre*, and his "explanation" of his (ultimately unsuccessful) attempt can be interpreted as a staged exhibition. My thanks to Paolo Stellino for pointing me to this reference.

complaints ... and in this really beautiful position, like in mid-leap—in flight ... but on her side, helpless, finished ... nose toward her getaway forests, up there where she came from, where she'd suffered ... God knows!"

"Oh, I've seen plenty of death throes, here ... there ... everywhere ... but by far nothing so beautiful, discreet ... faithful ... the trouble with men's death throes is all the fuss [*c'est le tra-lala*] ... somehow man is always on stage ... even the plainest man."

"The trouble with men's death throes is all the fuss." What a line! And: "somehow man" is always on stage." Don't we all recall the ghoulish drama of those famous "last words" on the deathbed? That's how it is: even in the throes of death, man is always on stage. And even "the plainest" of them, the least exhibitionist, because it's not always the man himself who climbs on stage. If he doesn't do it, someone will put him there. That is his fate as a man. (Kundera 2009, pp. 22–23)

Kundera sees in Céline's style the expression of his *"life utterly devoid of fuss."* Notice, however, that the absence of fuss in Céline's style does not necessarily imply the impossibility of representing the dog's death aesthetically. Try as one might, in fact, one can never achieve an alleged ideal point of aesthetic *adiaphoron*, a zero degree on the aesthetic scale, a wholly objective and impartial representation. Even when seemingly silenced or nullified, an aesthetic "turning back" can always develop (whether deliberately or not), even when it stands in painful contrast to what we are living, experiencing, imagining, etc. In fact, Kundera points out how Céline is capable of grasping the *"sublime beauty* in a dog's death" (Kundera 2009, p. 24, my italics). This peculiar beauty seems to present itself while receding; Céline expresses it for the reader through a *how* immune to theatricality and yet describable in terms of a "really beautiful position, like in mid-leap—in flight": a death "so beautiful, discreet," unlike any seen before.

2.9 A True Story

To gain further clarity in this regard, let us delve into the complex relationship between aesthetic attitudes and images affected by belief, which we contrasted to those free of having to comply with any form of belief in actual existence. Previously, we had specified how, in aesthetic consideration, interest in the factual existence of the object under observation is put out of play. Husserl's 1912 manuscript on aesthetic consciousness undertakes a more nuanced analysis of this issue, ultimately acknowledging the possibility that consciousness of existence can legitimately affect aesthetic experience to a certain extent. This acknowledgment does not constitute a disavowal of the previous research. Rather, Husserl seems to say that aesthetic consciousness, which recognizes different degrees of value among modes of an object's or occurrence's manifestation, can and must also account for the element of belief that may imbue an image; in principle, this applies to both two-dimensional and three-dimensional images, including those "in the flesh."[136]

Differentiating between positional and fictional images certainly does not exclude the phenomenological possibility of manifold "hybrid" forms falling between the two poles—indeed, this distinction may even form the basis for such a possibility to develop. For example, a fictional *quasi*-reality might be intertwined with a form of belief in reality. Consider fictional films that open with a caption describing the work as "based on a true story." Even though such films still constitute phantasy productions that establish a fictional relationship toward the presentified reality—in other words, we are watching characters, not presentifications of actual people—these indications can serve to introduce a positional dimension that commonly impacts the feelings aroused through images. Such feelings might seem different to those "*quasi*-feelings" we supposedly experience when watching films that do not claim to reference reality (or perhaps even specify that "any similarity to real persons, places or events is purely coincidental").

In some cases, this "true story" claim is merely a gimmick to trigger a sentimental response and is often used in films lacking in aesthetic value.[137] In such circumstances, we may find the story moving despite never experiencing any form of aesthetic consciousness (once again, it is a matter of acknowledging differences: aesthetic/artistic enjoyment does not equal "the pleasure of weeping"[138]). Other times, the positional attitude elicited through the caption may even lead the viewer to overlook the fact that the filmic images did not originate from encounters with actual reality, that they are merely imaginative reconstructions (of varying degrees of reliability—many commercial films would be considered approximate at best and completely misleading at worst). The risk in such instances is that of reflexively adopting an uncritically positional stance toward many of the image elements, allowing them to impact our beliefs—whether we adopt these beliefs casually or through a process of rigorous reasoning.

---

136 In the sense (outlined before) of landscape and people seen as if they were images. But, even if it is a different phenomenon, this can of course regard the case of characters played by actors.
137 E.g., products made purely for entertainment purposes, featuring cliché stories and expressionless images. Of course, the fact that images are produced that way does not rule out the possibility that later some new point of view arises that can find some sort of aesthetic value in those productions (as we said, the aesthetic *adiaphoron* is only a limit point, and an aesthetic consciousness can in principle arise for every object/occurrence).
138 On the "pleasure of weeping" and its eighteenth-century roots, see Mazzocut-Mis (2012) and Mazzocut-Mis (2021).

The purpose of this digression is to emphasize the fact that iconic presentifications are never neutral or indifferent regarding their presentified *sujets*; in many cases, they affect our subsequent phantasy reproductions of those *sujets* in multiple ways. Our phantasy reproductions are in fact nourished on infinite occasions through reworkings of images, which can then obviously be combined with phantasy reproductions of perceptual realities. Husserl offers an example: "I phantasy 'freely' and in a purely playful way—if I 'daydream'—that I am walking on the Friedrichstrasse and there encounter Goethe, who addresses me amiably" (Hua XXIII, p. 310).[139] Moreover, it is interesting to note that in the mixed reproductions generated from such playful combinations, there seems to be no difference whatsoever on the object side between elements stemming from actual experiences and those stemming from iconic experiences. It might be difficult to distinguish which parts of the resulting composite originated based only on the appearance of the reproduced object.

Suppose, for instance, we watch a documentary about a lion and later envision ("reproduce") that lion walking down the street outside our house (which we see "in the flesh" every morning). Though stemming from different modes of consciousness, the components of this phantasy are perfectly fused in the scene "hovering before us." In terms of a pure description of the objectual side of the reproductive experience, there is little difference between a phantasy reproduction in which I see my friend (whom I know in person) getting out of a subway train, and one in which I phantasize Edmund Husserl (whom I cannot and will not ever meet in person) getting out of the same train.

This last remark points us to a more general phenomenon wherein image objects we experience within a positional attitude often (whether we realize it or not) influence our phantasy reproductions of reality. Indeed, there are plenty of living beings or things that we have never seen in person, yet have some *knowledge* of thanks to images "imbued with belief" that we have viewed at some point in our lives—for instance, we might *know* where to find them and would still *recognize* them if we saw them. In other words, our reproductive phantasies concerning reality also feed on images we encounter in everyday life.

Even if I had never seen a lion in the flesh, I could still have a reproductive intuition of it and could perhaps transport myself to the savannah in my imagination. We can further hypothesize that such a reproductive intuition would not be in black and white: having viewed photographic or video images of the savannah in color, I would likely draw upon these previous experiences in developing my phantasy reproduction of a lion. On the other hand, if I were attempting to picture

---

[139] On "mixed phantasies" see also Hua XXIII, pp. 537, 713.

World War I, the soldiers and trenches conjured in my phantasy would likely be tinged with unsaturated black and white—a result of conditioning through the many archive images passed down to us documenting the dramatic events of that period. Naturally, with a little effort, I can overcome this ingrained habit and imagine that same scenario in color. Colorized film would certainly help me in that regard: once I had viewed enough full-color presentifications of those past events, I would most likely shift my own phantasy presentifications of them into color.[140]

Clearly, presentifying a scene in a new way (by colorizing old film footage or making a historical movie using modern color film) might also affect how we feel about or value the presentified object. Here, depending on the filmic style of the images, viewing World War I scenes in color instead of grayscale might trigger a corresponding shift in emotional tonality. In any case, when watching historical films involving facts positionally established as true, we experience the filmic images as imbued with belief from the outset, which can make it hard to draw a line between emotions originating from our belief in the "what" and those triggered by the specific manner of appearance, the "how."

Furthermore, at this juncture, it is important to emphasize that there is also a third crucial dynamic at play in these cases: the narrative. The constitutive nature of this element may seem fairly obvious when we are talking about fiction, but as will gradually become clear, it can also help us define the genesis of what we call reality. The relationship between facts and cinematic narrative can shake out in innumerable ways, as a quick glance through cinematic history shows.

Take, for example, David Lynch's *The Straight Story* (1999), whose title reflects the close interconnection of real and phantasy elements characteristic of the film itself. The title refers to the name of the protagonist, Alvin Straight (Richard Farnsworth), a man who "actually existed," whose "true story" is being told, as well as to the adjective "straight," whose range of English meanings includes "sincere," "honest," and "exact."[141] Or consider Francesco Rosi's *Hands over the City* (*Le mani sulla città*, 1963), which closes with a caption stating that "the characters and the facts narrated here are imaginary, but the social and environmental reality that produces them is authentic"—a statement that would likely apply to many social critique films (among other genres, of course).

---

[140] Significant in this regard is Peter Jackson's 2018 *They Shall Not Grow Old*, a documentary on World War I comprised entirely of colorized film footage and archival interviews.
[141] See McGowan (2007, pp. 178–179) for an analysis of the film according to which Lynch applies a "fantasmatic distortion" to the *straight story* such that "the film encourages us to view the world that it depicts as a world of fantasy."

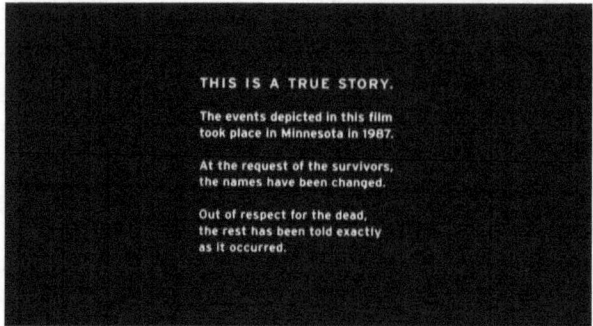

Figure 8: Still from Joel and Ethan Coen's *Fargo* (1996)

These myriad possibilities of articulation show us that even when the boundaries between reality and fiction are clear on one level, they can be shifted, blurred, or called into question at another. The narrative aspect will prove fundamental in shedding light on these considerations. The Coen brothers again clearly wink at these well-known codes by opening *Fargo* (1996) with the following caption: "This is a true story. The events depicted in this film took place in Minnesota in 1987. At the request of the survivors, the names have been changed. Out of respect for the dead, the rest has been told exactly as it occurred" (Figure 8). (Incidentally, that same caption now opens each episode of the television series of the same name, on which the Coen brothers serve as executive producers.)

However, the end credits of the film include the standard disclaimer that "The persons and events portrayed in this production are fictitious. No similarity to actual persons, living or dead, is intended or should be inferred." Concerning the "contradictory game" between the two statements, Luhr (2004, pp. 2–3) observes that "the first one is […] part of a complex strategy to guide the viewer's response to the film. Regardless of whether the first statement is true, it is certainly no joke. It sets a somber mood that is reinforced by the tone of the opening scenes. […] Fact-based or not, the film strives for the *feel* of actual events and invites the viewer to accept its story as such." Indeed, Joel Coen has commented that he and his brother were not interested in making *Fargo* a film with documentary value, but that they were well aware that "by telling the public that we took our inspiration from reality, we knew they wouldn't see the movie as just an ordinary thriller" (Ciment/Niogret 2004, p. 109). To put it into our terms, they wanted to make a film in the atmosphere of a particular mode of consciousness. In other words, they wanted to make a film inspired by the true story genre, in the "true story style."

One might initially assume that the positional nature of documentary cinema would be more clear-cut, but cinematic history is rife with examples of its contamination with fiction (Werner Herzog documentaries being one prime example), and recent filmmakers have experimented with new and unprecedented articulations of the relationship between image and belief. Two examples well known among cinema scholars include Pedro Costa's *In Vanda's Room* (*No quarto da Vanda*, 2000, though we might also mention his recent *Vitalina Varela*, 2019) and Joshua Oppenheimer et al.'s *The Act of Killing* (2012). These are but a few of the many examples of how cinematic reflection is aggressively investigating the gray areas in which phantasy and reality seem to merge or overlap.

Even in the documentary realm, the "what" cannot be separated from the "how." These two thematic poles are not abstractly separated. We can focus our attention in either or both directions; either may represent our main interest, but this does not mean that one is given without the other. Each of the two poles ("what" and "how") may be more or less developed, may remain latent and "virtual," may become the (implicit or explicit) focus of our experience.

2.10 Living in the Aesthetic Feeling

Before concluding our examination of Text no. 15h, we need to clarify one last important aspect we touched upon above. In this text Husserl specifies that, although aesthetic attitude puts existential interest out of play, it does not nullify positional attitudes (just as, in a more general sense, phenomenological *epoché* does not nullify reality); this may indeed contribute to the whole of the aesthetic experience.

Such an elucidation may seem paradoxical: if aesthetic feeling implies disinterest in existence, why ask what role belief in existence might play in the emergence of such a feeling? In this context, however, the remark does appear to pose a legitimate question. Though, as we have said, aesthetic feeling is essentially related to the "how," Husserl is aware that emphasizing this "how" in an abstracting approach may give rise to misunderstandings, which is why he specifies that the "what" can affect aesthetic feeling as well. We outlined the reasons for this above: firstly, because the "how" encompasses the "what," and the aesthetic turn is continuous movement between the two poles; secondly, because the sense and quality of what manifests itself can enhance or undermine our aesthetic feelings. Moreover, all modes of manifestation involve manifestations of things within a context of signification, in a horizon of sense, a system of mutual and interacting references that are also part of the "what." They cannot simply be abstracted from the "how."

Given that this manuscript is where Husserl specifies that the aesthetic turn cannot be abstractly detached from the object represented (that, indeed, it bears a responsibility toward that object), it seems less strange that Husserl is prompted to ask whether the presence or absence of belief in the actual existence of the "what" can ultimately affect aesthetic feeling.

It is essential that we attempt to clarify this point, which constitutes a re-evaluation of the dimension of belief in aesthetic consciousness—an aspect that his earlier approach, notably as epitomized in his letter to Hofmannsthal, risked dismissing in an excessively normative way. Of course, this issue does not pertain exclusively to images imbued with belief; it concerns all four of the dimensions listed above. Here, Husserl approaches the question by considering a natural landscape, a "what" in the flesh. As we have seen, he had used this example in previous manuscripts, suggesting that, in this attitude, we would view the landscape *as* an image. This time, however, Husserl explains that neutralization of the posited reality is not necessary: "if, for example, I contemplate *nature* aesthetically, then nature remains for me this determinate *actuality*." In other words, the fact

> that I do not live in the actuality consciousness does not mean that I exclude it by shifting into a corresponding "mere presentation." Rather, it means that I live in feelings that are determined by nature's manner of appearing, by this or that way of being conscious of nature. And in looking at these "subjective" modes of givenness, and in the shift from the focus on the object to this reflective focus and vice versa, I am conscious of the feelings as affective determinations of the object itself. (Hua XXIII, pp. 463–464)

There is no need for us to come to experience the landscape as an image. Rather, Husserl seems to leave open the possibility that belief in reality can itself be aesthetically co-determined. This, in conjunction with our observations on the intertwining of acts, speaks against the need to separate or mutually exclude different kinds of attitudes in such cases, although we can certainly continue drawing phenomenological distinctions between aesthetic feelings and feelings specifically related to the existence of objects. In the latter, it is the "belief in being [*Seinsglaube*] that grounds the feeling": we feel joy or love because something exists, that it has happened or will happen, without yet thematically addressing our interest in how it happened or will happen. Note that Husserl seems to view such feelings as directly related to actuality (though later we will examine the nature of these feelings when they arise in connection with fictional people or events). Aesthetic feelings, on the other hand, are elicited through the reflexive *fold* of our attention from the "what" to the "how" and vice versa. As we have said, aesthetic attitude does not pass through the manifestation giving exclusive attention to the object; rather, it considers the object by repeatedly "folding back" into the mode of manifestation.[142]

---

[142] This manuscript also seems to propose correlating terms that had previously been associated

As should now have become clear, Husserl's explorations of the relationship between the how and the what—as two distinguishable but not separate forms of interest—does not find its final formulation in his letter to Hofmannsthal. His subsequent analyses bring forth new possibilities of articulation, opening up further questions. Though his 1907 line of argumentation posited that passing to aesthetic experience automatically entailed setting aside the question of an object's existence, these new questions oblige us to reconsider other modalities of passage between the different attitudes we might experience toward an object. Later on, we shall attempt to develop these insights in the specific context of different possible ways to experience images.

Conversely, as Husserl explains, I can live in the aesthetic attitude (for example one elicited in me by a natural landscape), and then, *without having to abandon that aesthetic attitude*, I can shift into a consciousness of reality (for example, to explore my surroundings, my perceptual horizon). Phenomenological description must be able to account for these interweavings as well. In this sense, it is not surprising that this manuscript draws upon the idea of "thematic primacy," which clearly resonates with the *"domineering action"* notion we discussed above in context of *Philosophy I* and *Ideas II*.

Thus, we might suggest that Husserl comes to outline two possible senses in which one might refer to living in an aesthetic feeling: the narrower sense, which we have characterized as a dynamic folding toward the mode of manifestation; and a broader sense, in which the aesthetic attitude is the privileged thematic horizon against whose backdrop other acts may be performed—acts whose fulfillment would occur in a manner subordinate to the nourishment of the dominant aesthetic feeling. As we have seen, and as the following quote reiterates, "grasping actuality" can contribute to the aesthetic effect in this broader sense:

> *Living* in feeling has a double significance. In one sense, it means *turning toward:* here, in aesthetic feeling, turning toward the manner of appearing, which thereby gains a distinctive mode. In the other sense, it means *thematic primacy.* If I contemplate nature and progressively take cognizance of it, the aesthetic consciousness can nevertheless have thematic primacy (even though in the aesthetic consciousness I am not turned toward something in the first sense). The actuality is not the theme of my consciousness, but instead the beauty of its manner of appearing, or the actuality in the beauty of its manner of appearing. The grasping of

---

under a completely different approach. Here (as in the 1907 letter to Hofmannsthal), "aesthetic pleasure" is defined as compatible with theoretical interest. One example would be the joy of knowledge, such as mathematical knowledge—the joy one derives from the beauty one sees in ratios, theorems, proofs, etc. (there would be no apathetic *theoresis*; as Richir (1999, p. 22) notes, there would be a *Stimmung* proper to *theoria*).

actuality, the cognizance-taking, is not as such a thematic act. Only insofar as it carries on through the appearance series, which I taste in their aesthetic effect. (Hua XXIII, pp. 464–465)

2.11 The Portrait and Its *Sujet*

The 1912 Husserlian manuscript on aesthetic consciousness offers an even further declination of the discourse we have developed thus far concerning the relationship between image and copy vis-à-vis the notion of representation; I shall attempt to develop this line of thought in order to elaborate upon some of the key implications opened up by our previous phenomenological analyses. To this end, I will now turn to Diderot's *Salons*, the famous *comptes rendus* of the Paris Biennial Exhibition of the Académie Royale de Peinture et de Sculpture, which Diderot compiled for the *Correspondance littéraire* from 1759 to 1781 (1773, 1777, and 1779 excepted). I shall refer to the *Salons* several times in the present work. For now, suffice it to recall that Diderot's task consisted in drawing up a literary account of works on exhibit at the *Salon Carré* in the Louvre and that the pages he sent to the prestigious magazine were intended to provide updates on the great exhibition to its influential subscribers, a restricted circle of foreign aristocrats and sovereigns who could not admire the masterpieces on display in Paris "in the flesh."[143] Diderot's *Salons* strongly indicate what is at stake when it comes to the *choice* of mode of manifestation, of the specific "hows" through which different artists presentify the same pictorial *sujet*—consider, to refer to the *Salons*, the different renditions of *sujets* such as *Susanna and the Elders* or *Roman Charity*. We have seen that, in Husserl's view, this involves a problem of *expression*. More specifically, I suggest that in Diderot's work, the creative power of the genesis of forms and colors is more important to a painting than any external references in it (the full relevance of this question will become evident in the third chapter).

Indeed, even when striving to be faithful to a model in their work, the painter will always be "condemned" to *recreate* an *expression* on a canvas—in other words, to create their own *sujet*. Undoubtedly, the resulting expression may go in a different direction from the artist's original plan. For example, despite having good intentions to paint Christ, the artist's resulting work might depict a drowned man, his "head livid and rotten."[144] Sharp Diderotian irony aside, these "exchanges

---

[143] On the peculiar and original ekphrastic function of Diderot's *Salons*, see Mazzocut-Mis 2016.
[144] "Pierre, my friend, your Christ, with his livid and rotten head, is a drowned man who has sojourned at least fifteen days in the nets of Saint Cloud" (Diderot 2007 [1761], p. 122).

of person" point us to a phenomenon deeper than a simple lack of painterly control: the autonomous expressive power of the depiction.

The lesson I see in Diderot's work is that even the most faithful and accurate *Ab-bildung* always has an essential, inextricable element of *"Bildung,"* of *"figurativeness,"* which is always given through a mode of manifestation with its own expressive autonomy.[145] Portraits, seemingly representational art *par excellence,* are no exception in this regard; we might also say that the figurativeness expressed by the image is the same whether the person is real or fictional. In a similar vein, in the 1912 manuscript on aesthetic consideration, Husserl notes that "the portrait serves me as a presentification of the person: the description of the person is indifferent to being and nonbeing. The description is the same whether the person is an actual person or an imaginary one" (Hua XXIII, p. 463).

If I set aside the "position of being" that might be linked to the image—the *ab-* in *Abbildung* that denotes the possibility of the image finding its own fulfillment in an original for which the image is merely a depictive (representative) proxy—I am then living in "pure presentifications." In a "pure presentification," "it is irrelevant [...] whether or not I take the person to be an actual person" the way I would with a "portrait in the proper sense" (a portrait understood to be a presentification in the image of an absent original). This, as we know, does not "in itself" constitute an "aesthetic act" (Hua XXIII, p. 463); moving *toward* the mode of manifestation is what triggers the aesthetic feeling proper.

We have already mentioned the importance of not being overhasty in associating aesthetic attitude with neutrality. We have discussed how promoting disinterest in the being or nonbeing of an object is certainly not enough to generate aesthetic experience: "nondoxic" and "apositional" are not equivalent to "aesthetic." In a certain sense, Husserl's (necessarily brief) discussion of the topic in his letter to Hofmannsthal could give rise to this misunderstanding as Husserl in fact juxtaposes phenomenologists and artists in the name of neutrality. However, this notion turns out to be too broad, which suggests that additional analyses are necessary in order to define the major differences between phenomena that might otherwise be confusingly equated.

---

[145] Making reference to Brentano 1874 (pp. 170–172) and to Twardowski 1894 (pp. 12–15), Paolo Spinicci also rightly stressed a similar point: "when we say that a painting depicts something, we use an *ambiguous* expression. A portrait—*The Lady with an Ermine* by Leonardo—depicts Cecilia Gallerani, and here we mean to say that *it applies* to this person [...]. However, we must distinguish another meaning of the verb 'to depict,' since every image, regardless of whether it applies to the world or not, stages a spectacle that does not refer to something beyond itself [...]. I am referring in this regard to the *figurativeness* of images, and to the *figurative presence* of what manifests itself within them" (Spinicci 2008, pp. 23–24).

Let us start by clarifying that the positional image, as we have defined it, does maintain its dimension of neutrality as regards its nature of image. This neutrality is tied to its status as an image—as a presentification, not a presentation—and is not revoked by the ray of belief passing through it: I might believe what I see in an image, but I cannot physically touch it there where I am viewing it (in a newspaper or on screen, for example).

Hence, it is useful to distinguish between two ways of understanding the dimension of neutrality, as their inadvertent confusion could undermine analyses of these phenomena. As we will discuss in more detail in the third chapter, we can refer to a neutrality consubstantial to the image, to the image object construed as a nothing that appears without properly occupying a physical place, as unreality contrasting with the surrounding reality. But we can also speak of a neutrality with respect to the *sujet:* for example, as we have just seen, when faced with a positional image, we can decide to drop all reference to the actual belief of what is being presentified and live in a mere figurativeness.

The first type of neutrality, the consubstantial iconic neutrality, is common to all images. When watching a "positional" film in which a person is being harmed, we can suffer and feel the need to intervene, but actually doing so would require us to understand *where* the violence is actually happening. Even an image imbued with belief is essentially a nothing, and we cannot act upon it to stop the violence unfolding before us (unless, of course, the image had an interactive element, but this is a point we cannot linger upon here; either way our point stands as such situations would necessarily involve supplementary knowledge concerning the kind of *link* to the actual dimension).

The images themselves remain a nothing of actuality even when we view them as a direct reflection of actual facts occurring at the moment we observe them. Even though "whenever a picture is perceived as a mere portrait, as the copy [*Abbild*] of a reality, we remain in the doxic attitude" (Dastur 1991, p. 28), the positional attitude we experience in images always implies an involvement with neutrality that differentiates them from the doxic attitude commonly experienced within a perceptual regime. Let us repeat: in images defined as positional, imbued with belief, the neutrality characterizing image consciousness does not disappear by virtue of the ray of reality that passes through them. The condition of neutrality that characterizes image consciousness—specifically that of the image object—holds.

On the other hand—and this is perhaps the most controversial point in all of Husserl's research on the image—the neutrality that pertains to the image does not necessarily correspond to a neutral attitude toward belief in the *sujet*. That is why I am suggesting that our discussion of belief and neutrality distinguish between two directions: one addressed to the image object, the other to the *sujet*. Our discourse on neutrality must also explore the nature of the *sujet* and our implicit or explicit belief in it. According to the structure of seeing-in, we see the *sujet* in the image: we can intuit it by looking into the image, and it can in turn concern us. The image thus reveals a singular power, an implicit creative possibility.

In Chapter 1, we discussed how a photo of our friend is not, properly speaking, our actual friend in the actual world but rather our friend as we see her through the image object manifested when we look at the photo. The similarity between an image and its *sujet* is not technically a similarity between two things, but rather an "intrinsic" relationship: we see our friend according to the *perspective* opened up by that image, not as actually "there" in the place where we see her (on the page, on screen). Of course, the image object that we see on the photograph paper or our mobile screen is usually only a few inches tall; in the case of the black-and-white photos Husserl describes, it is also of an unnatural hue. Whether or not we have ever seen the person in a photo, we know that they are not actually gray- or sepia-toned in real life.

Yet, as we have just remarked, these were and are entirely legitimate considerations within a specific attitude, namely that of comparing the image object and its purported real-world counterpart. Saying an image does not resemble "the original" is, in fact, already relating to it in a specific way, within a particular attitude that does not exhaust its essence. If we shift to the aesthetic attitude, the matter changes considerably, as we can then feel a particular *value* connected to a particular *way of manifestation* of the image and the *sujet* it expresses—for example, toward a specific emotional tonality expressed by a black-and-white image.[146] In cinema, where "how" images are presented to us is a central part of the director's individual style, a colorized version of a black-and-white film like *Citizen Kane* would certainly not be the "same" film (let alone a "better" film by virtue of the "chromatic boost of similarity!").

In light of the considerations elaborated thus far, we can suggest that, although Husserl's initial reflections were written with general eidetic structures in view, his primary focus was on describing the essence of images that functioned specifically as an *Abbildung* of their *sujet*, and that this attitude also conditioned his understanding of artistic images at that time (this initial approach is also what gave rise to the questions listed in the Appendix to *Sacred Love* in Hua XXIII). Under this framework (which we have described as the delegation model), the image invites us to see into it, yet presents itself in place of another object for which it acts

---

146 Whole chapters could easily be devoted to the stylistic peculiarities of the grayscale *quasi*-worlds in black-and-white films. To name a few more recent examples, *Manhattan* (1979) by Woody Allen, *The Elephant Man* (1980) by David Lynch, *Dead Man* (1995) by Jim Jarmusch, *The Man Who Wasn't There* (2001) by the Coen brothers, and *The White Ribbon* (*Das weiße Band*, 2009) by Michael Haneke.

as a representative. The image manifesting itself has no intrinsic value; rather, it functions solely as a "representative [*Stellvertreter*]" (Hua XXIII, p. 26) for another object "like it or resembling it" (Hua XXIII, p. 22).[147]

As discussed in Chapter 1, the representative in such a paradigm is at most (and ideally) permitted equality with the original; it can never offer more than the original. However, this type of relationship functions exclusively within a specific system of meanings and practices, so it would be incorrect to apply it universally. In fact, I would like to stress that creation of a *sujet* seems to take place on the surface of every image, and in my view, Husserl's progressive meditations on the structure of seeing-in can ultimately lead us to conceive a potential space of "independent life" for every image—even portraits, whose autonomous expressive character thus seems perpetually capable of detaching from its possible subordinate relationship to the presumed original.

2.12 Failed Recognitions

The previous paragraphs highlighted the need for further investigation into the nature of the image's *sujet*. In this context, it may be useful to examine another paradigmatic Diderotian example of image description. We discussed how the triadic structure of image consciousness can be found in both an ordinary photograph and a painted portrait. Based on what we have learned regarding the "generalized" notion of phantasy as presentification, we can say that both cases involve

---

[147] This is not to say that Husserl views "Sujetintention" in image consciousness as implying a "signifying" or "symbolic" consciousness (nor, for that matter, is this a view I wish to espouse here). My position differs in this regard from Eldridge's (2017, cf §§ 2.1, 2.2), who refers to "Husserl's symbolic interpretation of the Sujetintention." Eldridge bases his interpretation on a short passage from Text no. 16 in Husserliana XXIII (likely written in Spring 1912) in which Husserl writes: "I have not sufficiently taken into account here that this symbolizing function is by no means unconditionally necessary for the possibility of an 'image' consciousness" (cf. pp. 555–556). According to Eldridge, this implies that Husserl considered the possibility of interpreting image consciousness symbolically before 1912 (the year when the text was written). However, in my view, this highly circumscribed remark refers to the fact that, in a certain sense, reproduction in simple depiction can continue the work of the image object by fulfilling a symbolic demand, construed as an *intuitive* (not symbolic) reproductive function that can accompany image consciousness and make up for the nonanalogizing moments of the image object. Thus, in my view, Husserl does reiterate how such symbolic moments are not absolutely necessary for the emergence of image consciousness, but this does not constitute resolving serious earlier doubts regarding an alleged symbolic-signitive interpretation of image consciousness. In any case, I do not see elements in this manuscript (or others) supporting Eldridge's view that Husserl "seems to equate an image's depictive function with a symbolizing function."

Figure 9: Louis-Michel Van Loo, *Portrait de Denis Diderot* (1767)

a phantasy complying with *perceptio*. Here, of course, phantasy is not meant to suggest that what is phantasized is wholly fictitious, lacking associations to another reality (consider, for example, "impressional" images, whose connection to another reality plays a central role indeed). Rather, it simply indicates that the image itself conflicts with the spatio-temporal context of reality.

The passage we will examine now is taken from the *Salon of 1767*, in which Diderot recounts the moment at the Louvre when he found himself viewing his own portrait, painted by Louis-Michel Van Loo (Figure 9). Despite the many moments of resemblance that seem to allow a viewer to conclude that the portrait does indeed depict Diderot—and despite the unequivocal title (*M. Diderot*)—the famous *philosophe* seems unable to recognize himself in the image. In his *compte rendu* for the *Correspondance littéraire*, he describes the Van Loo portrait as follows:

> Mr. Diderot. Me. I love Michel, but I love the truth still more. Quite similar. [...] Very much alive. [...] But too young, head too small. Graceful as a woman, leering, smiling, cute, lips pursed, simpering. [...] But what will my grandchildren say when they compare my sad works with this laughing, graceful, effeminate pretty boy? My little ones, I warn you, this is not me. In the course of a day, I took on a hundred different physiognomies, depending on what affected me. I was serene, sad, dreamy, tender, violent, passionate, enthusiastic. But I was never as you see me here. (Diderot 2008 [1767], pp. 81–82)

Evidently, this is a case of "nonrecognition." On the one hand, we certainly cannot say that the picture painted by Louis-Michel Van Loo *does not* (or better: *cannot*) *depict* Denis Diderot: we can reasonably say that its expressed *sujet*—what I shall call a *noema*—is Diderot. In fact, *we believe* that the person depicted in the portrait reproduced above is Diderot and, in several respects, *that* man with the mysterious smile resembles him. No one would say that he possesses no resemblance to the *philosophe* whatsoever.

In our case, of course, it is only thanks to other images of Diderot or other written accounts that we are able to say that this image resembles him. For example, we can see a *certain* similarity to other portraits or busts of Diderot that we have seen before in the same sense that we can say such things about a person whom we know only from images and second-hand accounts, and whom we are accordingly able to recognize despite having never seen them in the flesh.[148] At any rate, it seems at least *prima facie* obvious that this portrait could not function as a depiction of Nietzsche, whose *noema* likewise is produced by images of him we have seen before.

Even so, Diderot refuses to recognize himself in that portrait—and his reaction openly reminds us of the other, previously mentioned potential sense of the term *depiction*: as "piction," so to speak. More generally, it is worth underscoring how the *Salons* inaugurate a spectatorial experience (Diderot's, but through him, as Lyotard [1979, pp. 466–467] notes, ours as well) in which, I maintain, the *sujet* we see in the image is always a *sujet* expressed and produced by the image itself—what I have called a *noema*. This *noema* acquires a certain autonomy vis-à-vis the *sujet* that the image is supposed to—or "claims to"—depict.

Such cases highlight a difference that is less about image object vs. image *sujet* (which contributes to the phenomenon of contrast in the delegation model) than about *sujet* referenced by the image vs. *sujet* produced by it. Here, the creative power of depiction—its figurativeness—emerges, and the *sujet* expressed appears to claim difference from the original it purportedly references. We have already suggested that the image object is always "condemned" to create its own *sujet* in a way; now, we find ourselves likely expanding the boundaries of Husserl's own theories by proposing that we use this very lens to reconsider his phenomenon

---

148 As Louis Marin has noted, Diderot previously alluded to this "resemblance without original" in connection with another painting by Louis-Michel Van Loo. Diderot writes: "Louis-Michel Van Loo: the first painting that caught my eye was the *Portrait of the King*. It is beautiful, well painted, and it is said to be a fine resemblance." But "this 'it is said,'" writes Marin, "would deserve a whole gloss: how can I say, me, that the *Portrait of the King* resembles [the king], given that I have never seen the king "in the flesh"? To me, it only looks like resemblant: failure of *mimesis* whose powers are hollowed from the absence of the real [*défaillance de* mimesis *dont les pouvoirs sont creusés de l'absence du réel*]" (Marin 1993, p. 76).

of seeing-in. When Husserl states that seeing-in pertains to the essence of image, he actually goes far beyond his own intentions.

We might consider the image object a manifestation not in contrast to the *sujet* but rather that gives the *sujet* in its unreality (as phantasy in the proper sense). We might view the image object as either one specific adumbration or profile (*Abschattung*) (for fixed images) or a complex of several coherently connected adumbrations or profiles (*Abschattungen*) (for moving images), usually contrasting to the perceptual surroundings, allowing us to see an expressed *noema*, i.e., the *sujet*. It should be emphasized that, even in perception, we never get to see a *sujet* throughout. Properly speaking, the *sujet* is incorporeal, an invisible pole arising from adumbrations; it is sense arising from them and revealing them as a whole.

The phenomenological object, which can be given in all evidence, is an ideality that always exceeds the effective (*reell*) givenness of the sensible manifestation. However, such an ideality *is neither separate from the sensible manifestation nor expressible without it*; the *noema* surpasses the effective impressional content without being separable from it. As such, the phenomenological approach goes beyond the Humean approach, under which genuine evidence seems to be reduced to genuine impressions.¹⁴⁹ The *sujet* is not another effective manifestation, to be distinguished from the image object manifestation; rather, the *sujet* is the object that I see when I look *into* the image object. The *sujet* is the Paul I see when I look at a picture of Paul, with all the shades of meaning opened up by that manifestation (Paul as sad, absorbed, with dark hair, etc.)—an ideality certainly intertwined with the actual mode of manifestation, but an ideality nonetheless. When I meet Paul, when I see him in the picture, when I recall him: it is always Paul manifesting himself, but in different modes of givenness, in different modes of consciousness. Each of these manifestations can modify the *noema* Paul, which is a dynamic essence perpetually constituted and reconstituted by the different manifestations. This is the sense in which every depiction produces its own *sujet:* we see in every depiction its own *noema*, which enjoys a degree of independence from any alleged connection to actual reality or any other manifestation of the same *sujet* (in the same or different modes of consciousness).

Against this background, let us return to the *Salons* passage for some final remarks on the matter of failed recognition. Here, the *sujet* produced in the philos-

---

149 Regarding the intrinsic relationship between effective sensible givenness and exceeding sense, our proposal is in keeping with Costa (2007, pp. 123–124): "This is a crucial point: here, the term 'transcendence' does not refer to a 'being beyond the phenomenon,' which would imply a separateness; rather, it refers to an excess directly linked to the manifestation but not reducible to it, because it is the other side of the sensible, it is sense, it is *noema*." As I pointed out above, I construe the *noema* as the expressed of the sensible.

opher's portrait gives rise to a phenomenon of nonrecognition, despite the painter's explicit intentions to the contrary. The converse is obviously possible as well: the painter might inadvertently render a faithful depiction. In the same *compte rendu* in which Diderot describes viewing Van Loo's portrait of that "stranger" claimed to be himself (a stranger who shares many moments of similarity with Diderot yet betrays him in essence), Diderot refers to a different portrait that he believes captures him accurately. Curiously, however, the painter in question was not a particularly masterful one—Diderot, at least, describes him as "a poor devil named Garant [sic],[150] who captured me the same way a fool sometimes comes up with a witty remark" (Diderot 2008 [1767], p. 83).[151]

One might reasonably assume that this second portrait (which is unfortunately lost to time; we are left with only a drawing by Garand and an engraving by Chenu; Figure 10[152]) presents fewer moments of resemblance to the *sujet* it purportedly presentifies, yet Diderot considers it a more faithful rendition than Van Loo's. How? Let us recall Descartes' remarks that a less-detailed portrait can be more accurate than a highly detailed one. Diderot's explanation is, in a similar vein, very simple: "The one who sees my portrait painted by Garand sees me. *Ecco il vero Polichinello*[153]" (Diderot 2008 [1767], p. 83). In other words, he sees a *noema* that expresses some of what he considers his essential traits, and therefore he recognizes himself.

Let us now return to our discussion of theater and come full circle as regards the productive dimension of the image. As mentioned, Husserl acknowledges that theatrical images can assume a depictive function. For example, when watching a play in which one of the characters is a real historical figure, it would not be incorrect to say that that person is depicted in the scene. What Husserl suggests, however, is that the delegative attitude is not essential to our aesthetic and artistic experience of that representation (though we can certainly focus our attention on the depictive relationship if we choose). In the shift in thematic attitude through which theater invites us into the fictional and artistic/aesthetic spheres (I continue to draw such distinctions, though they often overlap), even moments of so-called dissimilarity (which Husserl's 1904–05 analysis cited as key to defining the con-

---

150 Jean-Baptiste Garand portrayed Diderot in September 1760 at Mme d'Épinay's dwelling at La Chevrette. Note what Diderot writes to Sophie Volland relating to this portrait: "I am represented [...] as someone who is meditating. I am indeed meditating on this canvas. I am alive, I am breathing, I am animated; the thinking shows through the forehead" (Diderot 1955–1970, Vol. 4, p. 73).
151 For a comparison between the two portraits on the basis of this *compte rendu*, with a particular focus on the theme of absorption, see Fried (1988, pp. 111–115).
152 Cf. Dieckmann (1952, pp. 6–7).
153 In Italian in the original text.

Figure 10: Pencil drawing on the left: Jean-Baptiste Garand, *Portrait de Diderot* (ca. 1760). On the right: Pierre Chenu, engraving by Jean-Baptiste Garand, *Portrait de Diderot* (ca. 1760)

trast between image object and image *sujet*) can take on seminal importance for expressing a *sujet*, a *noema*, and can fit perfectly into the overall image world pre-sentified in the play. This is equally true for portraits and their expressive capacities.

It is against this background that we can understand Husserl's remark in Text no. 18b that theater does not constitute "a presentation [*Darstellung*] in the sense in which we say of an image object that an image *sujet* is presented in it" (Hua XXIII, p. 616). That is, we can construe theatrical image as bypassing the relation between image object and image *sujet* conceived on the *Abbildung* model, under which the former would be a subordinate image of the latter:

> Neither the actor nor the image that is his performance for us is an image object in which another object, an actual or even fictive image *sujet*, is depicted. (The performance of the actor here means the *production* of an "image" by means of his real actions, and among these are his movements, his change of expression, his external "appearance," which is his production). An actual depicting presents itself in the case of a portrait, which, moreover, can just as well be the portrait of an imaginary person as of an actual person. And furthermore, the depictiveness here may itself fall into the aesthetic consciousness as aesthetic. But when a play is presented, no consciousness of depiction whatsoever needs to be excited, and what then appears is a pure figment complying with *perceptio*. (Hua XXIII, pp. 616–617, my italics)

Husserl is not claiming that the character of image (*Bildlichkeit*) falls under theatrical experience; rather, he insists that what falls under it (since it becomes inessential) is the character of depiction (*Abbildlichkeit*), thus leaving room for an experience of image in the sense of a phantasy complying with *perceptio*, an immediate *imaginatio:* the actor creates the *noema* of the character, which we can then see directly. In the first chapter, we mentioned this in the context of Proust discussing the actress Berma's creation of Phaedra. What happens on stage is thus not conversion into image (*Verbildlichung*) as a proxy for absent persons and objects but a presentation of *ficta* to be lived directly in the "as if"—an immediate *imaginatio* in the sense of immediate phantasy, a direct seeing of what is manifested in the temporality consciousness of *as if it were*. As we have just seen, this is also true of a portrait construed as a phantasy complying with *perceptio* and not in its depictive function, not in its role (one among several others) as a proxy for something (real or fictitious) that precedes it and purportedly serves as a guideline for it.

We noted how, elsewhere in Text no. 18b, Husserl expressly distinguishes between perceptual illusion (in the sense of a deceptive *belief* in reality) and artistic illusion (in the sense of conscious "entry into a playful dimension" having aesthetic value). At this juncture, let us elaborate further by recalling how Husserl draws this distinction in Appendix L (1912) to Hua XXIII, Text no. 16, which offers precious insights into the notion of phantasy complying with *perceptio:* Husserl differentiates between 1) cases that can be traced back to "the example of the mannequin/human being,"[154] in which there are "unmodified apprehension tendencies, belief tendencies fighting with belief tendencies"—the consciousness set out to determine and fix a belief among two or more possibilities—and 2) cases ascribable to "image apprehensions, specifically the ordinary aesthetic image apprehensions," in which we do not have "real belief tendencies" clashing with one another, but

> Rather, the situation is just like that in which I vivaciously project something into reality from phantasy. The difference consists only in the fact that the "phantasy image" is a reproductive image, the seen image an image complying with *perceptio*. Both [*scil*. Reproductive image and

---

[154] Husserl references his well-known example of a wax mannequin being mistaken for a woman as early as in the *Logical Investigations:* "Wandering about in the Panopticum Waxworks we meet on the stairs a charming lady whom we do not know and who seems to know us, and who is in fact the well-known joke of the place: we have for a moment been tricked by a waxwork figure. As long as we *are* tricked, we experience a perfectly good percept: we see a lady and not a waxwork figure. When the illusion vanishes, we see exactly the opposite, a waxwork figure that only *represents* a lady. Such talk of 'representing' does not of course mean that the waxwork figure is modelled on a lady as in the same waxworks there are figure-models *of* Napoleon, *of* Bismarck etc." (Hua XIX/1 Vol. 2, pp. 137–138).

image complying with *perceptio*] *are cases of imaginatio*. This must *never* be forgotten and is absolutely *certain*. (Hua XXIII, p. 570)

Here, again, Husserl alludes to a universalized phantasy consciousness grounding phantasies with and without iconic images; Husserl categorizes both as *imaginatio* (*Imagination*), but we might as well say they are both examples of phantasy since here he is talking about *imaginatio* in the second of the two meanings derived through his Göttingen analysis. As we have seen, by the end of the third *Hauptstück*, Husserl had come to distinguish between an "*imaginatio* in the proper sense," conceived in the manner of a "conversion into an image," and an "*imaginatio* as phantasy," the sense under investigation here.[155]

2.13 Rise of the Mannequins? Illusion and Art

Though Husserl does not use his "mannequin-man" example expressly to discuss phantasy consciousness, it can certainly contribute a variety of interesting insights on artistic and fictional experiences. For one thing, we can mistake not only a wax mannequin for a man, but a work of art for a man or, more generally, a work of art for something else—especially when viewing it out of context. A friend of mine who works in a museum told me that one morning he spotted a stranger in a room used for restoration. My friend was taken aback at first, but then the alleged intruder's rigid posture betrayed "his" true identity: it was a sculpture by Duane Hanson. Illusions can even be elicited in an exhibit context, and not only through hyperrealistic sculptures but also by large paintings (for example), as Sartre reports in *The Imaginary:*

> At the museum in Rouen, suddenly entering an unfamiliar room, I happened to take the people in a large picture for actual men. The illusion was of very short duration—a quarter of a second, perhaps—it remains nonetheless that I did not have, during this negligible lapse of time, an imaged consciousness [*conscience imagée*], but on the contrary, a perceptual consciousness. Without doubt, the synthesis was poorly made and the perception false, but that false perception was nonetheless a perception. (Sartre 1940, p. 22)

Up to this point, the way Sartre characterizes his experience is fully in line with Husserl's descriptions. Yet the conclusions he draws from this *perceptual* illusion lasting "a quarter of a second" seem to go in the opposite direction:

---

[155] Cf. *supra*, Chapter 1.9. Accordingly, in this same Appendix L, Husserl talks about the "ground of phantasy, of *imaginatio*" (Hua XXIII, p. 569).

> It is the case that, in the picture, there is the appearance of a man. If I approach it, the illusion disappears, but the cause of the illusion persists: the picture, made to resemble a human being, acts on me as would a man, whatever attitude of consciousness I took towards it in other respects; this knitting of the brows, on the canvas, directly moves me, because the cleverly prepared synthesis "brows" is itself carried out even before I make these brows "image brows" or real brows; the *composure* [*calme*] of this figure *moves me* directly whatever interpretation I may give it. In brief, these elements in themselves are neutral; they can enter into a synthesis of imagination or of perception. But although they are *neutral*, they are *expressive*. If I decide to continue to perceive it, if I look at the painting purely aesthetically, if I consider the relations between the colours, the form, the brush strokes, if I study the purely technical procedures of the painter, the expressive value does not disappear for all that; the person in the painting solicits me gently to take him for a man. Likewise, if I know (*connais*) the subject of the portrait, the portrait will have, before any interpretation, a real force, a resemblance. (Sartre 1940, p. 22, my italics)

What specifically could cause confusion here is Sartre's assertion that "the person in the painting solicits [him] gently to take him for a man." From a Husserlian standpoint, art should not deceive—even though, as Sartre notes, it can make us feel as if we were face-to-face with a presentified person. Art can undoubtedly play with deception or illusion; it is not for us to decide whether this is true or not as its own history says so. We must choose our words carefully when describing such experiences. There is a sharp difference between "as if"/*quasi* and perceptual illusion, one that becomes evident under phenomenological analysis. The "as if" experience—here, the one in which I look at a face in a painting "as if it were there in front of me"—is always tinged with an awareness of fictionality that prevents us from falling victim to the genuine perceptual illusion (see Hua XXIII, p. 45).

Obviously, art is not the only context in which perceptual illusions can occur; one object that looks similar to another object may be all that is required. This discussion concerns the more general problem of describing the genesis of our *belief* in reality. As we have begun to see, this cannot be based solely on some privilege afforded to flesh-and-blood presence; rather, it hinges on how we articulate the difference between reality and phantasy. Earlier, I went as far as to say that the capacity to consider other possibilities besides what "there is," to vary what manifests itself to us, is a transcendental condition for the emergence of the concept of reality itself.

Along these lines, one might *in primis* retort to Sartre that the picture does not "act on me as would a man" in context of habitual perception (although one might explore the common structures between the two experiences). In any event, beyond the Sartrian experience just described, perceptual illusions seem to have found a place in contemporary art, and some may see this as a crisis for the Husserlian approach to artistic phenomena, especially when it comes to hyperrealism.

Truth be told, however, this view is based more on Husserlian aesthetic consciousness as articulated in 1904–1905 than on any real attempt to understand it in the context of subsequent developments.[156] Approaches from this perspective are primarily focused on the facts that Husserl's Göttingen analyses state i) that image consciousness must always involve a difference between image and thing, lest it shift into a consciousness of illusion (see Steinmetz 2011, p. 126); and ii) that "the delight in blunt disappointment or in the crude conflict between reality and semblance, in which now semblance passes itself off as reality, now reality as semblance [...] is the most extreme antithesis to aesthetic pleasure, which is grounded on the peaceful and clear consciousness of imaging. Aesthetic effects are not the effects of annual fairs" (Hua XXIII, p. 44; see Steinmetz 2011, pp. 138–140).

Let us make a few brief clarifying observations on this alleged contradiction. As we have seen, describing a phenomenon eidetically (perceptual illusion, in this case) is one matter; asking how artistic practices can bring that phenomenon into play (within the context of specific historical dynamics in the art world) is another. We should begin by recalling that Husserl primarily uses his "mannequin-man" example to describe situations involving perceptual deception, such as when we confuse one thing for another or when someone plays a joke on us. As Husserl remarks, the "mannequin-woman" who winks at him from a staircase at the *Panoptikum*, playing a brief trick on him, is specifically "calculated to deceive."[157] Conversely, a famous person might pretend to be a statue at a wax museum and then suddenly "come to life"; the surprise this would evoke in spectators would represent the "pendant" to the surprise Husserl experienced on the staircase at the waxworks. Clearly, this does not exclude the possibility of the artist elaborating on these expectation structures in their work as well. I recently visited the exhibition *Shift. AI and a Future Community* at the Kunstmuseum Stuttgart.[158] As I came to Louisa Clement's "Repräsentantin" (2021; Figure 11), which I immediately recognized as a female mannequin, I was not expecting her to move. When I approach-

---

[156] For an example of these critiques, see Steinmetz (2006); they are explored and expounded upon in Steinmetz (2011), a broader volume devoted to Husserl's "phenomenological aesthetics" (see pp. 119–160).
[157] In another 1912 manuscript from Hua XXIII, Husserl returns to the experience he had years prior at the Berlin *Panoptikum*, which he had previously mentioned in the *Logical Investigations* (see note 154 above): "I *remember* the scene at the waxworks in Berlin: How startled I was when the all-too-amiable "lady" on the staircase beckoned to me. But how, after somewhat regaining my composure, I suddenly recognized that this was a mannequin calculated to deceive me" (Hua XXIII, p. 497).
[158] *Shift. AI and a Future Community* (Feb. 4, 2023–May 21, 2023), Kunstmuseum Stuttgart.

Figure 11: Louisa Clement, *Repräsentantinnen* (2021). Installation view of the exhibition *SHIFT. AI and a future community* (04.02.–21.05.2023), Kunstmuseum Stuttgart, Foto: Gerald Ulmann, Stuttgart

ed her, she turned her head and looked at me, creating an uncanny effect "for a quarter of a second".

Such considerations should firstly interest us on an eidetic level as they describe phenomena we have all experienced many times—whenever our positional consciousness takes something for something else or vacillates uncertainly between two (or more) *perceptual* possibilities. It is not by chance that Husserl devotes considerable space to this phenomenon in his lectures on "passive synthesis", making extensive use of the mannequin-man example.

The danger here is in erroneously asserting that Husserl "claims to say *a priori*, in advance, what [art] is" (Steinmetz 2011, p. 141); if we can be certain of one thing, it is that this was not his intention. As Brough (1988) suggests, in order to examine the constitutive laws of the artistic sphere from a phenomenological perspective—with the goal of describing the "spiritual world" of the art world—it is probably best for us to turn to the *Crisis*. As regards the specific question of the threat that hyperrealist works (as an art form that tends to suppress the contrast between image and thing ostensibly required for image consciousness to develop) might represent for a Husserlian approach to art, let us recall that, even when Husserl notes the need for "consciousness of difference" (Hua XXIII, pp. 44, 162) between image object and image *sujet* in his Göttingen lectures, he does not exclude the possibility of cases in which the representative and the represented are identical.[159] In fact, another 1912 manuscript (Hua XXIII, Text no. 17, Section A, p. 581ff.)

---

[159] "If the appearing image were absolutely identical phenomenally with the object meant, or, bet-

contemplates the possibility for image consciousness to arise even with an image object having identical traits to those of the depicted person;[160] in Section C of that same text, he goes as far as to write, "I must be on guard against generalizing improperly: as if image and conflict were necessarily connected" (Hua XXIII, p. 589).

As such, the fact that contemporary art often tests the limits of conventional boundaries between perception and image does not detract from the eidetic descriptions we have developed thus far; our concern here should instead be with examining how the elucidated structures apply to those gray areas of intersection between phantasy and reality, those mixed experiences for which we often lack vocabulary beyond the merely metaphorical. Daniel Buren's "work *in situ*," Marina Abramović's performances exposing her own body, Sophie Calle's "mises en scène" that present "stories" blurring "the line of demarcation between the field of reality and that of the imaginary" lies (cf. Steinmetz 2011, p. 132), Duane Hanson's and John De Andrea's sculptures (cf. Steinmetz 2011, p. 160): these and other examples should represent not counterarguments to Husserlian phenomenological research on artistic image, but rather invitations to develop new levels of descriptions.

2.14 Expressive Elements

Let us conclude this chapter by returning to Sartre's description of his "encounter" at the museum to highlight one final aspect that will be relevant to our discussion in Chapter 3. Even though we have been unwilling to concede to Sartre's assertion that paintings have a tendency toward illusion (at least in the sense that the person presented in image "solicits me gently to take him for a[n actual] man"), should we not agree when he describes the "appearance of a man" at the Rouen museum as having a "composure," a "knitting of the brows" that "directly moves [him]"?

In keeping with our previous considerations regarding the *noema*, I would like to suggest that these effects do not in themselves undergo modification relative to a

---

ter, if the image appearance showed no difference whatsoever from the perceptual appearance of the object itself, a depictive consciousness could scarcely come about. This is certain: A consciousness of difference must be there, albeit the *sujet* does not appear in the proper sense. The appearing object is not just taken by itself, but as the representant of another object *like it or resembling it* [*ihm gleiches oder ähnliches*]" (Hua XXIII, p. 22, my italics).

160 "The spatiality of the image object and the spatiality of the image *sujet* can coincide [...], as in the case of the bust's head, which has a human being's natural size. [...] Colors can also enter into the analogizing. And there is even more in drama: it goes much further. Human beings, living human beings, analogize, depict human beings *without illusion*" (Hua XXIII, pp. 583–584, my italics).

position of existence; indeed, as Sartre points out, they seem more originary than the various modalizations they can undergo. (As we have read, he notes that the "synthesis 'brows' is itself carried out even before I make these brows 'image brows' or real brows.") We can, in fact, feel the breath of that "composure" regardless of the regime in which it manifests itself (perceptual, iconic, or even merely reproductive, with the various levels of *belief* that might be at play in each). Although it is legitimate to say that we are looking at a presentification of a man in this particular case, it would not be correct to *eo ipso* infer that we are viewing a presentification of "composure." As we can also see from the previous *Imaginaire* passage, this calm is a "neutral element," "expressive," something that can arise for us equally through a flesh-and-blood face we believe to be real or a painting of a face with no real-world reference whatsoever.

This capacity for expression is fundamental to many forms of art. For example, through imaginative variation, art can open us up to experiencing *neutral events*, which we can then recognize in everyday life, and which can in turn be re-expressed through new phantasy deformations (we shall investigate this more thoroughly in Chapter 3). As we shall see, this movement triggers a continuous exchange between art and life that we could define as chiasmatic; such an exchange plays a decisive role in our infinite inquiries into *sense* and what we call "truth." This neutral expressive dimension also captured the attention of Merleau-Ponty, who, considering a passage about the "long-dead monarch's smile" in Sartre's *Nausea*, develops the idea of a painting that "scrambles all our categories" insofar as it *expresses events* resistant to changes in attitude by our consciousness:

> Consider, as Sartre did in *Nausea*, the smile of a long-dead monarch which keeps producing and reproducing itself [*de se produire et de se reproduire*] on the surface of a canvas. It is too little to say that it is there as an image or essence; it is there as itself, as that which was always most alive about it, the moment I look at the painting. The "world's instant" that Cézanne wanted to paint, an instant long since passed away, is still hurled toward us by his paintings. His *Mont Sainte-Victoire* is made and remade from one end of the world to the other in a way different from but no less energetic than in the hard rock above Aix. Essence and existence, imaginary and real, visible and invisible—painting scrambles all our categories, spreading out before us its oneiric universe of carnal essences, actualized resemblances, mute meanings. (Merleau-Ponty 1960–1961, p. 130)

Here, Merleau-Ponty refers to a smile that is "producing and reproducing itself on the surface of a canvas […] as that which was always most alive about it." We could also describe the smile of *Nausea*'s monarch as one that *is* always new and alive, since it is not tied to a specific chronological reference point. Though *de facto* bound to the lifespan of the surface material, the smile shines *de jure* with an eternity continuously recreated. In this sense, we can say that this smile "is still hurled

2.14 Expressive Elements — 143

toward us," impassive to the difference between reality and phantasy, perception and image.

Before moving on to Chapter 3, let us address one last point concerning the relationship between the sensible texture of an image or work of art and these "neutral qualities" that cannot be reduced to merely physical features. Emphasizing this expressive dimension is by no means intended to disenfranchise the sensible dimension. This clarification also holds as regards Husserlian characterization of aesthetic experience. In principle, as we have seen, every stance, judgment, or feeling concerning the existence or nonexistence of the thing manifested is put out of play in aesthetic consciousness; we can shift thematically toward an attitude not affected by the belief in the actual existence or nonexistence of something. Yet this does not mean that the quality and nature of the sensible material expressing the *ideal noema* are of no importance. For instance, I might like how a certain blue door looks from a certain angle at a certain time of day, but despite what all this talk of "putting reality out of play" might lead us to believe, this is not to say that the emergence of the aesthetic experience is independent of the object's materiality. The sensible texture of a manifestation (the blue grained door's materiality) contributes toward the constitution of the "how" and the expression of the *noema*.

This is also true when it comes to images. On the one hand, an interpretation of the Husserlian image consciousness based entirely upon the delegation model might well deny that the material plays any role in the *sujet*'s presentification on the basis that the physical image never comes to manifest itself in image consciousness. It is true that Husserl specifies that the material content is taken away from perceptual consciousness and put in service of manifesting the image object, which is no longer something perceived (*wahrgenommen*) but rather merely a *perceptum*. However, in a note in the margins of the Göttingen course, he also mentions that the material dimension can contribute to the aesthetic effect.[161] At most, we might say that our purely aesthetic feelings do not seem to be based on materiality conceived as something *positionally existing*—in other words, not based on the perceived but on the *perceptum*. This also holds true with, for example, a nonfigurative, monochromatic image. In this respect, a gray monochrome painting by Gerhard Richter can become an "image object" if understood in the sense that the "grey, which presents itself in image and as image, is not posited

---

[161] "Since I did not talk about it earlier, I call attention to the aesthetic function of the means and materials of reproduction, for example, the bold brushwork of many masters, the aesthetic effect of marble, and so on" (Hua XXIII, p. 55).

as *real.*"¹⁶² We might more simply say: *perzeptive Phantasie*. Nevertheless, despite the differences in modality of consciousness with respect to the wall behind the painting, the material continues to act in all its sensible richness.

Were we in a museum, we could follow the concordant synthesis of a perceptual experience that progresses from the white ceiling along the wall to, say, Richter's gray or Yves Klein's patented International Klein Blue (IKB). Properly speaking, this perceptual synthesis—which takes its manifestation as real (*wahrnehmend*)—does not continue into that gray or that blue, although it *could*. Though image boundaries are usually well defined (for example by a frame, yet *not necessarily* by one), we can make perceptive synthesis cross the ideal boundaries of the painting and instead perceive—take as existing—the material that supports the creation of the painting, its physical paint different from the paint on the wall yet perceptible in the same way that the wall paint is.

Now, suppose we heard someone complain that this monochromatic work is nothing but paint slapped onto canvas—"certainly not art," as the cliché goes. Phenomenologically, that person had their *own* valid reason for making such a complaint: they were merely perceiving the paint as existing in its synthetic qualitative continuity with the rest of the wall. Rather than perceiving the image, they merely perceived the physical thing hanging on the wall and the paint spread across it. Perhaps it was a legitimate experience after all. Be that as it may, the fact is that no aesthetic or artistic consciousness arose in their experience, no thematic shift in consciousness took place. Properly speaking, we do not perceive (*wahrnehmen*) the object in aesthetic experience. In principle, it is not a matter of seeing an existing color, even though it manifests itself in a manner complying with *perceptio* and even though its reality is not denied.

This is the reason one might argue that—as can be said of the image object— Richter's gray or Klein's blue are not "subject to the laws of physics" (Wiesing 2005, p. 35), even though their manifestation rests on the *de facto* condition of physical materiality.¹⁶³ I would contend that this point is of paramount significance for the

---

162 Lotz (2010b, p. 178). See also Lotz (2010b, pp. 174–175): "Even a monochrome painting remains a painting, because 'a' color, e.g., gray, presents itself in this gray as an image object. Thus the painting, e.g. one of Gerhard Richter's gray paintings, becomes an image object in which 'the' gray shows itself."

163 As regards color specifically, I believe that the issue concerning passage to a nonperceptual dimension can be profitably associated with what Heidegger and Deleuze say about the intensive dimension of color (Deleuze 1968, p. 244). In *The Origin of the Work of Art*, Heidegger remarks that "to be sure, the painter [...] makes use of pigment; [...] however, in such a way that the colors are not used up but begin, rather, for the first time, to shine" (Heidegger 1980 [1936], p. 25). In *Difference and Repetition*, Deleuze talks about this "splendor" bringing out the idea of an "intensive space." In Deleuze's view, it is a matter of bringing the sensible to a "superior coherence" that

comprehension of artistic works—particularly when it comes to artistic works that produce events, i.e., expressive qualities that, while emerging from sensibility, cannot simply be reduced to it.

Significantly, Merleau-Ponty's reading of the monarch's "Sartrian" smile can be connected to Deleuze's remarks on the potentiality of art in *What Is Philosophy?*, in which he and Félix Guattari examine art's power to preserve what we have called neutral, expressive qualities:

> The young man will smile on the canvas for as long as the canvas lasts. Blood throbs under the skin of this woman's face, the wind shakes a branch, a group of men prepare to leave. In a novel or a film, the young man will stop smiling, but he will start to smile again when we turn to this page or that moment. Art preserves, and it is the only thing in the world that is preserved. It preserves and is preserved in itself (*quid juris?*), although actually it lasts no longer than its support and materials—stone, canvas, chemical color, and so on (*quid facti?*). The young girl maintains the pose that she has had for five thousand years, a gesture that no longer depends on whoever made it. The air still has the turbulence, the gust of wind, and the light that it had that day last year, and it no longer depends on whoever was breathing it that morning. If art preserves it does not do so like industry, by adding a substance to make the thing last. The thing became independent of its "model" from the start, but it is also independent of other possible personae who are themselves artists-things, personae of painting breathing this air of painting. And it is no less independent of the viewer or hearer, who only experience it after, if they have the strength for it. What about the creator? It is independent of the creator through the self-positing of the created, which is preserved in itself. What is preserved—the thing or the work of art—is *a bloc of sensations, that is to say, a compound of percepts and affects.* (Deleuze/Guattari 1991, pp. 163–164)

This is an important passage, as it thematizes the question of the self-sufficiency of the work—its independence from the model (the gesture on the canvas "no longer depends on whoever made it"), from personal experience ("the air [...] no longer depends on whoever was breathing it that morning"), and from the creator (the "created [...] is preserved in itself"). To a certain extent, we addressed this question earlier when discussing the autonomous expressive power of the image. In Chapter 3, we will explore it more thoroughly with a specific focus on artistic images. An entity seems to emerge in the artistic image that is independent of whatever model may have supplied the artist with source material or inspiration. In Deleuze's words, these expressive elements are also neutral in that they lose any specific

---

makes qualities attain the state of pure expression. It is a matter of "retain[ing] of extensities only what combines with the original depth." Only in this way will "the final prediction of the *Phaedo* [...] be realised, in which Plato promised to the sensibility disconnected from its empirical exercise temples, stars and gods such as had never before been seen, unheard-of affirmations" (Deleuze 1968, p. 244).

reference concerning their agent. In phenomenological terms, we might say that the individual existence of the "expressor" no longer really matters. Again, this does not mean that the physicality of the gesture is irrelevant—only that the gesture has been worked to a point that it has come to exceed that reference: it is no more mine than it is yours or the artist's. In this sense, Deleuze reveals his own phenomenological orientation when he writes that art "mobilize[s] pure thought as a faculty of essences" (Deleuze 1964, p. 98), thus allowing access to new and higher perspectives: it acts as a multiplier of perspectives that cannot be unified once and for all, yet they are neither arbitrary nor aleatory.

3 Toward Perspectival Images

3.1 What Kind of Sameness?

Living in the "how" of the manifestation when experiencing art aesthetically does not necessarily mark the end of the reception process, as if this "how-pleasure" were a static ultimate goal closing the relationship between work and spectator. In particular, the moment of aesthetic-axiological enjoyment we experience in art (as is becoming clear, we also mean "aesthetic value" in the sense of a *value produced aesthetically*) can and must elicit our return to a reality we then contemplate through "new eyes"—just as Diderot's love of Vernet stems partly from the latter's having allowed him to find the *same* thing in the real world that Vernet manifested upon the canvas. Again, as we shall see, this is not to imply that this journey is either static or unidirectional.

In this context, let us recall a passage from the *Salon of 1769* that touches upon a point that will be essential to our discussion in this chapter. The passage offers an emblematic topos that I will call the "Vernet window," and it immediately calls into question the classical concept of nature as art and vice versa. Diderot had previously thematized the relationship between nature and art in his 1766 *Essays on Painting*, in a passage that clearly echoes the Husserlian reference to nature *as image* discussed above: "If we happen to be walking [...] and we find ourselves at the end of a beautiful day," Diderot writes, it may happen that

> the passages from darkness to shadow, from shadow to light, from light to the most luminous splendor [are] so sweet, so touching and wonderful that the appearance of a branch, of a leaf, attracts the gaze and interrupts a conversation even at its most interesting moment. [...] We walk with our gaze along that magical canvas and exclaim: "What a painting! Oh, how beautiful it is!" Conversely, if it happens that the painter is capable of recreating that same enchantment on the canvas, we seem to view something that is the product of art as though it were the product of nature. It is not at the Salon, but in the depths of a forest, among the mountains shadowed and illuminated by the sun, that Loutherbourg and Vernet are great. (Diderot 2007 [1766], p. 27)

Clearly, the theme of nature as a painting has emerged frequently throughout the history of aesthetics. What I want to highlight here is how Diderot's comparison questions the nature of this *sameness* between nature and image, a sameness not to be construed as merely metaphorical. Rather than simply pasting one atop the other or saying that one can be lived *as if* it were the other, I suggest that Diderot's approach illuminates how the mutual influence between art and nature gives rise to a *sameness* that plays out on the eidetic plane—a relationship that only the ceaseless interplay between the two poles of *nature* and *canvas* can generate: "moonlight is not only beautiful in nature: it is also beautiful on the trees and waters of Vernet, on the hills of Lutherbourg" (Diderot 2007 [1766], p. 28).

In keeping with the theories we developed in Chapter 2, we might say that neither of the two—neither art nor nature—can exhaust the moonlight phenomenon, the *noema* "moonlight." Like the monarch's smile as referenced by Sartre, I suggest that this *noema* is an expressed idea, one that resonates through the differential combination of art and nature, through the differences between the two. It can never be reduced to one or the other.

Let me stress that it is art's capacity for creating variations or deformations of reality (rather than merely copies of it) that allows this dynamic resonance between nature and art to arise. From a noematic standpoint, neither of these two elements precedes the other in terms of expressivity; the two resonate in intersubjective virtuality, in a "chiasmatic exchange" (Starobinski 1991, p. 30). This is the direction in which I am inclined to construe what happens to Diderot at his window, where he comes to see the moonlight as the *thing itself*, something to be grasped both in Vernet's painting and in nature:

> Listen to a fact, but a true fact, to the letter. It was night, everything was asleep around me. Having spent the morning at the Salon, I was recalling what I had seen that evening. I had picked up my pen; I was about to write that Vernet's *Moonlight* was a little dry, that the clouds seemed to me too black and not deep enough, when suddenly, through the window, I saw the moon among some clouds—the *same* thing the artist had imitated on his canvas was there in the sky. Imagine my surprise, when, recollecting the painting, I could discern no difference between it and the phenomenon I had before my eyes, the same *blackness in nature*, the same *dryness*. I had been preparing to slander art and blaspheme against nature. I stopped and said to myself that no one should accuse Vernet of falsehood without having looked carefully. (Diderot 2009 [1769], p. 54)

Note how Diderot refers to *sameness* in the specific sense of *blackness* and *dryness*—qualities expressed in both nature and the painting. Again, at an expressive level, neither of the two resonant poles precedes the other in terms of either time or importance; one cannot be described as more expressive than the other. Rather, they are both capable of expressing these qualities, and they do so in their interrelation. Here, the emphasis is on the artistic variation's ability to highlight moments of expression. Art can then teach us to "look better." This ties in strongly with the Sartrian/Deleuzian considerations we discussed at the end of the second chapter.

Proust echoes Diderot's views on this subject,[164] suggesting that the possibilities opened up by art have important repercussions for how we view everyday reality. In a pre-*Recherche* text on Chardin's style—the same style that bewitched Diderot two centuries prior—Proust shows that an artistic journey can be construed as a journey of initiation into the real, a "journey of initiation into the unknown life within the still life, which each of us can make if we let Chardin be our guide, as Dante was guided by Virgil" (Proust 2009 [1895], pp. 21–22). The "same" beauty we feel in a painting, he invites us to find in encountering the "real" object. Again, this line of aesthetic thought is not a one-way journey from the real to the image or vice versa—it is a continuous exchange between two elements that feed off one another, each participating in the production of a common expressive element that is not self-contained in either. Such expressive elements, as we shall see, are not exclusive to the dynamic between nature and art; they can also develop between two works of art, two images, or two objects, and so on.

Along these lines, we can suggest that the experience to which an artistic image gives life becomes a moment of *recreation*, not so much in the "momentary relief from the burden of reality" sense as in the sense of "new creation." Touched by the beauty of a particular manifestation of reality, the artist may feel the need to recreate that expression. In turn, the image that arises from the artist's creation is not merely a pale copy of reality: it must prolong its effects upon a renewed perception.

In the pre-*Recherche* text devoted to Chardin, Proust, imagining himself talking to a bored young man, says that "the pleasure you take in his painting of a [...] sideboard, is the same pleasure—seized in passing, detached from the moment, deepened, eternalized—that he took in seeing a sideboard" (Proust 2009 [1895], p. 13). Here, once again, we have the concept of *sameness*. The two pleasures "are so inseparable that if he [Chardin] was unable to content himself with the initial pleasure in what he saw and wished to give himself and others the second sort, then you,"—here we have the obligatory return to reality—"cannot be content with only the second and will inevitably return to the first" (Proust 2009 [1895], p. 13).

The effects that a Chardin painting arouse in us can undoubtedly allow us to view what once seemed like aesthetically insipid realities with new eyes: "If you can say, looking at a Chardin: this is as intimate and comforting and vital as a kitchen, then as you walk through a kitchen you will say: this is intriguing, this

---

164 In Rozzoni (2015) I delved into the relationship between Diderot and Proust on this point, comparing their respective descriptions of Chardin's *La Raye* in an effort to highlight similarities and differences in their respective understandings of the relationship between nature and art.

is grand, this is as beautiful as a Chardin'" (Proust 2009 [1895], p. 13). This applies to Chardin's cupboards no less than to Vernet's moon. Proust, in a line drawn from Diderot by way of Baudelaire,[165] is referring here to the "danger" of no longer knowing how to recognize beauty in everyday objects, in the spectacle of the real as it manifests itself in even the humblest reality.

As we noted in Chapter 2, of course, Kundera/Céline remarked upon an inverse "danger" to the one Proust cautions us against, namely employing a process of undue or unnecessary aestheticization of reality. The spectacularization that results from such an approach threatens inappropriate *exhibition* of the *how*, especially when it comes to forms of reality that, as Pedro Costa puts it, we ought to have the "decency" to avoid phonily aestheticizing (see Costa 2020). Later, we will explore in greater detail how the tensions generated between these opposite tendencies can take shape in photography and cinema as well.

3.2 Opening Perspectives

Art can become a place in which we develop (including in the photographic sense) and express the invisible "traces" of a "life" that might otherwise go unheard or unacknowledged in the regime of our ordinary world. As we suggested in our Proust/Chardin example, it is often an aesthetic experience of reality in all its "mute" richness that prompts the artist to answer this silent call with an act of creation.[166]

In Chapter 2, we pointed out how an experience offered to us in image does not prevent us from experiencing a noematic sense that goes beyond the modifications related to belief-modulations. Likewise, we noted that the fact of viewing an image is no barrier to our *Wertnehmung*, our *valueception*—a process seemingly impassive to distinctions between perceptual and phantasy dimensions. Now, we can say that the essential sameness that we feel in the chiasm between world and art (which is often given in that very chiasm between the world and its forms of presentification) can in fact be given as having a certain value, one not reducible to the individual manifestation expressing it. Indeed, as we have remarked, this sameness is expressed through a relation rather than some hidden common quality intrinsic to either individual.

---

[165] See also Rozzoni (2015) for further discussion of this continuity.
[166] In his 1954 "Cours du jeudi" on "Le problème de la parole" at the Collège de France, Maurice Merleau-Ponty insisted on this Proustian theme of the "mute call" of things to the artist (see Merleau-Ponty 1954, pp. 135–143). See also Merleau-Ponty 1996, p. 16.

We have said that, as far as the expressive axiological plane is concerned, the image experience is not second to actual reality. Even if it arises on a presentificational basis, the axiological significance of what we experience as expressed through an image can in turn affect our everyday experience. This might be expected, considering that what we experience as real in our world clearly cannot be reduced to a simple collection of facts—such facts are inseparable from the correlated senses that manifest itself to us. Over and over again, we encounter this sense dimension as a web of meanings and ideas, always manifesting as having different values. What we call the real world is not the sum of facts entirely reducible to sensible-causal laws. Rather, sensible facts and things are already imbued with, and constituted within, a web of interrelated senses. Hence it is no exaggeration to say that the valuable new perspectives we acquire when reading a novel or watching a movie actually can change the world for us. Each new perspective opens up a new noematic sense, and we perceive this aperture as having value (whether positive, negative, or neutral).

In other words, originally, each perspective (*sensu stricto*: cognitive/narrative dimension) on the world has a value that always pertains to it and an emotional dimension that always characterizes it. The essential interconnection among these three elements can be construed as a noematic dimension (perspective *lato sensu* as a narrative-cognitive/axiological/emotional *whole*) and, as such, experienced in not only the actual perceptual environment but also in nonperceptual (e.g., iconic or fictional) contexts. Art is a medium through which this fundamental possibility can develop. When we transpose ourselves into *quasi*-worlds created through art, we can obtain new perspectives and experience new values within them. These shifts in perspectives can open us up to new forms of valorization that manifest themselves at an emotional level.

As with the expanded perspectives opened up through phantasy, we reshape and recreate our vision as we traverse new styles. Having lived these experiences, our eyes return to the real world attuned to new aspects—we literally find new meaning and new values in things. Through this continuous, dynamic exchange between life and art, we can recognize the essential qualities they both express, the eidetic regions that resist differences between real and phantasy domains.

It bears repeating here that artistic experience in image can have cognitive or moral value as well and that such experiences can have more than exclusively aesthetic value. But it should equally be emphasized that art expresses these values by producing them through the *aesthetic creation* of sense; it is more than some simple "message in a bottle" format for communicating preexisting, self-contained ideas or values. What art seeks to express are those very senses that defy mere propositional or analytical boundaries.

Elicited through fertile encounters with the world, the urge to create is heard on an emotional level—it is felt as a value even before it can be deliberately judged to hold any. But this does not mean that such an axiological opening can be reduced to a mere emotional state. Such a value can have cognitive significance at a pre-propositional level: before any attempt to find ways to formulate it, it *implies* a perspective on the world, an understanding undergoing a process of valorization felt emotionally.

3.3 Expressive Coherent Deformations

As we have suggested, the artist can restore the essence of a thing by creating not a copy or *Abbildung* of it but a variation of it. And not just any arbitrary variation, either: altering something does not per se equal producing its essence. In a manner of speaking, the variation must be able to shake the emphasis on individual facts and instead produce an essential noematic sense that can be felt in both the real world and the artistic one. Merleau-Ponty notes that, in order for the painter Elstir to bring out the essence of the hawthorns in Proust's *Recherche*, he must *deform* them; only in doing so can Elstir cause *Recherche*'s narrator to feel something beyond what the merely empirical, non-"varied" hawthorns alone can elicit.[167]

Again, however, this deformation is not haphazard. Artistic movement must give rise to what Merleau-Ponty, quoting Malraux, called a *coherent deformation*.[168]

---

[167] Again, these reflections can be found in Merleau-Ponty's preparatory notes for his 1954 "Cours du jeudi" at the Collège de France. There, Merleau-Ponty recalls the passage in the *Recherche* in which the narrator wishes Elstir, the "painter of the Recherche," would explain to him the essence of the hawthorns, saying that his own efforts to discover this essence had been in vain. Merleau-Ponty then hypothesizes that, had he engaged in the "enterprise," Elstir would not have rendered the essence of hawthorns in terms of features exclusive to those flowers but rather would have painted the movement capable of generating "the hawthorns in what they have of the essential of something else than the hawthorns, by making them appear through what they are not [*naître les aubépines dans ce qu'elles ont d'essentiel d'autre chose que les aubépines,*" "*les faisant apparaître à travers ce qu'elles ne sont pas*]" (Merleau-Ponty 1954, p. 153): the essence of hawthorns could only be found in something other than hawthorns, through one of their possible variations.

[168] This expression appears in several places in his work. See, in particular, Merleau-Ponty (1969, p. 60). He revives the expression in his final Collège de France courses before his untimely death, for example in reference to Paul Klee: "It is necessary that a line, as a trace of movement, must be a rhythm, a law—a law not only of a real displacement in space but also of a field of possibilities beyond the probable. This spatiality is meta-spatial. The line speaks to a field of existential possibilities within us, like a certain gap [*écart*] in relation to it. Klee: 'genius is the error within the system'. It is a systematic error, 'coherent deformation'" (Merleau-Ponty 1996, p. 18, transl. slightly modified).

After all, "mere" deformation is well within anyone's capabilities. As Deleuze (1981, p. 63) writes regarding Bacon, "great painters know that it is not enough to mutilate, maul, or parody the cliché in order to obtain a true laugh, a true deformation." Deforming with coherence, on the other hand, is a bit more complicated. As we shall try to show, it is a way to get to experience the "event," inexhaustible by definition. Facts are not merely causal occurrences in a physical space: they manifest themselves equally in a virtual space teeming with possibilities, and infinite, perpetually shifting possibilities are consubstantial to their manifestations. That is why "to write *what one has seen* is in reality to shape it," "*coherent*[ly] deform" it (Merleau-Ponty 1996, p. 132), bearing in mind that what is given is not "once and for all." A deformation expresses an idea that is more the effect of the difference between its variations than a fixed, stable core within each.

Of course, we usually perceive things in a predominantly ordinary flow—we live steeped in habitualities in which we constantly recognize objects as familiar. We saw in the second chapter that the aesthetic experience is given mainly through a change of attitude constituting a break in the chain of ordinary habitualities, in which other interests frequently prevail over the aesthetic one (which can nonetheless also play an ancillary background role to these primary practical thematic interests). Aesthetic attitude entails a qualitative change in our experience, through which our attention is captured at a specific moment by the particular *noema* expressed by the way something is happening. Something creates a "vertical cut" in the weave of *passive syntheses* (infinite fulfillment of infinite anticipatory expectations). Within the *schematism of habits* through which we recognize or quickly come to recognize the innumerable things manifesting around us, in an ordinary experience sedimented through innumerable reconfirmations, we can recognize a new yet familiar sense seemingly concealed from our awareness until that moment.

3.4 The Silent Axiological Appeal

Let us attempt to characterize that "vertical cut" in the "flow" in context of our further analysis, particularly as regards our earlier point on the essential interrelation of *perspective* (*stricto sensu*, cognitive/narrative), *value*, and *emotion*. We can now say that aesthetic experience emerges when a particular mode of manifestation is observed from a particular perspective, allowing a specific value to manifest itself that is not purely practical but still bears a close relation to that particular "how" of manifestation. The value grasps our attention, and we in turn can grasp this value. For example, appearance may manifest itself as beautiful (though this is obviously not the only type of valorization that can arise).

In such cases, valueception is not simply related to a perspective construed as a vantage point from which we perceive a concrete matter of fact. Let us say instead that we are interested in that precise "how," that precise perspective, insofar as it expresses a particular noematic sense experienced as having value. Crucially, however, this is not tantamount to affirming that the *noema* results from a simple process of abstraction wherein we seek to extract from the manifestation an abstract universal, under which we then subsume the individual experience. Rather, as we have already remarked, we are dealing here with a noematic sense that is closely *related* to that particular way of manifestation, but not strictly *reducible* to it.

It is a moment of rupture: our attention is displaced toward something that captures it, something "never before noticed" yet given as having always "been there" for us to grasp. We can experience it as having always been there because we grasp the expressed *noema as* eternal, not confined to the moment of actual individualization. The individual thing can be perceived as a part of the chronological flow we relentlessly define as a community (our common shared time). Even so, the sense expressed through an individual occurrence can be grasped as impassible, not reducible to a chronological position. The temporality of the *noema* is qualitatively different from individual chronological temporality (defined as a chronological succession of instants). In this respect, in his final course on Cartesian ontology at the Collège de France, Merleau-Ponty spoke of "a trans-temporal core—Visible or World—a kind of eternity of the visible, like a container that secretly 'leaks' [*perd*], and thus is always ahead of and late to the present, never on time" (Merleau-Ponty 1996, p. 126).

Significantly, this description resonates with the Deleuzian characterization of time in *Logic of Sense*, which also offers crucial insights concerning an overcoming of the "chronological line" in favor of a timeline that is "never punctual" (note the similarity to Merleau-Ponty's remarks)—that is, transcending the timeline of *Chronos* for that of *Aion*, "the milieu of surface effects or events" (Deleuze 1969, p. 166).

The aesthetic experience involves surprise at the manifestation of the phenomenon, its pure event, its sense inseparable from its manner of manifestation, which we paradoxically recognize as something new. Indeed, it entails the paradoxical *recognition* of something that *was not there*, something unknown and yet familiar, a break in the experience. This kind of "breach" is masterfully described in another passage from Proust's *Recherche*:

> The tiled roof cast upon the pond, translucent again in the sunlight, a dappled pink reflection which I had never observed before [*je n'avais encore jamais fait attention*]. And, seeing upon the water, and on the surface of the wall, a pallid smile responding to the smiling sky, I cried aloud in my enthusiasm, brandishing my furled umbrella: "Gosh, gosh, gosh, gosh! [*Zut, zut,*

zut, zut]." But at the same time I felt that I was in duty bound not to content myself with these unilluminating words, but to endeavour to see more clearly into the sources of my rapture. (Proust 1913, pp. 169–170)

Here, the inarticulate exclamation ("Gosh, gosh, gosh, gosh!") indicates how the aesthetic-axiological moment cleaves the ordinary perceptual fabric of our experience, a silent appeal that demands to be written, filmed, photographed, and that would vanish unexplored if left unheeded. I propose that such a call can be answered through an act of creation, through a *variation* that will allow others to live that "same" experience—a "sameness" expressed in the variation insofar as it is brought to the impassible eidetic plane. Whenever another person reads those words, watches that film, views that photograph, etc., it will open up the possibility of establishing an "intersubjectivity that is at the same time, as Husserl describes it in the second volume of *Ideas*, aesthetic, affective, spiritual": a space that assumes a founding character for a "communion of subjects based on a historical-productive commonality that is constituted between networks of spiritual motivations" (Franzini 1997, p. 149) and values that, "one could add, […] maintain in themselves the world of life that generated them, the sense, sensitive and symbolic, of sentiment" (Franzini 1997, p. 154).

3.5 Cinematic *Quasi*-worlds

Hopefully the above considerations shed light on the sense in which we meant our previous remarks about how fictional art's potential for giving rise to originary experiences in spectators relies on its potential for expressing sense through *ficta* rather than through a representational link with a presupposed reality. It should now be clear that passing from reality to iconic phantasy need not preclude us from experiencing the dimension of neutral events. In the *quasi*-worlds created through images and words, we can experience noematic senses given in that essential connection among perspective, value, and emotions now under consideration. An atmosphere is not affected by differences in *modalization*; a gaze is no less inherently a gaze when expressed in an image.

Similarly, cinema can allow the creation of *quasi*-worlds in which we discover the productive power of the "nothingness of the image," worlds aimed less at duplicating reality than at developing a variation through which experiences can acquire new essences and values. If, as we have proposed, the condition of possibility of a world's manifestation is the essential connection among a perspective, values, and emotions, then we can ask whether cinema can become a privileged field in which to experience the transcendental significance of this connection and explore its nature.

In cinema, even though the manifestation under consideration is purely presentificational in nature, we can witness how this triadic interrelation opens up new possibilities of being in the world, and we can experience new perspectives emotionally as having various values. (As we have said, the word "perspective" also includes an element of cognition or comprehension.) In our terms, the screen could then be considered an eidetic field within which we experience that essential relationship among value, perspective, and emotion. When we live that experience in the regime of *quasi*-consciousness, this allows us to focus our attention on the sense produced by the on-screen actions rather than on the practical consequences of those individual actions. Cinema allows us to experience possibilities and explore the nature of what we call reality, to experiment with the infinite perspectives that continuously participate in the constitution of what we think of as our shared world.

Moreover, in cinema, our playful phantasy finds ample opportunity to give intuitiveness—in accordance with *perceptio*—to our phantasy movements. It affords us various possibilities to create fictional worlds on a *perzeptiv* basis, modified variations presentifying occurrences to us that we tolerate or even enjoy within this iconic fictional regime, although we would not accept them in the "real" world.

This is not to say that other art forms had not previously demonstrated these possibilities for varying our shared reality—that the novel, for instance, had never previously succeeded in freeing the imagination by giving rise to movements, connections, effects (in a word, narrative montage) that would later find renewed expression in cinema. In this regard, Eisenstein (1988 [1943]) suggested that Diderot already "wrote about cinema";[169] similarly, Deleuze (1985, p. 39) stated that Proust "sp[oke] [...] in terms of cinema." But film is qualitatively different from literature in how it allows our phantasy to find freedom of movement even along the terrain of *perceptio*, prompting us to intuit iconic presentifications.

The technical opportunities that have supported and inspired camera work have led cinematographers to explore new possibilities, such as passing through solid objects (consider the well-known shot in *Citizen Kane* in which the camera's gaze enters the El Rancho nightclub through the skylight) or showing us things from vantage points we could previously only imagine in a reproductive or nonintuitive way, not in a manner complying with *perceptio*. Our gaze can now literally whirl around (as in the opening of *Touch of Evil* [1958], another Welles film), insin-

---

[169] "Strange as it may seem, this is a fact. Diderot wrote about cinema!" (Eisenstein 1988 [1943], p. 383.

uate itself into the most recondite of spaces, and see things impossible to observe with the naked eye (like the journey through the man's ear canal at the beginning of the Coen brothers' *A Serious Man*). In principle, it could intuitively explore even the infinitely small and the infinitely large. Such developments are far from exhausted, of course; these paths are still under development.

Manovich (2001, 2016), for example, discusses the pictorial possibilities afforded by the advent of digital media: practically every movement, every iconic occurrence can be simulated via computer. Against this background, filming physical reality directly—using genuine impressional images—becomes but one among several cinematic possibilities,[170] which means a burgeoning variety of ways to offer the viewer experiences of *perzeptive* phantasies. The gap between the limits of what can be shown to the public intuitively and what can only be phantasized privately is shrinking all the time, which clearly feeds into the previously discussed mutual exchange between reproductive and *perzeptiv* phantasy. As new media allows us to experience an ever-increasing array of *perzeptive* phantasies, these experiences in turn shape our own private reproductive phantasies.

In principle, VR seems to suggest the possibility of making reproductive experiences *comply fully with perceptio*. In other words, it seems to open up (or at least point toward) the phenomenological possibility of producing *perzeptive* phantasies

---

[170] Of course, in keeping with what we said in the second chapter, this is a point that can also affect our belief habits. For example, we cannot exercise a light-hearted documentary consciousness toward a film that we *know* is composed of many digitized elements. Without the possibility of relying on "lens-based recordings of reality" (Manovich 2016, p. 21), it seems harder to know which details we should or should not approach with documentary consciousness. Nonetheless, as Manovich notes (see Manovich 2016, p. 28), this certainly opens up the possibility of experiencing an as-if "documentary consciousness," in the sense that we can experience a scene that appears genuinely photographic (although we know it is not) *as if* it were direct footage (shot from a "lens-based recording" device). However, this would still constitute a consciousness of fiction (as-if documentary). Conversely, when viewing films that prompt us to exercise documentary consciousness from the first moment onward, any form of digital creation or manipulation of the image, while obviously easy to achieve, might be perceived as deception.

Clearly, this also implies the possibility of making "re-enactments," fictional films about real past events, using seemingly "faithful" manifestations of the actual protagonists' bodies. In the previous century, such re-enactments were achieved using actors or animation; now, we can create digital presentifications of the "original" subjects with "perfect photographic credibility" (Manovich 2016, p. 22), i.e., such that it would be impossible to tell whether or not such manifestations were genuine photographic images. Such reconstructions, if accompanied by positional rays, would then have an even stronger effect on how we frame our shared past privately and publicly.

at will. To draw upon a Husserlian idea, we could also call this the possibility to hallucinate at will,[171] to dream *while knowing that one is dreaming.*

Cinematic developments lead us to discover new ways of seeing things. Cinematic imagination inaugurates an exercise of vision by allowing us to visualize all sorts of possible scenarios for anyone. Though others might not see my reproductive phantasies, I can create shareable *perzeptive* phantasies on the basis of those phantasies. This might not bear on the actual causality (the gun I fire in a VR fictional environment does not hurt anyone), but it can surely bear upon the sense that constitutes reality since phantasy dramatization can use several forms of narrative to make us think, to expand our usual perception. (Consider the possibilities that merely juxtaposing one sequence with another can offer in terms of expanding our way of thinking.)

3.6 Between "Real" and "Ideal"

We have seen how an aesthetic attitude can not only occur within a regime perfectly uncontaminated by any positional stance, but it can also arise while "tolerating," exploiting, recomposing in itself some degree of belief. Along these lines, beauty and existence are not mutually exclusive in the Kantian sense; we shall soon see the level at which this type of interaction may be achieved.

Firstly, if it is true, at least *prima facie*, that a purely fictitious film with no claimed links to actual reality poses no particular impediments to the enjoyment of its fictional *quasi*-world in an attitude of complete neutrality, it is equally true that (as Fink never ceased to insist, albeit mostly in relation to theater), in this attitude, what happens on-screen often entails an element of "regarding"—both in the sense of "looking back at" us and of "concerning" us.[172] Indeed, this "regard," this "concern" can occur even with phantasies completely free of any positional reference.

Moreover, we must always keep in mind that our experience of cinematographic, theatrical, and literary works can often be imbued and mingled with beliefs about reality, beliefs that can change from genre to genre; a similar argument

---

171 In this regard, let me quote a short but important passage from Hua XXIII (p. 625), where Husserl notes that *"perceptio [Perzeption]* as such determines nothing. One sees this in the fact that we would not live with one another in a pure phantasy world and that obviously nothing at all would change in what has been said if we had the same immediate freedom of phantasy complying with *perceptio* as we do of reproductive phantasy: hence if we could hallucinate at will."

172 See Fink (1971 [1968], p. 104). This is clearly an Aristotelian theme, which Fink develops in his phenomenology of play.

applies to the personal reproductive fantasies we consider free from any form of belief (for example, we might phantasize about a "water nymph" and then realize that she has the face of a woman we have seen before [see Hua XXIII, p. 611]). Appendix LIX to Text no. 18 of Hua XXIII—which, as indicated above, consists of two pages likely written in 1916 or 1918 (stemming from the aforementioned Ms. A VI 1)—deals specifically with the possible links that fictional art can have to what we consider our common reality.

In this manuscript, Husserl refers to a pair of opposite extremes that delimit fictional art's scope of movement vis-à-vis its referencing of reality. At one extreme, it can present the reality of a "given world" in a given "time [...], for example, Berlin of today." At the other, it can transport us to a world of "once upon a time, somewhere, in some fable land, in some time, in some world with entirely different animal beings, even different natural laws, and so on" (Hua XXIII, p. 651). Occurrences set in that world are wholly unconnected to our shared chronological time; they do not even pretend to fit into our commonly established past.

In principle, we can also think of cinema as oscillating between these two extremes, outlining a vast range of blends and hybrids as it traces that arc. A film may naturally tend toward the first pole, which Husserl associates with "realistic [*realistische*] art" or "realistic fiction." He mentions the latter in reference to Arthur Schnitzler, saying of his work that "within the indefinite horizon belonging to a given world and time, more concretely, belonging to a given city, Vienna, a series of events is clearly phantasized and presented in a vital way" (Hua XXIII, p. 652).

We can coherently position cinematic occurrences within a precise era in our shared world, along our common timeline (consider, in this context, the previously mentioned caption to *Hands over the City* (*Le mani sulla città*): "the characters and the facts narrated here are imaginary, but the social and environmental reality that produces them is authentic"). Significantly, Husserl specifies how such a series of occurrences is "not described, but represented in such a way that we witness a situation, a life's destiny, and so forth, in the as-if, as if we were present. We are 'spectators as it were'; we are present, as it were, in the society" (Hua XXIII, p. 652).

In other words, we can participate in the unfolding of these realistic *quasi-worlds* and be involved in their narratives within a nexus web articulating the intimate relationships among perspectives, values, and emotional dimensions. For example, we are invited to enter into the context of a society, to experience some of its imagined perspectives on life and feel the values that may emerge therefrom. Works of this kind (i.e., those nearer to the "realistic" pole) can teach us something about "what it was like" to live at a certain historical time: "it is art, not science [*Wissenschaft*], though in its own way it does mediate knowledge [*Wissen*]." Although realist art creates figures by means of phantasy, it "constructs" within these fictions "characteristic types belonging to the time present themselves" (Hua XXIII, p. 653). To use the phenomenological terminology we have discussed thus far, we can also speak of worlds presenting noematic senses that always connote emotional and axiological involvement.

As mentioned, the noematic possibilities of lives expressible through art can "regard" us even though the stories to which they give life do not have the positional mark of facts, things that "actually happened." The specific individuals are fictional, imaginary, but what escapes distinction between imaginary and real is the *expressed type*, the *noema*, which has the nature of a sense impassive to that difference. From an eidetic point of view, every "realistic" reference to existing people or facts is *never* purely coincidental. More specifically, in a realistic attitude, art "produces formations" of phantasy, but "as types with respect to times and world epochs" (Hua XXIII, p. 653). At a very general level, it can make us see characteristics of human culture, "types" that we can then return to *see* in the real world: "*theoria* [θεωρία] in the original sense" (Hua XXIII, p. 653).

However, Husserl says, the sphere of realistic art *stricto sensu* (which aims to be as faithful as possible to the "types" of its own epoch) leaves little room for "beauty." At most, he suggests, beauty would serve as an accessory stimulus to a "scientific" vision that penetrates the characteristic structure of a given epoch, a mere means to an "artistic empiricism or positivism" aimed at showing "the matter of factness" of the spirit of a time (Hua XXIII, p. 653). From a cinematographic point of view, this pole could be exemplified through a phantasy image of a realistic vocation, aiming to express *historical* "verisimilitude": roughly put, presentification of something that could have happened without any primary regard for beauty in the manner of appearance.

At the opposite extreme from realistic art, Husserl situates "idealistic [*idealistische*] fiction," which he construes as art that is "purely a matter of phantasy, producing phantasy formations in the modification of pure neutrality. At least producing no concrete depictive image" (Hua XXIII, p. 651). No image claiming to be a faithful presentification of a fact or an aspect of the world is involved here.

We previously specified that, when used in the context of fictional iconic phantasy, the term "neutrality" is not a reference to the work's representational status but rather to the status of *belief* toward a *sujet* which, in keeping with this "idealistic" pole, is wholly out of the equation. In this sense, no *Abbildung* is involved at the idealistic pole of Husserl's continuum. Husserl (writing primarily in reference to the literary *côté* here) notes that "the idealistic author" is under no constraints with respect to the faithful rendering of "facts and types belonging to regions of the empirical world and empirical life." Rather, he or she undertakes to catch sight of "ideas and ideals, and, in seeing them, values them and sets them forth as values" (Hua XXIII, p. 653).

Of course, even when making this rigid analytical distinction between an artistic fiction attempting to be as realistic as possible and one entirely without references to anything that "really happened," it should be noted that being "free" of historical obligations does not affect artistic fiction's ability to work with ideals and values. In the previous chapter, we observed how, even though we can rightly distinguish between these two extremes for descriptive purposes, works of art often interweave the two in various ways; innumerable examples of this can be found in visual art, literature, theater, and cinema. Crucially, such works are highly concerned with both poles rather than being relegated to one or the other. In fact, even a "realistic" artist can show us that "human beings have ideals and can be guided by them" (Hua XXIII, p. 653).

In any case, in the passage under examination, Husserl stresses the distinction between a realistic artist "ha[ving] a positivistic focus" and an idealistic artist "ha[ving] a *normative* focus" (Hua XXIII, p. 653). The latter, he specifies, "presents value types in concrete images, or he 'embodies' values in characters, and the values battle against disvalues in real *quasi*-situations" (Hua XXIII, p. 653). While working with fictions, the artist can "present values and the conflict of good and evil," and does so "without moralizing or preaching" (Hua XXIII, p. 654). As mentioned, art must be capable of generating axiological possibilities, perspectives manifesting themselves as having some degree of value; it does not serve merely to communicate some established maxim about good and bad (which would indeed make art superfluous).[173]

As I am emphasizing, it is only through free imaginative variation (and, in particular, through the deformation of reality) that art allows us to access an ideal, axiological, philosophical dimension, indifferent to distinctions between reality and fiction. Looking beyond the task of identifying and distinguishing these two polar tendencies (realistic and idealistic), I wish to stress the possibility of charac-

---

[173] Here, Husserl also seems to characterize "idealistic art" as a "philocallistic art" expressing its values through "beauty" that "is opposed above all to realistic art understood as philocharacteristic, philopositivistic art" (Hua XXIII, p. 654). Yet although this distinction is viable in a certain sense, it cannot be considered exhaustive. For one, we must remember that the source of this characterization is far from extensive (a single short manuscript page), and it is linked to a highly general and insufficiently articulated concept of "beauty." However, these brief pages do offer another important clarification regarding the difference between "aesthetic" and "callistic." Husserl writes that all art is "'aesthetic'," insofar as it "is delight in what is seen *in concreto*," and yet "not all art is callistic." At the same time, he also specifies that "not all callistic art is, in addition, idealistic, normative, portraying the ideal and transfiguring it through beauty," but "in a still higher stage, art can also be philosophical, metaphysical" (Hua XXIII, p. 654). This remark seems to be more in keeping with my thesis concerning the artistic possibility of an aesthetic genesis of ideas, a particular focus of this third chapter.

terizing both experiences in axiological terms. In other words, even realistic art wholly focused on "facts" does not avoid presentifying a world through a perspective from which specific values may emerge on an emotional level. Both realistic and fictional presentifications can set values in *motion*, can offer perspectives that are grasped axiologically. The value itself can be expressed using either realistic or idealistic approaches, on a level preceding distinctions concerning different existential modifications. As we have noted, value-ception (*Wert-nehmung*) does not involve differences that play out at the level of "*Wahrnehmung*," or more generally at the level of positional intention. It is, so to speak, impervious to the distinction between reality and unreality. Even so, we have observed how our attitude toward reality can influence our reception of a film in various ways; this is true of films we would consider "works of art" as well as those we would be more inclined to call "simple entertainment."

3.7 *Quasi*-emotions as Modified Emotions

Even in the consciousness of image that distinguishes it, even in the aesthetic value emerging from its modes of manifestation, a film can arouse in us a positional interest in existence that characterizes the story being told. Earlier, we mentioned the possibility of distinguishing between documentary and fictional attitudes toward images. Now, let us begin exploring the possibility of such a distinction eliciting a qualitative change concerning the emotional and axiological dimensions of experience. When it comes to cinematic images, the "classical" distinction between documentary and fiction might prompt us to distinguish between emotional reactions to each, thereby creating a divide between emotions aroused by real and fictive occurrences. Such a demarcation between emotions has now become a major focus in multiple fields, particularly in analytic philosophy within the past 40 years (cf., for instance, Currie 1990; Gendler/Kovakovich 2005; Walton 1978, 1990). Several influential authors have come to distinguish between "genuine emotions" elicited by real situations and "*quasi*-emotions" elicited in fictional contexts (cf. Konrad et al. 2018). Significantly, however, Husserl had already used "*quasi*-emotions" to describe emotions elicited through phantasy, thereby distinguishing them from those we experience in real contexts.[174]

---

[174] It is also appropriate to recall that other Brentano students, such as Alexius Meinong (and his own student, Stephan Witasek), studied and developed the notion of "*quasi*-emotions" extensively. Vendrell Ferran (2010) offered a detailed account of the debate on fictional emotions developed in the Graz School and also proposed insights for a dialogue between such a debate and the one emerging within the analytic field.

Indeed, the current debate on *quasi*-emotions could find in its largely forgotten phenomenological precursor a philosophical account that may help disentangle some of the most challenging puzzles raised within it. My goal here is to shed light on several phenomenological issues that may prove beneficial when questioning the nature of the relationship between film images and reality by considering, among other things, whether and how the emotions experienced with fictional films are qualitatively different from those we experience with documentaries and, ultimately, in reality. No exploration of this relationship would be complete without also examining the one between fictional emotions and values, such as by weighing the usefulness of distinguishing between "genuine values" experienced in reality and allegedly "*quasi*-values" experienced through fiction (in keeping with our earlier discussion of emotions).

When raising the issue of emotions in Hua XXIII, Husserl suggests that judgments "made on the basis of impressional images"—i.e., a "positing [...] pictorial [*bildlich*] exhibiting"—are not the same as those made when confronting a "pictorial exhibiting" pertaining to a fictional *sujet* (see Hua XXIII, p. 533). This might well hold true for our emotional reactions to such images as well. We may feel threatened by positing images that, despite their presentifying nature, we find frightening or upsetting in a very different way than if we were told that everything presentified in them was merely fiction. Are the emotions we experience in response to fictional images different from those intertwined with a consciousness of reality, and if so, how?

If we see one person show compassion toward another in a documentary, we might feel admiration for that gesture; upon seeing someone harass someone else, we might respond with indignation. Keeping in mind our previous remarks on the possibility of experiencing images positionally, we might say that the emotions we feel in these instances are "actual," unmodified (Hua XXIII, p. 554) emotions since they are based upon a form of existential position-taking: presentification and belief.[175] To put it roughly, we generally do not question the reality of those emotions; we take them for real emotional responses to real (or, at least, believed-real) facts.

But how are we to process emotions grounded in *presentifications* of fictional *sujets*? To return to our previous example, we might ask how our responses of admiration and indignation might change upon learning that the film we were watching in a "documentary mode" was, in fact, a work of fiction. Do emotions change in nature depending on whether they are grounded in presentifications in-

---

[175] This is not to say that our emotional encounters with a *sujet* in image and the same *sujet* in the flesh are the same. This is a separate topic deserving further specific inquiry. For example, it could be valuable to explore the difference between what Fuchs (2014, p. 156) calls "*primary*, intercorporeal empathy" and empathy grounded in what we called "positional images."

volving belief in the existence of the *sujet* or the situation? If so, then what kind of emotions do fictional films elicit?

According to Husserl, if I feel scared or joyous while in phantasy, my "emotions [*Gefühle*]" are "modified" insofar as they are "not relating to reality but to a phantasized world" (Hua XXIII, p. 448).[176] Following on from Husserl's remarks,[177] suppose that I am in a movie theater watching a fictional film,

> and in it a jungle appears to me. A man sits on the ground and searches for bugs. And then suddenly a huge lion emerges, and the man laughs cheerfully. While [...] this series of [iconic] phantasies runs its course, I feel astonishment, perhaps even fear. This is not fear or astonishment in the ordinary sense. They are certainly not reproductive acts (phantasy acts), but actual acts [*wirkliche Akte*], grounded in the actually executed phantasy. On the other hand, I am not feeling "actual astonishment" [*wirkliches Erstaunen*], "actual fear" [*wirkliche Angst*], but modified acts [*modifizierte Akte*]. (Hua XXIII, pp. 447–448)

Note that in this context, "modified" is not meant in reference to the "emotion" itself, as if to suggest that (for example) tears shed over a phantasized character were somehow inherently different from those shed over a "real person." When in a patently fictional situation, I *know* that my tears fit the phantasy actions I am experiencing, and I am aware that those phantasy actions are not actually occurring, nor have they ever occurred. In other words, my tears are not *motivated* by a consciousness of reality as regards the existence of the individual characters: their actions affect only the specific *quasi*-world unfolding in our iconically phantasized experience.

What matters here is the sense and network of meanings of the actions unfolding, and though the fact that we are dealing with fictional elements does not prevent motivational relations concerning many of the elements expressed from arising, it clearly leaves others out. It leaves out of play several motivational relationships that might elicit certain belief-related reactions in me. For example, if one of the characters were to shoot toward the camera, it might startle me (the way Husserl describes being startled by the lion), but it would not prompt me to run screaming from the theater, fearing for my actual safety. This also holds

---

[176] Rather than addressing the complex issue of distinguishing between emotions and feelings at this level of analysis, I am more generally focused on the alleged change of status that can influence our affective "reactions" (Hua XXIII, p. 461) when shifting from a documentary to a fictional attitude and vice versa. This clearly leaves open the possibility of exploring whether any change of status might occur for certain types of feelings/emotions and not for others.

[177] I am slightly modifying his example concerning reproductive phantasy by referring to "iconic phantasy" (cf. Hua XXIII, p. 456 ff.), which, as we have seen, is the kind of phantasy we might consider involved in fictional film.

true for desires elicited through iconic phantasies: if we see "a beautiful woman" on screen "and desire her love [...]," even though we "actually feel this 'desire,'" we "certainly cannot 'actually' desire that *this* woman, who does not even exist, love [us]" (Hua XXIII, p. 448, my italics).

To return to our earlier example of Hitchcock's *Vertigo*, we might fall under Madeleine's (or Judy's) spell and desire her just as Scottie does. That act would not be irrational. What *would* be irrational would be desiring that specific person—say, seeking the fictional character of Madeleine/Judy in the real-world city of San Francisco (or elsewhere, for that matter) in the hopes of asking her out. Of course, this does not preclude someone from seeking in real life what is expressed in the film through the figure of Judy. Consider Charles Swann, another character in *Recherche:* as the narrator explains, though "Odette's physical charms had at first failed to inspire in him" any desire, Swann develops an attraction to Odette after noticing her resemblance to Sephora, daughter of Jethro, as depicted in a Botticelli fresco (Proust 1913, p. 245).

3.8 Are Emotions in Fiction "Paradoxical"?

That said, when considering this issue through the lens of the above-mentioned "paradox of fiction," one might well conclude that emotions aroused through documentary images (grounded in a *belief* in the real existence of the *sujets* presentified) are fully justifiable and "genuine," whereas emotions aroused by phantasized characters (whom we do not actually believe to exist) cannot be justified. In fact, one of the premises underlying this paradox is that (a) "in order for us to have an emotion we *must* believe that the object of our emotion exists." The paradox famously comprises three premises, each considered plausible in itself but mutually contradictory when considered as a group—in other words, each individual statement is allegedly true, yet they cannot all be true at the same time. The other two premises are as follows: (b) "we do not believe that fictional characters exist"; (c) "we have emotional responses toward what we know to be fictional objects." (The a, b, and c labels are taken to be arbitrary here because the three premises are of equal importance; what matters is their mutual irreconcilability.)

In view of this paradox, problems concerning the nature of our emotions seem to arise when considering fictional presentifications. In the 1975 essay that gave rise to this paradox, Colin Radford claimed that "there is no problem about being moved by historical novels or plays, *documentary films, etc.* For these works depict and forcibly remind us of the real plight and of the real suffering of real people, and it is for these persons that we feel. What seems unintelligible is how we could have a similar reaction to the fate of Anna Karenina, the plight of

Madame Bovary or the death of Mercutio. Yet we do" (Radford 1975, p. 69, my italics). According to Radford, this *kind* of reaction "involves us in inconsistency and so incoherence" (Radford 1975, p. 78). To continue with our *Vertigo* example, the idea of reacting emotionally to Scottie's or Judy's fate should seem "unintelligible" to us because they have never existed.

However, I believe that a phenomenological account as outlined above can put this very inconsistency into question. On the one hand, we might say that our phenomenological analysis above supports the assertions in premises (b) and (c). They present results that can be expressed through "phenomenological data" (Hua XXIII, p. 2). Premise (b) states that one can tell the difference between believing in a person's actual existence and phantasizing about the existence of a made-up character. As for (c), it is merely a statement of fact: our awareness of characters' and stories' fictional nature does not prevent us from having reactions elicited by these *quasi*-people and their *quasi*-actions.

Premise (a), on the other hand, is an *explanatory* proposition. It alludes to a "theory of emotion" postulating a specific cognitive basis: namely, that belief in the existence of the object of an emotion is a prerequisite condition for the "authenticity" of that emotion.[178] Embracing this hypothesis might even mean presuming the existence of something like nongenuine emotions, a new and qualitatively different type of emotion elicited by fictional situations (as is well known, this is the thesis presented in Walton [1978]).[179] Nevertheless, from a phenomenological perspective, this assumption appears to be unjustified: the process of phenomenological description reveals that our experiences, whether positional or fictional, *always* manifest themselves through emotional connotations.

In *Being and Time*, Heidegger maintains that *Befindlichkeit*, our "affective state," is an essential aspect of our "being-in-the-world."[180] Specifically, it is not our *belief* in the world but our *involvement* in it that Heidegger emphasizes: emotions do not presuppose beliefs but rather this original relationship of "involve-

---

[178] Stecker (2011, p. 295) pointed out that "the paradox was formulated during the heyday of the cognitive theory of emotions" and that "now virtually no one accepts" that "to pity someone, one must believe that they exist and are suffering." Cf. Vendrell Ferran (2018, p. 206) on the possibility of discussing the "paradox" as a profitable "heuristic tool to shed light on problems regarding our involvement with fiction."

[179] For a discussion of the attempts that have been made to solve the paradox, including those that have done so while trying to maintain the validity of premise (a), see D'Angelo (2020).

[180] "Mood assails. It comes neither from 'without' nor from 'within', but rises from being-in-the-world itself as a mode of that being" (Heidegger 1927, p. 133).

ment."[181] This also holds true for our worldly "involvement" in phantasy, our phantasy states.

This also leads us back to a key aspect of the structure of phantasy experience: phantasy acts do not consist solely of the intuitive presentification of the phantasized object. Rather, they essentially imply the reproduction of a subjective act that *quasi*-perceives that object, thereby generating a splitting of consciousness between a real and a phantasy ego. It may be beneficial to underscore two key facets of this splitting phenomenon.

Firstly, the ego-splitting pertaining to phantasy experience is not to be construed as a sort of schizophrenic process involving a real ego and a phantasy ego unable to communicate.[182] The emergence of a split ego as a condition of possibility of a "phantasy life" does not automatically mean that emotions have completely separate "reality" and "phantasy" sides—it is not as though acting as a phantasy ego causes me to lose *all* awareness of my real ego's emotional life or vice versa. There are undoubtedly cases in which the real and phantasy egos have sharply contrasting emotional responses, as though they were "strangers," so to speak. For example, we might be puzzled by the fact that fictional movies allow us to *quasi*-participate in phantasy actions that we would never carry out in real life for various reasons. Indeed, we might be surprised to find ourselves enjoying a fictional situation that, at least *prima facie*, we would likely condemn in reality.

This is not necessarily a symptom of egological incompatibility. Even though we refer to experiencing the "same" action in reality and phantasy, the real and phantasy egos are not, strictly speaking, in the "same" situation. Our phantasy ego knows it is not *actually* taking that action, and thus we need not concern ourselves with the various real-world consequences we might face for having taken it. Accordingly, our emotional responses in phantasy situations might *fit* this kind of awareness.

Secondly, the very possibility of this discordance causing puzzlement is grounded in the fact that what we call the "real" ego can touch upon on the "phantasy" ego's phantasy experiences, and despite this split, the "real" ego appears to bear sole responsibility for both. The "real" ego has the last word, so to speak,

---

[181] Spinicci (2014, p. 86) also insists: "Prior to believing that a certain state of affairs exists, and prior to being able to doubt that there are sufficient reasons to assert it, we are already engaged by certainties that have to do with our being in a given situation. Now, emotions are forms in which our rooting in the *situation* is made manifest: they do not call for beliefs but only for the original relationship of *involvement*."

[182] For a discussion on the "discontinuity and permeability" between real and phantasy ego, cf. Summa (2017).

on what significance to assign these experiences. This view can also offer relevant insights into the phenomenon of "imaginative resistance" (cf., for instance, Moran 2017, pp. 18–25), in which, despite its almost inexhaustible ability to generate phantasy experiences, the phantasy ego is incapable of even imagining some specific situations, of even *quasi*-carrying out certain specific *quasi*-acts of phantasy. In such cases, it seems that it is in fact the real ego that refuses to allow itself into a phantasy that it finds unbearable. This suggests once again that phantasy egos are not *tabulae rasae*, abstract subjects *fully* alien to the real one that start from scratch every time we begin phantasizing. We might go as far as to say that a phantasy ego is always possible as a variation of the real ego, an imaginative variation that can in turn affect and shape what we call the real one in a relationship that is more articulated than the analytical distinction between the two might suggest.

3.9 *Quasi*-values and Axiological Effects

To expand upon these ideas, let us consider another passage from Proust's *Recherche*, in which the narrator considers the nature of the emotions elicited through fiction. On the one hand, *Recherche*'s narrator has no problem admitting that "it is true that the people concerned in" fiction are "not what Françoise would have called 'real people'" (Proust 1913, p. 91). We might propose that, in *Recherche*, the maid Françoise represents the uncontested and unproblematized natural attitude. Clichés and popular wisdom are sculpted in her with the force of sedimentation over time, repeatedly reinforced through the silent perseverance of "habit" (Beckett 1931, p. 9).[183]

It is not by chance that, in this context ruled by the natural attitude, the young narrator is granted the "pleasures of reading" only on Sundays, days of rest on which labor is banned—in other words, days where any activity is permitted as long as it is nothing "serious" or "concrete": no work, only pastimes. According to this sedimented view, then, no serious activity or emotion can be elicited in fiction (the same goes for watching fictional film, a perfect Sunday activity under this perspective): "I was reading in the garden," the narrator writes, "a thing my great-aunt"—another voice of the uncontested natural attitude—"would never have understood my doing save on a Sunday, that being the day on which it is unlawful to

---

[183] "Habit is like Françoise, the immortal cook of the Proust household, who knows what has to be done, and will slave all day and all night rather than tolerate any redundant activity in the kitchen" (Beckett 1931, p. 9). In the same vein, Robert Pippin (2005, p. 320) depicts her as "the rock of ages in the book, outside modern, historical time, supremely self-confident, unchanging, full of the opinions and the superstitions her ancestors would have expressed."

indulge in any serious occupation, and on which she herself would lay aside her sewing (on a week-day she would have said, 'What! Still amusing yourself with a book? It isn't Sunday, you know!'—putting into the word 'amusing' an implication of childishness and waste of time)" (Proust 1913, p. 139).

However, Proust's response to these clichés points in the direction we described above: in the emotional process, he suggests, involvement in a world (be it "fictional" or "real") takes precedence over the moment of belief in existence. Before delving specifically into Proust's argument, let us first return to and expand upon several Husserlian points that may add to the phenomenological account of emotion we developed earlier, offering insights that will aid us in drawing connections between Proust's views and the iconic dimension implied in movies.

As mentioned in Chapter 1, in his 1918 manuscript on theater, Husserl finally seems to recognize the productive power images can acquire when dramatized (as is also the case in fictional film)—that is, when the generative power of the *narrative* allows meanings and values to originate through images, irrespective of whether these images depict our "objective" reality or not. A fictional film can lead us, as phantasy egos, to experience new perspectives—new variations of what we call a real ego, as discussed in the previous section—whence we are able to experience values that can either corroborate or contradict the values that help shape our "real life" and motivate our day-to-day decisions.[184]

Cinema can make us perceive values that run contrary to our own; it can show us standpoints and narratives that help us understand and feel differently about things. (Of course, as any propagandist knows, its narrative capacity can also be exploited to steer viewers toward specific perspectives or processes of valorization.) And even though a film is presenting "facts" that have never empirically existed and that we believe will never exist as such, the contrary values we feel while *quasi*-living a cinematic dramatization can prompt us to question our "own" values, i.e., the values that appeal to us. They do this not by making a logical point, but by triggering a process of emotional evaluations that hold cognitive value despite not being fully articulable in predicative thought or reducible to propositional knowledge: an "aesthetic mode of understanding" (Pippin 2020, p. 11).

In other words, although I, as a phantasy subject, can be said to act in a neutral and "protected" situation (*qua* unaffected by the question of whether a char-

---

[184] For reasons of space, I will not be systematically addressing all of the various values (artistic, aesthetic, ethical, etc.) such a discussion might take into consideration. However, it may be useful to remark that the point we are making here need not be confined to artistic cinema or literature —it could certainly incorporate, say, literary and cinematic entertainment products and how their respective consumers evaluate or respond to them differently in light of the considerations elaborated here.

acter in a story really exists or not), I cannot be considered unaffected by the counter-values and alternative perspectives expressed in that story. Moreover, as we suggested earlier, these axiological effects cannot be simply confined to the phantasy boundaries of my egological dimension—they also can concern me as a "real" ego.

The key point here is that, despite not believing in the existence of what we see in the image, we can still be *involved* in another *interest*, namely what we have called a "valuing interest in the broadest sense of the term," one that concerns not only the aesthetic sphere but any axiological sphere.

As we have seen, this kind of interest is not preconditioned upon a belief in existence: *valueception* (*Wertnehmung*, value-taking) is not founded upon *perception* (*Wahrnehmung*, "taking as existent")—both are originary modes of givenness. *Accordingly, from a phenomenological point of view, we as the quasi-audience are not axiologically separated from what is quasi-happening on the screen.* Within a fictional context, we can describe ourselves as axiologically "interested" despite our disbelief in the factual existence of what we are experiencing. A fictional film can express a world in a way that invites our phantasy ego to *quasi*-live perspectives opening onto different values that can expand, confirm, restrict, or subvert our axiological horizon.

However, this is not tantamount to simply handing predetermined senses and values to the audience in a fictional context, as if film were simply a means of "translating" these into a cinematic language (this would hardly make for a good film). We do not "have" values as though they were a handful of coins, nor do works of fiction function as some sort of jar through which the author conveys their own collection of value-coins to the audience. Rather, we feel value in connection with our involvement in a *quasi*-world. The world is always given through perspectives that are perceived through a certain axiological orientation (whether positive or negative); a narrative is always given by gaining or losing value, and this axiological movement is essentially related to the different structures of sense we continually encounter (even in the form of an apathetic, unworthy absence of sense). In other words, the world is always given through processes of valorization or devalorization, which are intertwined and mutually influential.

As we have suggested, these cinematic perspectives develop a form of cinematic thinking that is more than merely formal or propositional: an "a-conceptual"[185] thought is developed through a word/image narrative implying an axiological-emotional dimension. Therefore, a "quasi-value" expressed through a fictional situa-

---

[185] "A-conceptual" in that no *determinate concept* can exhaust their sense, as is the case with Kant's aesthetic ideas.

tion is not to be considered a *quasi*-value in the sense of being nongenuine, a "make-believe" value, or a copy of a value—for, as we have seen, a value is something that attracts the subject before the issue of something's factual existence arises.

3.10 Same Body, Different Persons

All this might also serve to help us better interpret Proust's responses to the Françoise-like stubborn mistrust of fictional people. In fact, *Recherche*'s narrator seems to prompt his reader to go a step further by shifting the emphasis to the *imaginative source of emotion.* Proust makes a key remark on the genesis of our emotions when he points out how "none of the feelings [*sentiments*] which the joys or misfortunes of a real person [*personnage réel*] [...] arouse in us can be awakened except through an image [*image*] of those joys or misfortunes" (Proust 1913, p. 91, transl. slightly modified).

Of course, "image" in this sense does not specifically refer to an iconic manifestation, but to the narrative construction of fragments that we piece together every day to try to comprehend others. According to Proust, this alone can prompt us to care for or despise other people,[186] thereby suggesting that the sense of our narratives takes precedence over the real existence of our "objective" bodies.[187] On this basis, the narrator affirms that "the ingenuity of the first novelist lay in his understanding that, *as the image was the one essential element in the complicated structure of our emotions* [*émotions*], so that simplification of it which consisted in the suppression, pure and simple, of real people [*personnages réels*] would be a decided improvement" (Proust 1913, p. 91, my italics, transl. slightly modified). This same mechanism is at work in Hitchcock's *Vertigo*,[188] in which Madeleine and Judy, despite sharing one body, are in fact two different persons—or two dif-

---

[186] This clearly calls for further phenomenological inquiry into the role "narrative perspective taking" can play in the empathic process, a topic explored by Breyer (2019), for instance.
[187] "A real person, profoundly as we may sympathise with him, is in a great measure perceptible *only through our senses*, that is to say, remains *opaque*, presents a *dead weight* which our sensibilities have not the strength to lift. [...] The novelist's happy discovery was to think of substituting for those *opaque* sections, impenetrable to the human soul, their equivalent in *immaterial* sections, things, that is, which one's soul can assimilate" (Proust 1913, p. 91, my italics, transl. slightly modified).
[188] For a rich analysis of the relationship between Proust's *Recherche* and Hitchcock's *Vertigo*, cf. Goodkin (1987).

ferent "characters," since they emerge from two different narratives (Figures 12 and 13).

Figure 12: Still from Alfred Hitchcock's *Vertigo* (1958): Madeleine (Kim Novak)

Figure 13: Still From *Vertigo* (1958): Judy (Kim Novak)

Proust provides an apt demonstration of this dynamic in which, upon discovering that two people we know in completely different circumstances and perspectives are actually the same person, we struggle to reconcile the two manifestations, to view them as the same person. We can understand their identity from a deductive standpoint yet persist in thinking of them as different people, as two incompatible *noemata:*

> I am convinced that it is Albertine whom I find there, the same who used often to come to a halt in the midst of her friends during their walks against the backdrop of the sea; but *all those more recent images remain separate from that earlier one* because *I am unable to confer on her retrospectively an identity* which she did not have for me at the moment she caught my eye; whatever assurance I may derive from the law of probabilities, that girl with the plump cheeks who stared at me so boldly from the corner of the little street and from the beach, and

Figure 14: Still from *Vertigo:* Judy (Kim Novak) dressed as Madeleine

by whom I believe that I might have been loved, *I have never, in the strict sense of the words, seen again.* (Proust 1919, pp. 904–905, my italics)

In *Vertigo*, when Scottie, still pining desperately for Madeleine (the "fake wife" whom he believes dead), meets a girl who looks exactly like her (Judy Barton, the woman who had previously been impersonating Madeleine, as the audience has now come to understand), he actually re-encounters Madeleine's physical body, but this is clearly not enough for him to find Madeleine again. Obsessed with Judy's resemblance to Madeleine, Scottie begs her to dress her as Madeleine and mimic Madeleine's physical mannerisms in a frantic effort to recreate a narrative that will allow him to see Madeleine again (Figure 14). In Proust's terms, he tries to reconstruct her "image."

At the end of *Vertigo*, even after discovering that Madeleine was Judy Barton all along, Scottie still calls her by the old name: "I loved you so, Madeleine"—thereby indicating that "the grip of a fantasy, a projected image, a theatrical persona, can survive with a life-altering intensity, even after the 'truth' is known" (Pippin 2017, p. 120). Though Madeleine never truly existed except as a character performed by Judy, the corporeal Judy is not enough for Scottie, despite the fact that her physical body and Madeleine's are one and the same.

3.11 Fragmented Reality

Cinema can also serve as a means of exploring the dynamics of the *constitution of reality* that often go unnoticed in our daily lives. Michael Haneke's 1997 adaptation of Kafka's *The Castle* (*Das Schloß*) offers a paradigmatic example of this process by exploring the idea of reality and more specifically allowing its perspectival nature to emerge. *The Castle* is one of Haneke's lesser-known projects, and also his last work for television as of this writing;[189] he has always described it as a TV film adaption, "an honorable enterprise" aimed at "bring[ing] literature closer to an audience" (Haneke 2020a, p. 33). At the time he was making *The Castle*, Haneke had already strongly denounced both the ever-increasing speed with which TV and "electronic media" in general present images to the audience as well as the formal indistinguishability in their treatment of highly dissimilar content, especially regarding the stylistic similarities among representations. In our terms, Haneke denounced how presentifications of real and fictitious occurrences are offered to audiences in increasingly similar ways, thereby neglecting the different attitudes that he felt ought to characterize each individual experience.

Haneke has also raised this issue in connection with mainstream cinema and its mutually influential relationship with "electronic media" (see especially Haneke 2008a, pp. 577–578). In his view, "cinema tried to counter the overwhelming omnipresence of the electronic media by intensifying its own means, which television—as much as it was technically able—then immediately integrated into its system again. The compulsion to trump one another led to the permanent paroxysm of attempted intensity and, thus, indirectly to the further blurring of the boundary between reality and image as well" (Haneke 2008a, p. 578). This point resonates with a remark of Baudrillard's: "No blanks, no gaps, no ellipses, no silence, just like television, with which cinema has become increasingly assimilated by losing the specificity of its own images. We are moving ever closer to high definition, in other words to the useless perfection of images" (Baudrillard 1997, pp. 112–113).

Haneke insists that this lack of regard for difference in presentifications has created perilous consequences for the recipients' consciousnesses, a major one being that even those images purportedly depicting actual occurrences are "deprived of reality" (Haneke 1998, p. 60), experienced as devoid of much of the complexity characterizing our encounters with real situations (see Haneke 2020c,

---

[189] In 1967, well before he gained international fame as a film director, Michael Haneke began working for television (Holmes 2007, p. 109). His first TV film, *...und was kommt danach?* (*After Liverpool*, 1974), was released long before his first feature film, *Der siebente Kontinent* (*The Seventh Continent*), which came out in 1989. This should not come as a surprise since "practically every German-speaking filmmaker" at that time "started out directing films for television, taking advantage of the relatively generous system of subsidies and the general openness of German and Austrian state television channels to aesthetic innovation" (Speck 2010, p. 63). In any case, Haneke later specified that directing for television was not solely a matter of opportunity but also offered a fitting milieu in which to develop his own style (see Haneke 2001).

p. 25). In such "pollut[ed] iconospheres," he says, the audience becomes progressively "blind"[190] to the dimension of reality that those images still claim to show —another remark clearly reflective of Baudrillard's positions, particularly those concerning forms of "modern iconoclasm," of destroying images through profusion: multiplication resulting in annihilation.

Adapting Kafka's novel was Haneke's idea (see Haneke 2020a, p. 33; Haneke 1998, p. 45), and he did so for reasons that resonate with our endeavors here: he was particularly interested in Kafka's approach to "the question of how literature can reflect reality" through a "fragmented narration" (Haneke 1998, p. 45; *The Castle* itself is, of course, an unfinished work, written in 1922[191]). The relationship between fragmentation and reality is one of the key issues informing Haneke's own cinematic explorations as well, so delving into "Kafka's *fragmentary*, ambiguous perception of reality" affords him an opportunity to reflect cinematically on his own style by working with another person's style, another person's *perspective* —an opportunity "to remain true to [his] convictions and yet do the work of someone else" (Haneke 2020a, p. 33, my italics).[192]

Like the 1922 original version of the book, the film opens *in medias res*—as with Diderot's *Jacques the Fatalist*, we do not know "where K. is coming from" or "where he was truly headed" (Diderot 1798)—and ends *ex abrupto*, with text on a black screen reading, "Franz Kafka's fragment ends here [*An dieser Stelle endet Franz Kafkas Fragment*]." Haneke's use of black frames underscores *The Cas-*

---

[190] "The eyes have become a little blind, overfed with images. Of course there is acoustic pollution, but it's less, and it can be cleansed with good music. In case of the eyes, it's more difficult" (Kusturica/Testor 2004).

[191] *The Castle* famously tells of a man, K., who arrives in a village late one evening and enters an inn looking for a place to spend the night. Shortly thereafter, a young man claiming to be "the son of the castle warden" tells him that the village belongs to "the castle" and, unless he has a permit, he must leave. Although initially puzzled, K. affirms that he has been summoned by the castle as a land surveyor (*Landvermesser*), adding that his two assistants are supposed to be joining him the following day. The young man immediately seeks confirmation by calling the castle. A representative of the castle initially seems to deny any association with the so-called land surveyor, but another phone call soon follows to acknowledge the possibility of such a request having been made. (At this point, we do not know for sure whether K. was truly summoned by the castle, or whether he made up the story and the castle is playing along; in fact, this question is never answered.) From that point on, K. attempts to gain the castle's recognition as a land surveyor, albeit without success (at least until the end of the novel, which, as mentioned, breaks off mid-sentence).

[192] On Haneke's declared interest in Kafka's fragmented style see also Haneke (2008c, p. 24): "I'm working on an adaptation of *The Castle* by Kafka. What interests me about Kafka's work is the fragmentation of all our perceptions. I'm looking for a way to translate this Kafkaesque literary trope to television."

tle's fragmented cinematic style,[193] which articulates the film in "segments." These interruptions create an "in-between" space, breaking the flow of the audience's vision and, ideally, kick-starting the viewer's imagination by leaving blanks for it to fill.[194] Given Haneke's explicit reference to TV audience expectations, we might call these moments of black emptiness the antithesis of commercial breaks, in which advertising content overloads viewers' potential space for free imagination.

Significantly, there are no establishing shots to provide the audience with an overarching framework through which to unify the many fragmentary scenes into a cohesive whole—a choice that seems to underline the impossibility of finding a totalizing point of view on the different perspectives, a point of view that is not in turn a *perspective*. In a manner clearly evocative of Bresson (one of Haneke's most influential sources of inspiration), the characters' bodies are sometimes "fragmented" as well.

Even when *The Castle*'s indoor cinematography implies more "in-depth" inspection than panoramic views, it seems that going deeper does not equate to forward progress: zooming in brings us no closer to the "truth" than the lateral motion of the outdoor shots but rather just creates new possibilities for fragmentation, for a multiplicity of perspectives. This suggests that, as with the outdoor spaces, the indoor spaces might extend into infinity without ever arriving at a nonperspectival truth. As Nietzsche famously puts it, "every cave […] *must* […] have […] an even deeper cave behind it—a more extensive, stranger, richer world above the surface, an abyss behind every ground, under every 'groundwork'" (Nietzsche 1886, p. 173). Hence, regardless of whether our search progresses laterally (through tracking shots) or in profundity (by zooming in), there seem to be no endpoints representing either the beginning (source) or the end (goal) of the process in which the viewer is invited to participate.

---

[193] Let us recall that this is a technique that Haneke already experimented with in his *Der siebente Kontinent* (*The Seventh Continent*, 1989) and *71 Fragmente einer Chronologie des Zufalls* (*71 Fragments of a Chronology of Chance*, 1994)—his first and third films in his "glaciation of feelings" (*Vergletscherung der Gefühle*) trilogy, the second being *Benny's Video* (1992). He employs this technique again in *Code Unknown* (*Code inconnu: récit incomplet de divers voyages*, 2000). Tellingly, the titles of the 1994 and 2000 films explicitly refer to the dimension of *fragmentation and incompleteness*.

[194] On the function of black frames in *The Castle* cf. the following passage in Haneke's 1997 interview with Willy Riemer: "Riemer: Though film is so strongly iconic, nonetheless, the viewer's imagination is exercised between the images and shots. Haneke: Yes, in between, exactly. Certainly. In this film as well, I have two seconds of black film between scenes, the film is divided into segments, and one could say that the contradiction between these individual fragments produces that which goes beyond it" (Haneke 2020a, p. 34).

Phenomenologically, the camera movements and montages (diachronic and synchronic) present possibilities for staging directions of thought, ways of comprehending reality that can then become part of and affect our understanding of the world, which is never a neutral, privileged point of view—never untouched by its surroundings, never "external" to the action. Even iconically phantasized movements (such as these) can set in motion movements and possibilities of thought that can react with our perspective on the intentional correlations punctuating our commerce with the so-called real world.

Just as *The Castle* presents no single (neutral, external) perspective that absolutely encompasses all the others, it never resorts to a neutral or omniscient voice speaking from a nonsituated, "outside" perspective. Rather than helping connect the fragments to create unequivocal order, the voiceover is itself a part of the fragmented whole. Such interplays help establish mutual control between the two dimensions while also serving Haneke's aim of "slowing down the [audience's] speed of reception" (see Haneke 1998, p. 46), thus creating contrast with the rapid and overwhelming deluge of information transmission that Haneke describes as the standard for TV—a challenge he confronts "from within" the medium itself. (Notably, in the same year that Haneke made *The Castle*, he also launched an analogous, though certainly more widely known, challenge "from within" to mainstream cinema audience expectations in the form of *Funny Games* (1997; 2007, US remake); we shall return to that film later.)

Clearly, Haneke makes no concessions to what he considers to be TV audience expectations. *The Castle* uses no embellishment, no extra-diegetic music or dramaturgical signposting to lead the audience to the "correct" interpretation—nothing about it caters to popular tastes acquired through standardized patterns in entertainment. Many films, for example, include a sequence intended to reveal the misleading nature of previous sequences by showing the audience "what really happened," the "objective" truth as viewed by what the spectator assumes to be an omniscient eye—as if this "truthful" framing were not itself produced from a certain perspective. In *The Castle*, on the other hand, spectators are deprived of any fixed, reassuring points of reference from which to interpret on-screen events—they have no more insight into "what really happened" than does the character of K.

Nor does Haneke cater to conventional assumptions of what makes something "Kafkaesque": it is Kafka as a *"great realist"* Haneke is interested in. Kafka's realism, of course, gave rise to the "Kafkaesque," but only as one of the most peculiar effects of its faithful penetration into the structure of our existence. In Haneke's view, merely "transpos[ing]" this effect "into a scenic effect" would yield overly theatrical, illustrative results that would cause the film to "lose [...] its quality of realism," thereby undermining the goal of his exercise. If elements of the Kafkaesque, as a peculiar kind of "grotesque," are to be found in *The Castle*, they do not come in the form of ready-made clichés (e.g., a series of visual artifices commonly used to induce a sense of the grotesque in the audience). This does not mean that *The Castle* is incapable of expressing the "grotesque," but rather that it does so as an effect of Haneke's very precise realist approach.[195] The Kafkaesque, then, must be a result of a fragmented cinematic style—it is an *expressed* effect that emerges from "describ[ing] reality with [...] *precision*" (Haneke 2020a, p. 33), i.e., as it usually presents itself, through fragmentation.

This adaptation can thus also represent a sort of study, a cinematic critical-thinking activity examining a way of exploring reality (i.e., Kafka's) to which he strongly relates—which is in keeping with cinema's ability to elicit an "aesthetic mode of understanding, or an aesthetic perspective on what philosophy traditionally tries to pursue at the more conceptual level" (Pippin 2020, p. 11), a type of cinematic reflection. This is why such a strategy might not only trigger audiences to pick up (or revisit) Kafka's book but also to question their own receptivity as spectators toward the structure of the real. In fact, Haneke's *The Castle* is evidently not aimed exclusively at people who are unfamiliar with Kafka's novel (which might well imply an assumption that uncultured television audiences need Haneke's help discovering Kafka, whereas arthouse film audiences are well-read and require no such invitation—a patronizing blanket judgment indeed). His film, *qua* selective fragmentation, is a possible *variation* of the novel played through another medium, one that might prompt viewers to consider, through a cinematic lens, *forces* and *values* that they cannot usually detect but which imbue the structure of their everyday lives.

As we have said, a film cannot limit itself to communicating preexisting ideas. It has to be able to produce a new sense, which, according to my hypothesis, implies a necessary correlation between perspective (narrative), emotion, and

---

[195] "Now if you become theatrical in film in order to transport the grotesque, then you lose the sense of reality. If you look at most of the Kafka films, reality withdraws from the viewer into something oversized and surreal. Take the adaptation by Orson Welles. His film is very impressive, but in my opinion, it does a disservice to the book, to Kafka. Because of his enormous talent, it turned into a great film by Orson Welles. But he works under the standard of the book because he abandons reality, and Kafka *is nothing if not real.* That means, if one decides to convey this *real level of Kafka*, then one has to sacrifice the grotesque. The grotesque then only appears, so to speak, in the contradictoriness between the individual components, but not in each scene itself. Everything that has been described about the grotesque is in my film, but my film has the look of a wholly naturalistic film. The grotesque appears only through what happens. In my adaptation there are none of these curiously exaggerated zombies that one frequently sees in Kafka films. All that is gone. It is an entirely realistic film, and I believe that it comes closest to the spirit of Kafka's work" (Haneke 2020a, pp. 33–34, my italics).

value. Every constitution of a world implies a *perspectival process of valorization/ devalorization*. This sense is not something hidden behind a veil, an extant meaning that merely needs to be revealed and communicated. Rather, it must be disclosed through a process that brings one to *recognize* it, paradoxically, as *something that was not there before*.

3.12 Perspectival Truths

Our purpose in referencing Haneke/Kafka is also to further our examination of perspectivism as a possible approach to the nature of truth. In this context, it may prove beneficial to inquire a bit further into the nature of "The Castle" and its "true" manifestation. More specifically, *The Castle*'s fragmented style appears to question a metaphysical construal of "Truth" and "Values" as self-sufficient dimensions that exist unaffected behind the sensible world of appearances. Elaborating on this point may aid us in our efforts to characterize the expressive processes concerning production of sense and valorization.

The castle, the presupposed "true thing," is never rendered entirely visible, and its alleged fragments do not seem to be well-defined parts fitting into a classically hierarchical structure. Indeed, on closer examination, it does not even seem to look like a castle. At the beginning of their 1975 text on Kafka—after the well-known passage characterizing the Czech writer's work as a "rhizome"—Deleuze and Guattari remark that "the castle has multiple entrances whose rules of usage and whose locations aren't very well known" (Deleuze/Guattari 1975, p. 3). These entrances are not governed by any specific order whereby one is assigned more importance than another—none of the castle's entrances can be deemed, *a priori, more valuable* than any other, though they may differ greatly in appearance; in principle, every fragment of the castle has the power to *lead* us into it.[196] In fact, even without having consciously chosen to enter the castle, one might later learn or realize that they have stepped through one of its manifold entrances—as might be the case with K., who ends up in castle territory seemingly by chance.

Nevertheless, although it is possible to enter the castle from any of the fragments belonging to it, it seems that one can never reach "the" castle, properly speaking. As viewers, we *cannot* know if K. actually sees it at any point. We are

---

[196] "We will enter, then, by any point whatsoever; none matters more than another, and no entrance is more privileged even if it seems an impasse, a tight passage, a siphon" (Deleuze/Guattari 1975, p. 3).

only allowed to know fragments of truth. In the film, as in the novel, we meet only representatives of the castle, people who allegedly speak on its behalf—no one gets to reveal the "thing in itself." If anything, Haneke's adaptation makes this point even more forcefully, as though to emphasize that the castle is everywhere and yet nowhere. It is ultimately invisible and impossible to grasp; in principle, everything can signify it, and yet every sign of it essentially points elsewhere, beyond itself. The castle manifests itself only through its representatives (people, letters, phone calls)—that is, by delegation. Its representatives and signs may emerge from anywhere, at any time, but the alleged original castle, the alleged Truth beyond its manifestations, remains perpetually out of reach.

I would like to suggest that the word "castle" stands less for a thing than a *process*. As a *moving structure*, "The Castle" is unreachable, "untouchable" insofar there is nothing "behind its veils." In fact, experiencing Kafkan fragmentation might lead the audience to question the alleged transcendent nature of "the Castle." In other words, "the Castle" as metaphysical "Truth" might be the result of a kind of illusion, one that leads its "victims" to consider the ideal dimension we experience in reality in a Platonistic way, as a "Castle in itself" *qua* fixed Truth preceding and originating the process. This would be the consequence of a "deceptive movement," as Nietzsche remarked in *Twilight of the Idols*: "No error is more dangerous than that of *confusing the cause with the effect*" (Nietzsche 1889, p. 176). From this standpoint, the idea of the "Castle" as an independent principle might also turn out to be the result of a temporal illusion produced by the *après coup* phenomenon of projecting the effect of a process into the past, retroactively deeming it the metaphysical origin of that process. This is not to imply that such retrospective movement is erroneous *per se*, but it carries the risk of blindness to the way an effect may be inadvertently hypostatized as a fixed, separate origin of the process—what Bergson would call a "retrograde movement of the true" (Bergson 1934).

Of course, pointing the finger at an illusory backward-projection of truths and values emerging through a process could potentially deceive us into considering those values merely projectional—and thus relative—in nature. However, this relativistic stand would represent an overly simplistic upheaval of the classical, Platonistic view, one still caught within the framework of a true-false dichotomy. On the one side, we have the idea of a fixed, stable Truth that is the real cause of every appearance we encounter, a Truth that is always "beyond," just as the Castle is never originally present within its fragments but always presupposed beyond them—in other words, the primacy of the Castle's hidden essence over the appearances of its representatives. On the other side, we have the notion that the negation of one metaphysical Truth must result in the negation of any essential Truth whatsoever in favor of a relativistic (and nihilistic) outcome. Under this second dichotomic pole, without any metaphysical yardstick, we might be led to surmise that no single appearance can be claimed truer than any other; accordingly, truth must be arbitrary. This nihilist/relativistic conception of truth (one often too hastily linked to Nietzschean famous adage, "there are no facts, only interpretations") suggests that, if there is no Truth, *anything*—and, therefore, *nothing*—can be true.

Nietzsche was already well aware of the potential pitfall here: warning against the construal of a process's effects as its metaphysical origin need not *ipso facto* imply the reverse, i.e., the relativistic omnipresence of the false.[197] Indeed, Nietzsche famously remarks that *"along with the true [world] we got rid of the illusory [one]"* (Nietzsche 1889, p. 171). Thus, moving beyond a Platonistic approach cannot simply mean declaring that all discourse about truth is illusory and that *all* values are merely the result of arbitrary, subjective projections induced through a process of ever-changing appearances. Rather, appearances themselves must be *reassessed*[198] and reappraised. In our terms, they must undergo new processes of valorization (which can also entail devalorization, revalorization, etc.):

> it is no more than a moral prejudice that the truth is worth more than appearance; in fact, it is the world's most poorly proven assumption. Let us admit this much: that life could not exist except on the basis of perspectival valuations and appearances; and if, with the virtuous enthusiasm and inanity of many philosophers, someone wanted to completely abolish the "world of appearances,"—well, assuming *you* could do that,—at least there would not be any of your "truth" left either! Actually, why do we even assume that "true" and "false" are intrinsically opposed? Isn't it enough to assume that there are levels of appearance and, as it were, lighter and darker shades and tones of appearance—different *valeurs*, to use the language of painters? (Nietzsche 1886, p. 35)

Affirming the essential perspectivism of our experiences (their way of manifesting themselves and the values we can potentially recognize through them), then, is not tantamount to taking a relativistic stance; rather, it can offer a powerful alternative to the dichotomies of true vs. false, essence vs. appearance, or fact vs. interpretation.

Haneke's work develops this point extensively, especially through his abovementioned theme of fragmentation. Though reality is an enigma to him (see Kus-

---

[197] This would amount to a naïve reversal of Platonism. See also Smith (2012, p. 4), who points out the possibility of it producing positivistic outcomes, a danger against which Heidegger had already warned: "Plato, it is said, opposed essence to appearance, the original to the image, the sun of truth to the shadows of the cave, and to overturn Platonism would initially seem to imply a reversal of this standard relation: what languishes below in Platonism must be put on top; the super-sensuous must be placed in the service of the sensuous. But such an interpretation, as Heidegger showed, only leads to the quagmire of positivism, an appeal to the *positum* rather than the *eidos*."
[198] On this point see also Gori (2016, p. 38).

turica/Testor 2004), and though he makes no hasty concessions to any metaphysical notion of reality independent of appearances, this does not lead him to dismiss the value of the quest to describe reality—the "different *valeurs*" of the diverse possible but nonarbitrary *narratives* through which we weave our fragmented experiences from our perspectives, continuously redefining the scope of what we consider real. He constantly denounces the phony sense of safety many mainstream directors give audiences through dramaturgical patterns thought to convey an expected outcome—always presupposing the existence of, if not directly disclosing, an objective and truthful narrative underlying the manifold appearances presented to the viewer.

Instead, the world essentially appears as a multiplicity of "connected" and "broken" fragments that no surveying eye seems capable of resolving into a cohesive and definitive whole. In fact, as Merleau-Ponty points out, the ideal of an all-embracing eye, a *"kosmotheoros"* capable of objectively measuring reality from above and encompassing all its elements, is ultimately "forced into the bifurcation of the essence and the fact" (Merleau-Ponty 1964, p. 113)—analogous to the Nietzschean "bifurcation" of truth and appearance described above. For such a panoptic conception of truth, "good" images would be those most suitable for objectively and exhaustively measuring the truth—"land surveying images," so to speak. However, this kind of abstract, overarching eye betrays the nature of truth, for our experiences of truth are *essentially* perspectives, and the perspectival view should not be considered a deficiency requiring the adjusting influence of an omniscient eye. At the same time, these various perspectives can interweave at different levels and show varying levels of sedimentation, giving rise to a profundity and superficiality of perspective, including in a "geological" sense. Hence, *some of our perspectives are fleeting and temporary, while others are deeply rooted and affect us on a habitual and latent level.*

3.13 Perspectivism, Not Relativism

Cinematically (and iconically in general), renouncing this construal of truth signifies abandonment of the "organic" description Deleuze offers in his second book on cinema, specifically in the chapter devoted to "the powers of the false." This organic approach presupposes an "independent" and "pre-existing reality" to which "good" images—"land surveying images"—"truthful[ly] [...] claim [...]" to conform, "even in fiction" (Deleuze 1985, pp. 126–127). Within this framework, the "good" narration disqualifies all others.

In the example mentioned earlier in which a (documentary or fictional) film purportedly shows us "what really happened," such moments tacitly imply a neutral cinematic eye capable of seeing the truth objectively—as though this eye were not in turn perspectival. It is this allegedly omniscient cinematic eye that Haneke avoids using. In *The Castle*, the word "land surveyor [*Landvermesser*]" is bandied about throughout the film, a reference to an old function now rendered meaningless, though its name is still recognizable: everyone in the village refers to K. as the *Landvermesser*, without apparently knowing what the work entails or whether he will ever end up doing it (probably not). We, in turn, are thus invited to ponder the fragmentary nature of our own knowledge and how it develops.

In the above-mentioned chapter on "the powers of the false," when referring to the style of Bresson (whose influence on Haneke, as we have already noted, is evident in *The Castle*[199]), Deleuze describes his cinematic reconfiguration of fragments in terms of "Riemanian spaces," a "connecti[on] of parts" that "is not predetermined but can take place in many ways" (Deleuze 1985, p. 129). Interestingly, Bresson's oeuvre is well within that "crystalline" regime that Deleuze contrasts against the "organic" (see Deleuze 1985, pp. 127–137). In "crystalline narration" (of the type found in Haneke's work), the "fracture" (Deleuze 1985, p. 128) or *fragmentation* becomes the essential element that "puts the notion of truth into crisis" (Deleuze 1985, p. 130). Deleuze, explicitly drawing inspiration from Nietzsche, warns that, under this new and "fundamentally falsifying" regime, "the truthful man dies" and "every model of truth collapses" (Deleuze 1985, p. 131).

However, I consider it paramount to specify that the models of truth collapsing are those construed as metaphysically separate from their narrative interpretations; even from a Nietzschean standpoint, this need not mean the collapse of *any* concept of truth whatsoever. Analogously, the general idea that "the very possibility of judging is called into question" (Deleuze 1985, p. 138) in the fragmented regime need not lead to the equally untenable assertion that no judgment is possible whatsoever. Nietzsche's well-known appeal to the creation of new values must imply the possibility of a new way of assessment and judging[200]—in our terms, new processes of valorization.

---

[199] In this respect cf. also Grundmann et al. (2020, p. xi).
[200] In contradiction to Deleuze's well-known interpretation, I would argue that this also holds true regarding Welles' worlds. In fact, in the *The Powers of the False* chapter, Deleuze famously refers to Welles' "Nietzscheanism," saying that he "constantly constructs characters who are unjudicable and who have not to be judged, who evade any possible judgement. If the ideal of truth crumbles, the relations of appearance will no longer be sufficient to maintain the possibility of judgement. In Nietzsche's phrase, 'with the real world we have also abolished the apparent world'" (Deleuze 1985, p. 139). However, as we have already remarked, this quote of Nietzsche's is not wholly incompatible with the philosopher's endeavors toward a *revaluation* of appearances.

In fact, once we have dismissed the idea of a Truth independent of appearance, every manifestation *can* acquire some specific value without being thereby rendered true or false—though this, obviously, does not prevent it from being considered good or bad.[201] Each fragment participates in the movement through which only truth constitutes itself. This could certainly be one light in which to view Haneke's appreciation of Kafka's fragmented style: a fragmented approach might be more faithful to reality because reality itself is constituted through a series of fragmented perspectives, fragments we reconfigure through our changing yet nonarbitrary narratives. This is also true axiologically in that, for instance, "the same" narrative can take on different values when incorporated into other narratives or reacting to them. Against this background, I believe that Deleuze's concept of "the powers of the false" risks becoming unduly fixated (both terminologically and philosophically) upon a dichotomic and ultimately simplistic reversal of the Platonistic stance. In fact, his interpretation of Nietzsche undeniably tends to disqualify truthful narratives in favor of "falsifying" ones (Deleuze 1985, p. 131).

Instead, I wish to advocate for a "perspectivism of truth" implying perspective-related (but nonarbitrary), continuously interactive axiological and emotional levels of understanding, levels potentially imbued with different qualities of truth and/or falsehood depending on the nature and complexity of the perspective from which they are experienced. For this reason, I would avoid the term "falsifying" in relation to the *fragmented image* as it is still too closely tied to the very dichotomy we are striving to avoid. In fact, a fragment of the world can be experienced as an appearance of greater or lesser value, one involved in a reconfiguration of reality that is continuously redefined through intersections and interactions among different perspectives, each of which may be attributable to the same subject or different subjects when they share and participate in "views of the world."[202] A "genius" in one environment can be a "fool" in another (another point masterfully illustrated by Proust). Again and again, new perspectives can interact through contrasts, fractures, incorporations, and so on. Although this process may in principle be infinite (as there are no all-encompassing perspectives), it is not arbitrary. *The decisive question becomes this: under what conditions, from what perspectives, is it possible for a subject to experience the world (cognitively/*

---

[201] A point Deleuze makes explicitly in reference to Nietzsche (see Deleuze 1985, p. 141).

[202] "The one knows the other not only in what he suffers from him, but more generally as a witness, who can be challenged because he is also himself accused, because he is not a pure gaze upon pure being any more than I am, because his views and my own are in advance inserted into a system of *partial perspectives*, referred to one same world in which we coexist and where our views intersect" (Merleau-Ponty 1964, p. 82, my italics).

emotionally/axiologically) in that way, to undergo different processes of valorization and correspondingly react in that manner?[203]

The richness of the perspectives a subject considers when forming conceptions of reality becomes decisive in this regard, although no overarching point of view can incorporate all of these perspectives at once: however exhaustive a subject's position may be, there is always an *a priori* possibility of another perspective encompassing it. *The subject, then, is more a point of intersection of several perspectives than a fixed substance producing and projecting interpretations*; even when the subject experiences conflicting perspectives, the richness of these perspectives shapes the spectrum of what the subject calls truth. In principle, each of these perspectives affects the constitution of the "palette" of "different *valeurs*." Moreover, perspectival subjective sources are always made up of multiple understandings and beliefs. Some perspectives can grasp others because they are more comprehensive—they share their vision but encompass other possibilities as well. They are, so to speak, richer in sense.

To return to the previous example, the circumstances under which someone might be a "fool" in one context and a "genius" in another might be perfectly evident to a third party (working from a different perspective). In the *Recherche*, the narrator, an extremely rich perspectival entity, can shed light on why Charlus might be highly respected in high society and yet a fool within Mme Verdurin's *petit clan*. There are laws to be described that can motivate such seemingly irreconcilable contrasts. Clearly, the third instance (the narrator, in this case) can also only provide insight on these laws from his or her own perspectival situation—which can by its nature always change and develop.

Again, such perspectivism does not amount to a relativistic stance. In this regard, Haneke goes as far as to describe postmodernism—or, *at least, the postmodernism epitomized* in the "claim that all the existential and moral questions are behind us"[204]—as "dangerous nonsense," as a "Fun-Ideology" (Haneke 2008b, p. 122). Haneke places great importance on this point. At the same time, we have noted his insistence on avoiding imposing unique, "truthful" explanations of the on-screen action. Rather, he says, directors must leave space for viewers to develop their own narratives and images and to experience values essentially related to those perspectives.

Some might perceive a certain element of patronization in Haneke's stated goal of shaking TV audiences awake from their "iconically embedded sleep," but

---

[203] Haneke's considerations on violence in Haneke (2009) can also be viewed within this framework. See also Haneke (2020b, pp. 38–39).
[204] For a description of "postmodernism" in the context of a larger discussion of "modernism" that does not dichotomically oppose the two, cf., for example, Franzini (2018).

though there may be a pedagogical element to his intentions, didacticism is certainly not a factor. He does not view his work as a medium through which to snobbishly hand nuggets of clearly defined truths to the audience "from above," but rather as an attempt to renounce the specific dramaturgical devices and tricks aimed at providing reassuring answers about reality and its complexity. Haneke's audiences are not given more freedom so much as more responsibility:[205] they have to form their own ideas while grappling with the fragments presented to them. In fact, Haneke even rejects the notion that he, as the creator of the film, possesses the objective truth regarding the motives behind his characters' actions.[206] The absence of ready-made truths obliges the viewer to make an effort to reconfigure the fragments, to make connections by shifting between imagination and memory, by confronting public and personal narratives—just as occurs in our day-to-day construction and configuration of the real.

3.14 Shipwrecks at a Distance

We have seen that, even in the consciousness of the image that distinguishes it, a film can arouse in us a positional interest in the existence of the *sujet*, a consciousness of reality that characterizes the story being told. The complex nature of this connection becomes particularly evident in cases where the tragic nature of a real event for which we hope to provide an image-based account clashes with the delicate question concerning our chosen modality of representation. The reality of the tragic fact, one might suggest, delimits boundaries on the freedom of those who intend to present that fact in images; it implies a different responsibility. In Chapter 2, we referred to questions Rivette raised on a famous tracking shot by Pontecorvo; from there, we touched upon Kundera's reading of a Célinian passage to examine the inherent risk in a human "exhibition" of occurrences whose representation would be, to recall Bazin's words, "obscene" in nature (for example, the death of the toreador Manolete).[207] This inescapable danger forces cinema to make choices regarding the representational "how" whenever a being's suffering

---

205 See also Grundmann (2010, p. 384).
206 See, for instance, Haneke's remarks on the *Caché* (2005) characters Georges (Daniel Auteuil) and Majid (Maurice Bénichou): "We don't know if Georges is telling the truth, and we don't know if Majid is telling the truth. We don't really know which one of the characters is lying—just as we don't know in real life" (Haneke 2020b, p. 80).
207 "The cinema has given the death of Manolete a material eternity. On the screen, the toreador dies every afternoon" (Bazin 1949–1951, p. 31).

and death are presentified in film. Cinema is invested with this responsibility when it comes to the sense of what it shows.

We shall now re-examine some aspects that we deliberately left open earlier, while also considering the converse question: how is this responsibility affected when we are dealing with fictional, apositional works? These, one might think, ought to keep us from that bond to reality for which we assume responsibility when viewing images with positional connotations. When the representation of pain and death unfolds "on our terms," on a purely fictional plane—that is, when we witness *quasi*-suffering or a *quasi*-death not referencing allegedly real events—how does this affect our representation options? Do such circumstances entail a qualitatively different type of responsibility from positionally marked instances? Are the creators of fictitious works afforded unlimited license (of the type taken by the Marquise de Sade, for example) in their depictions, and are their audiences exempt from the responsibility that comes with bearing witness to violence or death? Absent this bond to reality, are spectators free to phantasize and enjoy the content of *any* type whatsoever?

In approaching these questions, we must keep in mind our previous analysis of *quasi*-emotions and *quasi*-values, along with the relationship we discussed between "real" and "phantasy" ego. We might start by noting that fictional images pose no genuine threat to us with their *quasi*-presences or *quasi*-actions given that we do not believe that their *sujets* exist or have ever existed. We have seen that the fact that fictional situations do not have actual consequences in themselves can alter the way we react to them (e.g., we respond to on-screen gunfights differently from real ones). The theme of the safe, protected spectator condition—a point of sufficient distance from which one can enjoy observing a tragic event—is one possible reading of Lucretius's well-known "shipwreck with spectator" *topos*, a metaphor used throughout Western tradition (see also Blumenberg 1979). Consider this well-known passage from *De rerum natura* (II, 1–4): "Pleasant it is, when on the great sea the winds trouble the waters, to gaze from shore upon another's great tribulation: not because any man's troubles are a delectable joy, but because to perceive what ills you are free from yourself is pleasant" (Lucretius 1992, p. 95). Note that Lucretius links pleasure not to the "what" of the presentation ("not because any man's troubles are a delectable joy") but to the *distance* that protects us from an otherwise-menacing occurrence.

This brief but necessary aside is aimed at introducing a final series of analyses: even when we restrict our spectrum of interpretations to the one just described, a wide variety of phenomena seem to fall under the "shipwreck with spectator" trope. As we shall see, despite having some degree of kinship among them, these phenomena display profoundly dissimilar traits when viewed through a phenomenological lens.

Let us consider the filmic image in this context: does it allow us to maintain distance from what it presentifies? And if so, what type of distance? We could start by suggesting that the dimension of unreality distinguishing film images (neutrality at the level of their status as image object, a feature common to every image, whether positional or not) could be considered a condition that *eo ipso* allows the viewer to feel safe with respect to what is happening on-screen. But this argument could prove a slippery slope: what does it mean to say that something *is happening* on-screen? There are several senses in which we might say that the cinematic screen allows us to maintain a certain distance from reality, regardless of whether we are given the opportunity to reflect consciously on this condition while watching.

We have seen that, from the Husserlian point of view, film images are like other physical images in that they do not show perceptual objects: what manifests on screen are images, not "flesh-and-blood" things. Properly speaking, we could not physically touch the things we see on-screen even if we wanted to: they are exclusively visible, intangible.[208] Though Diderot said that the fruit in Chardin's painting is just like fruit *in the flesh*,[209] neither we nor Diderot have any illusions about whether we can actually sample *that* specific fruit. This type of distance is consubstantial to the image as such.

Yet this is far from an exhaustive account of our experience of images, of the possible avenues through which they can become part of how we understand and experience the real. Even though we cannot actually taste Chardin's apple, the image might forever change the way we view (or even taste) real apples—and like Isaac Davis's character in Woody Allen's *Manhattan* (1979), we might include "those incredible apples and pears by Cézanne" on our list of things worth living for. Merleau-Ponty notes how Cézanne, Braque, and Picasso were able to create objects that "hold our gaze," force it to stop, "question it, convey to it in a bizarre fashion the very secret of their substance, the very mode of their material existence and which, so to speak, stand bleeding before us" (Merleau-Ponty 1948,

---

[208] Although we can certainly characterize vision as having a "haptic" dimension, the term (as Deleuze and Guattari recall, making explicit reference to Riegl [1901]) "does not establish an opposition between two sense organs but rather invites the assumption that the eye itself may fulfill this nonoptical function" (Deleuze/Guattari 1980, p. 492). As regards the tactile dimension, further analysis is warranted regarding virtual reality experiences—which, as mentioned, will be the subject of a dedicated study and will not be specifically addressed in this book.

[209] "The porcelain vase is porcelain; the olives are really separated from the eye by the water in which they drown; you just have to take those cookies and eat them, that bitter orange, open it and squeeze it, that glass of wine, drink it, that fruit, peel it and put the knife in the pâté" (Diderot 2007 [1763], p. 220).

p. 93, transl. slightly modified). Again, despite knowing that we cannot physically touch that blood, we can "feel it with our eyes," or better, feel it "in itself"—these are "painting[s... that lead] us back to a vision of things themselves" (Merleau-Ponty 1948, p. 93).

Though we cannot physically grab objects we see on-screen in a film and share them with the people around us, we can certainly phantasize ourselves in a world where such things are possible—something akin to the *quasi*-world presented in *The Purple Rose of Cairo* (1985). We could even think of a phantasy complying with *perceptio* involving a world like this, for example, through virtual reality. Even so, when we watch movies, we are not confronted with reality as the domain of perception. We know that the on-screen knife is merely presentified, so it cannot actually harm us—and if it is presentified in a fictional world, it cannot actually harm anyone.

On the heels of the questions raised above, we might ask whether this level of iconic distance ought to suffice to make us feel safe with respect to what is happening in the image, including when it comes to fictional images having no positional relationship to a presentified *sujet* and thus not presumed to pose an actual threat. Let us begin by considering *actual* occurrences *distanced* through images (the Latin *distanza* refers to a "not being there").

3.15 Actuality at an Iconic Distance

We have said that if we know that what we are about to see is a film in a documentary attitude, our position as spectators seems more complex than what a fictional situation would require. Knowing that the film in question is a documentary immediately gives us a different sense of responsibility toward what we are watching; we may even feel threatened by the on-screen images that, despite their presentificational nature, intimidate or unsettle us in a very different way than they would in a fictional context. Let us recall that the etymology of responsibility also refers back to the Latin *respondere* [to respond]; different types of images may call for different responses. In other words, we believe in the actual existence of what we see in the images, and that form of belief affects how we experience them. We know that what is manifested on-screen is not physically in the room with us at that moment, but we believe that it was there "in the flesh" at the moment of filming. With live broadcasts, we know that the on-screen action is actually happening in front of the on-scene cameras; as we mentioned earlier, this might entail real consequences for our "real lives," our "real egos," and our habits and beliefs might be called to respond as a result.

In keeping with what we said in the first chapter, we can characterize watching such footage as a type of "seeing at a distance" that allows us to intend something that claims a place in what we call "objective time and space"—whether in the present moment (for example, if we are watching a live broadcast) or the past (if the footage is pre-recorded). From a phenomenological perspective, and without prejudice to the contrast that characterizes it, an image imbued with belief can interact with the synthesis of perceptual continuity[210] (as opposed to an image without the mark of belief, whose concrete individuality is not actually framed within our shared world and does not aspire to be).

Strictly speaking, the Lucretian motif recalled above seems to reflect the documentary viewing experience rather than that of viewing images in a fictional context. Within that paradigm, the spectator remains at a protective distance from something that is *actually* happening, albeit elsewhere. In the documentary regime, we can live an experience strictly analogous (though obviously not identical) to the one presented in the Lucretian *topos:* we can sit in our armchairs and observe someone or something that *is* or *has been there*, at a spatial (and potentially temporal) distance.

Clearly, we can experience this *belief* in different ways, depending on the different styles involved—for, as we have stressed, the "how" of our experience is inseparable from the "what." This belief can be conveyed through images edited *ad hoc* to elicit some form of enjoyment in viewers, who in this case become consumers of presentification that is literally spectacularized. Music, editing, and voice-over narration are just a few of the mechanisms that can help define the sense of the positional images shown to us. But though the various types of films we might accurately describe as "documentaries" differ in many ways, we can still affirm that they have one thing in common: they *claim* to be presentifications of reality.

This is a key factor in our reception of live television and of news reporting in general, though the truthfulness and significance of such images is becoming an increasingly complex question amidst today's ever-expanding range of official and unofficial channels (newspapers, websites, etc.)

As we have remarked, "seeing at a distance" can be experienced in "real time" (present). In the case of live broadcasts, we see something "happening *there, now*". People viewing the live on-screen footage can observe something presentified and believe that it is really happening at that moment, a possibility that can give rise to collective experiences of image-mediated reality. Consider, for example, a live

---

[210] On the identifying synthesis between perception and image, see also Ferencz-Flatz (2009b, p. 490).

sporting event watched simultaneously (or at least approximately so) by millions of people around the world: streets in various cities might empty in advance of the event as people gather around their screens, celebrating or lamenting the events as they unfold, and many will likely return to the streets to celebrate afterward—but only a few thousand of the people experiencing the event are actually there "in the flesh."

Let us note that spectating a tele-visual experience can also give rise to a "seeing in proximity" through which certain details of an event are revealed that remain invisible to "in-the-flesh" observers. As such, TV viewers may experience that event very differently from those on scene, including in terms of distance/proximity. For instance, while watching a sports event or a concert on television, we may see—notwithstanding the iconic distance intrinsic to presentifications—the athlete's or musician's facial expressions from just a few feet or even mere inches away, depending on where and how the camera crew chooses to direct our attention (for now, anyway; we might, at least in principle, conceive of future scenarios wherein viewers might influence or even make such decisions). This shows us how some dichotomies (distance and closeness, for example, or opacity and transparency) can manifest themselves differently at different levels: for example, the iconic *distance* intrinsic to images can allow us to experience a *proximity* we could never achieve with the naked eye.

Moreover, nowadays we encounter more and more situations wherein we attend events in person yet choose to follow some or all of the action on some sort of screen. To stay with our sporting event/concert example, many of the spectators may follow and record the experience using a smartphone, a device that can capture image fragments to save or share with others—and these thousands of images, recorded from many different angles, can theoretically be sent to millions of other people's screens instantaneously. All of this qualitatively and quantitatively multiplies the range of possible perspectives constituting our experience of the real.

3.16 A Twenty-First-Century Portrait

The different perspectives involved in how an event unfolds are examined in *Zidane: A 21st Century Portrait*, an experimental film on retired French footballer Zinédine Zidane which was presented out of competition at Cannes in 2006. Made by two contemporary artists, Douglas Gordon and Philippe Parreno, the film not only serves as a noteworthy examination of the very concept of portraiture[211] but also, in its own way, explores the notion of "happening": when something happens, what is it that is actually "happening"?

The film was made during the Real Madrid vs. Villareal match held at Santiago Bernabéu Stadium in Madrid on the evening of April 23, 2005, using 17 synchronized movie cameras (including two prototype zoom models developed by Panavision for the US Army) coordinated by the famous photography director Darius Khondji. The filmmakers arranged the cameras around the field, "ready" to portray their *sujet*. In preparation for filming, Parreno organized a private tour of the Prado Museum with the entire camera crew so that they could analyze the details of certain portrait masterpieces. During the match itself, Gordon and Parreno were stationed in a trailer outside the stadium, monitoring the camera transmissions in real time and interacting with the operators, for example, to request specific types and modalities of framing (Figure 15).[212]

Figure 15: Still from Douglas Gordon and Philippe Parreno's *Zidane: A 21st Century Portrait* (2006)

Finally, together with editor Hervé Schneid (known for his collaboration with Jean-Pierre Jeunet), the artists put together a ninety-minute film—exactly the length of a soccer match—in which, instead of following the phases of the match like a normal television broadcast, the cinematographic eye focuses solely on Zidane. The flow of images following the single protagonist around the field is occasionally *fragmented* through the inclusion of television footage of the match, as if to mark the difference between the typical TV broadcast and the undergrowth of sounds, expressions, and interjections that this peculiar intrusion allows us to experience from the field of play.

---

211 Michael Fried writes: "I was curious to discover whether or not the designation of the film as a 'portrait' could be taken seriously—whether it meant simply that the film was a biopic or whether it had some deeper resonance. I hoped the latter was the case, and when I saw the film, my hopes were fulfilled" (Fried 2008, pp. 227–228).
212 See Parreno's commentary on the DVD version of the film.

As such, this portrait is not given through visual images exclusively, but also through sounds that are in turn "re-edited" into a rhythm that pushes them into the foreground one moment, the background the next—an alternation of proximity and distance that plays out on the acoustic level as well. This gives viewers the sense of having a peculiar "zoom" feature that allows them to perceive new sounds, to experience acoustic "close-up" shots wherein their attention is directed toward the rustling grass, the athlete's breathing, the foot colliding with the ball. (As an aside, we note that many such sounds became the object of attention during the pandemic, when microphones captured them in the silence of the spectatorless stadiums.) The extradiegetic music in the original soundtrack (composed by the Scottish band Mogwai) also helps *direct attention* toward these myriad aspects of the event.

The viewer's attention is thus continually redirected to the "how," to the perspective modalities through which reality necessarily constitutes and manifests itself for us.[213] Shifting our attention to the "how" also means examining the continuous genesis of our "what" (what we might call the polyvalent dimension concerning our determination of what really happened). At the same time, continuous return to the perspective modes of manifestation necessarily changes the essence of the thing, leaving us with the question of "what" really happened that day. Significantly, at one point (corresponding to the halftime break), the filmmakers show us an approximately three-minute series of images representing a cross-section of the many other events of Saturday, April 23, 2005, from which they could potentially have selected.

The images of these occurrences flow, accompanied by relatively "neutral" captions as follows: "Saturday, April 23rd, 2005 / a puppeteer brings Bob Marley back to life in Ipanema beach puppet show / hundreds of homes are destroyed in Serbia-Montenegro during the worst floods in forty years / Elian Gonzalez speaks on Cuban national TV…" and so on. Although confined to the short symbolic space of a "halftime," the list could obviously continue, potentially into infinity (with different values depending on how these occurrences emerge within strictly personal and shared narratives).

Within the infinite (but certainly not arbitrary) nexus web constituting our reality, certain events are showcased to the viewer, while others are omitted—even for a single player of a game living a complex, absorbed, fragmented reality, some

---

213 In this respect, Parreno (2014) affirms: "Pier Paolo Pasolini explained that the best way to record reality is to endlessly multiply the subjective points of view around the event. The first idea was to have 80,000 video cameras and to give one to each spectator in the stadium! The challenge could have been even greater."

events are sanctioned as "having happened," while others are not.²¹⁴ Each subject is a monad individualized by many different folds, different senses of understanding and habits constituting their possible perspectives. In this sense, a perspective cannot be arbitrary, since it is already a way of reflecting the world and responding to it (the whole world as lived through that singular monad, which is itself part of the world).

The struggle to decide what really happened in each moment also passes through the constitution of reality through images imbued with belief—such as the ones shown during the halftime section that in principle, as we have just said, could have been infinite. Infinite and yet not unrelated, each perspective can only emerge in a nexus with other perspectives, and individual readers might have their own insights on things that happened to them that day, which in turn might intersect with other "facts"—it is always possible to identify nexuses among different facts and perspectives. Our past is not fixed but continually in flux, determined by the continuous work aimed at unearthing what happened, and this applies to what happened "yesterday" as well as to "millions of years ago" (humanity's shared past, for example, is now decidedly more extensive than it was in the eighteenth century).

In keeping with the point we are making here, this film is a portrait, yet despite referencing an actual body, it is not a depiction in the delegative sense. Rather, this artistic portrait comes to express its own *sujet*, one that in its neutrality exceeds explicit references to the actual football player. Here, the multiple angles focusing on the "how" reveal a sensitivity to expressive qualities ultimately irreducible to the mere facts that express them.

3.17 A Temporal Portrait: Singular Expressive Qualities

It may be beneficial at this juncture to emphasize a facet of Diderotian aesthetics that Fried brought up when reflecting on the concept of "theatricality" and its opposite, "absorption" (see Fried 1988). He developed these ideas further in Fried (2008) in the context of photography, also offering a detailed analysis of Gordon and Parreno's portrait of Zidane.²¹⁵ Under this paradigm, *absorption* is a dimen-

---

214 In Zidane's words: "The game, the event, is necessarily experienced in 'real time.' My memories of games and events are fragmented" (Gordon/Parreno 2006).
215 Fried (2008) summarizes the 1988 thesis on absorption as follows: "starting in the mid-1750s in France a new conception of painting came to the fore that required that the personages depicted in a canvas appear genuinely absorbed [...]. Any failure of absorption—any suggestion that a painted

sion that allows for representation *without exhibition* (at least on the part of the one being filmed). Diderot, anticipating the remarks by Céline we mentioned earlier, asserts that the moral failure jeopardizing a tableau's artistic value is not a failure to comply with heteronomous ethical precepts external to the creative process, but rather the manifestation of *bad* taste revealing *exhibitionist* tendencies, rendering the work "inauthentic."

As Pippin (2021, p. 102) rightly points out, Diderot's concept of inauthenticity refers to the kind of fraudulence "at issue when we say of a person that he or she is false, not genuine, [...] especially when we say he or she is playing to the crowd, playing for effect, or is a poseur." When this is the case, the work betrays its falseness by lingering on the beholder's expectations, by aiming to appease the viewers' clichéd taste, "posing" for them.[216] In principle, this issue was also at stake in Gordon and Parreno's experiment given that Zidane knew he was going to be filmed.

We might say that absorption into action can foster the expression of qualities that are not affected by such posing. Conversely, an action performed merely to imitate a previous gesture or to conform to an expectation, on the other hand, would result in expressive poverty. *Using the terms we described earlier, there is no genuine expression without variation or deformation.* Thus, a lack of authenticity goes hand in hand with a lack of expression. We can say that Gordon and Parreno's is a productive portrait since it aims to bring out not the fact as an occurrence but the expressive qualities that emerge as "evenemential" qualities—qualities that, as we shall see, are neither merely individual nor merely abstract but *singular*, in the sense of expressing a singular perspective that is always the expression of a world.

The term "singular" refers to a dimension that cannot be reduced to either the individual or the universal. This is tantamount to trying to understand the dimension of expression. We are often tempted to assume a need to choose between universality and individuality, "collective and private, particular and general" (*tertium non datur*). Here, however, I suggest the importance of a *tertium*, a singular dimension which is "both collective and private, particular and general, neither individ-

---

personage was acting for an audience—was considered theatrical in the pejorative sense of the term and was regarded as an egregious fault" (Fried 2008, p. 26).

216 This Diderotian point need not apply exclusively to paintings; it can be extended to other artistic forms and generally maintains its validity outside the specific context in which Diderot brought it up: "Las Vegas lounge singers theatricalize jazz standards, even soul and blues songs, by fitting phrasing and expression into extremely predictable, narrow conventions, all in a way clearly designed to fit the elevator music assumptions and expectations of a middlebrow audience" (Pippin 2021, p. 113).

ual nor universal" (Deleuze 1969, p. 152). In other words, absorption seems to favor the emergence of these singular expressive qualities, or, more precisely, it represents a way to avoid phony expression, gestures bereft of their original expressive capacities and left with a merely conventional function.

In this case, Zidane knew he was going to be filmed in this specific way, that he would be the protagonist of this experiment. However, the absorption induced by his being caught up in the game (in the *performance*, we might also say) causes him to forget the multiple camera eyes pointed at him;[217] we shall return to this point soon in reference to Bresson's and Jeff Wall's "cinematography."

In this case, it is no coincidence that the filmmakers' choice has fallen on Zidane, who seems particularly attuned to this experience—to the dimension of absorption the match draws him into. At several key moments of the film, Zidane's own words are displayed in subtitles; in one such instance, he says: "It was not the game of my life, but I was in my game; why did I say yes? Because *I wasn't playing a role*" (Gordon/Parreno 2006, my italics). In another, he expressly refers to the "immersive" motion of his own attention during the game, in an absorptive regime:

> When you step onto the field, you can hear and feel the presence of the crowd. There is sound. The sound of noise. [...] you don't really hear the crowd. You almost decide for yourself what you want to hear. You are never alone. I can hear someone shift around in their chair. I can hear someone coughing. I can hear someone whisper in the ear of the person next to them. I can imagine that I hear the ticking of a watch. (Gordon/Parreno 2006)

The camera's eye focuses on the explication (in the sense of *ex-plicare*, allowing something virtually unnoticed to unfold) of the expressive qualities emerging from public, shared play. Like Zidane's own attention, the camera is drawn to these moments. Still more importantly, the camera's eye allows the qualities that the absorbed player expresses to emerge. By permitting interplay between proximity and distance, the eyes of these cameras also offer expressive possibilities not normally perceptible to the naked eye. As Benjamin (1936) notes, cinema, perhaps more than any other art, seems to allow entirely new possibilities for explication of the senses constituting what we call "the world." These new manners of explication mean that cinema can change our relationship with reality, our visual, auditory, and emotional ways of perceiving. The camera makes otherwise "unencounterable" expressiveness possible. Cinematographic effects like zoom or

---

[217] See also Conte (2020, p. 284): "It is also like the portrait of a moving unconscious mind, a portrait in which the subject does not pose; a portrait in which he is acted on by the game more than he acts. Thus, he is not playing a role as an actor but remains in a performing situation."

slow-motion are more than just a way to modify the data "already available": they allow us to experience space and time in new ways, to discover new forms of expression.[218] (Interestingly, the German word for slow motion is *Zeitlupe*, or temporal magnifying glass, which points to the temporal potential inherent in this cinematographic technique whereby it helps "make time visible." Didi-Huberman [2000] touches upon this peculiarity when elaborating upon Benjamin's notion of the optical unconscious.)

The *sujet* to be expressed is, of course, the athlete Zinédine Zidane, but this name is no longer the name of an individual—it is the name of a *singularity portrayed in its expressive qualities*, participating in an expressive rhythm. Hence, we might suggest that the viewer is given a chance to experience a moving portrait in which this condition of "absorption" elicits the on-screen appearance of those neutral and impersonal elements untouched by the difference between existence and nonexistence: the "physiognomy," the "impassibility," the "expression."[219]

3.18 Images without Belief: A Double Distance?

Now, how are we to read the Lucretian paradigm with regard to the spectatorial attitude when describing images not marked by belief, images that have never claimed to presentify something in existence? Should we perhaps surmise that such situations give us "even more distance" from what is being presentified? What essentially changes in the considerations made so far if the people involved in the filmic action are "just" characters rather than "actual people"? In this case, it would not be so much the iconic distance from the action that would make us feel safe but the fact that nothing is actually happening.

Myriad fictional works invite the viewer in various ways to relinquish responsibility toward what they are watching. Viewers are drawn into the game (positional belief in the image's *sujets* is suspended), and upon crossing the threshold to enter the "playing field," they are granted access to every conceivable scenario, or at least exponentially more than they could tolerate if the consciousness of reality were involved—after all, nobody actually gets hurt in the "play" world. Even if the fictional iconic phantasy were imbued with realistic forms and layers of positional prior knowledge, everything would essentially be transformed according to

---

218 Consider Danish director Jørgen Leth's "sports films," experimental films that make extensive use of such techniques in an effort to highlight the expressive qualities of athletic movement. One particularly notable example is his cinematographic portrait of the Danish football player Michael Laudrup, which anticipates Gordon and Parreno's experiment in some ways.
219 Fried (Fried/Griffin 2006, p. 334) points this out as well.

consciousness of play, giving rise to a *quasi*-world in which nothing real happens, so it seems permissible to allow anything to *quasi*-happen. To what extent can cinema lead us to phantasize intersubjective situations and lead us to enjoy them even though we would find them intolerable in real life? In our status as phantasy egos experiencing "as-if" worlds, do we really have unlimited freedom, with no consequences whatsoever?

In these circumstances, we do not take a positional attitude with respect to what we see. Our spectatorial status as a "fictional ego" appears to prepare us for anything we might want to live in that playful status since no real responsibility seems to be involved.[220] Right from the start, we transpose ourselves into the "as if," at an ontological distance to any reality actually posited. After all, when we experience a fictional film, we find ourselves in the attitude of *quasi*-positionality, in a dimension of destinies "played out" rather than actually experienced.

From a Husserlian point of view, as we have seen, we experience "modified" situations in such cases; in fact, I would go so far as to say that these are no longer the "same" situations in the first place, since the world in which we are acting changes—as also evidenced from the practical point of view concerning what we are "willing to do." Our responsibilities—also construed as our possibilities for response—change. We find ourselves *both* at an iconic distance from the events and at an absolute distance concerning the neutralization of belief in the actuality of the facts we see unfolding in the images. Not only can we do nothing about what is happening on screen (since none of the "things" involved are tangible objects), but the intended action is not *actually* happening, nor did it happen in the past. *Double neutralization*, we might say. Or *double distance*: the iconic distance inherent to the presentificational dimension, and the fictional distance related to the nonactual existence of the *sujets* and the presentified actions. Against this background, we might think that we as spectators are freed of those implications for reality that we have to acknowledge when viewing positional images (as with Bazin's example of the real, positional death of the bullfighter Manolete and the "obscene" dimension of its representation).

---

[220] Consider, for example, the TV series *Westworld*, which was created by Jonathan Nolan and Lisa Joy for HBO in 2016 (and in turn was inspired by the 1973 Michael Crichton film of the same name). The title refers to a kind of Wild-West-themed live-action amusement park populated by androids practically indistinguishable from human beings. Within park boundaries, visitors are permitted to act as they please, including "killing" the androids. It is true that Westworld's example refers to visitors taking an ostensibly far more active role in *quasi*-violence, not merely spectating from the gallery. However, the same question still applies: do fictional environments (filmic, theatrical, virtual, "play" spaces) give participants a "pass" to *quasi*-do whatever they like?

However, based on our previous analysis, we can say that the playful nature of such images devoid of any positional implications does not imply that they cannot participate in the nexus of senses and values (axiological interest) that continuously contribute to the constitution of reality. Questions concerning boundaries may emerge even in such an attitude of play or *quasi*-positionality. For instance, can we freely enjoy violence when in a fictional attitude? Is there an aesthetic/ethical limit to the imaginable—or even simply a limit of the will, a line we refuse to cross even in a regime of playful phantasy?

For a more detailed exploration of these cinematic effects on sense (and therefore on reality), let us return to Haneke, who dedicated a substantial part of his cinematic reflections to examining the difference between what we have called positional and fictional images.

3.19 *Quasi*-Guilty: Haneke and the "Reality of Fiction"

Investigating the ways we can experience (and participate in) extreme situations and violence within a fictional regime is a major theme in the works of Michael Haneke, a director known to confront his audiences with such questions directly, sometimes forcing them to experience the sheer impossibility of enduring violence even when mediated by this iconic-fictional double distance. Haneke seems to question this very double neutralization and the protection it allegedly offers us —a two-turn lock on the door to the audience's safe space from which they can enjoy otherwise-threatening situations, particularly those involving violence and death.

Before delving into Haneke's "cinematic argument," it is beneficial to recall our earlier remarks concerning the nature of a phantasy ego living moments of fiction that do not actually reference individual reality. We noted that distinguishing between real and phantasy egos does not automatically constitute advocating for an impenetrable separation of the two. Rather, what we call the phantasy ego can be considered a (more or less free) variation of what we consider our "real" self, and the "real" ego can itself be composed of continuous narratives which these phantasy variations can affect. Real and phantasy egos can be considered mutually permeable according to certain laws, and our concept of "self" is continually fed by results obtained through the experiences of phantasy—so much so, in fact, that if we were asked to provide an inventory of the ideas, beliefs, desires, and values that constitute our real ego, we would find it difficult to determine which of those ideas, beliefs, desires, and values originated exclusively from real-ego experiences and which stemmed from phantasy ego experiences.

Haneke seems to believe that experiencing *quasi*-worlds while sitting comfortably in an armchair, at a "double-locked" distance from the on-screen action, does not necessarily render us either completely passive or completely innocent. In his view, "film, in general," can "put the viewer in the position of perpetrator [*Täter*]" (Haneke 2008a, p. 576), in the place of the one performing the act (in this case, the person committing the acts of violence).[221]

Obviously, Haneke is not claiming that we, as viewers, *actually* perpetrate the violent *quasi*-actions we believe we are merely watching, nor is he accusing us of taking sadistic enjoyment in the violence, of putting ourselves in the perpetrators' shoes rather than the victims'. (Though the latter is possible, at least in principle, we will not go into that here—nor does Haneke, who relegates it to a "pathological [...]" dimension.[222]) Nevertheless, he goes as far as to affirm that "in Coppola's *Apocalypse Now* supported by Wagner's 'The Ride of the Valkyries', we are riding along in the helicopter, firing on the Vietnamese scattering in panic below us, and we do it without a guilty conscience because we—at least in the moment of the action—do not become aware of this role" (Haneke 2008a, p. 576).

What violent acts are we then committing? Can it be said that we viewers do in fact carry out such actions somehow? Ought we not claim our innocence, that very ontological innocence arising from our distance from *quasi*-worlds edified in the "as if" regime? In Husserlian terms, as we have seen, such presentifications essentially imply a splitting: the production of a *quasi*-ego performing *quasi*-acts. Interestingly, we can see this same intentional structure at work in the childhood memory that Haneke mentions when recalling his first encounter with cinema's unique power to "transport" us into *quasi*-worlds, allowing us to *quasi*-belong to them, as *quasi*-egos who are led to perform *quasi*-actions:

---

[221] Let us remark that, for Haneke, this is not what usually happens with the "still image," which "generally shows an action's *result*" and "usually appeals to a viewer's solidarity with the *victim*" (Haneke 2008a, p. 576). For our purposes, the point is not to determine how static and moving images differ in terms of the direction of our participation in them (though this question is far from irrelevant and should be extended to more recent formats of image manifestation as well). Rather, the point is to discuss the nature of the phantasy ego and its emergence out of an iconic phantasy experience, going as far as to question whether this double distance can or should allow our phantasy egos unrestricted freedom in their *quasi*-actions.

[222] See Haneke (2008a, p. 576). Even so, the fact that sadists can also take pleasure in violent images while identifying with the person committing the violence is still relevant to our discourse. For example, some people might take sadistic (or masochistic) pleasure in identifying with explicitly iconically phantasized violence, yet they might only indulge this desire in contexts without real-world consequences. The nature of sadism and masochism and their relationship with reality and phantasy is another area of potential future analysis.

I spent three months in Denmark for "recreation" as part of an aid program for children from countries that had lost the war. [...] In an effort to cheer me up, my Danish foster parents took me to the movies. It was a murky, rainy, late fall day, cold and cheerless, and the film, the title and plot of which I've forgotten, took place in the jungle and savannah of Africa. Here, too, I can exactly remember the long, narrow, gloomy theater with doors along the side that opened directly on to the street. The film comprised a number of traveling shots, obviously filmed from inside a jeep, before which fled antelopes, rhinoceroses, and other creatures I'd never seen before. I, too, was seated in that car, captivated with astonishment and joy.

Finally the film came to an end and the lights went on, the doors were opened to the twilit streets, outside rain was pouring down, the noise of traffic filled the theater, and the moviegoers opened their umbrellas and stepped out of the theater. But I was in a state of shock: I could not understand how I, who scant seconds before had been in Africa in the sun amidst the animals, had been transported back so quickly. How could the theater, which for me had been like a car I was traveling in, have driven back—and especially so quickly—to northern, cold Copenhagen? (Haneke 2008c, pp. 565–566)

Based on our analyses thus far, we can characterize such experiences in terms of *quasi* (*quam si*). We might therefore be inclined to consider the *quasi*-actions performed in them as pertaining exclusively to *quasi*-characters, which would then not make us responsible for them. However, even as he affirms (in cinematographic terms) that splitting process we have described phenomenologically, Haneke seems eager to prompt us viewers to question our presumed innocence.

In particular, what happens to that power of transposition leading to the rise of a fictional ego when we pass from an innocuous safari scene to one of raw violence? Should we take responsibility for consuming fictional *quasi*-violence from our privileged place as viewers? Haneke suggests that perhaps we should: in a way, he says, by enjoying *quasi*-acts of violence, we become *quasi*-accomplices in their perpetration even if only unconsciously, in the form of "as-if."

One paradigmatic example of this is Haneke's previously mentioned *Funny Games*, with which he expressly intended to "slap the viewer in the face" (Haneke 2008b, p. 72). In this work, Haneke initially invites the audience to believe that they are about to experience canonical filmic enjoyment of violence, equipped with those anesthetizing codes that leave viewers free to participate in *quasi*-violent action without the collateral effects that greater awareness might awaken. As the film progresses, however, it gradually becomes clear that Haneke does not intend to keep this implicit "promise of stylistic safety"; he is going to force the audience to *quasi*-experience the horror unfolding on screen without the assistance of typical directorial solutions aimed at making it enjoyable to watch. Those well-established forms of mainstream cinematic representation employed to render violence and horror "fit for audience consumption" do indeed come into play during the film—only to be subverted, thus rendering viewers "prisoners," defenseless against violence that proves unbearable even in the context of a *quasi*-experience (unless they leave their seats, of course). Viewers are thus trapped in a game that is impossible to find "funny," and if they stay in the theater in hopes of attempting to enjoy it, Haneke adds, then the "slap in the face" is well-deserved.[223]

One crucial example in this regard is the "rewind scene": at the moment when a member of the tortured family (the mother) manages to kill one of the two villains with a spectacular rifle shot, the other one grabs the remote control in the living room where the scene is taking place, rewinds the film to a moment just before the mother grabs the rifle, and then restarts the action, this time preventing the mother from reaching the firearm. The seemingly averted carnage can thus resume unabated, smothering any budding sense of liberating revenge the viewer may have felt.

By looking into the camera, breaking the "fourth wall," the two antagonists provoke the audience in an effort to shake them awake from their silent passivity. In the 1997 version, one of them even winks at the camera conspiratorially, as though to suggest that spectators, too, are part of the game (Figure 16). Realizing they are involved confronts audience members with a new choice, a new responsibility: given this new awareness, do they stay in the game or not?

Figure 16: Still from Michael Haneke's *Funny Games* (1997)

Generally, however, the Austrian director's work is not merely a provocation aimed at testing the limits of our tolerance as viewers. It is a cinematographic practice helping investigate the relationship between experiences in images and real experiences. Haneke has insisted on several occasions that fictional images (despite their nonpositional status, their being presentifications of fictional characters) can make us feel reality; this point, in fact, seems central to his cinematic oeuvre. Haneke, therefore, seems to reject the notion that this double distance (iconic and fictional) to violent *quasi*-events can sufficiently shelter us from reality's grip. In

---

223 "*Funny Games* cynically plays with the viewer, because the film tells them: this slap in the face is well-deserved, because you're still here" (Haneke 2008b, p. 77).

fact, he says, for violence to be enjoyable, it must be divested of reality—a process that usually goes unnoticed by spectators. Mainstream productions know this all too well: in order to be "a good sell," violence must be "deprived of that which is the *true measure of its existence in reality:* deeply disconcerting fears of pain and suffering" (Haneke 2008a, p. 576, my italics). Iconic and fictional distance in themselves are not enough to protect us from reality. Such pain and suffering are *expressible* in an iconic fictional experience, and this expressibility renders them "non-consumable" (Haneke 2008a, p. 576)—as is the case in films like *Funny Games*, which want to slap their audiences in the face.

As such, even when perpetrated on a fictional level in fictional images, violence must undergo a further process of "exorcism" to make it digestible for viewers. Without going into the full "vocabulary of forms used" in pursuit of such a goal, Haneke identifies *"three dramaturgical* premises, of which at least one must be satisfied in order to attain a large audience with the display of violence":

> First, the *disengagement* of the violence-producing situation from the viewer's own immediate life experiences that elicit identification [...], Second, the *intensification* of one's living conditions and their jeopardization, which allows the viewer to approve of the act of violence as liberating and positive [...], Third, the *embedding* of the action *in* a climate of *wit and satire* [...]. (Haneke 2008a, p. 576)

Consider, for example, *Kill Bill (Vol. 1,* 2003; *Vol. 2,* 2004), a Quentin Tarantino film that combines many "revenge film" genre *topoi* and that, in many respects, also belongs to that "climate of *wit and satire"* mentioned in the third of the dramaturgical stratagems Haneke refers to. (Haneke himself names *Pulp Fiction* (1994) as another example). While watching Beatrix Kiddo's experiences unfold, the audience can innocently and justifiably co-participate in her violent deeds since the very first scene shows us that her fury is motivated by the violence she has previously endured. Of course, we go into the movie knowing that we are not watching actual violence and death, but rather *quasi-*violence and *quasi-*killing—"as-if" killing in which the aestheticization sought in the virtuosity of the "how" plays a primary role. Indeed, we might suggest that aesthetic pleasure is a factor in these acts. There is no doubt that Hattori Hanzo's katana never actually kills anyone. Nevertheless, as Haneke suggests, we might not realize that we are also *quasi-*there, *quasi-*grasping its handle.

In Haneke's view, such an experience is made possible not because iconic fiction provides *eo ipso* ontological protection but rather thanks to certain dramaturgical choices aimed at "exorcising" violence and death of their "real" expressed qualities. Violence and death are rendered consumable by being transfigured into something that does not touch their essence: "Through irony, Tarantino makes violence consumable for intellectuals. The real danger lies not in the individual film but in the permanent presence of violence. Sickness and death have been exiled from our lives. They are presented to us in film and television, but not as reality, rather as images without a scale of values" (Haneke 1998, pp. 59–60).

3.20 Phantasy as a Protected Field of Experimentation

Even when accounting for Haneke's warning about the phantasy ego's implicit involvement in *quasi*-violent acts, one might draw conclusions contrary to Haneke's based on the possibilities that phantasy worlds allow. For example, we might claim that the possibility of phantastically carrying out any action (even one we would consider unthinkable if associated with any real consequences) represents a beneficial opportunity. As viewers (or authors, or even performers—when playing video games, for example, though also from the perspective that we as viewers are already *quasi*-performers), we might be specifically interested in deliberately experimenting with *quasi*-actions that we would never take in real life through free variations capable of producing some form of knowledge without having actual consequences for others.

This point is raised *in nuce* in a passage of *Recherche* in which Albertine asks the narrator, "but did he ever murder anyone, Dostoievsky? The novels of his that I know might all be called *The Story of a Crime*. It is an obsession with him, it isn't natural that he should always be talking about it" (Proust 1923, p. 385). The narrator's answer is not really directed at Dostoevsky specifically; rather, he represents one example of the possibility for a writer (and, we can add, for a reader, spectator, performer, etc.) to unlock *quasi*-worlds and *quasi*-lives in order to *quasi*-explore "forms of life" they cannot actually live:

> I don't think so, dear Albertine, I know little about his life. It's certain that, like everyone else, he was acquainted with sin, in one form or another, and probably in a form which the laws condemn. [...] Perhaps it wasn't necessary for him to be criminal himself. I am not a novelist [*sic!*]; it's possible that creative writers are tempted by certain forms of life of which they have no personal experience. (Proust 1923, p. 386)

Here, Proust articulates the possibility we have just mentioned for phantasy egos (authors, readers, spectators, or simply "phantasy performers"), as variations of their "real" egos, to *quasi*-live experiences that they could not live as real egos and thereby potentially gain otherwise-unattainable forms of knowledge. Indeed, the sense and the value of these *quasi*-experiences can in turn inform the continuous constitution of what we call our real ego.

Proust's thematization of this topic is also linked to his well-known thesis postulating a separation between artists' everyday lives and their work, a position that he strongly defended at the beginning of the twentieth century in *Contre Sainte-Beuve* (see Proust 1971, pp. 221–222). Yet we must be careful not to conflate these two conceptual dichotomies: the distinction between real and phantasy egos is not equivalent to the one between real and artistic egos, though the two can often overlap, such as when art arises by constituting possible worlds (which is not the case with all art). In any case, we might suggest that Proust essentially considers this a distinction between the social/public ego (the empirical "Marcel Proust," the one known to his friends and enemies, which can be measured against social mores) and the artistic ego (which is known by encountering a work of art, and which grows and develops along with the process constituting the artist's work)—what we call "Marcel Proust" as the *expression* of his work. Accordingly, the narrator's argumentative response to Albertine continues as follows:

> If I come with you to Versailles as we arranged, I shall show you the portrait of the ultra-respectable man, the best of husbands, Choderlos de Laclos, who wrote the most appallingly perverse book [*scil. Les Liaisons Dangereuses*], and just opposite it the portrait of Mme de Genlis who wrote moral tales and, not content with betraying the Duchesse d'Orléans, tortured her by turning her children against her. (Proust 1923, p. 386)

In any case, fiction (artistic or not) can offer a powerful means of inhabiting different perspectives, thus opening up possibilities for the growth of what we call our "self," since variations of the phantasy self are always variations of what we call our real self. The boundaries of that self are neither static nor well-defined, and the (emotional or cognitive) knowledge we glean from phantasy worlds perpetually shapes our relentless constitution and re-constitution of reality. Participating in these variations of phantasy can therefore have a positive impact in at least three respects:

i) By opening up new avenues for self-understanding we can move within a "safe" environment while experiencing actions in new ways and using a different focus, paying particular attention to the *sense* of those actions. This possibility has some essential similarities with *epoché*, as we have seen in the Hofmannsthal letter; analytical literature has also referred to it as an "off-line situation" (see, for instance, Sitch/Nichols, 1997). We can experience perspectives from which a specific understanding of the world can arise emotionally as valuable (or valueless). All of this facilitates our comprehension of the world, our grasp of its possible meanings.

ii) By opening up new avenues for understanding others we come away with a better idea of what it is like to be in others' situations, where their perspectives on the world come from. We might learn what emotional experiences and valueceptions are possible from their points of view.

iii) By opening up new opportunities to focus on the impersonal dimension of the sense in which it is less important whether a particular experience is our own (first person) or someone else's (third person)—for example, a perspective may have multiple and inviolable individuations but also shed light on an understanding of the world that exceeds the historical fact of a personal viewpoint. Again, this sense is neither specific to an individual nor an abstract generalization; though expressed by an individual experience, it cannot be reduced to that individual narrative. Our final section will focus on this third dimension, but let us first lay the groundwork for our analysis by considering one final element highlighted in Haneke's work.

3.21 Dramaturgically Manipulative Presentifications

The modalities of presentification used in fictional cinema to make violence more "consumable" can also be used in the sphere of actuality in the iconic presentifications of actual violence. As mentioned in Chapter 1, anesthetizing techniques are regularly employed in the real world in various ways to create tolerable (or even enjoyable, as in the case of infotainment) iconic presentifications of an otherwise unbearable reality. Spectacularizing reality for tele-spectators at an iconic distance —making it "clickable," so to speak—can serve a variety of political or economic goals, and this process can substantially influence how we feel about and experience our belief in the positional images in question. Haneke notes that the "hows" in which real and fictitious acts of violence are presentified in image form are growing increasingly similar:

> Did the *similarity between the forms* through which real and fictional violence are represented influence our perception and especially our sensitivity in such a way that we are no longer able to distinguish between the *contents* of either, so that the value of authenticity of the corpses of Grozny and Sarajevo approximate that of *The Terminator*, and that *Star Wars* can only be distinguished from the media event of the blitz invasion of Kuwait by the timeslot in which it goes on the air? But how is such commingling and indistinguishability possible? (Haneke 2008a, pp. 577)

Haneke places particular emphasis on the ways in which nominally positional images (those for which we believe in the existence of what we see) are tendentially presented using stylistic or dramaturgical choices that remove those elements that concern the nexus constituting our actual experience. This creates the danger that, when viewing those images, we still posit a reality, but without critically reflecting on the fact that our experience of the presentified facts (the what) is heavily shaped by the specific manner of presentification and the deliberate omission of troubling or disturbing elements. We have little room for maneuver in our interpretations—the images impose what is happening or what happened upon us in a deliberately biased manner that makes us find what we see tolerable.

Of course, the effects of the "how-indistinguishability" between reality and fiction are already at work on the developmental psychology level. We need to describe the effect that screens have on our constitution of (what we call) reality and on the sense in which we can maintain awareness of the distinction between positional and nonpositional on-screen images, or at least avoid being passively subjected to unquestioned conflation. Haneke, for example, wonders "to what degree children, who—at least in highly industrialized countries—experience the world primarily *via* the viewing screen, can still develop this capability to distinguish" (Haneke 2008a, p. 577). Haneke's own work has explored this question as well, for example, in *Benny's Video* (1992).[224]

Given the ceaseless barrage of images marking the contemporary era, one of the issues at stake is defining the phenomenological conditions under which presentified reality and unreality are currently discernible. According to Haneke, the exacerbation and homologation of these forms of presentification (toward what we have called the "how") render the content (the "what") "an interchangeable variable"—they bring about the "*absolute equivalency of all the contents* stripped of their reality," which "ensures the *universal fictionality* of anything shown and, with it, the coveted *feeling of security* of the consumer" (Haneke 2008a, p. 578).

It is not our purpose here to judge the general accuracy or thoroughness of Haneke's analysis; Haneke, for his part, specifies that his position is not "as a sociologist or a media critic, but rather as a filmmaker" compelled to investigate the "reality-value [*Realitätswert*]" (Haneke 2008a, p. 579, transl. slightly modified) of these forms of presentification. (Note that some of the themes in Haneke's argument echo Baudrillard's and Sontag's ideas.) More generally, within a context of phenomenological perspectivism such as the one I support here, it is clear that the "how" and the "what" are two inseparable sides of the same experience. There is no "what" without a "how" (there is no prior pure objective fact that would *subsequently* be perceived in infinite different ways, each more or less adequate reflections of that allegedly straight fact).

Still, as noted, this is not to say that perspectives are all perfectly equal and indiscriminate, which would imply naïve relativism. The various perspectives are not solipsistically separated; even when they "agree to disagree," they can still rectify, develop, enrich, intersect, and encompass one another. They are always

---

[224] Indeed, the text I am referring to (Haneke 2008a) was originally a lecture given in 1995 on the occasion of a presentation of *Benny's Video* at the Marstall Theater in Munich.

intertwined and in flux, as are the narratives, values, and emotions that constitute them.

3.22 *Sub Specie Sensus*

At one level, we (through Haneke) have highlighted the need to recognize and defend against implicit interpretations of the images we are offered, to reactivate our critical capacity to describe the difference between reality and fiction. At another level, however, we have pointed to art's ability to bypass the boundaries between these two dimensions, offering us an avenue through which to investigate and explore the dimension of sense. (This separate approach does not invalidate the one developed above with Haneke.) Indeed, questions of sense can apply to both fiction-oriented and belief-oriented films, as well as the myriad hybrids of the two. When considered *sub specie sensus*, from the point of view of the *sense*, all these forms can have the same rights.

Along these lines, cinema as art (either fictional or not) can think *aesthetically* (Deleuze/Guattari 1991, p. 55). Films or other works of art can prompt the viewer to participate in creating a perspective (*lato sensu*) construed as an essential interrelation between a narrative (implying a comprehension of a nexus of meanings and their relations: perspective *stricto sensu*), values, and emotions exhibited aesthetically, i.e., through an aesthetic (*aisthesis*) form of presentation. This type of thinking is certainly also capable of expressing itself through logical-propositional thought, but it cannot be reduced to it (art is no mere vessel through which to communicate logical-propositional content). This can foster involvement with worldly possibilities and trigger a process of investigation that is at once cognitive, emotional, and axiological without being conceptually mediated or circumscribable. Art opens up the possibility of producing senses that react with our own perspectives from the intimately related dimensions of comprehension, emotion, and valorization that constantly figure in our everyday processes of grasping the world. Clearly, this can also mean that spectators can live a process of devaluation in which they recognize disvalues, empty repetitions without coherent deformation, static rhetorical values—in short, in which they determine that the perspectives opened up by the work are falsely pretentious, ill-advised, stupid, etc.

Shifting our focus to the sense images express or produce may help us move past any naïve distinctions between documentary and fiction, especially those overemphasizing the "real facts themselves," despite the fact that (to paraphrase Aristotle's famous remark in *Poetics*) poetry—i.e., productive imitations of *actions*, not facts—can be "more philosophical and more serious than history" (Aristotle 1996, p. 16). This will also help us prevent any factitious separations between form and content—separations that, as we have shown, often betray a tendency to conceive the form as something that "comes after" the content and must comply with it, as if they were completely distinct things. What we have called a *noema* is not separable from the form through which it is expressed and still cannot be reduced to it.

In this chapter we have emphasized that expression can be produced in either a perceptual or a presentificational regime—one marked by belief or free of it. In this regard, let me emphasize that, in *Cinema I* (1983), Deleuze characterizes film images *sub specie sensus* when, referring to what he calls "affection-images," he writes that

> The Stoics showed that things themselves were bearers of ideal events which did not exactly coincide with their properties, their actions and reactions: the edge of a knife... The affect is the entity, that is Power or Quality. *It is something expressed:* the affect does not exist independently of something which expresses it, although it is completely distinct from it. (Deleuze 1983, p. 97, my italics)

Deleuzian reference to the Stoics goes back to the 1969 *Logic of Sense*. Here, as there, the use of the term "expression" indicates a relationship between "form and content" that is different from the one which the etymology of the verb "to express" (*ex-primere:* "to press out," "to squeeze out") might suggest—that is, as if the form squeezed out content that "was already there," hidden but *self-contained*. In *Logic of Sense*, referring to the Stoics, Deleuze distinguishes between two qualitatively different dimensions of our experience. On the one hand, there are "bodies with their tensions, physical qualities, actions and passions, and the corresponding 'state of affairs'" (Deleuze 1969, p. 4). On the other hand,

> All bodies are causes in relation to each other, and causes for each other—but causes of what? They are causes of certain things of entirely different nature. These *effects* are not bodies, but, properly speaking, "incorporeal" entities. [...] They are not things or facts, but events. We cannot say that they exist, but rather that they subsist [*subsistent*] or insist [*insistent*] (having this minimum of being which is appropriate to that which is not a thing, a nonexisting entity). (Deleuze 1969, pp. 4–5)

Thus, the verb "to insist" is used to highlight the inseparability between the expressed and that which expresses it. (Though inseparable, they remain distinguishable because the sense insisting in the bodies or words is a quality not reducible to what expresses it.) From the perspective of the sense expressed, the distinction between documentary and fiction is no longer relevant: documentaries can contain fabrications in terms of expression without being *ipso facto* compromised in their aspirations for truth. Likewise, fiction can contain material with documentary value, yielding an iconic dramatization that seeks to acquire value for what it expresses rather than for which reality it presentifies.²²⁵ Deleuze uses the analogous concept of *fabulation* to denote a function through which art can reveal the sense expressed by facts, whether they are real, remembered, or merely imagined (see Deleuze/Guattari 1991, p. 171). *Qua* art, cinema can overcome the distinction between real and fictional to produce a horizon of not only aesthetic valorizations but cognitive and ethical ones as well—and not as heteronymous values referenced to justify the work's existence but as processes of valorization emerging from the cinematic *quasi*-world (believed or not in its factual-individual actuality).²²⁶ Cinema thus has a seminal ability to participate in the continuous constitution of what we call truth and the world.

This, of course, is not to say that the distinction between documentary and fiction is wholly irrelevant—that in cases of violence or death, to mention two critical points discussed above, it does not matter whether the depicted victim genuinely suffered. Rather, the issue at hand is the *artistic power* to cause viewers to feel the incorporeal sense that the images express. It is this sense that is impervious to the difference between documentary and fiction: on the expressive level, it is not important whether what we are watching is "a true story."

Art must be able to overcome factual individuality by *expressing* the not-merely-individual character of a specific experience, a sense that can be found in every individual occurrence, including the extreme case in which someone dies—which brings us back to our earlier discussion of representations of death. According to Deleuze, even when depicting death—the presentification of which seemed to be

---

225 Consider Werner Herzog's notion of ecstatic truth as he explains it in his 1999 *Minnesota Declaration*. Reproaching *cinéma vérité* for confounding fact and truth, Herzog introduces his notion of "poetic, ecstatic truth," defining it as "mysterious and elusive," something that can be reached "only through fabrication and imagination and stylization" (Herzog 2002 [1999], p. 301). Herzog underlines that what is important is not the factual but rather the ecstatic truth disclosed by the filmic experience. As Eric Ames points out, "by cinéma vérité, he [Herzog] means not the French movement of the 1950s associated with Jean Rouch (whose work Herzog admires) but rather the American brand of observational cinema espoused by Robert Drew, Richard Leacock, D.A. Pennebaker, and Fred Wiseman, or what Albert and David Maysles called 'direct cinema'" (Ames 2012, p. 9). This is how Herzog can ask Fini Straubinger, the main character in the 1971 documentary film *Land of Silence and Darkness* (*Land des Schweigens und der Dunkelheit*), to recount a fake memory of a ski-jumping competition as her own (see Cronin 2002, pp. 240–241), yet also insist that a real ship be pulled over a mountain in the jungle for the 1982 fiction film *Fitzcarraldo* because he refused to shoot the sequence in a studio. As Herzog explained to Paul Cronin: "So for me, the boundary between fiction and 'documentary' simply does not exist; they are all just films. Both take 'facts,' characters, stories and play with them in the same kind of way. I actually consider *Fitzcarraldo* my best 'documentary'" (Cronin 2002, p. 240).
226 Gilles Deleuze (1985, p. 150): "What cinema must grasp is not the identity of a character, whether real *or* fictional."

impossible *qua* obscene—the artist must be capable of expressing the "impersonal" dimension (the French *on meurt*[227]) "insisting" in it, as Deleuze and Guattari (1991, pp. 171–172) put it in the *Logic of Sense*'s vocabulary.

As Deleuze and Guattari (1991, p. 171) observe, "it is always a question of freeing life wherever it is imprisoned":[228] a singularity whereby that death is also "a" death—not a universal concept, but the *noema* expressed in that particular death. In the same vein, Deleuze refers to other literary descriptions of animal deaths, such as "the death of the porcupine in Lawrence and the death of the mole in Kafka"[229] (Deleuze/Guattari 1991, p. 171). More specifically, Deleuze refers to the ways Lawrence's and Kafka's *styles* use an act of "creative fabulation" to define a certain "vision" about life—a sense, a singular, sharable perspective on our world experience which an overly fact-focused approach might well overlook. Regardless of how important or unimportant a fact may be considered in everyday life, an act of artistic "fabulation" can "extract" the "Life in the living or the Living

---

[227] Drawing upon Blanchot's *L'espace littéraire* (a reference that re-emerges in Deleuze 1983, p. 102), in *Logic of Sense* Deleuze states that "death has an extreme and definite relation to me and my body and is grounded in me, but it also has no relation to me at all—it is incorporeal and infinitive, impersonal, grounded only in itself. On one side, there is the part of the event which is realized and accomplished; on the other, there is that 'part of the event which cannot realize its accomplishment'. [...] Every event is like death, double and impersonal in its double. 'It is the abyss of the present, the time without present with which I have no relation, toward which I am unable to project myself. For in it *I* do not die. I forfeit the power of dying. In this abyss they (*on*) die—they never cease to die, and they never succeed in dying' [*en elle on meurt, on ne cesse pas et on n'en finit pas de mourir*]. How different this 'they' [*on*] is from that which we encounter in everyday banality. It is the 'they' [*on*] of impersonal and pre-individual singularities, the 'they' is the splendor of the event itself or of the fourth person. This is why there are no private or collective events, no more than there are individuals and universals, particularities and generalities. Everything is singular, and thus both collective and private, particular and general, neither individual nor universal" (Deleuze 1969, pp. 151–152).

[228] See also Deleuze (1995, pp. 28–29): "The life of the individual gives way to an impersonal and yet singular life that releases a pure event freed from the accidents of internal and external life, that is, from the subjectivity and objectivity of what happens: a 'Homo tantum' with whom everyone empathizes and who attains a sort of beatitude. It is a haecceity no longer of individuation but of singularization: a life of pure immanence, neutral, beyond good and evil, for it was only the subject that incarnated it in the midst of things that made it good or bad. The life of such individuality fades away in favor of the singular life immanent to a man who no longer has a name, though he can be mistaken for no other. A singular essence, a life..."

[229] Deleuze refers here to Lawrence's *Reflections on the Death of a Porcupine* and to Kafka's *The Burrow* (*Der Bau*). The same reference can also be found in Deleuze (1993, p. 2): "Literature begins with a porcupine's death, according to Lawrence, or with the death of a mole, in Kafka: 'our poor little red feet outstretched for tender sympathy.'" Here, Deleuze is quoting a letter Kafka sent to Max Brod (dated August 28, 1904).

in the lived" and "fabricate[...]" a "giant" from them. The artist turns an individual person into a "character" not as a universal concept abstracted from the individual, but rather as a singular character indivisible from the individual expressing it —a character through which the audience can "attain" the "sense" surrounding the individual, "insisting" in it.

3.23 By Chance, Balthazar

Deleuze's remarks on the deaths of the porcupine (Lawrence) and the mole (Kafka) clearly echo the way Kundera characterizes the dog's death in Céline. The notable thing here is that, when characterizing a novelist's description of an animal's death, Deleuze and Kundera both emphasize the importance of "style" in creating the possibility of expressing a truth "insisting" in the mere "fact" of death. To elaborate on this parallel between Deleuze (Lawrence and Kafka) and Kundera (Céline), we might also draw upon Michael Haneke's writings and note that what Lawrence, Kafka, and Céline do through literature, Bresson does in his *Au hasard Balthazar*, in which he films the life and death of a donkey. Haneke's remarks are highly reflective of our discourse thus far—his writings on Bresson's film stress this very point about the singular (not merely individual) character of Balthazar's life and death and how it enables participation:

> What does the film tell? Balthazar is a donkey. The film tells the story of his life, his suffering, and his death. And it tells—*in fragments*—the story of those who cross Balthazar's path. [...] *A life* that, in its sad simplicity, stands for those of millions, a life of small pleasures and great efforts, banal, unsensational, and because of its depressing ordinariness, apparently unsuitable for exploitation on the silver screen. In fact, the film is not about anyone, and thus about everyone—a donkey has no psychology, only a destiny. The title is the precise reflection of the film's intention: "By chance, for instance, Balthazar." It could be anyone else, you or I. (Haneke 2008c, pp. 567–568, my italics)

Haneke's goal of scrubbing images of all those dramaturgical expedients, those convenient elements of cinematographic spectacularization that make images easier for consumers to "digest" in exchange for "losing reality," finds in Bresson one of its most influential sources of inspiration. Notably, Haneke stresses the anti-exhibitionist nature of Bresson's work, describing the French director's films as the precious results of indefatigable efforts to eliminate all traces of theatricality (in the pejorative sense underlined above with Diderot/Fried). These efforts are also reflected in the director's decision to work with nonprofessional actors and his use of "characters mov[ing] with the monotony of marionettes" (Haneke 2008c,

p. 571)—another step aimed at making individuality work as a singularity, i.e., simultaneously particular and general.

For Haneke, this "not-acting" and "monotony of their manner of talking and moving, their existence reduced to mere presence [*ihr auf bloße Präsenz reduziertes Vorhandensein*]" amount to "a liberating experience" (Haneke 2008c, p. 569, transl. slightly modified). As with the phenomenological/Deleuzian line drawn above, what is at stake here is the possibility of liberating a life, a sense expressed through specific manifestations. The fold on the essential and invisible dimension of the event can also be seen as a way to avoid, even eschew the inclination to "fuss" or "tralala," which Kundera (via Céline) says relentlessly undermines human actions: "No one had to pretend anymore to make visible emotions that, because acted, could only be a lie anyway" (Haneke 2008c, p. 569). More specifically, as Haneke recalls, Bresson scrubs images of all superfluous (and often misleading) dramaturgical expedients proffered as reassuring yet meaningless clichés, signposts for preconceived ideas rather than manifestations producing their own inseparable sense.[230] In his *Notes on Cinematography*, to which Haneke explicitly refers, Bresson endeavors to contrast the idea of *cinema*, which he considers an outgrowth of theater (acting, actors, scripts), with the idea of the *cinematographer*, who seeks to dispense with those very elements in order to "use the camera to create."[231] In *cinematography*, he says, one turns away from actors to work with "models"[232] in an attempt to prevent phony, contrived acting, theatrical in the sense Diderot condemned above.[233]

---

[230] For instance, even when some scenes of nudity or violence may seem *prima facie* gratuitous, they actually serve a precise purpose in Bresson's cinema. In *Une femme douce*, when Dominique Sanda drops her towel in front of the television and remains naked for a moment, "it isn't gratuitous," according to Bresson, because "a certain kind of sensuality can't be evoked without nudity" (Bresson 2013, p. 206). Similarly, Arsène's epileptic fit in *Mouchette* is shown in its entirety rather than merely suggested because "it's a dramatic event that cannot be suspended or divided into pieces" (Bresson 2013, p. 187). Even the opening sequence of *Lancelot du lac*, which consists of three gruesome murder scenes (with blood gushing profusely from a decapitated neck, a groin, and a helmet, respectively), is not gratuitously shocking, but rather serves to emphasize the striking coexistence of inner spirituality and brutal violence in the quest for the Holy Grail: "it was Lancelot's very particular inner adventure that I found striking, combined with the violence and blood spilled during the search" (Bresson 2013, p. 237).
[231] "Two types of film: those that employ the resources of the theater (actors, direction, etc.) and use the camera in order to *reproduce*; those that employ the resources of cinematography and use the camera to *create*" (Bresson 1975, p. 2).
[232] According to Bresson, *cinematography* gives up on actors to work with "models": "No actors. / (No directing of actors). / No parts. / (No learning of parts). / No staging. / But the use of working models, taken from life. / BEING (models) instead of SEEMING (actors)" (Bresson 1975, p. 1).

Contrasting such "nonacting" with the principles Diderot discusses in *Paradox of the Actor* could be another fruitful line of discourse, but this goes beyond the scope of this text. Suffice it to say that Bresson's "models" and the actor in *Paradox* are figures aimed at avoiding theatricality, exhibitionism, and inauthenticity, i.e., an ill-concealed desire to parade around that ultimately relies on clichés. Mainstream works often resort to such received ideas as a way of telling spectators what to think of the images, thereby eliminating the recipient's chance to reflect on the perspectival richness of phenomena.

Gratuitous embellishments frequently serve to divert attention from the phenomena's essential features. We might even say that the proliferation of spectacular details renders viewers blind to much of the sense of what they are looking at—to what Adorno's *How to Look at Television* (1954) calls "latent content." (In this instance, we might say, the latent content would be the sense expressed despite the manifest content that a TV show aims to convey).[234] Divested of all theatricality, Bresson's art serves as an attempt to reconquer the "dignity" of reality without "any form of aesthetic pretense" or "lie" (Haneke 2008c, p. 569). A year after Balthazar the donkey's death, we have the death by suicide of a young girl named Mouchette (*Mouchette*, 1967), whose destiny Bresson strives to express without resorting to rhetorical devices (Figures 17 and 18).

Figure 17: Still from Robert Bresson's *Au hasard Balthazar* (1966)

---

233 "The animal Balthazar, along with the knights in the director's later *Lancelot du lac*, locked up in their clattering suits of armor to the point of being unrecognizable, are Bresson's most convincing 'models' simply because they are by definition unable to pretend" (Haneke 2008c, p. 569).

234 Here Adorno refers to television fiction, showing how it too can have important effects on our conception of reality. Television is a medium that helps delimit the boundaries of the social field and produce ideologically determined representations of it. Television fiction tends to keep viewers in a safe zone—whatever adventures it takes consumers on, they must never feel too deeply unsettled. Even so, television fiction creates a tension between its manifest, explicit content and the latent, implicit content that affects viewers without their full awareness, penetrating and shaping their world.

Figure 18: Still from Robert Bresson's *Mouchette* (1967)

Analogously to what Kundera saw in Céline, Haneke recognizes in Bresson "an almost manic rejection of 'beautiful', that is, pleasing images" (Haneke 2008c, p. 569), a refusal of every form of gratuitous aestheticization of the *how* not strictly essential to its *what*.[235] Needless to say, this does not preclude a *style* potentially arising from such renunciation (and, correlatively, an aesthetic feeling that grasps the style's *value*). Through subtraction and essentiality, such a style consistently follows the "rigorous aesthetic concept" of a "precision" without "beauty" (Haneke 2008c, p. 570)—or perhaps it would be more accurate to say without embellishments, for as Haneke notes there is indeed a beauty that emanates from "precision."[236] Rendering things without exhibiting them—"Nothing too much, nothing deficient," as Bresson puts it (Bresson 1975, p. 20)—is a delicate balancing act between the "how" and the "what," the form and the content. Specifically, such efforts strive to make the two inseparable, though this inseparability must be more than mere confusion: it should result from a cinematographic gesture capa-

---

235 See also Bresson (2013, p. 73): "I shun the beautiful image. All this is to say that I'm not looking for beautiful shots; I'm looking for necessary shots, which is not the same thing. [...] It's true that if you want to affect the viewer of a film, the image itself must be in order. Just as all the elements of the film must be so. It's possible, then, that there is some concern for composition—which is, come to think of it, my main concern, but not at all in the sense of the beautiful image."

236 "Precision means: one must go as deep as possible into a theme and recreate it, into what is essential. Why does an image strike us? It's a question of precision. One could even say that intensity comes from precision in detail. This is why precision is as much a moral category as it is an aesthetic category. It presents an obligation. The moral imperative of art, so to speak" (Haneke 2008b, p. 46). Similarly, "I can scrape away the patina of attractiveness from images, look for 'precise' and 'dirty' images instead of 'beautiful' and 'interesting' ones. For 'banal' images, which only acquire their own dignity and beauty in context. [...] Why do director-designers produce work so devoid of intellectual tension? Why have advertisement aesthetics become the goal and trademark feature of today's films? Conversely, in my opinion, keeping an eye out for the reality value of the image is one of the most difficult tasks in cinematographic art. In fact, we are all surrounded almost exclusively by artificial images of an embellished reality" (Haneke 1994, p. 67).

ble of giving the spectator a "measured image" (Bresson 1975, p. 45), the *necessary minimum of image* required to express the sense, to make the "event" graspable, to put it in Deleuzian terms.[237]

Striking that delicate balance is how art avoids the threat of "obscenity," even when rendering death. For Haneke, what is "obscene" is art that leaves no room for interpretation, that does not open up a sense in order to stimulate thought but instead tells viewers what to think, how to see, which values to feel:

> It had always struck me as *obscene* [*"obszön,"* a term resonating with the Bazinian vocabulary introduced above] to watch an actor portray, with dramatic fury, someone suffering or dying—it robbed those who were truly suffering and dying of their last possession: the truth. And it robbed the viewers of this professional reproduction of their most precious possession as viewers: their imagination. They were forced into the humiliating perspective of a voyeur at the keyhole who has no choice but to feel what is being felt before him and think what is being thought. (Haneke 2008c, p. 569, my italics)

3.24 The Polyvalence of Truth

Yet creating truth requires more than mere subtraction. As Bresson himself points out, "The crude real will not by itself yield truth" (Bresson 1975, p. 66). Hence, as Herzog remarks, naïvely documentary cinema is wrong in thinking that showing "mere facts" is sufficient to reveal their truth. We have seen that art must be able to express the sense that constitutes our world—a world that cannot be wholly described in purely factual terms but that rather emerges from the intimate relationship between perspective (narrative), value and emotion. Paraphrasing Proust, one might say that a cinema "which contents itself with 'describing things,' with giving of them merely a miserable abstract of lines and surfaces, is in fact, though it calls itself realist, the furthest removed from reality" (Proust 1927, pp. 920–921). Such a style would amount to the impoverished result of a naïve re-

---

[237] "One must always find the appropriate form. That's why Robert Bresson's films are immense, because with him you never know what was there in the first place. First of all, was it the form that yielded the story, or did the story find the form? Bresson is always the same in all his films. He only looks for stories that could be told within his formal horizon, that were suitable for it. Absolutely perfect" (Haneke 2008b, p. 47). Regarding the notion of event, see also two passages from Deleuze: "If we want to grasp an event, we must not show it, we must not pass along the event, but plunge into it, go through all the geological layers that are its internal history (and not simply a more or less distant past)" (1985, pp. 254–255); "A purely optical and sound situation does not extend into action, any more than it is induced by an action. It makes us grasp, it is supposed to make us grasp, something intolerable and unbearable" (1985, p. 18).

alism based on the presumption that our world can be reduced to a list of facts. "If reality were indeed a sort of waste product of experience," he notes,

> more or less identical for each one of us, since when we speak of bad weather, a war, a taxi rank, a brightly lit restaurant, a garden full of flowers, everybody knows what we mean, if reality were no more than this, no doubt a sort of cinematographic film of these things would be sufficient and the "style," [...] that departed from the simple data that they provide would be an artificial *hors d'œuvre*. But was it true that reality was no more than this? (Proust 1927, p. 925)

Clearly not—this is Proust's answer—and "truth will be attained by [the writer] only when he takes two different objects, states the connexion between them [...] and encloses them in the necessary links of a well-wrought style" (Proust 1927, pp. 924–925). In this regard, *only art* is capable of revealing new senses, new perspectives that would otherwise remain unseen in everyday life.

For Bresson, too, truth can be found not by copying reality but by searching for essential relationships. Like Proust's, Bresson's style avoids separating form and content, rejecting strict dichotomies that posit reality as a pre-existing content to which form should passively comply, as though the content were an autonomous body and the form merely the clothing tailored to fit it—or perhaps concealing it through inessential embellishment. Rather than deeming form inessential to content, Bresson works from the perspective that form produces its own content. In Husserlian terms, we might suggest that cinematographic presentifications are there to produce their own new *sujets*, to broaden our perspectives and open our eyes to new ways of understanding the world, new *possibilities for valorization*. Through "rhythm and combination of images," they "express" a sense that cannot be reduced to allegedly pure facts or to their ready-made interpretations (clichés).[238] The image *per se*, as we have seen, does not do anything: "the cinema must express itself not with images, but with relationships between images, which is not at all the same thing" (Bresson 2013, p. 48).

Bresson understands the cinematographer as a medium holding specific possibilities of creation, a machine producing effects through combinations—"relationships"—of images. It must be able to create genuine (in the sense of nonsimu-

---

[238] "What I'm looking for is not expression by gestures, by speech, by mimicry, but rather expression by way of the rhythm and combination of images, their position, relation, and number" (Bresson 2013, p. 42). In another interview, he reiterates that "cinematography doesn't exist, films don't exist to copy life, but to transport us with a rhythm that must at all times remain under the control of the auteur. We shouldn't look for truth in facts, in beings or things ('realism,' as it's generally construed, does not exist), but in the emotions they provoke. Emotional truth is what teaches and guides us" (Bresson 2013, p. 90).

lated) emotions that cannot be abstracted from the form producing them: "There is an image, then another, and they have relative values: so the first image is neutral, but if put in the presence of another, it vibrates, life erupts from it. And it isn't just the life of the story, of the characters—it's the life of the film. Beginning with the moment when the image vibrates, we are making cinema" (Bresson 2013, p. 48). For Bresson (as in the phenomenological-Deleuzian approach outlined here), how one thing acts *causally* upon another is less important than the structure of sense that motivates a given action, the emergence/loss of a value through a process of valorization/devalorization—an axiological-emotional structure of sense (what we have also called "a perspective *lato sensu*"). Without that, nothing is truly happening yet. Bresson's aesth(ethical) "Jansenism"[239] implies a rigorous quest for the simplest relations able to express, "make visible what, without you, might never have been seen" (Bresson 1975, p. 39). Such productive simplicity is far from being simplistic,[240] however; it is built upon essential relations composed through a long process of distillation and "compression"[241] resulting in the *necessary minimum of image*—or better, the *necessary minimum of rhythm* able to give rise to the unexpected: "a thing expressible solely by the cinematographically new, therefore a new thing" (Bresson 1975, p. 31).

---

[239] The label "Jansenism" has been used to describe Bresson's *rigor* and *austerity*—in *Cinema 1*, Deleuze himself refers to Bresson's "extreme Jansenism" (Deleuze 1983, p. 114). From the aesthetic point of view, this specific aspect emerges (for example) in Bresson's response when Godard proposed describing him as a "Jansenist" cinematographer: "Jansenist? Well, in the sense of the *starkness*..." (Bresson 2013, p. 152, my italics). Here *starkness* stands for the French *dépouillement*: the idea of stripping oneself (*se dépouiller*) of anything not strictly necessary, which carries both ethical and aesthetic connotations. See also what Bresson says in his interview with Godard: "I am persuaded that all of our lives are made in exactly the same way: out of predestination and chance. We're well aware that the essence of who we are is already formed by the age of five or six. By that point it's more or less finished. At twelve or thirteen, it starts to become visible. And after that we continue to be what we've been, taking advantage of different opportunities [*en utilisant les différents hasards*]. We use them to cultivate what was already in us, what—if we don't get the chance to cultivate it—might not be visible about us" (Bresson 2013, p. 156). On Jansenism's role in Bresson's filmography, see also Schrader (2018, pp. 114–119).
[240] "You know that I lean toward the side—not intentionally, mind you—of simplification. And let me clarify right away: I believe that simplification is something one must never seek. If you've worked hard enough, simplification should arrive of its own accord. But you must not look for simplification, or simplicity, too soon, for that's what leads to bad painting, bad literature, bad poetry..." (Bresson 2013, p. 142).
[241] "Expression through compression. To put into an image what a writer would spin out over ten pages" (Bresson 1975, p. 47).

Haneke adopts Bresson's compositional rigor, renouncing those visual and acoustic signs aimed at imposing interpretations upon viewers[242] in favor of creating situations that present possible perspectives, but without attaching labels to the occurrences presented. In Haneke's films, the *quasi*-accidents do not escape the "polyvalence of real life [*Polyvalenz des wirklichen Lebens*]," "the polyvalence of (...) motives [*Die Polyvalenz der Motive*]" (Haneke 2008c, p. 571, transl. slightly modified), the *polyvalence*—but not the relativism—*of truth*.

Ordinary "media victim" viewers who may not be accustomed to this polyvalent understanding of the world may find it highly disturbing to confront and explicate the real instead of being (explicitly or implicitly) fed an objectivistically impoverished or tritely relativized reality. But unlike with the *Funny Games* experiment (where viewers who remain in their seats get deservedly slapped in the face), staying in one's seat could turn out to be the right choice in such cases:

> Spectators accustomed to and luxuriously accommodated within the lies, leave the theater aghast. Starved for a language capable of capturing the traces of life, and with hearts and minds suddenly opened, the remaining spectators wait for a continuation of the stroke of luck that has unexpectedly taken place. (Haneke 2008c, p. 573)

3.25 Beyond Documentary and Fiction

Many of the themes discussed thus far are intertwined in the oeuvre of Canadian photographer Jeff Wall, and his work can thus offer profitable source material for our final analyses. Wall has often been portrayed as a "photographer of modern life," and rightly so; in fact, he has explicitly named Baudelaire's *The Painter of the Modern Life* as a major influence on his work, saying that he seeks to continue the Baudelarian legacy in his own way. Specifically, Wall is interested in Baudelaire's "modernity"—though he describes it not as a concept worth "returning" to or restoring, but rather as an approach to reality worth revisiting in relation to the present day: "When I talk about the 'painting of modern life', people often think I'm referring to the nineteenth century, but I'm not. I am talking about now. [...] The idea of the painting of modern life is always about the now" (Wall 2007 [1996b], p. 265).

---

[242] As we have seen, Haneke believes that "a director is not there to tell the viewer how things are," saying that he gets "very irritated when someone in a film or book tells [him] how to think and feel" (Haneke 2008b, p. 66). He likewise asserts: "Only in bad movies does one know immediately who lied. The actor recites a kind of commentary: 'Now I'll show you that my character is lying'" (Haneke 2008b, p. 27).

In Wall's view, photography can trigger a kind of meta-reflection on what we described in the previous chapter as its "zero degree." Wall's work continuously explores the idea of the "snapshot" *qua* photograph that anyone can take immediately with no preparation, organization, or collaboration—"the most characteristic type" of photography, the "fundamental type" against which all other types of photography are necessarily compared. In this sense, snapshots are also construed as mere reflections of reality, and as a format they seem to allow anyone to capture reality as it is in order to "tell" us what was on the other side of the lens: "innocent takes" immediately afforded a documentary status ("that has been").

Wall explicitly states that he considers many of his photographs meditations on the nature of this *regulative* concept of photography. He pursues this by creating photographs that *look* like snapshots (thereby generating that Diderotian effect of reality mentioned in the second chapter) without actually *being* snapshots. Wall calls these "near documentary photographs."[243] To produce these images, photographic practice enters into an intimate relationship with cinematography, so much so that we can say that Wall considers the "near documentary" "a subcategory of the cinematographic" (Fried 2007, p. 514, note 28).

Inheriting that same Bressonian approach that inspired Haneke, the Canadian photographer finds in cinema (and particularly in the notion of *cinematography*)[244] a source of inspiration for experimenting with a peculiar form of photography, which he himself defines as *cinematographic:*

> I began to call my photography "cinematography." [...] "Cinematography" referred simply to the techniques normally involved in the making of motion pictures: the collaboration with performers (not necessarily "actors," as neorealism showed); the techniques and equipment cinematographers invented, built, and improvised; and the openness to different themes, manners, and styles. It was probably an overstatement to identify these things strictly with filmmaking and not with still photography, since photographers, to a greater or lesser extent, have used almost all the same techniques and approaches; but it helped me to concentrate on what was needed to make pictures with the kind of physical presence I wanted. (Wall 2007 [2003], p. 179)

---

243 Which is not to say that Jeff Wall forbids himself from taking actual "snapshots"; *Pleading* (1984; printed 1988) is one such example. In some cases, a composition can be directly recognized and 'taken' without any intervention by the photographer (as happens, for example, in *Concrete Ball*, 2002): "cinematographic photographs" do not exhaust Wall's production. Wall has also taken "documentary photographs" and has no problem defining them as such (e.g., *Steve's Farm, Steveston,* 1980; *Diagonal Composition,* 1993; *Dawn,* 2001).

244 Bresson (in particular *Mouchette,* 1967) is quoted directly by Jeff Wall as one of his cinematic inspirations, among other equally important filmmakers such as Pasolini, Fassbinder, and Eustache (*La maman et la putain,* 1973).

Wall thinks of cinematography also as "the art of photography for motion pictures," as an art form developed by cinematographers (directors of photography), especially those who worked closely with "auteurs" like "Bergman, Pasolini, Bresson, Buñuel, and so on, the ones who made up the 'art cinema' of the time" (Wall 2002, p. 31). He considers some of these cinematographers to be outstanding photographers, and he takes great inspiration from their work.[245]

Alongside this aspect, however, the Bressonian lineage explored above finds a unique form of development in Wall's "cinematographic" experimentation with a photographic process involving collaboration with performers (not actors, as the quotation above stresses). We might summarize his concept of "cinematographic near documentary" photographs as two moments: *preparation* and *collaboration* (Wall 2013).

These two directions mark a different step with respect to what one might consider the purely documentary sphere, for which, at least in principle, reality should not need to be "touched" and "retouched." In this sense, Wall's cinematographic photographs are reconstructions, expressive moments whose advent is the result of advance preparation. Before arriving at the final shot, Wall intervenes in reality itself, *collaborates* with it (yet *without predetermining* it, as we shall see). In *Volunteer* (1996), for example, he "didn't just choose a suitable place with ordinary colors and photograph it in black and white; instead, he built a room painted with gray tones, as film sets in the 1930s required specific control of colors and light in order to shoot the black-and-white films of the time" (Graziani 2013, p. 235; Figure 19).

Still, Wall considers cinematographic photography more than just a way to repurpose film techniques for static images; rather, it represents a means of working toward the production of the near-documentary genre. When one of these cinematographic photographs creates the impression of being a "snapshot," we enter the dimension Wall dubs "near documentary." Looking at *Man with a Rifle* (2000), for example, we may have the impression that we are viewing a snapshot of a real scene from everyday urban life (Figure 20). What is important to Wall is not whether or not his images have a documentary status;[246] he is focused on the in-between expressive dimension, the possibility of "not choosing between fact and artifice" (Wall 2007 [2003], p. 181).

His cinematographic work explores the possibility that the recreation of a meaningful moment can have value in itself, regardless of its relationship to any

---

[245] "Sven Nykvist, Nestor Almendros, are among the important photographers of our time" (Wall 2002, p. 32).
[246] "Cinematography as such did not suggest a choice to be made between the imaginary space of the studio and the seamless actuality of the documentary approach" (Wall 2007 [2003], p. 180).

Figure 19: Jeff Wall, *Volunteer*, 1996, silver gelatin print (original in black and white), 221.5 x 313.0 cm, Courtesy of the artist

actual referent, of what actually "has been" in front of the lens. As we said in Chapter 2 in context of Husserl and Diderot, it is a question of finding the maximum of expression in a single instant, in a specific gesture. As Wall notes in his 1984 essay *Gestus*, "my work is based on the representation of the body. In the medium of photography, this representation depends upon the construction of *expressive gestures* which can function as emblems" (Wall 2007 [1984], p. 85, my italics).

This creates a paradoxical relationship: even though such a photograph may tend toward ("near") a reality effect ("documentary"), it is not subject to that "indexical" constraint that would constitute its essence from a Barthesian point of view:

> I have always thought of my "realistic" work as populated with spectral characters whose state of being was not that fixed. That, too, is an inherent aspect, or effect, of what I call "cinematography": things don't have to really exist, or to have existed, to appear in the picture. (Wall 2007 [1996a], p. 254)

This can amount to expressing one's "caring" about even the most humble things (*Siphoning Fuel*, 2008, see Wall 2014b), the nature of an element (the liquid dimension in *Milk*, 1984[247]), the tension of gravitational force through stillness (*Boy Falls From Tree*, 2010), and even absence.[248]

---

[247] On the notion of "liquidity" see Wall (2007 [1989]).
[248] "Photographs either record an occurrence—like one of my pictures where something human is happening: let's call it an occurrence—or they are made in the absence of an occurrence, so it might just be a place [...]. It seems to me that in terms of photography both are equal. Photography

Figure 20: Jeff Wall, *A Man with a Rifle*, 2000, transparency in lightbox, 226.0 x 289.0 cm, Courtesy of the artist

I do not think it is a stretch to say that these remarks are in line with a position we discussed earlier—that is, with how art's expressive capacities elevate an image from a mere depiction "running after a fact" (an *Abbildung*, if we wish to continue using that term) to a figuration (*Bildung*), a "piction," so to speak, that produces its own *sujet*:

> The claim that there is a necessary relationship (a relationship of "adequacy") between a depiction and its referent implies that the referent has precedence over the depiction. This "adequacy" is what is presumed in any imputed legitimation of what you're referring to as representation. [...] I don't think depictions, or images, can be judged that way, and I don't think they're made in those terms, or at least not primarily. Depiction is an act of construction; it brings the referent into being. All the fine arts share this characteristic, regardless of their other differences. (Wall 2007 [1996a], p. 255)

It is important to note that, when Wall describes cinematography in terms of *preparation* and *collaboration*, this is not to imply a need to maintain rigid control over a scene in order to ensure that the instant presented photographically is a manifestation of something already blueprinted in the artist's mind. Rather, it is a question of *working* with reality artistically through movements and additions aimed at facilitating the emergence of an occurrence the artist then recognizes as the right one (without knowing its definitive form before its manifestation).

---

is quite happy to record an occurrence and photography [...] is quite happy to record another thing where there is no occurrence" (Wall 2015a).

224 — 3 Toward Perspectival Images

Figure 21: Jeff Wall, *Overpass*, 2001, transparency in lightbox, 214.2 x 273.3 cm, Courtesy of the artist

Once again, the moment must be recognized as a new variation of an essence that is enriched by the novel manifestation. This, too, involves the possibility of *recognizing something that was not there:* in this case, a *composition* that is not recognized in its value until the moment of its manifestation. As suggested, Wall's use of the adjective cinematographic strongly echoes Bresson's in that he categorically refuses to define this type of photography in terms of "staged photography."[249] Here, unlike on stage, there are no actors, there is no blocking, and, most importantly, there is no script.

In *Overpass* (2001), for example, the four people walking are not actors (Figure 21). Wall asked them to perform actions—but not to act them out. He asked his "models" to repeat the agreed-upon path several times until he recognizes the expressive richness of that pregnant moment. In this regard, Wall remarks that *Overpass* "does resemble a candid photo" (Wall 2015a). There is *collaboration* and *preparation* involved, but not exclusively: as in reality, there is also an element of

---

[249] Cf. the conversation with art historian Thierry de Duve held on the occasion of the traveling Jeff Wall exhibit *Tableaux Pictures Photographs 1996–2013* (presented in Amsterdam, Begrenz, and Humlebæk), available on the website of the Louisiana Museum of Modern Art in Humlebæk (Denmark). In this conversation, Wall states, "I have always disliked the term 'staged photography,' maybe because it implies a 'stage,' the presence of a 'stage'" (Wall 2015b). He makes similar suggestions when commenting on some of his works at the Stedelijk Museum in Amsterdam on the occasion of the same exhibition. Against this background, the only photograph of his that he would define in terms of "staged photography" is *Monologue* (2013), in which three men (one of them Wall's brother) in conversation are actually arranged on a sort of stage, through which the reality represented behind them is essentially reconfigured as a backdrop (cf. Wall 2014c).

chance outside our control. The white truck that we see in *Overpass* at the top right is an element incorporated without preparation or setup, and the same clearly goes for the ever-changing cloud shapes. However, this recognition is not an arbitrary process: the accidental component is recognized as valuable in the final composition[250] (as shown in Chapter 2, the artist works in the "valuing interest").

Wall searches for his chosen image and waits for it to manifest itself by manipulating real material the way a sculptor works with marble, a painter with paint, or a musician with sound. Within such endeavors, variables (such as material resistance) and unexpected occurrences are not only obstacles to the creative process, they can also, to varying degrees, yield opportunities for developing new forms. Phenomenologically speaking, as we pointed out earlier, matter teems with virtual possibilities that can be explicated through variation.

Here, there is a plastic process of creating a photographic form without a script (cf. Wall 2015b)—what some have described as "constructed authenticity" (Weski 2010, p. 14). This process, however, does not detract from the veracity of the shot: "truth is not a work of seconds" (Albig 1996, p. 129). Photography therefore becomes the result of a compositional process in which, similarly to what happens in other arts, the author's shaping work collides with chance, which continually both hinders and stimulates it.

This process of striving to create an expressive moment takes place over time and can often be repetitive (as when those involved are obliged to perform their assigned actions over and over).[251] Though the model's gesture may initially resemble an act in some ways, thereby coming close to that theatrical dimension Wall wishes to avoid at all costs, through repetition it acquires an element of spontaneity and automatism that makes it similar to many of our everyday behaviors—a sort of absorption, we might say, recalling our earlier discussion of absorption and expressiveness[252] (again echoing Bresson, who had his models repeat specific gestures as a way of "rediscovering the automatism of real life"[253]).

---

[250] This is another aspect that can be read in continuity with Bresson's cinematography. In his *Notes*, Bresson writes, "*Shooting.* Wonderful chances, those that act with precision. Way of putting aside the bad ones, to attract the good ones. To reserve for them, in advance, a place in your composition" (Bresson 1975, p. 17).

[251] *Overpass* is just one of many examples here; another would be *A View from an Apartment* (2004–2005).

[252] Cf. Wall (2015b), where he points out that in *Volunteer* (see above) the presence of the performative element is almost annulled by the daily repetition of a gesture that acquires a new, albeit induced, spontaneity.

[253] "Your models [...] will get used to gestures they have repeated twenty times. The words they have learned with their lips will find, *without their minds taking part in this*, the inflections and the lilt proper to their true natures. A way of recovering the automatism of real life. (The talent of

For this reason, Wall is no more willing to describe his work as "fiction" than he is to use the term "staged photography." Rather, his work seeks to illuminate some of the hidden associations that constitute our world, links that are ontologically impassive to the difference between perception and phantasy. He creates an expressive form that offers the viewer the freedom to choose from among multiple possible (albeit nonarbitrary) interpretations. To return to Haneke's remarks, we can also describe this in terms of a "polyvalence of real life" that the observer can "breathe" into the image. In other words, the image opens up a series of implicit virtual possibilities to be developed. The person viewing the photograph can feel the virtual relationship expressed in the image and become its narrator, developing some of the virtual possibilities implicit in it.

In this regard, we could say that Diderot's *salonnier*, the author of extraordinary narrations around the *Salons* paintings we mentioned in the previous chapter, would constitute Jeff Wall's ideal viewer. For Wall, the viewer is the one ultimately tasked with using the fecundity of the instant expressed in the photograph to compose the narrative. The viewer is the *storyteller*, while the stories that arise from the photographs are open to multiple perspectival narrations:

> The only narrative element in the picture is supplied by the viewer, not the "director" or "screenwriter". In the moment of aesthetic experience, aesthetic appreciation of the picture, the viewer writes the scenario; he or she doesn't read it. That writing is done instantaneously, in the quickness of liking and responding to the qualities of the picture. (Wall 2014a, p. 32)

In the terms developed here, we can say that the viewer perceives the value of the image as essentially related to its narrative. However, when Wall says that the viewer "writes" the image's script in the immediacy of the aesthetic experience, this writing clearly must be construed as pre-propositional. Appreciation of the image emerges through the production of a perspective (narrative, value, emotion) that strikes the viewer in a given moment. Such appreciation precedes any deliberate efforts toward possible logical-propositional "explications" of the experience

---

one or several actors or stars no longer comes into it. What matters is how you approach your models and the unknown and the virgin nature you manage to draw from them)" (Bresson 1975, p. 32). The boundaries between fiction and documentary can be artistically explored in various ways. I will limit myself here to referring to Molder (2017) for an analysis of how, in Víctor Erice's *Vidros partidos* (*Broken Glass*, 2012), the director (in a path that in some ways represents the pendant of Bresson's approach) collects testimonials from workers at the historic *Fábrica de Fiação e Tecidos do Rio Vizela* (Textile Factory of the Vizela River) (which was founded in 1845 and closed its doors in 2002), "working with these people as if they were actors" (Molder 2017, p. 253), writing for them, and making them repeat them the dialogues of their testimonies until they "learned the part" (see Molder 2017, pp. 254–256).

("I love that piece, it's good. […] I love that piece means I think it's good," Wall 2015a). The image strikes the viewer in all its implicit and manifold senses, which the viewer then unfolds to create new possibilities for development.

Within the world as a totality of meaningful (or meaningless) nexuses, there is always the possibility for a valuable idea (axiological comprehension) to emerge on an emotional horizon—the dimensions are intimately linked. In this artistic context, a "faithful image" is not necessarily one that tells us what definitely happened in front of the lens but rather is one capable of expressing the complexity and richness of reality, allowing multiple possible (yet nonarbitrary) interpretations, multiple narratives that can perpetuate the sense opened up by the image through new variations. Let us note how our reflections on the different perspectives opened by near documentary images can also shed light on our reception of positional images and their pretense of showing viewers "what has been." As has become clear, images in themselves do not present objective facts but only manifestations that can take on perspectival meanings: beyond the element of *belief* that characterizes positional experience of images, we can always ask ourselves *what* and *how* "has been"—we can ask what kinds of perspectives such facts originated from.[254]

Wall's process of creation does not take place on the spot. Creating and recognizing the pregnant moment is often the result of a process triggered by an aesthetic experience, which in turn is elicited through an encounter with reality. Perceiving a silent aesthetic call opened up by a particular perspective does not lead to him taking an immediate snapshot in the hopes of capturing that vision the moment it presents itself—Wall is not a photographer *à la* Cartier-Bresson, practicing "direct-photography" in the vein of "art-photojournalis[m]" (Wall 2007 [1996b], p. 263); he seems to counter the Cartier-Bressonian (1952) idea of a "decisive moment" with that of a "pregnant moment." Paradoxically, his photographic process "begins by not photographing" (Wall 2007).

> I developed that phrase—I begin by not photographing—because it just described something I really do. So, if I see something on the street, let's say, I don't photograph it. So I could be looking and hunting for things, but I just don't photograph them. It's only a small difference, really. The actual event disappears as a photograph. It vanishes as a potential photograph. It doesn't happen. But it doesn't disappear because I am the photographer. So, therefore, what I do with it is still photography, it's part of my process; and so I do remember it and then you just deal with what memory is all about. (Wall 2007)

---

[254] In this regard, it is also interesting to consider the work of German photographer Barbara Probst, who explicitly thematizes this question in her works, exploring the "explosion" of perspectives that can implicitly constitute what we call *a* "fact" (see Probst 2021, pp. 44–46).

In the same Diderotian and Proustian vein expounded above, Wall's creative process starts from his own memory. It is triggered by an encounter with a reality expressing potentialities, an encounter breaking the usual flow of life. Wall obsesses over that moment—which haunts his memory, so to speak—and responds to the urge through a process aimed at rediscovering that expression by recreating it. Indeed, as we have seen, the "originary" moment floating virtually in Wall's (or anyone's) memory can be obtained only through *variation:* the fruitful instant can return as the same only in *variation*, only *differently the same*. In our terms, the *noema* can be recreated only by *varying* it.

Indeed, artistic recreation also implies a passage from personal recollection to an impersonal *noema:* once recognized in its essence, the moment expressed is no more Wall's than it is the viewer's. It becomes a "neutral," "expressive" element. It does not matter, at that point, whether the image specifically refers to one of Wall's memories. We have also referred to this as a singular dimension—productively more than individual (which would miss its intersubjectivity) and productively less than a general abstraction (which would miss its specificity). In the same vein, such a singular impersonality proves refractory to the difference between documentary and fictional consciousness (despite the fact that we know we are dealing with images).

Referencing Bresson can be useful for understanding the sense in which Wall's creative process can reach this neutral dimension. When creating cinematographic photographs, Wall can introduce conditions favoring the emergence of the "fruitful" moment, but he does not yet know precisely what will happen or when; there is no script, no predetermined "plot." In this respect, Wall's participation (to a greater or lesser extent) in giving rise to the propitious occurrence does not change the status of these photographs—it does not make them more fictional than documentary.

As in Proust, the encounter with reality engenders the creative process through which the sense of that encounter can be re-expressed through variation. On the one hand, there is a fidelity to the silent appeal of things, to the implicit virtualities reality expresses. On the other hand, as we have tried to show, expression is possible only through pregnant variation (see also Wall 2007), and the expressive power of reality is not by rights greater than that of fiction. At the level of the sense expressed, *once created*, the work lives a life of its own, independently of specific references regarding its genesis. In a photo like Wall's *In Front of a Nightclub* (2006; Figure 22), the club we see is "only" a reconstruction of the one that originally caught Wall's attention and inspired the work. However, this had nothing to do with ontological considerations potentially affecting the status of this photograph. Rather, it was a banal question of logistics: Wall would gladly have photographed the "original" club, but it would have taken

Figure 22: Jeff Wall, *In Front of a Nightclub*, 2006, transparency in lightbox, 226.0 x 360.8 cm, Courtesy of the artist

too much time (see Wall 2015a). According to him, the fact that he opted for a "copy" does not change anything about the sense of the experience he hopes to offer to the viewer: "there is no one way to create a realistic photo, you can go on location or create a replica" (Wall 2015a).

This does not constitute a form of deception, as Wall points out that even the *ad hoc* club possesses a certain "documentary quality" in its own right. More precisely, as he is fond of emphasizing, we are in the gray area of "near documentary," which tends to emancipate itself from fiction (Bresson) but does not aspire to documentary status. Here, the image opens up a perspective as a zone of productive ambiguity in which the existence or nonexistence of what is experienced does not affect the manifestation of the *noema*.

Let us conclude by remarking that, in Wall's work, the neutrality of expression comes to concern the art of the portrait in a direction that resonates strongly with the ideas explored earlier through Diderot. Let us consider *Adrian Walker, artist, drawing from a specimen in a laboratory in the Department of Anatomy at the University of British Columbia, Vancouver* (1992; Figure 23). On the one hand, as the title itself seems to underline, *Adrian Walker* might be considered a documentary photograph depicting an individual. On the other, if one thinks in terms of a *sense consciousness* (where *consciousness is not the source of the sense, but a condition for the sense of the world to manifest itself*):

> The fact of it being or not being a "portrait" of a specific real person, again, may be secondary in the structure. The title, because it names him, makes it appear that he is such a specific, real person. But it's easily possible that *Adrian Walker* is simply a fictional

Figure 23: Jeff Wall, *Adrian Walker, artist, drawing from a specimen in a laboratory in the Department of Anatomy at the University of British Columbia, Vancouver*, 1992, transparency in lightbox, 119 x 164.3 cm, Courtesy of the artist

> name that I decided to make up to create a certain illusion, like "Emma Bovary." Even though that's not true and there is such a person, and that is him, I don't think there is necessarily any resonance of that in the structure of the work. (Wall 2007 [1993], p. 230)

It is all the more significant that Wall himself, when commenting on this portrait, references the theme of *absorption* we introduced above concerning Zidane's *21st Century Portrait*. Wall refers directly to Michael Fried's characterization of absorption, suggesting that, when considering portraits of *sujets* "absorbed in some activity" (Wall 2007 [1993], p. 231), unaware of the gaze of the artist and the viewer, one "begin[s] to move outside of the boundaries of the portraiture, strictly speaking" (the portrait "in the proper sense," in Husserl's words) to arrive at a "kind of picture in which people are identified, and identified with, primarily by their physiognomy and their actions and the less by their names, less by their personal, empirical, historical, social identity and more by the generic identity as controlled by the type of picture they're in" (Wall 2007 [1993], p. 231). This is in keeping with the thesis of images producing their own *sujets*.

At this level, it no longer matters much whether a model (Adrian Walker, in this case, but this also applies to the "real" restorers in *Restoration*, 1993) is actually himself/herself or not. The *sujet* "breathing" in the image belongs to an order that is no longer affected by the difference between reality and phantasy, and every time we "look into" the image and undergo a valueception, we can rediscover the *de jure* eternity of those "neutral" and "expressive" faces and bodies. This is also the case for those films that do reference individual characters but only for purposes of expressing a singular and shareable *noema*. In these cases, the proper noun denotes not so much an individual narrative as a perspective, a possibility of being in the world,[255] an expressed *sujet* apprehended in an axiological-emotional-cognitive opening. In our terms: these are cinematic creative portraits.

---

[255] Consider, for example, the Dardenne brothers' *Rosetta* or *Le silence de Lorna*. In this regard, see also Robert Pippin's insightful discussion of how the Dardennes' cinematic thought is capable of "intimat[ing] an unusual picture of human subjectivity" (Pippin 2015, p. 758).

References

Husserl's Writings

Husserl's Writings Not Included in the Husserliana Series

Husserl, Edmund (1910): "Philosophie als strenge Wissenschaft." In: *Logos* 1 (1910–11), 289–341; – "Philosophy as Rigorous Science." Eng. transl. ed. by Lauer, Q. In: *Phenomenology and the Crisis of Philosophy*. New York, NY: Harper Torchbooks, 1965, 69–147.
Husserl, Edmund (1939): *Erfahrung und Urteil*. Ed. Landgrebe, Ludwig. Prag: Academia; – *Experience and Judgment. Investigations in a Genealogy of Logic*. Eng. transl. ed. by Landgrebe, L., Evanston: Northwestern University Press, 1973.
Husserl, Edmund (1956): "Persönliche Aufzeichnungen." In: *Philosophy and Phenomenological Research* 16, 3, 293–302.
Husserl, Edmund (1994): "Brief an von Hofmannsthal. 12.I.1907." In: *Husserliana Dokumente, III, Briefwechsel*, Vol. VII: *Wissenschaftskorrespondenz*. Ed. Schuhmann, Karl. Dordrecht: Kluwer, 133–136; – "Letter to Hofmannsthal (Göttingen, January 12th, 1907)." Eng. transl. Wallenstein, S.O. In: *Site* 26–27 (2009), 2.

Manuscripts

Ms. A VI 1 (1906–1918) – Husserl Archive Leuven.

Secondary Literature

Albig, Jörg-Uwe (1996): "Wahrheit ist kein Werk von Sekunden." In: *Art. Das Kunstmagazin* 6, 14–25.
Aldea, Andrea S. (2013): "Husserl's Struggle with Mental Images: Imaging and Imagining Reconsidered." In: *Continental Philosophy Review* 46, 371–394.
Alloa, Emmanuel (2011): *Das durchscheinende Bild. Konturen einer medialen Phänomenologie*. Zürich: Diaphanes; – *Looking Through Images. A Phenomenology of Visual Media*. Eng. transl. Scott, N.F., New York: Columbia University Press, 2021.
Ames, Eric (2012): *Ferocious Reality. Documentary According to Werner Herzog*. Minneapolis/London: University of Minnesota Press.
Aristotle (1996): *Poetics*. Eng. transl. Health, M., London: Penguin.
Barthes, Roland (1973): "Diderot, Brecht, Eisenstein." In: *Revue d'esthétique*, 26, 2–3–4, 185–191; – "Diderot, Brecht, Eisenstein." Eng. transl. Heath, S. In: *Image, Music, Text*. London: Fontana Press, 1977, 69–78.
Barthes, Roland (1980): *La chambre claire. Note sur la photographie*. Paris: Cahiers du cinéma-Gallimard-Seuil; – *Camera Lucida*. Eng. transl. Howard, R., New York: Hill and Wang, 1981.
Barthes, Roland (2003): *La Préparation du roman, suivi des séminaires La Métaphore du labyrinthe et Proust et la photographie*. Paris: Seuil/IMEC; – *The Preparation of the Novel: Lecture Courses and Seminars at the Collège de France (1978–1979 and 1979–1980)*. Eng. transl. Briggs, K., New York: Columbia University Press, 2010.

Baudrillard, Jean (1991): *La guerre du Golfe n'a pas eu lieu*. Paris: Galilée.
Baudrillard, Jean (1997): *Illusion, désillusion esthétiques*, Paris: Sens & Tonka; – "Aesthetic Illusion and Disillusion." Eng. transl. Hodges, A. In: *The Conspiracy of Art. Manifestos, Interviews, Essays*. New York: Semiotexte, 2005, 111–129.
Bazin, André (1949–1951): "Mort tous les après-midi." In: *Qu'est-ce que le cinéma?* Paris: Cerf, 1958, 65–70; – "Death Every Afternoon." Eng. transl. Cohen, M.A. In: *Rites of Realism: Essays on Corporeal Cinema*. Durham/London: Duke University Press, 2003, 27–31.
Beckett, Samuel (1931): *Proust*. London: Chatto & Windus.
Benjamin, Walter (1936): "Das Kunstwerk im Zeitalter seiner technischen Reproduzierbarkeit." In: Tiedemann, R., Scweppenhäuser, H. (Eds.): *Gesammelte Schriften. I/2, 1974–1989*, Frankfurt am Main: Suhrkamp, 1974, 471–508; – "The Work of Art in the Age of Mechanical Reproduction." Eng. transl. ed. by Arendt, H. In: *Illuminations*. New York: Schocken, 1968, 217–251.
Bergson, Henri (1934): "Introduction (première partie). Croissance de la vérité. Mouvement rétrograde du vrai." In: *La pensée et le mouvant*. Paris: Alcan, 7–31; – "Introduction (Part I). Growth of Truth. Retrograde Movement of the True." Eng. transl. Andison, M.L. In: *The Creative Mind*. New York: Philosophical Library, 2007, 1–17.
Bernet, Rudolf (2004): *Conscience et existence. Perspectives phénoménologiques*. Paris: PUF.
Bernet, Rudolf (2006): "Reine Phantasie als freie Selbstentzweiung bei Husserl." In: Fonfara, D. (Ed.): *Metaphysik als Wissenschaft. Festschrift für Klaus Düsing zum 65. Geburtstag*. Freiburg/Munich: Karl Alber, 408–426.
Besoli, Stefano (2007): "Il tradimento di un'eredità. Franz Brentano a confronto con l'originaria vocazione aristotelica." In: Brentano, Franz: *La psicologia di Aristotele, con particolare riguardo alla dottrina del 'nous poietikos'*. Ital. transl. ed. by Besoli, S., Macerata: Quodlibet, xi–lxi.
Blumenberg, Hans (1979): *Schiffbruch mit Zuschauer. Paradigma einer Daseinsmetapher*. Frankfurt am Main: Suhrkamp.
Boehm, Gottfried (1986): "Der stumme Logos." In: Métraux, A., Waldenfels, B. (Eds.): *Leibhaftige Vernunft. Spuren von Merleau-Pontys Denken*. Munich: Fink, 289–304.
Boehm, Gottfried (1994): "Die Wiederkehr der Bilder." In: Boehm, G. (Ed.): *Was ist ein Bild?* Munich: Fink, 11–38.
Boehm, Rudolf (1966): "Einleitung." In: Husserl, Edmund: *Zur Phänomenologie des inneren Zeitbewusstseins (1893–1917)*. Boehm, R. (Ed.), Den Haag: Martinus Nijhoff, xiii–xliii.
Brentano, Franz (1874): *Psychologie vom empirischen Standpunkte: in zwei Bänden*. Vol. 1. Leipzig: Duncker & Humboldt; – *Psychology from an Empirical Standpoint*. Eng. transl. ed. by Crane, T., London/New York: Routledge, 2015.
Brentano, Franz (1959): *Grundzüge der Ästhetik*. Mayer-Hillebrand, F. (Ed.), Bern: Francke.
Bresson, Robert (1975): *Notes sur le cinématographe*. Paris: Gallimard; – *Notes on Cinematography*. Eng. transl. Griffin, J., New York: Urizen, 1977.
Bresson, Robert (2013): *Bresson par Bresson*. Bresson, M. (Ed.), Paris: Flammarion; – *Bresson on Bresson: interviews 1943–1983*. Eng. transl. ed. by Moschovakis, A., New York: Review Books, 2016.
Breuer, Irene (2018): "Aristotle and Husserl on the Relationship between the Necessity of a Fact and Contingency." In: *New Yearbook for Phenomenology and Phenomenological Philosophy* 15, 269–296.
Breyer, Thiemo (2019): "Self-Affection and Perspective-Taking: The Role of Phantasmatic and Imaginatory Consciousness for Empathy." In: *Topoi* 39, 803–809.

Brough, John B. (1988): "Art and Artworld: Some Ideas for a Husserlian Aesthetic." In: Sokolowski, R. (Ed.): *Edmund Husserl and the Phenomenological Tradition. Essays in Phenomenology.* Washington: Catholic University of America Press, 25–45.

Brough, John B. (2005): "Translator's Introduction." In: Husserl, Edmund: *Phantasy, Image Consciousness, and Memory (1898–1925).* Eng. transl. ed. by Brough, J., Dordrecht: Springer, 2005, xxix–lxviii.

Brough, John B. (2011): "Showing and Seeing. Film as Phenomenology." In: Parry, J.D. (Ed.): *Art and Phenomenology.* London/New York: Routledge, 192–214.

Brough, John B. (2012): "Something That Is Nothing but Can Be Anything: The Image and Our Consciousness of It." In: Zahavi, D. (Ed.): *The Oxford Handbook of Contemporary Phenomenology.* Oxford: Oxford University Press, 545–563.

Brunet, François (2012): "La photographie, éternelle aspirante à l'art." In: Heinich, N., Shapiro, R. (Eds.): *De l'artification. Enquêtes sur le passage à l'art.* Paris: Éditions de l'Ehess, 29–46.

Caminada, Emanuele (2020): "Developing Digital Technology at the Husserl Archives. A Report." In: Desideri, F., Zaccarello, B. (Eds.): *Reading Philosophy Through Archives and Manuscripts. Aisthesis* 13, 2, 79–86.

Carbone, Mauro (2016): *Philosophie-écrans. Du cinéma à la révolution numérique.* Paris: Vrin; – *Philosophy-Screens. From Cinema to the Digital Revolution.* Eng. transl. Nijhuis, M., New York: SUNY Press, 2019.

Cartier-Bresson, Henri (1952): *Images à la sauvette.* Paris: Verve; – *The Decisive Moment.* Eng. transl. New York: Simon and Schuster, 1952.

Casey, Edward (1971): "Imagination: Imagining and the Image." In: *Philosophy and Phenomenological Research* 31, 475–490.

Cavallaro, Marco (2017): "The Phenomenon of Ego-Splitting in Husserl's Phenomenology of Pure Phantasy." In: *Journal of the British Society for Phenomenology* 48, 162–177.

Chateau, Dominique/Moure, José (Eds.) (2016): *Screens. From Materiality to Spectatorship – A Historical and Theoretical Reassessment.* Amsterdam: Amsterdam University Press.

Chateau, Dominique/Moure, José (Eds.) (2020): *Post-cinema Cinema in the Post-art Era.* Amsterdam: Amsterdam University Press.

Ciment, Michel/Niogret, Hubert (2004): "Closer to the Life than the Conventions of Cinema: Interview with the Coen Brothers (conducted in Cannes on May 16, 1996)." In: Luhr, W.G. (Ed.): *The Coen Brothers' Fargo.* New York: Cambridge University Press, 109–118.

Cometti, Jean P. (2002): "Merleau-Ponty, Wittgenstein, and the Question of Expression." In: *Revue internationale de philosophie* 1, 73–89.

Cometti, Jean P. (2010): "Frames and Bodies – Notes on Three Films by Pedro Costa: Ossos, No Quarto da Vanda, Juventude em Marcha." In: *Afterall: A Journal of Art, Context, and Enquiry* 24, 62–70.

Conte, Richard (2020): "The Zidane Film." In: Chateau, D., Moure, J. (Eds.): *Post-cinema. Cinema in the Post-art Era.* Amsterdam: Amsterdam University Press, 281–292.

Costa, Pedro (2020): "Interview: Pedro Costa, dir. Vitalina Varela." In: *Cinevue* 9 (https://cine-vue.com/2020/03/interview-pedro-costa-dir-vitalina-varela.html, last accessed June 15, 2023).

Costa, Vincenzo (2007): *Il cerchio e l'ellisse. Husserl e il darsi delle cose.* Soveria Mannelli: Rubbettino.

Costa, Vincenzo (2010): "Per una fenomenologia dell'immaginazione." In: Feyles, M. (Ed.): *Memoria, immaginazione e tecnica.* Rome: NEU, 127–139.

Costa, Vincenzo (2014): "Verso una fenomenologia delle tonalità emotive." In: Matteucci, G., Portera, M. (Eds.): *La natura delle emozioni.* Milan: Mimesis, 129–143.

Cronin, Paul (Ed.) (2002): *Herzog on Herzog*. London: Faber and Faber.
Crowell, Steven (2013): *Normativity and Phenomenology in Husserl and Heidegger*. New York: Cambridge University Press.
Crowther, Paul (2022): *The Phenomenology of Aesthetic Consciousness and Phantasy: Working with Husserl*. London/New York: Routledge.
Currie, Gregory (1990): *The Nature of Fiction*. Cambridge: Cambridge University Press.
D'Angelo, Paolo (2020): *La tirannia delle emozioni*. Bologna: Il Mulino.
Daney, Serge (1992): "Le travelling de Kapò." In: *Trafic* 4, 5–19.
Dastur, Françoise (1991): "Husserl et la neutralité de l'art." In: *La Part de l'Œil* (Dossier : Art et phénoménologie) 7, 19–29.
de Warren, Nicolas (2009): *Husserl and the Promise of Time*. New York: Cambridge University Press.
de Warren, Nicolas (2010): "Tamino's Eyes, Pamina's Gaze: Husserl's Phenomenology of Image-Consciousness Refashioned." In: Ierna, C., Jacobs, H., Mattens, F. (Eds.): *Philosophy, Phenomenology, Sciences. Essays in Commemoration of Edmund Husserl*. Dordrecht: Springer, 303–332.
Deleuze, Gilles (1964): *Proust et les signes*. Paris: PUF; – *Proust and Signs: The Complete Text*. Eng. transl. Howard, R., London: Athlone Press, 2000.
Deleuze, Gilles (1968): *Différence et répétition*. Paris: PUF; – *Difference and Repetition*. Eng. transl. Patton, P., London/New York: Continuum, 1994.
Deleuze, Gilles (1969): *Logique du sens*. Paris: Les Éditions de Minuit; – *The Logic of Sense*. Eng. transl. Lester, M., Stivale, C., New York: Columbia University Press, 1990.
Deleuze, Gilles (1981): *Francis Bacon – Logique de la sensation*. Paris: Éditions de la Différence; – *Francis Bacon. The Logic of Sensation*. Eng. transl. Smith, D.W., London: Bloomsbury, 2017.
Deleuze, Gilles (1983): *Cinéma 1. L'Image-Mouvement*. Paris: Les Éditions de Minuit; – *Cinema 1: The Movement-Image*. Eng. transl. Tomlinson, H., Habberjam, B., London: Athlone, 1986.
Deleuze, Gilles (1985): *Cinéma 2. L'image-temps*. Paris: Les Éditions de Minuit; – *Cinema 2: The Time-Image*. Eng. transl. Tomlinson, H., Galeta, R., Minneapolis: University of Minnesota Press, 1989.
Deleuze, Gilles (1993): *Critique et Clinique*. Paris: Les Éditions de Minuit; – *Essays Critical and Clinical*. Eng. transl. Daniel, W., Smith, D.W., Greco, M.A., London/New York: Verso, 1997.
Deleuze, Gilles (1995): "L'immanence : une vie...." In: *Philosophie* 47, 3–7; – "Immanence: A Life." Eng. transl. Boyman, A. In: *Pure Immanence. Essays on A Life*. New York: Zone Books, 2001, 25–33.
Deleuze, Gilles/Guattari, Félix (1975): *Kafka. Pour une littérature mineure*. Paris: Les Éditions de Minuit; – *Kafka: Toward a Minor Literature*. Eng. transl. Polan, D., Minneapolis: University of Minnesota Press, 1986.
Deleuze, Gilles/Guattari, Félix (1980): *Capitalisme et schizophrénie 2 : Mille plateaux*. Paris: Les Éditions de Minuit; – *A Thousand Plateaus: Capitalism and Schizophrenia*. Eng. transl. Massumi, B., Minneapolis/London: University of Minnesota Press, 1988.
Deleuze, Gilles/Guattari, Félix (1991): *Qu'est-ce que la philosophie?* Paris: Les Éditions de Minuit; – *What Is Philosophy?* Eng. transl. Tomlinson, H., Burchell, G., New York: Columbia University Press, 1994.
Denson, Shane/Leyda, Julia (2016) (Eds.): *Post-Cinema: Theorizing 21st-Century Film*. Falmer: Reframe.
Deodati, Marco (2010): "Immagini in movimento, emozioni in immagine." In: *Fata Morgana* 12, 71–82.
Descartes, René (1637): "La Dioptrique." In: Adam, Ch., Tannery, P. (Eds.): *Œuvres de Descartes*. Vol. 6. Paris: Cerf, 1902, 81–147; – "Optics." Eng. transl. ed. by Cottingham, J., Stoothoff, R., Murdoch,

D. In: *The Philosophical Writings of Descartes*. Vol. 1. Cambridge, MA: Cambridge University Press, 1985, 152–175.

Desideri, Fabrizio (2004): *Forme dell'estetica. Dall'esperienza del bello al problema dell'arte*. Rome/Bari: Laterza.

Diderot, Denis (1798): *Jacques le Fataliste et son maître*. Vol. 1/2. Paris: Maradan.

Diderot, Denis (1875 [1761]): *Éloge de Richardson, auteur des romans de Paméla, de Clarisse et de Grandisson*. In: Assézat, J., Tourneux, M. (Eds.): *Œuvres completes*. Vol. 5. Paris: Garnier Frères.

Diderot, Denis (1951 [1830]): "Paradoxe sur le comédien." In: *Œuvres*. Billy, A. (Ed.), Paris: Gallimard.

Diderot, Denis (1955–1970): *Correspondance*. 16 Vols. Roth, G., Varloot, J. (Eds.), Paris: Les Éditions de Minuit.

Diderot, Denis (2007 [1761]): "Salon de 1761." In: *Essais sur la peinture, Salons de 1759, 1761, 1763*. Paris: Hermann.

Diderot, Denis (2007 [1763]): "Salon de 1763." In: *Essais sur la peinture, Salons de 1759, 1761, 1763*. Paris: Hermann.

Diderot, Denis (2007 [1766]): "Essais sur la peinture." In: *Essais sur la peinture, Salons de 1759, 1761, 1763*. Paris: Hermann.

Diderot, Denis (2008 [1767]): "Salon de 1767." In: *Ruines et paysages. III. Salon de 1767*. Paris: Hermann.

Diderot, Denis (2009 [1765]): *Salon de 1765*. Paris: Hermann.

Diderot, Denis (2009 [1769]): "Salon de 1769." In: *Héros et martyrs. IV. Salons de 1769, 1771, 1775, 1781, Pensées détachées sur la peinture*. Paris: Hermann.

Didi-Huberman, Georges (2000): *Devant le temps. Histoire de l'art et anachronisme des images*. Paris: Les Éditions de Minuit.

Didi-Huberman, Georges (2004): *Images malgré tout*. Paris: Les Éditions de Minuit; – *Images in Spite of All. Four Photographs from Auschwitz*. Eng. transl. Lissis, S.B., Chicago: The University of Chicago Press, 2012.

Dieckmann, Herbert (1952): "Description of Portrait." In: *Diderot Studies* 2, 6–8.

Dostoevsky, Fyodor (1869): *The Idiot*. Eng. transl. Pevear, R., Volokhonsky, L., New York: Vintage, 2003.

Dufourcq, Annabelle (2011): *La dimension imaginaire du réel dans la philosophie de Husserl*. Dordrecht: Springer.

Eldridge, Patrick (2017): "Depicting and Seeing-in. The '*Sujet*' in Husserl Phenomenology of Images." In: *Phenomenology and the Cognitive Sciences* 17, 555–578.

Eisenstein, Sergej M. (1988 [1943]): "Didro pisal o kino (1943)." In: *Teatr* 7, 112–120; – "Diderot ha scritto di cinema." Ital. transl. Bottone, L., Cioni, A., Montani, P. In: *Stili di regia*. Venice: Marsilio, 1993, 383–404.

Ferencz-Flatz, Christian (2008–2009): "Filmbewusstsein und Zuschauer im Bild. Ein husserlscher Ansatz zum Kinematographen." In: Vainovski-Mihai, I. (Ed.): *New Europe College Yearbook 2008–2009*. Bucharest: New Europe College, 91–117.

Ferencz-Flatz, Christian (2009a): "Gibt es perzeptive Phantasie? Als-ob-Bewusstsein, Widerstreit und Neutralität in Husserls Aufzeichnungen zur Bildbetrachtung." In: *Husserl Studies* 25, 235–253.

Ferencz-Flatz, Christian (2009b): "The Neutrality of Images and Husserlian Aesthetics." In: *Studia Phaenomenologica* 9, 477–493.

Ferencz-Flatz, Christian/Hanich, Julian (2016): "Editors' Introduction: What is Film Phenomenology?" In: *Studia Phaenomenologica* 16, 11–61.

Ferrarin, Alfredo (2007): "Immaginazione e memoria in Hobbes e Cartesio." In: Sassi, M.M. (Ed.): *Tracce nella mente. Teorie della memoria da Platone ai moderni*. Pisa: Edizioni della Normale, 159–189.
Ferrarin, Alfredo (2015): "From the World to Philosophy, and Back." In: Bloechl, J., De Warren, N. (Eds.): *Phenomenology in a New Key: Between Analysis and History. Essays in Honor of Richard Cobb-Stevens*. Dordrecht: Springer, 63–92.
Ferrarin, Alfredo (2018): "Productive and Practical Imagination: What Does Productive Imagination Produce?" In: Geniusas, S., Nikulin, D. (Eds.): *Productive Imagination: Its History, Meaning, and Significance*. London/New York: Rowman & Littlefield, 29–48.
Fink, Eugen (1930): "Vergegenwärtigung und Bild." In: *Studien zur Phänomenologie*. Den Haag: Martinus Nijhoff, 1966, 1–78.
Fink, Eugen (1955): *Grundphänomene des menschlichen Daseins*. Schütz, E., Schwarz, F.A. (Eds.), Freiburg/Munich: Karl Alber, 1979.
Fink, Eugen (1960): *Spiel als Weltsymbol*. Stuttgart: Kohlhammer; – *Play as Symbol of the World and Other Writings*. Eng. transl. Moore, A., Turner, C., Bloomington: Indiana University Press, 2016.
Fink, Eugen (1971 [1968]): "Maske und Kothurn." In: *Epiloge zur Dichtung*. Frankfurt am Main: Klostermann, 1–18.
Fitzner, Werner (2014): *Wertendes Erleben. Ästhetik aus der Perspektive von Edmund Husserls Phänomenologie*. Dissertation of Werner Fitzner. Greifswald (OPUS 4 | Wertendes Erleben. Ästhetik aus der Perspektive von Edmund Husserls Phänomenologie (uni-greifswald.de)).
Franzini, Elio (1997): *Filosofia dei sentimenti*. Milan: Mondadori.
Franzini, Elio (2002): "Introduzione." In: Husserl, Edmund: *Idee per una fenomenologia pura e per una filosofia fenomenologica. Libro primo: Introduzione generale alla fenomenologia pura*. Ital. transl. ed. by Costa, V., Turin: Einaudi, 11–51.
Franzini, Elio (2009): *Elogio dell'Illuminismo*. Milan: Bruno Mondadori.
Franzini, Elio (2018): *Moderno e Postmoderno. Un bilancio*. Milan: Raffaello Cortina Editore.
Fried, Michael (1988): *Absorption and Theatricality. Painting and Beholder in the Age of Diderot*. Chicago: University of Chicago Press.
Fried, Michael (2007): "Jeff Wall, Wittgenstein, and the Everyday." In: *Critical Inquiry* 33, 3, 495–526.
Fried, Michael (2008): *Why Photography Matters as Art as Never Before*. New Haven/London: Yale University Press.
Fried, Michael/Griffin, Tim (2006): "Absorbed in the Action." In: *Artforum International* 45, 1, 332–339.
Friedberg, Anne (2006): *The Virtual Window. From Alberti to Microsoft*. Cambridge, MA: MIT Press.
Fuchs, Thomas (2014): "The Virtual Other. Empathy in the Age of Virtuality." In: *Journal of Consciousness Studies* 21, 5–6, 152–173.
Gendler, Tamar Szabó/Kovakovich, Karson (2005): "Genuine Rational Fictional Emotions." In: Kieran, M. (Ed.): *Contemporary Debates in Aesthetics and the Philosophy of Art*. Hoboken, NJ: Blackwell, 241–253.
Goodkin, Richard (1987): "Film and Fiction: Hitchcock's *Vertigo* and Proust's 'Vertigo'." In: *Modern Language Notes* 102, 1171–1181.
Gordon, Douglas/Parreno, Philippe (2006): *Zidane: A 21st Century Portrait*. Gordon, D., Parreno, P. (Dir.), DVD.
Gori, Pietro (2016): *Il pragmatismo di Nietzsche. Saggi sul pensiero prospettivistico*. Milan: Mimesis; – *Nietzsche's Pragmatism. A Study on Perspectival Thought*. Eng. transl. De Sanctis, S., Berlin/Boston: De Gruyter, 2019.

Graziani, Stefano (2013): "Nota del curatore." In: Wall, Jeff: *Gestus. Scritti sull'arte e la fotografia.* Ital. transl. ed. by Graziani, S., Macerata: Quodlibet, 225–237.

Griffero, Tonino (2010): "Dal bello all'atmosferico. Tra estetica e atmosferologia." In: Russo, L. (Ed.): *Dopo l'Estetica.* Palermo: Aesthetica Preprint Supplementa, 133–146.

Grundmann, Roy (2010): "Between Adorno and Lyotard: Michael Haneke's Aesthetic of Fragmentation." In: Grundmann, R. (Ed.): *A Companion to Michael Haneke.* Malden: Wiley-Blackwell, 371–419.

Grundmann, Roy/Naqvi, Fatima/Root, Colin (Eds.) (2020): *Michael Haneke: Interviews.* Jackson: University Press of Mississippi.

Gunthert, André (2019): *L'image partagée. La photographie numérique.* Paris: Textuel.

Gurwitsch, Aron (2009 [1940]): "On the Intentionality of Consciousness." In: Kersten, F. (Ed.): *The Collected Works of Aron Gurwitsch (1901–1973),* Vol. 2: *Studies in Phenomenology and Psychology.* Dordrecht: Springer, 139–156.

Guyer, Paul (1978): "Disinterestedness and Desire in Kant's Aesthetics." In: *The Journal of Aesthetics and Art Criticism* 36, 4, 449–460.

Haneke, Michael (1994): "Notizen zum Film." In: *Stadtkino-Programm* 255.

Haneke, Michael (1998): "La negazione è l'unica forma d'arte che si possa prendere sul serio. Colloquio con Michael Haneke." In: Horwath, A., Spagnoletti, G. (Eds.): *Michael Haneke.* Turin: Lindau, 41–62.

Haneke, Michael (2001): "Michael Haneke: The Bearded Prophet of 'Code Inconnu' and 'The Piano Teacher', interview by S. Foundas." In: *Indiewire* (https://www.indiewire.com/2001/12/interviewmichael-haneke-the-bearded-prophet-of-code-inconnu-and-thepiano-teacher-2-80636/, last accessed June 15, 2023).

Haneke, Michael (2008a): "Gewalt und Medien." In: *Nahaufnahme Michael Haneke. Gespräche mit Thomas Assheuer.* Berlin: Alexander, 155–163; – "Violence and the Media." Eng. transl. ed. by Grundmann, R. In: *A Companion to Michael Haneke.* Oxford: Wiley-Blackwell, 2010, 575–579.

Haneke, Michael (2008b): "Michael Haneke – Gespräche mit Thomas Assheuer." In: *Nahaufnahme Michael Haneke. Gespräche mit Thomas Assheuer.* Berlin: Alexander Verlag, 7–182.

Haneke, Michael (2008c): "Schrecken und Utopie der Form – Bressons Au hasard Balthazar." In: *Nahaufnahme Michael Haneke. Gespräche mit Thomas Assheuer.* Berlin: Alexander Verlag, 135–154; – "Terror and Utopia of Form. Robert Bresson's *Au hasard Balthazar.*" Eng. transl. ed. by Grundmann, R. In: *A Companion to Michael Haneke.* Oxford: Wiley-Blackwell, 2010, 565–574.

Haneke, Michael (2009): "Michael Haneke on Violence. Interview by F. von Boehm." In: *Cine-fils magazine* (MICHAEL HANEKE on VIOLENCE – cine-fils.com – YouTube).

Haneke, Michael (2020a): "Beyond Mainstream Films." In: Grundmann, R., Naqvi, F., Root, C. (Eds.): *Michael Haneke: Interviews.* Jackson: University Press of Mississippi, 29–36.

Haneke, Michael (2020b): "Collective Guilt and Collective Responsibility." In: Grundmann, R., Navqi, F., Root, C. (Eds.): *Michael Haneke. Interviews.* Jackson: University Press of Mississippi, 78–82.

Haneke, Michael (2020c): "Modern Times. Interview by S. Blumenfeld." In: Grundmann, R., Naqvi, F., Root, C. (Eds.): *Michael Haneke: Interviews.* Jackson: University Press of Mississippi, 23–28.

Heidegger, Martin (1927): *Sein und Zeit.* Halle: Max Niemeyer; – *Being and Time.* Eng. transl. Stambaugh, J., Schmidt, D.J., Albany/New York: SUNY Press, 2010.

Heidegger, Martin (1980 [1936]): "Der Ursprung des Kunstwerkes." In: *Holzwege.* Herrmann, F.W. von (Ed.), Frankfurt am Main: Klostermann, 1–72; – "The Origin of the Work of Art." Eng. transl. ed. by Young, J., Haynes, K. In: *Off the Beaten Track.* Cambridge: Cambridge University Press, 2002, 1–56.

Herzog, Werner (2002 [1999]): "The Minnesota Declaration. Truth and Fact in Documentary Cinema." In: Cronin, P. (Ed.): *Herzog on Herzog*. London: Faber & Faber, 301–302.

Hillier, Jim (Ed.) (1985): *Cahiers du cinéma. The 1950s: Neo-Realism, Hollywood, New Wave*. Cambridge, MA: Harvard University Press, 59–70.

Hirsch, Rudolf (1968): "Edmund Husserl und Hugo von Hofmannsthal: eine Begegnung und ein Brief." In: Friedrich, C.-J., Reifenberg, B. (Eds.): *Sprache und Politik. Festgabe für Dolf Sternberger zum sechzigsten Geburtstag*. Heidelberg: Lambert Schneider, 108–115.

Holmes, Deborah (2007): "Literature on the Small Screen: Michael Haneke's Television Adaptations of Josef Roth's 'Die Rebellion' and Kafka's 'Das Schloß'." In: Preece, J., Finlay, F., Owen, R.J. (Eds.): *New German Literature: Life-Writing and Dialogue with the Arts*. Oxford: Peter Lang, 107–122.

Hyman, John (2006): *The Objective Eye. Color, Form, and Reality in the Theory of Art*. Chicago/London: University of Chicago Press.

Jansen, Julia (2005): "Phantasy's Systematic Place in Husserl's Work. On the Condition of Possibility for a Phenomenology of Experience." In: Bernet, R., Welton, D., Zavota, G. (Eds.): *Edmund Husserl. Critical Assessments of Leading Philosophers*, Vol. 3: *The Nexus of Phenomena: Intentionality, Perception and Temporality*. London/New York: Routledge, 221–243.

Jullier, Laurent/Leveratto, Jean-Marc (2016): "The Story of a Myth: The 'Tracking Shot in *Kapò*' or the Making of French Film Ideology." In: *Mise au point* 8 (https://journals.openedition.org/map/2069?lang=en, last accessed June 15, 2023).

Konrad, Eva-Maria/Petraschka, Thomas/Werner, Christiana (2018): "The Paradox of Fiction – A Brief Introduction into Recent Developments, Open Questions, and Current Areas of Research, Including a Comprehensive Bibliography from 1975 to 2018." In: *Journal of Literary Theory* 12, 2, 193–203.

Krauss, Rosalind E. (1985): "Notes on the Index: Part 1" and "Notes on the Index: Part 2." In: Krauss, Rosalind E.: *The Originality of the Avant-Garde and Other Modernist Myths*. Cambridge, MA: MIT Press, 196–219.

Kundera, Milan (2009): *Une rencontre*. Paris: Gallimard; – *Encounter. Essays*. Eng. transl. Asher, L., New York: Harper Collins, 2010.

Kusturica, Nina/Testor, Eva (2004): *Filmdokumentation: 24 Wirklichkeiten in der Sekunde. Ein filmisches Portrait von Nina Kusturica und Eva Testor*. Arte/ORF.

Lyotard, Jean-François (1979): "La philosophie et la peinture à l'ère de leur expérimentation. Contribution à une idée de la postmodernité." In: Cazenave, A., Lyotard, J.F. (Eds.): *L'art des confins : Mélanges offerts à Maurice de Gandillac*. Paris: PUF, 1985, 465–478.

Lohmar, Dieter (2006): "Synthesis in Husserls Phänomenologie. Das grundlegende Modell von Auffassung und aufgefaßtem Inhalt in Wahrnehmung, Erkennen und Zeitkonstitution." In: Fonfara, D. (Ed.): *Metaphysik als Wissenschaft. Festschrift für Klaus Düsing zum 65. Geburtstag*. Freiburg/Munich: Karl Alber, 387–407.

Lohmar, Dieter (2010): "On the Constitution of the Time of the World: The Emergence of Objective Time on the Ground of Subjective Time." In: Lohmar, D., Yamaguchi, I. (Eds.): *On Time – New Contributions to the Husserlian Phenomenology of Time*. Dordrecht: Springer, 115–136.

Lotz, Christian (2010a): "The Photographic Attitude. Barthes with Husserl." In: Luft, S., Vandevelde, P. (Eds.): *Phenomenology, Archaeology, Ethics: Current Investigations of Husserl's Corpus*. New York: Continuum, 152–167.

Lotz, Christian (2010b): "Im-Bilde-sein. Husserls Phänomenologie des Bildbewusstseins." In: Neuber, S. (Ed.): *Das Bild als Denkfigur. Funktionen des Bildbegriffs in der Philosophiegeschichte von Platon bis Nancy.* Munich: Fink, 167–181.

Lucretius (1992): *On the Nature of Things.* Eng. transl. ed. by Smith, M.F., Cambridge, MA: Harvard University Press.

Luft, Sebastian (2004): "Husserl's Theory of the Phenomenological Reduction: Between Life-World and Cartesianism." In: *Research in Phenomenology* 34, 198–234.

Luft, Sebastian (2019): "Introduction to the Translation." In: Husserl, Edmund: *First Philosophy. Lectures 1923/24 And Related Texts from the Manuscripts (1920–1925).* Eng. transl. Luft, S., Naberhaus, T.M., Dordrecht: Springer, xiii–lxxxii.

Luhr, William G. (2004): "Introduction." In: Luhr, W.G. (Ed.): *The Coen Brothers' Fargo.* New York: Cambridge University Press, 1–9.

Mamber, Stephen (1974): *Cinema Verite in America. Studies in Uncontrolled Documentary.* Cambridge, MA: MIT Press.

Manovich, Lev (2001): *The Language of New Media.* Cambridge, MA: MIT Press.

Manovich, Lev (2016): "What Is Digital Cinema?" In: Denson, S., Leyda, J. (Eds.): *Post-Cinema: Theorizing 21St-Century Film.* Sussex: Reframe, 20–50.

Marbach, Eduard (2000): "On Depicting." In: *Facta Philosophica* 2, 291–308.

Marbach, Eduard (2006): "Einleitung des Herausgebers." In: Husserl, Edmund: *Phantasie, Bildbewusstsein, Erinnerung. Zur Phänomenologie der anschaulichen Vergegenwärtigungen. Texte aus dem Nachlass (1898–1925).* Den Haag: Martinus Nijhoff, xxv–lxxxii.

Marin, Louis (1993) : "Entreglose 2. Le descripteur fantaisiste. Diderot, *Salon de 1765, Casanova n. 94, 'Une marche d'armée',* description." In: *Des pouvoirs de l'image. Gloses.* Paris: Seuil, 72–96.

Matteucci, Giovanni (2013): "Introduzione." In: Wollheim, Richard: *L'arte e i suoi oggetti.* Ital. transl. ed. by Matteucci, G., Milan: Marinotti, 5–13.

Matteucci, Giovanni (2017): "Everyday Aesthetics and Aestheticization: Reflectivity in Perception." In: *Studi di Estetica* 7, 207–227.

Mazzocut-Mis, Maddalena (2012): *How Far Can We Go? Pain, Excess and the Obscene.* Eng. transl. Coggan, J., Newcastle upon Tyne: Cambridge Scholars.

Mazzocut-Mis, Maddalena (2016): "Picture, Poetry and Theatricality. Writing the Salons Is 'Describing' the Salons." In: *Lebenswelt* 8, 68–80.

Mazzocut-Mis, Maddalena (2021): "The Pleasure of Weeping: The Novelty of a Research." In: Giacomoni, P., Valentini, N., Dellantonio, S. (Eds.): *The Dark Side: Philosophical Reflections on the "Negative Emotions."* Cham: Springer Nature, 159–175.

McGowan, Todd (2007): *The Impossible David Lynch.* New York: Columbia University Press.

Mensch, James (2010): "Retention and the Schema." In: Lohmar, D., Yamaguchi, I. (Eds.): *On Time – New Contributions to the Husserlian Phenomenology of Time.* Dordrecht: Springer, 153–168.

Merleau-Ponty, Maurice (1945): *Phénoménologie de la perception.* Paris: Gallimard; – *Phenomenology of perception.* Eng. transl. Smith, C., New York: Routledge, 2002.

Merleau-Ponty, Maurice (1948): *Causeries 1948.* Ménasé, S. (Ed.), Paris: Seuil, 2002; – *The World of Perception.* Eng. transl. Davis, O., London: Routledge, 2004.

Merleau-Ponty, Maurice (1954): *Le problème de la parole. Cours au Collège de France. Notes, 1953–1954.* Geneva: Metis.

Merleau-Ponty, Maurice (1959): "Le philosophe et son ombre." In: Van Breda, H.L., Taminiaux, J. (Eds.): *Edmund Husserl (1859–1949): recueil commémoratif publié à l'occasion du centenaire de la naissance du philosophe.* Den Haag: Martinus Nijhoff, 195–220; – "The Philosopher and His

Shadow." Eng. transl. ed. by McCleary, R.C. In: *Signs*. Evanston: Northwestern University Press, 1964, 159 – 181.

Merleau-Ponty, Maurice (1960 – 1961): *L'œil et l'esprit*. Paris: Gallimard, 1964; – "Eye and Mind." Eng. transl. ed. by Smith, M.B., Johnson, G.A. In: *The Merleau-Ponty Aesthetics Reader*. Evanston: Northwestern University Press, 1996, 121 – 151.

Merleau-Ponty, Maurice (1964): *Le visible et l'invisible*. Paris: Gallimard; – *The Visible and the Invisible*. Eng. transl. ed. by Lefort, C., Evanston: Northwestern University Press, 1968.

Merleau-Ponty, Maurice (1969): *La prose du monde*. Lefort, C. (Ed.), Paris: Gallimard; – *The Prose of the World*. Eng. transl. O'Neill, J., Evanston: Northwestern University Press, 1973.

Merleau-Ponty, Maurice (1996): *Notes des cours au Collège de France 1958 – 1959 et 1960 – 1961*. Ménasé, S. (Ed.), Paris: Gallimard; – *The Possibility of Philosophy. Course Notes from the Collège de France, 1959 – 1961*. Eng. transl. Whitmoyer, K., Evanston: Northwestern University Press, 2022.

Metz, Christian (1965): "À propos de l'impression de réalité au cinéma." In: *Cahiers du cinéma* 166 – 167, 74 – 83; – "On the Impression of Reality in the Cinema." In: *Film Language. A Semiotics of the Cinema*. Chicago: The University of Chicago Press, 3 – 15.

Meunier, Jean-Pierre (1969): *Les structures de l'expérience filmique : l'identification filmique*. Louvain: Librairie Universitaire; – *The Structures of the Film Experience by Jean-Pierre Meunier. Historical Assessments and Phenomenological Expansions*. Eng. transl. ed. by Hanich, J., Fairfax, D., Amsterdam: Amsterdam University Press, 2019.

Molder, Maria F. (2017): "Green Leaves, Green Sorrows. On Víctor Erice's Broken Glasses." In: Reeh, C., Martins, J.M. (Eds.): *Thinking Reality and Time through Film*. Newcastle upon Tyne: Cambridge Scholars, 244 – 265.

Moran, Richard (2017): *The Philosophical Imagination*. New York: Oxford University Press.

Nichols, Bill (2010): *Introduction to Documentary*. Second Edition. Bloomington: Indiana University Press.

Nietzsche, Friedrich (1886): *Jenseits von Gut und Böse*. Naumann: Leipzig; – *Beyond Good and Evil*. Eng. transl. ed. by Horstmann, R.P., Norman, J., Cambridge: Cambridge University Press, 2002.

Nietzsche, Friedrich (1889): *Götzen-Dämmerung*. Naumann: Leipzig; – "Twilight of the Idols." Eng. transl. ed. by Ridley, A., Norman, J. In: *The Anti-Christ, Ecce Homo, Twilight of the Idols, and Other Writings*. Cambridge: Cambridge University Press, 2005, 153 – 230.

Parreno, Philippe (2014): "Un prince du football ou le regard du modèle par Gordon et Parreno." In: *Point to Point*. June 16 (http://pointopoint.blogg.org/un-prince-du-football-ou-le-regard-du-modele-par-gordon-et-parreno-a116322804, last accessed June 15, 2023).

Peirce, Charles (1992): *The Essential Peirce. Selected Philosophical Writings*, Vol. 1: *1867 – 1893*. Houser, N., Kloesel, C. (Eds.), Bloomington/Indianapolis: Indiana University Press.

Peirce, Charles (1998): *The Essential Peirce. Selected Philosophical Writings*, Vol. 2: *1893 – 1913*. Peirce Edition Project (Eds.), Bloomington/Indianapolis: Indiana University Press.

Piana, Giovanni (1979): *Elementi di una dottrina dell'esperienza: saggio di filosofia fenomenologica*. Milan: Il Saggiatore.

Pippin, Robert (2005): *The Persistence of Subjectivity. On the Kantian Aftermath*. New York: Cambridge University Press.

Pippin, Robert (2015): "Psychology Degree Zero? The Representation of Action in the Films of the Dardenne Brothers." In: *Critical Inquiry* 41, 757 – 785.

Pippin, Robert (2017): *The Philosophical Hitchcock*. London/Chicago: The University of Chicago Press.

Pippin, Robert (2020): *Filmed Thought. Cinema as Reflective Form*. London/Chicago: The University of Chicago Press.

Pippin, Robert (2021): *Philosophy by Other Means*. London/Chicago: The University of Chicago Press.
Plato (1980): "Cratylus." Eng. transl. ed. by Hamilton, E., Cairns, H. In: *The Collected Dialogues of Plato*. Princeton: Princeton University Press, 421–474.
Probst, Barbara (2021): *Matters of Uncertainty. Thoughts on Photography and the World Behind It, 1997–2020*. New York: Edgewise.
Proust, Marcel (1913): *Du côté de chez Swann*. Paris: Grasset; – "Swann's Way." Eng. transl. Moncrief, C.K.S., Kilmartin, T. In: *Remembrance of Things Past*, Vol. 1: *Swann's Way, Within a Budding Groove*. London: Penguin, 1984.
Proust, Marcel (1919): *À l'ombre des jeunes filles en fleurs*. Paris: Gallimard; – "Within a Budding Groove." Eng. transl. Moncrief, C.K.S., Kilmartin, T. In: *Remembrance of Things Past*, Vol. 1: *Swann's Way, Within a Budding Groove*. London: Penguin, 1984.
Proust, Marcel (1920–21): *Le Côté de Guermantes*. Paris: Gallimard; – "The Guermantes Way." Eng. transl. Moncrief, C.K.S., Kilmartin, T. In: *Remembrance of Things Past*, Vol. 2: *The Guermantes Way, Cities of the Plain*, London: Penguin, 1986.
Proust, Marcel (1923): *La Prisonnière*. Paris: Gallimard; – "The Captive." Eng. transl. Moncrief, C.K.S., Kilmartin, T., Mayor, A. In: *Remembrance of Things Past*, Vol. 3: *The Captive, The Fugitive, Time Regained*. London: Penguin, 1983.
Proust, Marcel (1927): *Le Temps retrouvé*. Paris: Gallimard; – "Time Regained." Eng. transl. Moncrief, C.K.S., Kilmartin, T. In: *Remembrance of Things Past*, Vol. 3: *The Captive, The Fugitive, Time Regained*. London: Penguin, 1983.
Proust, Marcel (1971): *Contre Sainte-Beuve, précédé de Pastiches et mélanges, et suivi de Essais et articles*. Paris: Gallimard.
Proust, Marcel (2009 [1895]): *Chardin et Rembrandt*. Paris: Le Bruit du temps; – *Chardin and Rembrandt*. Eng. transl. Feldman, J., New York: David Zwirner, 2016.
Radford, Colin (1975): "How Can We Be Moved by the Fate of Anna Karenina?" In: *Proceedings of the Aristotelian Society, Supplementary Volumes* 49, 67–93.
Richir, Marc (1971): "La Défenestration." In: *L'ARC* 46, 31–42.
Richir, Marc (1999): "Commentaire de Phénoménologie de la conscience esthétique de Husserl." In: *Revue d'Esthétique (Esthétique et phénoménologie)* 36, 15–23.
Richir, Marc (2000): *Phénoménologie en esquisses. Nouvelles fondations*. Grenoble: Jérôme Millon.
Richir, Marc (2004): *Phantasia, imagination, affectivité. Phénoménologie et anthropologie phénoménologique*. Grenoble: Jérôme Millon.
Riegl, Alois (1901): *Die Spätrömische Kunstindustrie nach den Funden in Österreich-Ungarn*. Vienna: Kaiserlich-Königliche Hof- und Staatsdruckerei.
Rivette, Jacques (1961): "De l'abjection." In: *Cahiers du cinéma* 120, 54–55; – "On Abjection." Eng. transl. Phelps, D., Szaniawski, J. (http://www.dvdbeaver.com/rivette/ok/abjection.html, last accessed June 15, 2023).
Rodrigo, Pierre (2006): "L'image, l'analogon, le simulacre: la question des 'fictions perceptives' chez Husserl." In: *La Part de l'Œil (Dossier: Esthétique et phénoménologie en mutation)* 21–22, 95–105.
Rodrigo, Pierre (2009): *L'intentionnalité créatrice. Problèmes de phénoménologie et d'esthétique*. Paris: Vrin.
Rollinger, Robin D. (1993): "Husserl and Brentano on Imagination." In: *Archiv für Geschichte der Philosophie* 75, 195–210.
Rozzoni, Claudio (2012): *Per un'estetica del teatro. Un percorso critico. Con testi di Simmel, Merleau-Ponty, Fink, Deleuze*. Milan: Mimesis.

Rozzoni, Claudio (2015): "Disgustare gli occhi/gustare con gli occhi." In: Mazzocut-Mis, M. (Ed.): *Dal gusto al disgusto. L'estetica del pasto*. Milan: Cortina, 99–125.
Rozzoni, Claudio (2016): "L'antre de Diderot. Fantômes, sentiments, verité." In: Mazzocut-Mis, M., Messori, R. (Eds.): *Actualité de Diderot. Pour une nouvelle esthétique*. Milan: Mimesis, 61–77.
Rozzoni, Claudio (2020): "Seeing the Unreal: Husserlian Insights into the Nature of Images." In: Mion, R.N. (Ed.): *Kunstiteaduslikke Uurimusi. Studies on Art and Architecture* (Special Issue: Depiction: Contemporary Studies on Pictorial Representation) 29, 3–4, 55–70.
Rozzoni, Claudio/Conceição, Nélio (Eds.) (2021): *Aesthetics and Values. Contemporary Perspectives*. Milan: Mimesis.
Saraiva, Maria M. (1970): *L'imagination selon Husserl*. Den Haag: Martinus Nijhoff.
Sartre, Jean-Paul (1940): *L'imaginaire. Psychologie phénoménologique de l'imagination*. Paris: Gallimard; – *The Imaginary, A Phenomenological Psychology of the Imagination*. Eng. transl. ed. by Webber, J., London/New York: Routledge, 2004.
Scaramuzza, Gabriele/Schuhmann, Karl (1990): "Ein Husserlmanuskript über Ästhetik." In: *Husserl Studies* 7, 3, 165–177.
Schnell, Alexander (2007): *Husserl et les fondements de la phénoménologie constructive*. Grenoble: Jérôme Millon.
Scholz, Oliver R. (2004): *Bild, Darstellung, Zeichen. Philosophische Theorien bildlicher Darstellung*. Frankfurt am Main: Klostermann.
Schrader, Paul (2018): *Transcendental Style in Film. Ozu, Bresson, Dreyer*. Oakland: University of California Press.
Sepp, Hans R. (2014): "Prefazione." In: Fink, Eugen: *Presentificazione e immagine. Contributi alla fenomenologia dell'irrealtà*. Ital. transl. ed. by Giubilato, G.J., Milan: Mimesis, IX–XXI.
Shapiro, Roberta/Heinich, Natalie (2012): *De l'artification. Enquêtes sur le passage à l'art*. Paris: Éditions EHESS.
Smith, Daniel W. (2012): "Platonism. The Concept of the Simulacrum: Deleuze and the Overturning of Platonism." In: *Essays on Deleuze*. Edinburgh: Edinburgh University Press, 3–26.
Sobchack, Vivian (1999): "Toward a Phenomenology of Nonfictional Film Experience." In: Renov, M., Gaines, J. (Eds.): *Collecting Visible Evidence*. Minneapolis: University of Minnesota Press, 241–254.
Sobchack, Vivian (2004): *Carnal Thoughts. Embodiment and Moving Image Culture*. Berkeley/Los Angeles/London: University of California Press.
Sobchack, Vivian (2012): "Being on the Screen: A Phenomenology of Cinematic Flesh, or the Actor's Four Bodies." In: Sternagel, J., Levitt, D., Mersch, D. (Eds.): *Acting and Performance in Moving Image Culture. Bodies, Screens, Renderings*. Bielefeld: Transcript, 429–445.
Sokolowski, Robert (1992): *Pictures, Quotations, and Distinctions: Fourteen Essays in Phenomenology*. Notre Dame: University of Notre Dame Press.
Sontag, Susan (1977): *On Photography*. New York: Farrar, Straus and Giroux.
Sontag, Susan (2003): *Regarding the Pain of Others*. New York: Farrar, Straus and Giroux.
Speck, Oliver (2010): *Funny Frames. The Filmic Concepts of Michael Haneke*. New York: Continuum.
Spinicci, Paolo (2008): *Simile alle ombre e al sogno. La filosofia dell'immagine*. Turin: Bollati Boringhieri.
Spinicci, Paolo (2014): "The Concept of Involvement and the Paradox of Fiction." In: *Philosophical Inquiries* 2, 1, 77–94.
Starobinski, Jean (1991): *Diderot dans l'espace des peintres*. Paris: Réunion des Musées Nationaux.
Stecker, Robert (2006): "Aesthetic Experience and Aesthetic Value." In: *Philosophy Compass* 1, 1, 1–10.

Stecker, Robert (2011): "Should We Still Care about the Paradox of Fiction?" In: *British Journal of Aesthetics* 51, 3, 295–308.

Steinmetz, Rudy (2006): "La conscience d'image, l'attitude esthétique et le jeu de la mimésis chez Husserl." In: *La Part de l'Œil (Dossier : Esthétique et phénoménologie en mutation)* 21–22 (2006–2007), 107–117.

Steinmetz, Rudy (2011): *L'esthétique phénoménologique de Husserl. Une approche contrastée.* Paris: Éditions Kimé.

Stich, Stephen/Nichols, Shaun (1997): "Cognitive Penetrability, Rationality, and Restricted Simulation." In: *Mind & Language* 12, 297–326.

Strauss, David L. (2020): *Photography and Belief.* New York: David Zwirner.

Summa, Michela (2017): "Experiencing Reality and Fiction: Discontinuity and Permeability." In: Summa, M., Fuchs, T., Vanzago, L. (Eds.): *Imagination and Social Perspectives. Approaches from Phenomenology and Psychopathology.* London: Routledge, 45–64.

Taieb, Hamid (2018): *Relational Intentionality: Brentano and the Aristotelian Tradition.* Dordrecht: Springer.

Tinaburri, Egidio (2011): *Husserl e Aristotele. Coscienza Immagine Mondo.* Milan: Franco Angeli.

Twardowski, Kazimier (1894): *Zur Lehre vom Inhalt und Gegenstand der Vorstellungen: Eine psychologische Untersuchung.* Munich/Vienna: Philosophia, 1982.

Vågnes, Øyvind (2011): *Zaprudered: The Kennedy Assassination Film in Visual Culture.* Austin, TX: University of Texas Press.

Van Breda, Herman Leo (1962): "Maurice Merleau-Ponty et les Archives-Husserl à Louvain." In: *Revue de métaphysique et de morale* 67, 410–430.

Vendrell Ferran, Íngrid (2010): "Ästhetische Erfahrung und Quasi-Gefühle." In: Raspa, V. (Ed.): *The Aesthetics of the Graz School. Meinong Studies 4.* Heusenstamm: Ontos, 129–168.

Vendrell Ferran, Íngrid (2018): "Emotion in the Appreciation of Fiction." In: *Journal of Literary Theory* 12, 204–223.

Voltolini, Alberto (2013): *Immagine.* Bologna: Il Mulino.

Vongehr, Thomas (2007): "A Short History of the Husserl-Archives Leuven and the Husserliana." In: *Geschichte des Husserl-Archivs. History of the Husserl-Archives.* Dordrecht: Springer, 99–126.

Wall, Jeff (2002): "A Conversation Between Jeff Wall and Lynda Morris." In: Morris, L. (Ed.): *Jeff Wall. Landscapes.* Norwich: Norwich Gallery and Birmingham: Article Press, 27–33.

Wall, Jeff (2007): *I Begin by Not Photographing.* Video interview, San Francisco Museum of Modern Art, San Francisco (https://www.sfmoma.org/watch/jeff-wall-i-begin-by-not-photographing, last accessed June 15, 2023).

Wall, Jeff (2007 [1984]): "Gestus." In: *Jeff Wall. Selected Essays and Interviews.* New York: The Museum of Modern Art, 85.

Wall, Jeff (2007 [1989]): "Photography and Liquid Intelligence." In: *Jeff Wall. Selected Essays and Interviews.* New York: The Museum of Modern Art, 109–110.

Wall, Jeff (2007 [1993]): "Jeff Wall in Conversation with Martin Schwander." In: *Jeff Wall. Selected Essays and Interviews.* New York: The Museum of Modern Art, 229–233.

Wall, Jeff (2007 [1996a]): "Arielle Pelenc in Correspondence with Jeff Wall (1996)." In: *Jeff Wall. Selected Essays and Interviews.* New York: The Museum of Modern Art, 251–262.

Wall, Jeff (2007 [1996b]): "Dirk Snauwaert: Written Interview with Jeff Wall (1996)." In: *Jeff Wall. Selected Essays and Interviews.* New York: The Museum of Modern Art, 263–269.

Wall, Jeff (2007 [2003]): "Frames of Reference (2003)." In: *Jeff Wall. Selected Essays and Interviews.* New York: The Museum of Modern Art, 173–181.

Wall, Jeff (2013): *Künstlervortrag*. Munich: Ernst von Siemens-Auditorium, Pinakothek der Moderne, November 7, 2013 (https://www.youtube.com/watch?v=DxMoeYC1bs4, last accessed June 15, 2023).

Wall, Jeff (2014a): "A Long Novel in Pictures, An Interview with Jeff Wall (Interview by Y. Dziewior)." In: Dziewior, Y., Visser, H. (Eds.): *Jeff Wall: Tableaux Pictures Photographs 1996–2013*. Amsterdam/Bregenz/Humlebæk: Stedelijk Museum Amsterdam – Kunsthaus Bregenz – Louisiana Museum of Modern Art, 28–38.

Wall, Jeff (2014b): *Artist Talk. Chapter 6: Siphoning Fuel (2008)*. Stedelijk Museum Amsterdam (https://www.youtube.com/watch?v=U1XQ4pIpeaQ, last accessed June 15, 2023).

Wall, Jeff (2014c): *Artist Talk. Chapter 8: Monologue (2013)*. Stedelijk Museum Amsterdam (https://www.youtube.com/watch?v=RQ0lfz30w4A, last accessed June 15, 2023).

Wall, Jeff (2015a): *Pictures like Poems*. Video interview by Marc-Christoph Wagner at the Louisiana Museum of Modern Art, Humlebæk in March 2015 in connection to the exhibition "Jeff Wall: Tableaux Pictures Photographs – Works from 1996–2013." Louisiana Channel, Louisiana Museum of Modern Art (http://channel.louisiana.dk/video/jeff-wall-pictures-poems, last accessed June 15, 2023).

Wall, Jeff (2015b): *We Are All Actors*. Video interview by Thierry de Duve at the Louisiana Museum of Modern Art, Humlebæk in March 2015 in connection to the exhibition "Jeff Wall: Tableaux Pictures Photographs – Works from 1996–2013." Louisiana Channel, Louisiana Museum of Modern Art (https://channel.louisiana.dk/video/jeff-wall-we-are-all-actors, last accessed June 15, 2023).

Walton, Kendall L. (1978): "Fearing Fictions." In: *The Journal of Philosophy* 75, 1, 5–27.

Walton, Kendall L. (1990): *Mimesis as Make-Believe*. Cambridge, MA: Harvard University Press.

Weski, Thomas (2010): "I Always Try to Make Beautiful Pictures." In: Wall, Jeff: *Transit (Ausstellungskatalog der Staatlichen Kunstsammlungen Dresden)*. Bischoff, U., Wagner, M. (Eds.), Munich: Schirmer/Mosel.

Wiesing, Lambert (2005): *Artifizielle Präsenz: Studien zur Philosophie des Bildes*. Frankfurt am Main: Suhrkamp; – *Artificial Presence. Philosophical Studies in Image Theory*. Eng. transl. Schott, N.F., Stanford, CA: California University Press, 2010.

Wiesing, Lambert (2013): *Sehen Lassen. Die Praxis des Zeigens*. Berlin: Suhrkamp.

Wittgenstein, Ludwig (1980): *Bemerkungen über die Philosophie der Psychologie*. Vol. 1. Anscombe, G.E.M., von Wright, G.H. (Eds.), Oxford: Blackwell; – *Remarks on the Philosophy of Psychology*. Vol. 1. Eng. transl. ed. by Anscombe, G.E.M., von Wright, G.H., Chicago: University of Chicago Press.

Wollheim, Richard (1984): *The Thread of Life*. Cambridge, MA: Harvard University Press.

Zahavi, Dan (2002): "Merleau-Ponty on Husserl. A Reappraisal." In: Toadvine, T., Embree, L. (Eds.): *Merleau-Ponty's Reading of Husserl*. Dordrecht: Kluwer Academic, 3–29.

Zahavi, Dan (2003): *Husserl's Phenomenology*. Standford: Stanford University Press.

Zecchi, Stefano (1984): *La magia dei saggi*. Milan: Jaca.

Thematic Index

Absorption   39, 134, 194–197, 225, 230
Actor   45–47, 50, 54, 80–86, 119, 135f., 157, 196, 212–214, 216, 219–221, 224, 226
Aesthetic *adiaphoron*   97, 113, 118f.
Aesthetic experience   44, 47, 55–58, 91–96, 98–107, 110–114, 118, 123–127, 143f., 150, 153f., 226f.
Aesthetic pleasure/displeasure   27, 92, 94–98, 101, 103f., 110, 114f., 125, 139, 147, 149, 187, 203
Aesthetic "Turning Back"   99, 112–114, 118, 124
Apositional image   48, 53f., 61, 78, 99, 113, 127, 187, 202, 207
Aristotle   14f., 86, 158, 208
Artistic illusion   71, 136
Axiological Interest   94, 98–105, 112–114, 147, 151–153, 155, 160–162, 168, 170, 184f., 199, 208, 218, 227, 231

Barthes, Roland   52–54, 61f., 64–66, 68–71, 77, 79–81, 97, 222
Blind intuition   93, 101, 104
Body   44–46, 50, 64f., 84–86, 89, 96, 115, 141, 157, 171, 173, 176, 194, 209, 211, 217, 222, 230
Bresson, Robert   83, 176, 183, 196, 212–221, 224–226, 228f

Céline, Louis-Ferdinand (pseud. of Louis-Ferdinand Destouches)   117f., 150, 195, 212f., 215
Character   16, 25f., 31, 38, 46–48, 50f., 53, 64, 67, 75, 79–86, 88, 90, 107, 114f., 117, 119, 121, 130, 134, 136, 155, 159, 161, 164–166, 170, 172f., 176f., 183, 186, 188, 197, 201f., 210, 212, 218f., 222, 230
Chardin, Jean-Baptiste-Siméon   22, 149f., 188
Chiasm   142, 148, 150
Cinematic image   18, 76, 162
Conflict (phantasy) 21–23, 31–33, 43, 46, 50f., 56f., 75, 87–89, 96, 128, 131–133, 139–141, 190

Copy   28, 38, 41, 49, 56, 59, 126, 128, 149, 152, 171, 217, 229

Dark idea   101
Death and phantasy   61, 77, 82, 87, 89, 116–118, 166, 186f., 198f., 203f., 210–212, 214, 216
Delegation   19, 23f., 28, 30f., 34–36, 45, 56f., 129, 132, 134, 141, 143, 180, 194
Deleuze, Gilles   12, 144–146, 148, 153f., 156, 179, 182–184, 188, 196, 208–213, 216, 218
Depiction consciousness   20, 23f., 30, 33, 35, 43, 46, 50f., 53–57, 59f., 75, 82f., 86, 97, 99, 106, 110, 121, 126f., 130–136, 141, 160, 168f., 174, 187, 194, 210, 223, 229
Diderot, Denis   22, 70f., 74, 85f., 97, 126f., 130–132, 134f., 147–150, 156, 175, 188, 194f., 212–214, 220, 222, 226, 228f.
Digital image   55, 65f., 78, 80, 94, 157
Documentary consciousness   45f., 52, 63f., 69–71, 76f., 80–84, 87, 117, 120–123, 157, 162–165, 182, 189f., 208–210, 216, 219–222, 226, 228f.

Ego-splitting   38–40, 167, 200f.
Event   142, 145, 153–155, 209, 211, 213, 216
Exhibitionism   117n, 150, 186, 195f., 212–214
Expressive quality   97, 145, 194–197

Fictional consciousness   45, 49, 70f., 80, 82–84, 86–88, 90, 111–113, 119, 124, 127, 134, 137n, 151, 155–171, 182, 187, 189f., 197–199, 201–203, 206–210, 228f.

Heidegger, Martin   13, 102, 111, 144, 166, 181
Hitchcock, Alfred   89, 165, 171f.
Hofmannsthal, Hugo von   91, 93f., 98, 101, 124f., 127, 205

Iconic distance   15, 50, 56–58, 72, 89, 103, 186–191, 193, 196–200, 202f., 206
Iconic mediation   19, 21, 28–35, 38, 41, 46
Image-theory   28f., 34

https://doi.org/10.1515/9783110725766-008

Thematic Index — 247

Imaginatio   18–20, 25 f., 30 f., 33–35, 42, 136 f.
Impressional image   53 f., 61, 65–68, 71, 77, 79 f., 83 f., 131, 157, 163
Incorporeal   133, 209–211

Lucretius   187, 190, 197

Mannequin   136 f., 139 f.
Mental image   18 f., 28–30, 34 f.
Merleau-Ponty, Maurice   10, 12, 28, 43, 74 f., 81, 83, 85, 98, 102, 110, 142, 145, 150, 152–154, 182, 184, 188 f.
Models   213 f., 224–226, 230
Mode of manifestation   92, 94–96, 98 f., 105 f., 110 f., 113–115, 123–127, 133, 153, 162, 193
Modified consciousness   37, 41, 47, 106, 109 f., 113, 136, 156, 162–164, 198

Near documentary   220 f., 227, 229
Noema   41, 43, 132–136, 141, 143, 148, 150–155, 160, 172, 209, 211, 228–230
Noesis   41, 46, 75, 79

Obscene   116, 186, 216
One-fold intentionality   31–36, 43, 46 f., 136

Peirce, Charles Sanders   62 f., 65, 67, 70, 79
Perceptual flux   50, 89
Perceptual illusion   17, 23, 43, 88 f., 136–139, 141, 188
Performer   82, 204, 220 f.
Perspective   129, 146, 150–156, 159, 161 f., 169–172, 175–178, 182–186, 191–195, 204–208, 211, 216–219, 226 f., 229, 231
Perzeptive Phantasie   17, 42–47, 49, 58, 60, 87, 89, 106, 109, 131, 135–137, 144, 156–158, 189
Phantasy ego   38–40, 47, 88, 167–170, 187, 198–200, 204 f.
Phantasy hovering   15 f., 19, 30 f., 33, 35, 120
Phantasy image   18–20, 28–32, 34 f., 42, 136, 160
Phantasy intentionality   14 f., 17 f., 29 f., 33 f., 38, 41
Phantasy present   37
Photographic image   20, 62, 65, 68 f., 80, 157

Physical image   18–22, 28, 30–33, 42, 50, 53, 58 f., 94, 143, 188
Plato   23 f., 56, 88, 145, 180 f., 184
Polyvalence of Truth   216, 219, 226
Portrait   25, 46, 62, 77, 79, 86, 126–138, 191–197, 205, 229–231
Positional image   53, 61, 71, 76 f., 79, 84, 118, 128, 163, 190, 198, 206, 227
Presentification and belief   54, 58, 163
Proximity   191, 193, 196
Proxy   19, 28, 30, 46, 127, 130, 136

Quasi-emotion   162 f., 187
Quasi-value   163, 168, 170 f., 187
Quasi-world   29, 45, 50, 83, 85–88, 112, 151, 155, 158, 164, 170, 189, 198, 200, 204, 210

Reproduction   27, 35–40, 42 f., 47–49, 108 f., 117, 120, 130, 136, 142, 156–159, 164, 167
Retrograde movement of the true   179–181

Sartre, Jean-Paul   12, 26, 52, 81, 137 f., 141 f., 145, 148
Seeing-in   24 f., 28, 30 f., 52, 59 f., 76, 129 f., 133, 202
Sense   64, 83, 85, 89, 112, 123, 133, 142, 150–152, 154–156, 158 f., 160, 164, 170, 178 f., 182, 185, 187, 193 f., 196, 199, 204–206, 208–218, 227–231
Snapshot   63, 66 f., 220 f., 227
Sontag, Susan   61 f., 64, 76 f., 207

Tele-vision   71–73, 76 f., 190–192, 206
Temporal difference   16, 34, 37–39, 41, 45, 48 f., 56, 106, 136, 154, 180, 190, 194, 197
Theatrical image   45, 86, 90, 134–136
Theatricality   117 f., 136, 158, 173, 177 f., 194 f., 212–214, 225

Valueception   94, 98 f., 102–104, 113, 150, 154, 160, 170, 205, 230
Violence and phantasy   76, 128, 185, 187, 198–201, 203 f., 206, 210, 213

Wall, Jeff   64, 196, 219–230
Windowness   71–76, 85, 147 f.

www.ingramcontent.com/pod-product-compliance
Lightning Source LLC
Chambersburg PA
CBHW020227170426
43201CB00007B/344